S0-BTA-475

SHORT STORIES *for Students*

Advisors

Jayne M. Burton is a teacher of secondary English and an adjunct professor for Northwest Vista College in San Antonio, TX.

Klaudia Janek is the school librarian at the International Academy in Bloomfield Hills, Michigan. She holds an MLIS degree from Wayne State University, a teaching degree from Rio Salado College, and a bachelor of arts degree in international relations from Saint Joseph's College. She is the IB Extended Essay Coordinator and NCA AdvancEd co-chair at her school. She is an IB workshop leader for International Baccalaureate North America, leading teacher training for IB school librarians and extended essay coordinators. She has been happy to serve the Michigan Association for Media in Education as a board member and past president at the regional level, advocating for libraries in Michigan schools.

Greg Bartley is an English teacher in Virginia. He holds an M.A.Ed. in English Education from Wake Forest University and a B.S. in Integrated Language Arts Education from Miami University.

Sarah Clancy teaches IB English at the International Academy in Bloomfield Hills, Michigan. She is a member of the National Council of Teachers of English and Michigan Speech Coaches, Inc. Sarah earned her undergraduate degree from Kalamazoo College and her Master's of Education from Florida Southern College. She coaches the high-ranking forensics team and is the staff adviser of the school newspaper, *Overachiever*.

Karen Dobson is a teen/adult librarian at Plymouth District Library in Plymouth, Michigan. She holds a Bachelor of Science degree from Oakland University and an MLIS from Wayne State University and has served on many committees through the Michigan Library Association.

Tom Shilts is the youth librarian at the Okemos branch of Capital Area District Library in Okemos, Michigan. He holds an MSLS degree from Clarion University of Pennsylvania and an MA in U.S. History from the University of North Dakota.

SHORT STORIES *for Students*

Presenting Analysis, Context, and Criticism on Commonly Studied Short Stories

VOLUME 45

Kristin B. Mallegg, Project Editor

Foreword by Thomas E. Barden

Farmington Hills, Mich • San Francisco • New York • Waterville, Maine
Meriden, Conn • Mason, Ohio • Chicago

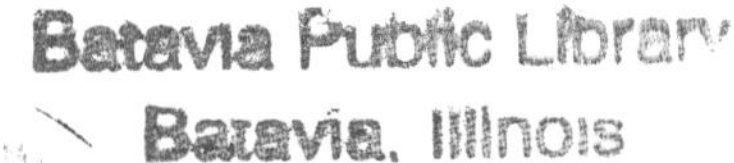

Short Stories for Students, Volume 45
Project Editor: Kristin B. Mallegg
Rights Acquisition and Management: Ashley Maynard
Composition: Evi Abou-El-Seoud
Manufacturing: Rita Wimberley
Imaging: John Watkins
Product Design: Pamela A. E. Galbreath, Jennifer Wahi
Digital Content Production: Edna Shy

Gale
27500 Drake Rd.
Farmington Hills, MI, 48331-3535

ISBN-13: 978-1-4103-2857-1
ISSN 1092-7735

This title is also available as an e-book.
ISBN-13: 978-1-4103-2862-5
Contact your Gale, a part of Cengage Learning sales representative for ordering information.

Printed in Mexico
1 2 3 4 5 6 7 21 20 19 18 17

Table of Contents

Why Study Literature At All?

Short Stories for Students is designed to provide readers with information and discussion about a wide range of important contemporary and historical works of short fiction, and it does that job very well. However, I want to use this guest foreword to address a question that it does *not* take up. It is a fundamental question that is often ignored in high school and college English classes as well as research texts, and one that causes frustration among students at all levels, namely why study literature at all? Isn't it enough to read a story, enjoy it, and go about one's business? My answer (to be expected from a literary professional, I suppose) is no. It is not enough. It is a start; but it is not enough. Here's why.

First, literature is the only part of the educational curriculum that deals directly with the actual world of lived experience. The philosopher Edmund Husserl used the apt German term *die Lebenswelt*, "the living world," to denote this realm. All the other content areas of the modern American educational system avoid the subjective, present reality of everyday life. Science (both the natural and the social varieties) objectifies, the fine arts create and/or perform, history reconstructs. Only literary study persists in posing those questions we all asked before our schooling taught us to give up on them. Only literature gives credibility to personal perceptions, feelings, dreams, and the "stream of consciousness" that is our inner voice. Literature wonders about infinity, wonders why God permits evil, wonders what will happen to us after we die. Literature admits that we get our hearts broken, that people sometimes cheat and get away with it, that the world is a strange and probably incomprehensible place. Literature, in other words, takes on all the big and small issues of what it means to be human. So my first answer is that of the humanist we should read literature and study it and take it seriously because it enriches us as human beings. We develop our moral imagination, our capacity to sympathize with other people, and our ability to understand our existence through the experience of fiction.

My second answer is more practical. By studying literature we can learn how to explore and analyze texts. Fiction may be about *die Lebenswelt*, but it is a construct of words put together in a certain order by an artist using the medium of language. By examining and studying those constructions, we can learn about language as a medium. We can become more sophisticated about word associations and connotations, about the manipulation of symbols, and about style and atmosphere. We can grasp how ambiguous language is and how important context and texture is to meaning. In our first encounter with a work of literature, of course, we are not supposed to catch all of these things. We are spellbound, just as the writer wanted us to be. It is as serious students of the writer's art that we begin to see how the tricks are done.

Seeing the tricks, which is another way of saying "developing analytical and close reading skills," is important above and beyond its intrinsic literary educational value. These skills transfer to other fields and enhance critical thinking of any kind. Understanding how language is used to construct texts is powerful knowledge. It makes engineers better problem solvers, lawyers better advocates and courtroom practitioners, politicians better rhetoricians, marketing and advertising agents better sellers, and citizens more aware consumers as well as better participants in democracy. This last point is especially important, because rhetorical skill works both ways when we learn how language is manipulated in the making of texts the result is that we become less susceptible when language is used to manipulate us.

My third reason is related to the second. When we begin to see literature as created artifacts of language, we become more sensitive to good writing in general. We get a stronger sense of the importance of individual words, even the sounds of words and word combinations. We begin to understand Mark Twain's delicious proverb "The difference between the right word and the almost right word is the difference between lightning and a lightning bug." Getting beyond the "enjoyment only" stage of literature gets us closer to becoming makers of word art ourselves. I am not saying that studying fiction will turn every student into a Faulkner or a Shakespeare. But it will make us more adaptable and effective writers, even if our art form ends up being the office memo or the corporate annual report.

Studying short stories, then, can help students become better readers, better writers, and even better human beings. But I want to close with a warning. If your study and exploration of the craft, history, context, symbolism, or anything else about a story starts to rob it of the magic you felt when you first read it, it is time to stop. Take a break, study another subject, shoot some hoops, or go for a run. Love of reading is too important to be ruined by school. The early twentieth century writer Willa Cather, in her novel *My Antonia*, has her narrator Jack Burden tell a story that he and Antonia heard from two old Russian immigrants when they were teenagers. These immigrants, Pavel and Peter, told about an incident from their youth back in Russia that the narrator could recall in vivid detail thirty years later. It was a harrowing story of a wedding party starting home in sleds and being chased by starving wolves. Hundreds of wolves attacked the group's sleds one by one as they sped across the snow trying to reach their village. In a horrible revelation, the old Russians revealed that the groom eventually threw his own bride to the wolves to save himself. There was even a hint that one of the old immigrants might have been the groom mentioned in the story. Cather has her narrator conclude with his feelings about the story. "We did not tell Pavel's secret to anyone, but guarded it jealously as if the wolves of the Ukraine had gathered that night long ago, and the wedding party had been sacrificed, just to give us a painful and peculiar pleasure." That feeling, that painful and peculiar pleasure, is the most important thing about literature. Study and research should enhance that feeling and never be allowed to overwhelm it.

Thomas E. Barden
Professor of English and Director of Graduate English Studies, The University of Toledo

Introduction

Purpose of the Book

The purpose of *Short Stories for Students* (*SSfS*) is to provide readers with a guide to understanding, enjoying, and studying short stories by giving them easy access to information about the work. Part of Gale's "For Students" Literature line, *SSfS* is specifically designed to meet the curricular needs of high school and undergraduate college students and their teachers, as well as the interests of general readers and researchers considering specific short fiction. While each volume contains entries on "classic" stories frequently studied in classrooms, there are also entries containing hard-to-find information on contemporary stories, including works by multicultural, international, and women writers.

The information covered in each entry includes an introduction to the story and the story's author; a plot summary, to help readers unravel and understand the events in the work; descriptions of important characters, including explanation of a given character's role in the narrative as well as discussion about that character's relationship to other characters in the story; analysis of important themes in the story; and an explanation of important literary techniques and movements as they are demonstrated in the work.

In addition to this material, which helps the readers analyze the story itself, students are also provided with important information on the literary and historical background informing each work. This includes a historical context essay, a box comparing the time or place the story was written to modern Western culture, a critical overview essay, and excerpts from critical essays on the story or author. A unique feature of *SSfS* is a specially commissioned critical essay on each story, targeted toward the student reader.

To further help today's student in studying and enjoying each story, information on audiobooks and other media adaptations is provided (if available), as well as reading suggestions for works of fiction and nonfiction on similar themes and topics. Classroom aids include ideas for research papers and lists of critical and reference sources that provide additional material on the work.

Selection Criteria

The titles for each volume of *SSfS* were selected by surveying numerous sources on teaching literature and analyzing course curricula for various school districts. Some of the sources surveyed include: literature anthologies, *Reading Lists for College-Bound Students: The Books Most Recommended by America's Top Colleges*; Teaching the Short Story: A Guide to Using Stories from around the World, by the National Council of Teachers of English (NCTE); and "A Study of High School Literature Anthologies," conducted by Arthur Applebee at the Center for the Learning and Teaching of Literature and sponsored by the National Endowment for the Arts and the Office of Educational Research and Improvement.

Input was also solicited from our advisory board, as well as educators from various areas. From these discussions, it was determined that each volume should have a mix of "classic" stories (those works commonly taught in literature classes) and contemporary stories for which information is often hard to find. Because of the interest in expanding the canon of literature, an emphasis was also placed on including works by international, multicultural, and women authors. Our advisory board members—educational professionals—helped pare down the list for each volume. Works not selected for the present volume were noted as possibilities for future volumes. As always, the editor welcomes suggestions for titles to be included in future volumes.

How Each Entry Is Organized

Each entry, or chapter, in *SSfS* focuses on one story. Each entry heading lists the title of the story, the author's name, and the date of the story's publication. The following elements are contained in each entry:

Introduction: a brief overview of the story which provides information about its first appearance, its literary standing, any controversies surrounding the work, and major conflicts or themes within the work.

Author Biography: this section includes basic facts about the author's life, and focuses on events and times in the author's life that may have inspired the story in question.

Plot Summary: a description of the events in the story. Lengthy summaries are broken down with subheads.

Characters: an alphabetical listing of the characters who appear in the story. Each character name is followed by a brief to an extensive description of the character's role in the story, as well as discussion of the character's actions, relationships, and possible motivation.

Characters are listed alphabetically by last name. If a character is unnamed—for instance, the narrator in "The Eatonville Anthology"—the character is listed as "The Narrator" and alphabetized as "Narrator." If a character's first name is the only one given, the name will appear alphabetically by that name.

Themes: a thorough overview of how the topics, themes, and issues are addressed within the story. Each theme discussed appears in a separate subhead.

Style: this section addresses important style elements of the story, such as setting, point of view, and narration; important literary devices used, such as imagery, foreshadowing, symbolism; and, if applicable, genres to which the work might have belonged, such as Gothicism or Romanticism. Literary terms are explained within the entry, but can also be found in the Glossary.

Historical Context: this section outlines the social, political, and cultural climate in which the author lived and the work was created. This section may include descriptions of related historical events, pertinent aspects of daily life in the culture, and the artistic and literary sensibilities of the time in which the work was written. If the story is historical in nature, information regarding the time in which the story is set is also included. Long sections are broken down with helpful subheads.

Critical Overview: this section provides background on the critical reputation of the author and the story, including bannings or any other public controversies surrounding the work. For older works, this section may include a history of how the story was first received and how perceptions of it may have changed over the years; for more recent works, direct quotes from early reviews may also be included.

Criticism: an essay commissioned by *SSfS* which specifically deals with the story and is written specifically for the student audience, as well as excerpts from previously published criticism on the work (if available).

Sources: an alphabetical list of critical material used in compiling the entry, with bibliographical information.

Further Reading: an alphabetical list of other critical sources which may prove useful for the student. Includes full bibliographical information and a brief annotation.

Suggested Search Terms: a list of search terms and phrases to jumpstart students' further information seeking. Terms include not just titles and author names but also terms and topics related to the historical and literary context of the works.

In addition, each entry contains the following highlighted sections, set apart from the main text as sidebars:

Media Adaptations: if available, a list of audiobooks and important film and television adaptations of the story, including source information. The list also includes stage adaptations, musical adaptations, etc.

Topics for Further Study: a list of potential study questions or research topics dealing with the story. This section includes questions related to other disciplines the student may be studying, such as American history, world history, science, math, government, business, geography, economics, psychology, etc.

Compare and Contrast: an "at-a-glance" comparison of the cultural and historical differences between the author's time and culture and late twentieth century or early twenty-first century Western culture. This box includes pertinent parallels between the major scientific, political, and cultural movements of the time or place the story was written, the time or place the story was set (if a historical work), and modern Western culture. Works written after 1990 may not have this box.

What Do I Read Next?: a list of works that might give a reader points of entry into a classic work (e.g., YA or multicultural titles) and/or complement the featured story or serve as a contrast to it. This includes works by the same author and others, works from various genres, YA works, and works from various cultures and eras.

Other Features

SSfS includes "Why Study Literature At All?," a foreword by Thomas E. Barden, Professor of English and Director of Graduate English Studies at the University of Toledo. This essay provides a number of very fundamental reasons for studying literature and, therefore, reasons why a book such as *SSfS*, designed to facilitate the study of literature, is useful.

A Cumulative Author/Title Index lists the authors and titles covered in each volume of the *SSfS* series.

A Cumulative Nationality/Ethnicity Index breaks down the authors and titles covered in each volume of the *SSfS* series by nationality and ethnicity.

A Subject/Theme Index, specific to each volume, provides easy reference for users who may be studying a particular subject or theme rather than a single work. Significant subjects from events to broad themes are included.

Each entry may include illustrations, including photo of the author, stills from film adaptations (if available), maps, and/or photos of key historical events.

Citing Short Stories for Students

When writing papers, students who quote directly from any volume of *SSfS* may use the following general forms to document their source. These examples are based on MLA style; teachers may request that students adhere to a different style, thus, the following examples may be adapted as needed.

When citing text from *SSfS* that is not attributed to a particular author (for example, the Themes, Style, Historical Context sections, etc.), the following format may be used:

"How I Met My Husband." *Short Stories for Students*. Ed. Sara Constantakis. Vol. 36. Detroit: Gale, Cengage Learning, 2013. 73–95. Print.

When quoting the specially commissioned essay from *SSfS* (usually the first essay under the Criticism subhead), the following format may be used:

Dominic, Catherine. Critical Essay on "How I Met My Husband." *Short Stories for Students*. Ed. Sara Constantakis. Vol. 36. Detroit: Gale, Cengage Learning, 2013. 84–87. Print.

When quoting a journal or newspaper essay that is reprinted in a volume of *SSfS*, the following form may be used:

Ditsky, John. "The Figure in the Linoleum: The Fictions of Alice Munro." *Hollins Critic* 22.3 (1985): 1–10. Rpt. in *Short Stories for Students*. Vol. 36. Ed. Sara Constantakis. Detroit: Gale, Cengage Learning, 2013. 92–94. Print.

When quoting material from a book that is reprinted in a volume of *SSfS*, the following form may be used:

Cooke, John. "Alice Munro." *The Influence of Painting on Five Canadian Writers*. Lewiston, NY: Edwin Mellen Press, 1996. 69–85. Rpt. in *Short Stories for Students*. Vol. 36. Ed. Sara Constantakis. Detroit: Gale, Cengage Learning, 2013. 89–92. Print.

We Welcome Your Suggestions

The editorial staff of *Short Stories for Students* welcomes your comments and ideas. Readers who wish to suggest short stories to appear in future volumes, or who have other suggestions, are cordially invited to contact the editor. You may contact the editor via E-mail at: **ForStudentsEditors@cengage.com.** Or write to the editor at:

Editor, *Short Stories for Students*
Gale
27500 Drake Road
Farmington Hills, MI 48331-3535

Literary Chronology

1812: Charles Dickens is born on February 7 in Landport, Hampshire, England.

1863: Arthur Machen is born on March 3 in Caerleon, Wales.

1866: Charles Dickens's "The Signalman" is published in *All the Year Round.*

1870: Charles Dickens dies of a stroke on June 9 at Gadshill, near Rochester, Kent, England.

1890: Katherine Anne Porter is born on May 15 in Indian Creek, Texas.

1895: Arthur Machen's "Novel of the Black Seal" is published in *The Three Imposters.*

1902: Kay Boyle is born on February 19 in St. Paul, Minnesota.

1909: Flannery O'Connor is born on April 13 in Savannah, Georgia.

1919: J. D. Salinger is born on January 1 in New York, New York.

1924: James Clavell is born on October 10 in Sydney, Australia.

1930: Katherine Anne Porter's "María Concepción" is published in *Flowering Judas.*

1937: Walter Dean Myers is born on August 12 in Martinsburg, West Virginia.

1940: Bharati Mukherjee is born on July 27 in Calcutta, India.

1941: Kay Boyle's "Defeat" is published in *New Yorker.*

1944: Alice Walker is born on February 9 in Eatonton, Georgia.

1947: Stephen King is born on September 21 in Portland, Maine.

1947: Arthur Machen dies of natural causes on December 15 in Beaconsfield, England.

1948: J. D. Salinger's "Just Before the War with the Eskimos" is published in *New Yorker.*

1954: Louise Erdrich is born on June 7 in Little Falls, Minnesota.

1956: Flannery O'Connor's "Greenleaf" is published in *Kenyon Review.*

1956: Ha Jin is born on February 21 in Liaoning Province, China.

1963: James Clavell's "The Children's Story" is published in *Ladies Home Journal.*

1964: Flannery O'Connor dies of lupus on August 3 in Milledgeville, Georgia.

1966: Katherine Anne Porter is awarded the Pulitzer Prize for Fiction for *Collected Stories.*

1980: Katherine Anne Porter dies after several debilitating strokes on September 18 in Silver Spring, Maryland.

1982: Louise Erdrich's "The World's Greatest Fishermen" is published in *Chicago* magazine.

1983: Alice Walker is awarded the Pulitzer Prize for Fiction for *The Color Purple.*

1985: Alice Walker's "Kindred Spirits" is published in *Esquire.*

1988: Bharti Mukherjee's "Orbiting" is published in *The Middleman and Other Stories.*

1992: Kay Boyle dies of natural causes on December 27 in Mill Valley, California.

1994: Stephen King's "The Man in the Black Suit" is published in *New Yorker.*

1994: James Clavell dies of complications from cancer on September 6 in Vevey, Switzerland.

2000: Walter Dean Myers's "The Streak" is published in *145th Street: Short Stories.*

2008: Ha Jin's "The House Behind a Weeping Cherry" is published in *New Yorker.*

2010: J. D. Salinger dies of natural causes on January 27 in Cornish, New Hampshire.

2012: Jean Kwok's "Where the Gods Fly" is published in *The Shortlist: The Sunday Times EFG Private Bank Short Story Award.*

2014: Walter Dean Myers dies of natural causes on July 1 in New York, New York.

Acknowledgements

The editors wish to thank the copyright holders of the excerpted criticism included in this volume and the permissions managers of many book and magazine publishing companies for assisting us in securing reproduction rights. We are also grateful to the staffs of the Detroit Public Library, the Library of Congress, the University of Detroit Mercy Library, Wayne State University Purdy/Kresge Library Complex, and the University of Michigan Libraries for making their resources available to us. Following is a list of the copyright holders who have granted us permission to reproduce material in this volume of *SSfS*. Every effort has been made to trace copyright, but if omissions have been made, please let us know.

COPYRIGHTED EXCERPTS IN SSfS, VOLUME 45, WERE REPRODUCED FROM THE FOLLOWING PERIODICALS:

Booklist, September 1, 2010. Copyright © 2010 American Library Association. Courtesy of American Library Association. — ***Booklist***, June 1, 2014. Copyright © 2014 American Library Association. Courtesy of American Library Association. — ***Publishers Weekly***, March 15, 2010. Copyright © 2010 PWXYZ, LLC. Courtesy of PWXYZ, LLC. — ***Independent***, September 8, 1994. Copyright © 1994 Independent Print LTD. Courtesy of Independent Print LTD. — ***Publishers Weekly***, July 26, 2010. Copyright © 2010 PWXYZ, LLC. Courtesy of PWXYZ, LLC. — ***Booklist***, April 1, 2010, 106:15, pp. 22. Copyright © 2010. Copyright © 2010 American Library Association. Courtesy of American Library Association. — ***Victorian Studies***, Spring 2001. Copyright © 2001 Indiana University Press. Courtesy of Indiana University Press. — ***Publishers Weekly***, September 3, 2007. Copyright © 2007 PWXYZ, LLC. Courtesy of PWXYZ, LLC. — ***Journal of Adolescent & Adult Literacy***, December 2007. Copyright © 2007 International Literacy Association. Courtesy of International Literacy Association. — ***Horn Book***, March 2000. Copyright © 2000 Horn Book Incorporated. Courtesy of Horn Book Incorporated.

COPYRIGHTED EXCERPTS IN SSfS, VOLUME 45, WERE REPRODUCED FROM THE FOLLOWING BOOKS:

Alam, Fakrul. From ***Bharati Mukherjee***. The Gale Group, 1996. Copyright © 1996, The Gale Group. —Bell, Elizabeth S. From ***A Study of the Short Fiction***. The Gale Group, 1992. Copyright © 1996, The Gale Group. —Bishop, Rudine Sims. From ***Presenting Walter Dean Myers***. The Gale Group, 1991. Copyright © 1996, The Gale Group. —Carb, Alison B. From ***Conversations with Bharati Mukherjee***. University Press of Mississippi, 2009. Copyright © 2009 University Press of Mississippi. —Carpenter, Richard C. From ***Critical Essays on Kay Boyle***. The Gale Group, 1997. Copyright © 1996, The Gale Group. —Graf, Susan Johnston. From ***Talking to the Gods:***

Occultism in the Work of W.B. Yeats, Arthur Machen, Algernon. State University of New York (SUNY) Press, 2015. Copyright © 2015 State University of New York (SUNY) Press. —Paulson, Suzanne Morrow. From ***Flannery O'Connor: A Study of the Short Fiction***. The Gale Group, 1988. Copyright © 1996, The Gale Group. —Tearle, Oliver. From ***Bewilderments of Vision: Hallucination and Literature, 1880-1914***. Sussex Academy Press, 2013. Copyright © Sussex Academy Press. —Wenke, John. From ***J.D. Salinger: A Study of the Short Fiction***. The Gale Group, 1991. Copyright © 1996, The Gale Group. —Winchell, Donna Haisty. From ***Alice Walker***. The Gale Group, 1992. Copyright © 1996, The Gale Group. —Yao, Steven G. From ***Foreign Accents: Chinese American Verse from Exclusion to Postethnicity***. Oxford University Press, 2010. Copyright © 2010 Oxford University Press.

Contributors

Susan K. Andersen: Andersen is a teacher and writer with a PhD in English literature. Entry on "Orbiting." Original essay on "Orbiting."

Bryan Aubrey: Aubrey holds a PhD in English. Entry on "Greenleaf." Original essay on "Greenleaf."

Charlotte Freeman: Freeman is a former academic, published novelist, and freelance writer who lives in Montana. Entry on "The Children's Story." Original essay on "The Children's Story."

Kristen Sarlin Greenberg: Greenberg is a freelance writer and editor with a background in literature and philosophy. Entries on "María Concepción" and "Where the Gods Fly." Original essays on "María Concepción" and "Where the Gods Fly."

Michael Allen Holmes: Holmes is a writer with existential interests. Entries on "Defeat," "The Streak," and "The World's Greatest Fishermen." Original essays on "Defeat," "The Streak," and "The World's Greatest Fishermen."

Amy L. Miller: Miller is a graduate of the University of Cincinnati. Entries on "The House behind a Weeping Cherry" and "Kindred Spirits." Original essays on "The House behind a Weeping Cherry" and "Kindred Spirits."

Michael J. O'Neal: O'Neal holds a PhD in English. Entry on "The Signalman." Original essay on "The Signalman."

April Paris: Paris is a freelance writer with a degree in classical literature and a background in academic writing. Entry on "The Man in the Black Suit." Original essay on "The Man in the Black Suit."

William Rosencrans: Rosencrans is a writer and copy editor. Entry on "Just Before the War with the Eskimos." Original essay on "Just Before the War with the Eskimos."

Bradley A. Skeen: Skeen is a classicist. Entry on "Novel of the Black Seal." Original essay on "Novel of the Black Seal."

The Children's Story

JAMES CLAVELL

1963

"The Children's Story" was first published in the *Ladies' Home Journal* in 1963, then republished as a stand-alone book in 1981. James Clavell claimed the story was inspired by his daughter Michaela, who came home from first grade proud of herself for having learned the Pledge of Allegiance and demanding a dime for reciting it accurately. When Clavell queried her on what the words meant, particularly the words *pledge* and *allegiance*, the child had no idea.

Clavell then began asking other Americans around him what they thought the pledge meant, and he found that while most of them could recite it from heart, very few could speak to its meaning. The early 1960s were a time of high tensions during the Cold War between the Soviet Union and the United States, and many people were worried that the United States could be taken over by a foreign power and be subjected to Communism. Clavell imagined such an event taking place and speculated via the story about how easy it would be to indoctrinate a classroom of small children, who had never been taught critical thinking skills or the true meaning of the Pledge of Allegiance.

The story is an allegory in which the classroom of children stands for a population of adults who also lack critical thinking skills. It dramatizes not only Clavell's worry that the population lacked qualities necessary to resist domination but also a general cultural worry about the same issue that

James Clavell (©Daniel SIMON / Gamma-Rapho / Getty Images)

was common at the time. While "The Children's Story" has not had the evergreen success that Clavell's blockbuster novels for adults have had, it lives on in the teaching community, where it has proved a useful tool for class discussion.

AUTHOR BIOGRAPHY

Clavell was born James Edmund du Maresq Clavell in Sydney, Australia, on October 10, 1924, to English parents who moved back to England when he was only a few months old. His father was an officer in the Royal Navy who had been tasked with helping to found the Australian navy. The Clavell men had served in the Royal Navy for generations, and when World War II broke out, Clavell tried to join up. Ultimately, he enlisted in the Royal Artillery, where he was sent to the Far East and was captured by the Japanese in Java in 1941.

Clavell was shipped to the notorious Changi prison camp in Singapore. At the beginning of the war, forty thousand men were interned at Changi, but by war's end, only one man in fifteen had survived the regimen of torture, starvation, and disease. Many soldiers were shipped out, some sent to build the Thailand-Burma Railway and others to Japan to work in mines; those left at Changi were put to work loading ships, clearing sewers, and building tunnels in which their Japanese captors planned to hide and defend themselves if the Allies took back Singapore. "Changi became my university instead of my prison," he later told an interviewer, quoted in the *New York Times*. He continued:

> Among the inmates there were experts in all walks of life—the high and the low roads. I studied and absorbed everything I could from physics to counterfeiting, but most of all I learned the art of surviving.

Upon gaining his freedom, Clavell returned to England and, after a motorcycle accident ended his military career, enrolled in university, where he met his wife, April Stride (with whom he had two daughters), and became interested in film. For several years he worked in film distribution, before immigrating to the United States, where he bluffed his way into a screenwriting job. Clavell wrote several popular movies, including *The Fly* (1958), *The Great Escape* (1963), and *To Sir, with Love* (1967). During the screenwriters' strike of 1960, he drew on his experiences in Changi for his first novel, *King Rat* (1962), the story of a British officer and an American non-commissioned officer who become friends and team up to survive. It was a huge success and launched Clavell's career.

Clavell wrote numerous detailed historical novels about Westerners' experiences in the Far East, from *Shogun* (1975), set in Japan during the 1600s, to *King Rat*, *Tai-Pan* (1966), and *Noble House* (1981), which follows the fortunes of several characters through World War II and into the following decades. "The Children's Story," published in 1963, is his only work ostensibly for children and was inspired by his daughter's first day of school, where she learned the Pledge of Allegiance by heart. Clavell died at age sixty-nine at his home in Vevey, Switzerland, on September 6, 1994.

PLOT SUMMARY

"The Children's Story" takes place entirely within an elementary school classroom during the first twenty-three minutes of the school day.

MEDIA ADAPTATIONS

- "The Children's Story" was made into a thirty-minute television movie in 1982 as part of the Mobil Showcase series. The script was written and the episode directed by Clavell, featuring his daughter Michaela, acting under the name Michaela Ross, as the New Teacher.

The story begins with a classroom full of students, waiting. The air is thick with apprehension. The teacher is terrified. The students are terrified. There has been an invasion, and their country has been conquered by a foreign force. Johnny is not frightened, however; Johnny is upset, feeling hatred. He is angry that the teacher is afraid, and he wants to shout at her. His father has told him not to be afraid, that giving in to fear will make him "dead even though you're alive."

They hear footsteps in the corridor. They expect the worst, a monster or a bogeyman. When the door opens, a young woman enters. She is beautiful and young and dressed in a neat and clean uniform. She has a warm smile and does not speak with any kind of an accent. The children are confused by this, as they have been told that the invaders are foreign and different.

The New Teacher walks through the classroom and surprises them by addressing one of the children and their teacher by name. She tells the teacher, Miss Worden, that she will be taking over the classroom now and that Miss Worden should go to the principal's office. Miss Worden is panicky and in tears, and the children are frightened by her outburst. Sandra tries to run after Miss Worden as she leaves the room, but the New Teacher catches her.

To calm the frightened children, including Sandra, the New Teacher suggests a song. Still cradling Sandra, she lowers herself to the floor and sings the children a very pretty song in a foreign language. She explains what the words mean and that it is a song about two children who are lost and afraid. A man on a horse finds them and tells them that the stars will always lead them home. The New Teacher explains what the story means, that if "you know the right direction, then there's never a need to be afraid." This is the first of the teacher's suggestions that if the children acquiesce to her definition of right thinking, if they follow her lead, everything will be fine.

The New Teacher sings the song again, and all the children seem to become calm and happy—all except for Johnny, who still hates the New Teacher, even as he agrees with her about not being afraid. The New Teacher then astonishes the children by naming them all. Johnny raises his hand to ask her how she knew their names, when she has never taken roll. She says she learned them all from a list, and, to impress them, she tells the children it took her three days to do so. She asks Johnny whether he thinks it is important for a teacher to work hard, and he agrees, although he still hates the New Teacher.

The New Teacher tells the class they will not need roll call anymore, because a good teacher should just *know* who is present and who is not. She then asks the children to stand and say the Pledge of Allegiance, which is what they always do after roll call. As the children begin to recite, the New Teacher interrupts them, asking what the words mean. The children are bewildered. Miss Worden never interrupted the pledge and certainly never asked them what it meant. The New Teacher asks them about the word *pledge* and about the word *allegiance*; when the children admit that no one has ever explained to them what the words mean, the New Teacher asks if they ever asked their parents. The children tell the New Teacher that their parents never explained it, although Mary said her father did give her a nickel for reciting it.

The New Teacher tells the children that *allegiance* means "promising or pledging support to the flag," but she then claims that pledging support is "saying that it is much more important than *you* are." She asks them what they think this means. "How can a flag be more important than a real live person?"

Johnny then recalls the next part, about "and to the republic, for which it stands." He searches for the correct term, and the New Teacher supplies it for him, telling him that the word he is looking for is *symbol.* She tells them that a symbol is like a sign to remind them of something, in this instance, that they love their country. She tells the children that of course they love their country, because they are good girls and boys; then she asks them whether they need a symbol to remind them that they are good. They think they do not, because they know they are good children.

Johnny, however, reminds them that it is their flag and that they always pledge. The New Teacher looks at the flag and notes that it is very pretty. She leads the children to the idea that the flag could be cut up, so that each of them could keep a piece of it in his or her pocket. Mary is allowed to cut off the first piece, and each of the children, in turn, gets a piece. They have destroyed the flag they were pledging to protect, although they do not seem to understand this. They do sense that the flagpole is very strange without a flag on it. The New Teacher allows them to push the now-useless flagpole out the window. The children shriek with joy at the shock of being allowed to do something so transgressive and begin to love the New Teacher for allowing them to do such a thing.

The New Teacher tells them they can ask her anything, and Mary is curious about her uniform. The New Teacher tells her, "We think that teachers should be dressed the same. Then you always know a teacher." She tells the children that free uniforms will be provided for them as well. When Johnny asks what happens if he does not want to wear those clothes, the New Teacher tells him it is not required. He tells himself he will never wear their clothes, even if that means that he will look different from the other children.

When Mary asks why their teacher was crying, the New Teacher says she was probably tired and that she is going to be sent off for a long rest. Then Danny asks if the war is over, and Mary asks if "we" won. The New Teacher tells them: "We—that's you and I and all of us—*we* won." What she has done here is quietly change the meaning of "we" from Mary's original question, where she used "we" to refer to the population of the country that has just been invaded, to a new definition of "we," in which the New Teacher includes herself as a representative of the invading forces along with the children.

Johnny senses this and objects, asking what they have done with his dad. It appears that someone has taken his father away; his mother has told him that he is gone forever. The New Teacher tells him that his father has gone "back to school" because he was trying to persuade others to believe "wrong thoughts." At first Johnny cannot believe that his father would have wrong thoughts, but when the teacher asks if he has ever been impatient with Johnny, the boy has to admit that he has. She tells him that is akin to a wrong thought and that they are all going to learn all about good thoughts together in school.

Next she tells the children that they are going to stay at the school overnight, like a kind of slumber party. When Jenny says that they will have to say their prayers before bed, the New Teacher leads them through an exercise where they pray for candy; when no candy appears, she suggests that instead of praying to God, they should pray to Our Leader. While the children pray even harder, she quietly puts a piece of candy on each of their desks. Johnny objects, because he saw her putting the candy there. The teacher replies that Johnny is right. Prayer is useless, and only people can provide for one another.

When she tells them that knowing that prayer does not work can be their secret, the children object that they are not supposed to keep secrets from their parents. The New Teacher asks if their parents have secrets from them; when they reply that, of course, they do, she says this is the same. The class will have "lots of wonderful secrets together."

She rewards Johnny for his cleverness in catching her with the candy by making him monitor for the week. As he chews his piece of candy, he decides that he likes the teacher after all. He had wondered many times why his prayers were never answered, but now he knows. He resolves to "work hard and listen and not to have wrong thoughts like Dad."

The New Teacher looks out the window and thinks with contentment about how well she is going to teach her students and what good citizens they are going to be. Mostly, though, she is contented by the thought that "throughout the land, all children, all men and all women were being taught with the same faith, with variations of the same procedures." A mere twenty-three minutes have passed since the beginning of the school day, and the New Teacher has persuaded the children to betray their flag, their parents, and their belief in God and to follow her lead. She has persuaded even Johnny.

CHARACTERS

Brian

Brian is one of the children in the classroom. He is the one who tells the New Teacher that Miss Worden had scissors in her desk. They use the scissors to cut the flag into pieces.

Dad

Johnny's father tells him not to be afraid, because giving in to fear will make him "dead even though you're alive." He has been taken away before the story begins, and Johnny does not know where he has gone. His mother has said that Dad is gone forever. The New Teacher tells Johnny that Dad has gone to a school for adults who need to be taught not to have "wrong thoughts" anymore. Johnny does not believe his father could have wrong thoughts, but the teacher uses examples of minor instances of wrongness to erode Johnny's faith in his father. She even tells Johnny that he can see his father, that he will have a holiday soon. Johnny is skeptical at first but comes to believe the New Teacher. However, since the New Teacher is indeed an agent of the invading regime, the reader is left in doubt about Dad's fate, despite Johnny's conversion to the New Teacher's version of events.

Danny

Danny is one of the children in the classroom. He has been to another school before this one, where the teacher also did not explain what the Pledge of Allegiance meant. He is sorry to find out that other children have been given nickels to recite the pledge, when his father did not give one to him. It is Danny who asks if the war is over, and he is pleased when the New Teacher tells him that it is and that their daddies will all be home soon. Danny confesses he once prayed for a puppy, which he did not get.

Hilda

Hilda is one of the children in the classroom. She is Mary's best friend, and they share many secrets. She has also been to other schools before this one and testifies that no one in any of those schools explained the pledge to her either; they just told her she had to learn it.

Jenny

Jenny is one of the children in the classroom. She is the one who tells the New Teacher that they need to say their prayers before they go to sleep during the school overnight.

Joan

Joan is one of the children in the classroom. She has been to another school before this one and relays her experiences when the New Teacher asks the children about what had happened at school before.

Johnny

Johnny is the only child in his classroom who is not afraid of the new regime. He is angry instead, full of hatred because the conquering forces have taken his father away. He begins the story angry at their teacher, Miss Worden, for being afraid and then for crying in front of the children. Johnny hates the New Teacher when she arrives and resists being taken in by her youth or prettiness or lovely smell. Bit by bit, the New Teacher chips away at Johnny's objections. When he says that it is *their* flag, the New Teacher uses that as a starting place for suggesting that it is so special they should cut it into pieces and each keep one. When he demands to know what they have done with his father, the teacher says he has gone off to school to learn to overcome his "wrong thoughts"; and when Johnny says his father would not have wrong thoughts, she gives him several minor examples of his father's being wrong. She then tells him that wrong thoughts are not bad thoughts; they are simply old-fashioned. That is why his father needs to go back to school, to learn the new ways. She extrapolates from those examples to cause Johnny to doubt his father and all the other children to doubt their parents as well.

During the exercise where the New Teacher has them pray first to God for candy and then to Our Leader for candy, Johnny peeks when the other children are praying. He catches the teacher putting the candy on their desks and tells the other children that is where the candy has come from. He is very frightened to confront the teacher and for a moment thinks he might be punished, but she answers his objection seriously and uses it as a means of telling the other children that God does not exist after all. She tells them that the fulfillment of their desires can come only from other people, not from divine intervention. Then the New Teacher rewards Johnny by making him the class monitor. It is by demonstrating that the God who has never answered Johnny's prayers does not exist that she wins him over at last. By the end of the story, Johnny has decided that he likes the New

Teacher after all, and he resolves to listen to her and to not think wrong thoughts.

Mary

Mary is one of the children in the classroom. She tries to answer the question of what the word *pledge* means. She says that it is when you promise to do something good, like not suck your thumb so you will not need braces later. It is Mary's birthday, and so she is allowed to cut off the first piece of the flag with the scissors. Mary worries about the cost of the new uniforms that the New Teacher tells them are available and is relieved and excited to learn they will be free.

New Teacher

The New Teacher is not the monster the children were expecting. She is young and attractive. Her clothes are neat and new and all in olive green, including her shoes. She smells nice. She knows their names and that it is Mary's birthday before she has even met any of them, knowledge that awes the children and adds to her air of omnipotence. She is nineteen years old, and she startles the children in several ways. The old teacher panicked, but the New Teacher is calm and collected. When Sandra panics and tries to run out of the room, the New Teacher does not punish her but treats her gently and even sits on the floor with her, thereby aligning herself with the children, for whom it is always preferable to sit on the floor. She sings to them and teaches them the meaning of her song. She is reassuring. Then, when she has begun to gain their trust, she systematically undermines all the authority figures upon which the children have previously relied. Her very arrival unhinges the old teacher.

When it is time to recite the Pledge of Allegiance, the teacher startles the children by challenging them to define the meaning of words like *pledge* and *allegiance* and then finally undermines the pledge itself by declaring it to be simply a symbol, and one they do not need. Then she examines the flag, which is by now the flag of a conquered nation. Instead of simply replacing it with the new flag, she leads the children into destroying their own flag under the guise of each saving a piece for themselves. Once the flag is destroyed, the New Teacher allows the children to throw the flagpole out the widow in a fit of transgressive exuberance they find thrilling. These actions serve to undermine the children's attachment to the nationalist symbols of their now-conquered nation, but in a way that leads the children to think it is their own idea. This is a far more powerful way to gain their allegiance to the new order than force would have been.

The New Teacher uses the same tactics to undermine the children's attachment to their parents, by calling into question their authority and encouraging the children to keep secret from them what happens at school. She further seeks to break the child-parent bond by telling the children that they are going to stay at school overnight, where the school will feed them and clothe them in new uniforms. Her final tactic is to undermine their childish faith in God by telling them to pray very hard for candy, a prayer she knows will not be answered. The New Teacher even turns Johnny's skepticism to her purposes by praising him for his cleverness and rewarding him for it by making him class monitor. By the end of the story, a mere twenty-three minutes after it begins, the New Teacher has brought the children around to her cause with her use of "variations of the same procedures" being used elsewhere, a process that brings her great calm and confidence.

Sandra

Sandra is the first child that the New Teacher addresses by name, surprising them all. When Miss Worden leaves the classroom in tears, Sandra tries to run to her but is caught gently by the New Teacher, who cradles her in her arms until she stops crying.

Miss Worden

Miss Worden is the original teacher in the children's classroom. She is an older woman, with gray hair and shabby clothes. She has never married and has dedicated her life to teaching children. In her moment of terror, it is the faces of her former pupils that she sees in her mind's eye, melding into the face of one generalized, nameless child. She dissolves in tears when the New Teacher arrives and she is sent to the principal's office. The New Teacher tells the class that Miss Worden has gone off for a rest, although her panic and the fact that the nation has just been taken over by invasion would suggest that her fate might be more sinister.

TOPICS FOR FURTHER STUDY

- At one time or another most people have thought, even idly, about what it would be like if they were confronted with the kind of war and invasion that can be seen happening around the world. Write a play about what it might be like if your town were taken over by a foreign force. You must have at least three characters, and although your play need not take more than fifteen minutes to perform, it should have three acts. In the first act, the main character discovers that the town has been conquered. In the second act the character experiences the challenges of learning to navigate a foreign social and political regime in his or her own town. In the third, the character must resolve these problems. Perform the play for your class.
- The New Teacher uses several classic propaganda techniques as she leads the children from resistance to acquiescence to the new regime. Research propaganda and, using your web skills, create a multimedia online presentation. Your presentation should contain definitions of propaganda techniques, examples from "The Children's Story," and links to real-life examples of propaganda in action, using news clippings and video clips to illustrate your presentation.
- During the Communist revolutions in Southeast Asia that inspired Clavell's allegory of an ordinary classroom taken over by a totalitarian regime, everyday language was very specifically subordinated to the political aims of the ruling party. People are confronted every day with language that has been subverted to specific purposes, whether by the government, popular culture, advertising, religions, or the military. Working in small groups and using the Internet, newspapers, and magazines for sources, collect ten examples of phrases that exemplify such subversion. Create a propaganda campaign of your own, designed to persuade your fellow students to replace one of their beliefs with a false belief. For your campaign, create content with at least two of these media: music, graphic design/posters, video, news media.
- Read Marjane Satrapi's graphic novel *Persepolis* (2004). While Satrapi's book is set in a different place and time than "The Children's Story," both authors seek to communicate the experience of life under a repressive political regime. Compare the characters of Marji and Johnny and write a short story in which they somehow encounter each other. Feel free to use graphics, as in the Satrapi novel, to illustrate how these two characters might recognize each other as young people rebelling against similar constraints.
- In *Between Shades of Grey* (2011), by Ruta Sepetys, a young Lithuanian girl named Lina has her life turned upside down when her home is invaded by Soviet soldiers, who take away Lina's father and send her, her mother, and her younger brother to Siberia. Read this book, research the Stalinist era in the Soviet Union, and write a paper comparing the political repression in that era with that evident in "The Children's Story." In light of your historical research, do you believe the New Teacher's promises? or do you think Johnny's fate might be darker than the story leads the reader to believe? Incorporate your answer into your paper.

THEMES

McCarthyism

Anxiety in the United States about internal Communist subversion in the 1940s and 1950s reached a fever pitch as the Soviet Union consolidated power over Eastern Europe after World War II. Government loyalty boards were established, thirty-nine states required loyalty oaths for teachers and public employees, and hundreds of

The story is set in a classroom, and the action takes less than half an hour *(©Areipa.lt / Shutterstock.com)*

actors, screenwriters, and directors were blacklisted either for their political beliefs or for their refusal to accuse others. Although the anti-Communist activities of that era are commonly known as "McCarthyism," fears of Communism had been used since the 1930s to stifle union organizing and civil rights activism.

Although the United States and the Soviet Union were allies during World War II, the alliance eroded as the Soviet Union consolidated power in Eastern Europe after the war ended. Several events of the late 1940s and early 1950s, including the Soviet nuclear bomb tests of 1949, the Communist victory in China that same year, and North Korea's invasion of South Korea in 1950, all seemed unbelievable to many people. In response, they decided there must be sympathizers in the US government and industry supplying aid to Communist parties abroad.

"The Children's Story" is a classic example of McCarthy-era anxieties. The story portrays a group of innocents who are easily swayed by the promise of food and clothing and candy for all, at the expense of freedom of thought. At the end of the story, the teacher is warmed not by the sun or the loveliness of the land itself, but by the thought that "throughout the land, all children, all men and women were being taught with the same faith," a faith predicated on the idea that everyone would be provided for. "Each according to his age group. Each according to his need." This is a deliberate echo of a statement by Karl Marx that a goal of Communist governments should be to spur the people collectively to provide for every person, "from each according to his ability, to each according to his needs." To those worried about a Communist takeover of the United States, the specter of a group of shabby children being swayed to the Communist cause was deeply frightening.

Totalitarianism

Totalitarianism is a political system in which the individual is completely subordinated to the control of the state. Totalitarian regimes enforce their views through the use of extensive surveillance by secret police, often reinforced by the systematic use of spies and informers. Every level of social interaction in a totalitarian society, from the workplace to the family, is undermined by spying in order to subordinate the citizenry to the control of a single party and a single leader. Totalitarianism originated in Germany in the 1930s and 1940s, finding its full expression under Adolf Hitler's Nazi regime. Following closely upon Hitler's heels were the regimes of Benito Mussolini in Italy, Joseph Stalin in Russia, and Mao Zedong in China. True totalitarianism is a modern phenomenon, relying on technologies of surveillance and the systematic erosion of family and community bonds. In the absence of these bonds, individuals can be more easily manipulated by propaganda to do the will of their leaders.

While the classroom in "The Children's Story" is not yet fully converted to a regime of totalitarian surveillance, there are hints that the New Teacher's intentions lie in that direction. First, she sets about undermining the symbols of authority upon which the children rely—their old teacher, the Pledge of Allegiance, the flag, and their parents. First, the old teacher is made to look ridiculous, and the children read her fear as betrayal of their trust. Teachers are supposed to protect their students, and the old teacher, like the old regime that has been defeated, is clearly incapable of that. The New Teacher casts doubt on the Pledge of Allegiance and, in so doing, causes the children to doubt the veracity of those previously charged with educating them while simultaneously convincing them that her own educational methods are more honest and true. She encourages them to cut up the flag and throw the flagpole out the window, an act of rebellion against the former authority that serves to sway them to her side. Finally she erodes their confidence in God and enlists them to keep this knowledge secret from their parents, thus also undermining the family bond. All of these are hallmarks of a totalitarian regime, one that seeks to control not just the actions but, indeed, the beliefs of its citizens.

STYLE

Allegory

Allegory is a narrative technique in which characters represent something other than their literal identity. Characters in an allegorical work often represent abstract ideas or are used to convey a message or teach a lesson. While allegory is typically used to teach moral, ethical, or religious lessons, it can also be used for satiric or political purposes.

The first sign that "The Children's Story" is meant to be allegorical is in the way the characters are named. The children have very generic names and, with the exception of Johnny, are not really distinguishable from one another. They are not characters so much as they are representative of "children" in general. The same holds for the teachers. We find out that the original teacher even has a name only because the New Teacher addresses her by it; to the children, hearing their teacher addressed by name is almost as startling as seeing her in tears. To them, and to the story, she is simply the teacher, identified by her role and representative of the regime that has just been conquered. The New Teacher, however, is representative of the new regime and of newness in general. She is young and pretty. Her clothes are new and tidy, and she smells good. She seduces the children with her newness. her energy, and her engagement. Johnny's resistance to her appeal is also allegorical and is meant to demonstrate the healthy skepticism that independent people should have of any force that has defeated their country. The other children in the story are not individualized—not because the author was incapable of characterization but because they are a kind of collective character; they are "the children." Their purpose is to show how easily some people can be led and to serve as a contrast to Johnny's resistance. All of the characters in this story remain types rather than individuals, which is a hallmark of allegory.

Symbol

A symbol is something that suggests or stands for something else, without losing its original identity. In literature, symbols combine their literal meaning with the suggestion of an abstract concept. The classroom flag in "The Children's Story" is a good example of how a symbol works in narrative fiction. The New Teacher, having cast doubt upon the Pledge of Allegiance, then moves her attention to the object of that pledge, the flag itself. Flags are always symbolic. It is in the literal definition of a flag to be a symbol of the nation for which it stands. This is why there are so many rituals surrounding how a flag is treated, rituals that dictate the proper way to handle the flag, fly the flag, and salute the flag. Since the physical object that is the flag stands for the larger political entity that is the nation-state it represents, actions toward the flag are seen as an extension of one's feelings toward the nation.

Thus, when the New Teacher leads the children to destroy their flag, she betrays her true political project. The New Teacher seems like an improvement over the old teacher. She is young and pretty and clean. She promises the children food and new clothing and an educational atmosphere where they will be allowed to ask questions and to participate openly. All of these seem like improvements, and yet her actions, especially toward the flag, demonstrate that she is indeed an agent of the new regime who has come to impose that regime on the children.

Satire

Satire is a mode of writing that is designed to expose the failings of individuals, institutions, or societies. Satirical writing can be direct, in which the writer addresses the audience, or indirect, where the author leaves it to the readers to draw their own conclusions about the meaning of the piece.

In "The Children's Story," the satire operates through allegory. The allegorical meanings in this story are not meant to be taken at face value, and in this respect the story can be considered satirical. For instance, the New Teacher is described as being pretty and clean and treats the children with respect and interest, all of which are positive qualities. The old teacher, by contrast, was old and unkempt and did not smell fresh and clean. If the allegory was to be taken at face value, this would indicate that the New Teacher is better than the old teacher; however, since the New Teacher leads the children to abandon their pledge, deface their flag, and agree to keep secrets from their parents, and also to perform bad actions, it is clear that the New Teacher is not a positive figure. It is because there is a doubleness to the meaning that this can be taken as a satirical characterization. The New Teacher is outwardly attractive while leading the children to acts of betrayal, demonstrating that the author is using her as a satirical figure, one whose meaning is in opposition to her signification.

HISTORICAL CONTEXT

Cold War

Although "The Children's Story" is set in an indeterminate time and place, it was published in the United States in 1963, and Clavell wrote a postscript describing how it came into being as a result of his daughter's experience with the Pledge of Allegiance. Depicting an unnamed nation that seems very American and that has been recently invaded by a foreign power with some hallmarks of Communist rule, it is not a stretch to read the work as being influenced by particular historical events.

Although the United States, Britain, and the Soviet Union had been allies during World War II, as the war came to an end and the Soviet Union encouraged Communist takeovers of the governments of Eastern Europe, tensions began to rise. After the Americans used nuclear bombs in Japan at the end of the war, nuclear weapons development grew into an arms race between the United States and the Soviet Union and each nation's allies. The term *cold war* was coined to denote the opposite of a "hot" war (in which weapons are actually used).

In the decades following World War II, the Cold War extended to all corners of the globe. In a 1954 press conference, explaining the strategic importance of Vietnam and why he believed the United States might need to intervene there, President Dwight Eisenhower explained what came to be known as the "domino theory": "You have a row of dominoes set up, you knock over the first one, and what will happen to the last one is a certainty that it will go over very quickly." The president's concern was that if Vietnam went Communist, then it could lead to the "loss of Indochina, of Burma, of Thailand, of the Peninsula, and Indonesia following." Although the United States did not formally enter into combat in Vietnam until 1965, this "domino theory" became and remained a central tenet of the nation's engagement with Communist nations throughout the Cold War.

Negotiations to reduce the nuclear arsenals of both the United States and the Soviet Union began in the early 1980s, and by the end of that decade economic crises inside the Soviet Union, in conjunction with overextension into the wars in Afghanistan and Central America, caused the government of the Soviet Union to collapse. The Berlin Wall, a symbol of the Cold War since its erection in 1961 to prevent East German citizens from defecting

COMPARE & CONTRAST

- **1963:** The Cuban missile crisis erupts in the last weeks of 1962, and the United States will enter 1963 still negotiating an end to the crisis. In October 1962 US surveillance planes discover Soviet intercontinental ballistic missile silos being installed on Cuba, an island a mere ninety miles from the United States. After several tense weeks, a naval blockade by the US Navy, and much diplomatic negotiation, the crisis is averted. It is not until decades later that the public is informed of how close the nation came to nuclear war or how long it took to actually resolve the crisis.

  Today: In July of 2015, the United States and Cuba restore full diplomatic relations between their governments. The United States reopens its embassy in Havana, while the Cuban government opens an embassy in Washington, DC. While there are still any number of issues to be worked out, opening diplomatic relations is an important first step to normalizing relations between the two nations.

- **1963:** Dr. Martin Luther King Jr. calls for a direct action campaign to attack the segregation laws in Birmingham, Alabama. Hundreds are arrested, including King himself, on Good Friday. Sentenced to solitary confinement, he pens his famous "Letter from a Birmingham Jail." By May, negotiations to end the protest include promises from local government to remove "Whites Only" and "Blacks Only" signs on bathrooms and water fountains and to desegregate lunch counters.

  Today: In response to the unjust deaths of several young black men and the massacre at a black church in Charleston, South Carolina, the hashtag #BlackLivesMatter begins trending on social media like Twitter and Facebook. This leads to the creation of a new kind of organized political activism, with young activists forming local chapters and taking local action. It is too early to tell how effective the movement will be in the long run, but it has mobilized and trained thousands of activists across the country to work for racial equality.

- **1963:** On November 22, John F. Kennedy is assassinated while riding in an open limousine in a motorcade through Dallas, Texas. As the motorcade passes through Dealey Plaza, three shots ring out, killing the president and seriously injuring Governor John Connally. The vice president, Lyndon B. Johnson, is sworn in as president that evening on Air Force One. Lee Harvey Oswald is arrested for the crime but is almost immediately killed by Jack Ruby. Oswald's ties to the Soviet Union and Ruby's ties to organized crime lead to decades of speculation and conspiracy theories surrounding the assassination.

  Today: The sheer volume of conspiracy theories surrounding the Kennedy assassination, which live on despite several congressional investigations into the matter, is a precursor to the ongoing conspiracy theories that have dogged the Obama administration for eight years, including groundless speculation about President Obama's nation of birth and eligibility for the office. Thomas J. Wood, a political scientist from Ohio State University who researches conspiracy theories, has noted, as cited in an article in the *Boston Globe* by Michael Levinson, that they are "a core way that Americans read about and explain political phenomena in response to uncertainty."

---

to West Berlin, was toppled in a night of joyous street riots in 1989. By the early 1990s the Cold War seemed to be officially dead, as the Soviet Union broke up into its constituent nations and even China opened its nation to capitalist investment.

Cuban Missile Crisis

In October 1962, a diplomatic crisis brought the United States and the Soviet Union perilously close to war. President John F. Kennedy and his advisers were informed that a Central Intelligence Agency (CIA) spy plane had verified photographic evidence that the Soviet Union had secretly installed nuclear missiles in Cuba, a mere ninety miles from the Florida coast. The United States considered several courses of action, including invading Cuba, which had been a Communist nation since Fidel Castro defeated the dictator Fulgencio Batista in 1959. Instead, the Kennedy administration instituted a naval blockade of the island of Cuba, aimed at preventing any more Soviet weaponry from entering the nation. This precipitated both a diplomatic and military crisis, and for thirteen long days it seemed that the United States and the Soviet Union might be on the brink of nuclear war.

Not until decades later, during a conference in Havana in 1992, did American diplomats and scholars learn exactly how close to nuclear war both sides had come. It was at that conference that Soviet officials admitted that in addition to the intermediate-range intercontinental ballistic missiles (ICBMs) that the CIA planes had detected, the Soviets had installed nine short-range tactical nuclear missiles and had authorized ground troops to use them in case of invasion. In the intervening decades, more information has come to light about the crisis itself and the diplomatic negotiations that brought it to a close on October 28, when Soviet leader Nikita Khrushchev agreed to remove the warheads from Cuba in exchange for a treaty guaranteeing that the United States would not invade the island. Although the Cuban missile crisis was portrayed at the time as an unforeseen crisis, masterfully resolved by John F. Kennedy, further historical research has shown that it was more complicated than originally portrayed. Nonetheless, it remains the closest brush with nuclear war the world experienced during the Cold War, and one that everyone is grateful passed without further incident.

Pledge of Allegiance

The Pledge of Allegiance has evolved as the nation itself has grown and changed. One of the first versions of the pledge was written in 1892 by a minister named Francis Bellamy. The World's Fair and Columbian Exposition was set to open in Chicago on the four hundredth anniversary of Columbus's arrival in the Americas, and patriotic fervor was at a high. Bellamy's intention was to form a pledge that all schoolchildren could recite in unison every morning, a recitation that he believed would inspire patriotism and assimilate immigrants. The original pledge was "I pledge allegiance to my Flag and to the Republic for which it stands—one nation, indivisible—with liberty and justice for all," and it was meant to be recited while the students raised their right arms in salute. By the mid-1930s, as Hitler's forces came to power in Germany, the salute was dropped in favor of the hand over the heart used now. It was not until 1954 that, with other minor revisions, the words "under God" were added to the pledge. In light of growing American fear about Communism, godlessness, and the rise of the Soviet Union, President Eisenhower suggested the amendment, which was ratified by Congress. It is this version of the pledge that schoolchildren recite to this day.

The story begins with the children's teacher being replaced with a different teacher well-versed in the propaganda of the new regime

(©DarkBird / Shutterstock.com)

CRITICAL OVERVIEW

Clavell is known for his extensively researched historical novels filled with plot twists. He is considered a popular novelist rather than a literary one, and thus there is not much critical material on his work.

"The Children's Story" was first published in 1963 in the *Ladies' Home Journal*, and caused quite some controversy, as it seems many readers did not understand that it was a cautionary tale about how easy it could be to indoctrinate a group of children. Readers responded by claiming that the tale was un-American and subversive and accusing both the *Ladies' Home Journal* and Clavell himself of advocating the sorts of tactics the New Teacher uses in the story.

It was not until the early 1980s, shortly after the election of Ronald Reagan as president, that Delacorte, Clavell's publisher, decided the time might be right to reprint the story as a stand-alone book. The United States was experiencing a period of patriotic fervor, and Delacorte thought the public might be primed for Clavell's story. They republished it in 1981 and added a facsimile of Clavell's handwritten note explaining that he had been inspired to write the story when his young daughter Michaela came home from school proud to have learned the Pledge of Allegiance, but without any idea of what the words actually meant.

The book has come in for criticism, notably from Eliot Fremont-Smith, writing in the *Village Voice*, who notes that there are a number of problems with the tale—most tellingly its basic assertion that small children who do not properly understand the Pledge of Allegiance are in danger of being swayed to a New World Order by lovely nineteen-year-old teachers. Fremont-Smith concludes his review by stating that the story "stinks." While "The Children's Story" is not the best seller Clavell's other, adult novels were, it has found a second life in classrooms, where it has proved a useful teaching tool.

CRITICISM

Charlotte Freeman

Freeman is a former academic, published novelist, and freelance writer who lives in Montana. In the following essay, she examines Clavell's use of allegorical satire in "The Children's Story."

> "ALLEGORIES WORK THROUGH THE USE OF SYMBOL, AS DO THE TECHNIQUES OF THE NEW TEACHER. SINCE A SYMBOL IS SOMETHING THAT REMAINS ITSELF WHILE ALSO SIGNIFYING A LARGER MEANING, THE CLASSROOM FLAG IS AN EXAMPLE OF HOW CLAVELL AND THE NEW TEACHER ARE USING SYMBOLS TO MAKE THEIR POINTS."

While the Allied victory over fascism in World War II was a triumph, that Communism arose so quickly in its wake caused enormous social anxiety in the nations of the West, particularly in people like Clavell, who had personally waged the fight against fascism. One characteristic shared by both fascist and Communist governments is a concern with social control and conformity. As the Soviet Union consolidated power in Eastern Europe and across Asia Major and the Chinese Communist Party aided Maoist rebels in east Asia, a pervasive fear of Communist invasion and subsequent brainwashing grew in the West.

In 1950, Edward Hunter, an officer in the OSS (the precursor to the CIA) and the man who coined the term *brainwashing*, told the House Un-American Activities Committee (as quoted in an article by Timothy Weiner in the *New York Times*) that "the Reds have specialists available on their brainwashing panels," characterizing these experts as adept in the use of "drugs and hypnotism." He told the committee that "the United States is the main battlefield" and warned that through brainwashing Americans would become subjects of a "'new world order' for the benefit of a mad little knot of despots in the Kremlin." Brainwashing began to appear in popular culture of the era. While social control had featured prominently in earlier novels like George Orwell's *Nineteen Eighty-Four* (1949) and Arthur Koestler's *Darkness at Noon* (1940), by the late 1950s, shortly before "The Children's Story" was published, novels like *The Manchurian Candidate* (1959), by Richard Condon, and *Naked Lunch* (1959), by William

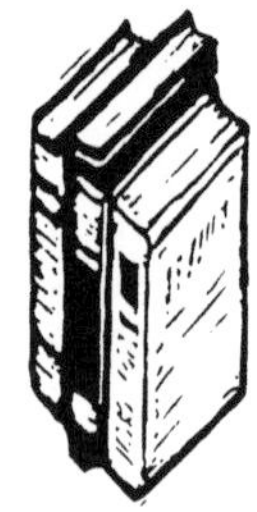

WHAT DO I READ NEXT?

- *Shogun* was the third novel published in Clavell's Asian Saga, but in the internal chronology of the saga it is the first installment in the story. Taking place in the 1600s in Japan, the novel follows John Blackthorne, an Englishman shipwrecked with his crew in isolationist Japan. It follows his rise to power as the right hand of the warlord Toranaga.
- In *Waves* (1985), Bei Dao turns to fiction to describe what life was like in the years just after the Chinese Cultural Revolution. In these six stories and a novella, Bei Dao describes not only the hopelessness and despair of life in a society gone mad but also the passion, anger, and hope that sustains his characters as they strive to remake their lives in the aftermath. Desperate to be a part of the society around them, his characters confront a society so hostile and corrupt that their best hope is to simply navigate it without falling into madness, despair, or suicide.
- Native American poet and novelist Sherman Alexie's *The Absolutely True Diary of a Part-Time Indian* (2007) is the story of a misfit adolescent who both resists and longs for assimilation. Arnold Spirit, known as Junior, was born with hydrocephalus (water on the brain). He is very bright and loves to draw, which, along with his geeky looks, makes him the target of bullies. When he transfers from the reservation school to a rich, white school, he expects the worst but finds, to his surprise, that he makes friends and even winds up on the basketball team. A game played against his old school causes Arnold to grapple with the meanings of tribe and community, even as he struggles to survive the deaths of several of his loved ones.
- Set in the dark end days of the Cold War, Elizabeth Kiem's *Dancer, Daughter, Traitor, Spy* (2013) is the story of Marina, a talented young ballerina who is forced to flee the Soviet Union with her father after her mother disappears into the security state. Svetlana, Marina's mother, was the star ballerina at the Bolshoi Ballet, and Marina is nearly as disoriented by finding herself living in Brighton Beach, New York, as she is by her mother's disappearance. Keim's novel is a clever mixture of coming-of-age story and spy thriller, as Marina must navigate young adulthood, the Julliard ballet school, and the arrival of her uncle Gosha with a suitcase full of secrets.
- Moying Li was only twelve years old when the Cultural Revolution swept across China. In *Snow Falling in Spring: Coming of Age in China during the Cultural Revolution* (2008), written for a young-adult audience, she tells the story of that traumatic time. Li takes refuge in books, but in a nation where all reading not specifically sanctioned by the Communist Party has been banned, even this activity puts her in danger.
- In *Reading Lolita in Tehran: A Memoir in Books* (2003), Azar Nafisi recounts the story of the illegal reading group she started after being forced to resign her professorship at the University of Tehran. She chose her seven best students to read through works by Jane Austen and William Faulkner and the great, if controversial, Vladimir Nabokov novel *Lolita*. The books were banned, so the women often share photocopies; as their group coheres, the shy become less so, and they find small ways to rebel against the oppressive government.

Burroughs, made popular the notion that a foreign power could take over the minds and bodies of American citizens.

It was into this general atmosphere of social anxiety about brainwashing, mind control, and foreign invasion, that Clavell's young daughter came home from school able to recite the Pledge of Allegiance but completely unaware of what it meant. Clavell seems to have found this disturbing on a number of levels. In "The Children's Story," he sets out to demonstrate the ease with which a foreign force could take over the hearts and minds of a group of unsuspecting children. That the story is allegorical is indicated by the way the characters are named, or rather how they are not named. The children all have the generic names characteristic of any group of 1950s elementary-school students; with the exception of Johnny, they are indistinguishable from one another. The lack of characterization flattens the children into a representation of "children" in general and demonstrates that Clavell is using these characters in an allegorical manner. On the literal level they are, of course, a group of typical 1950s schoolchildren, but they also represent a social fear prevalent at the time—that the American public had grown soft and pliable and had let their guard down.

That the teachers are also indistinctly named further signals that we are in the territory of allegory, a form that relies more on types than on individuals. The old teacher is referred to only as "the teacher" until the New Teacher addresses her by name. To the children, hearing their teacher addressed by name is almost as startling as seeing her in tears. To them, and to the story, she is simply the teacher, identified by her role and representative of the regime that has just been conquered. She is described as old, slightly unkempt, and emotionally unstable. It seems odd that Clavell would make the representative of the regime that has been defeated, a regime that would seem to be analogous to the United States, so unattractive; since he is trying to show how easy it is to sway people, it seems that he is making a point about the way people equate the new and beautiful with the good. The New Teacher represents the new regime and the promise of the new. She is young and pretty, wears an appealing uniform that is both new and tidy, and smells nice. She seduces the children with her newness, her energy, and her engagement. Johnny, the one child who appears to have a close relationship with his father, is the only child who resists the New Teacher's allure. His resistance to her appeal is meant to demonstrate the healthy skepticism that an independent person should have of any force that has defeated his country. And yet Johnny, too, is eventually led, step by step, to side with the New Teacher.

Allegories work through the use of symbol, as do the techniques of the New Teacher. Since a symbol is something that remains itself while also signifying a larger meaning, the classroom flag is an example of how Clavell and the New Teacher are using symbols to make their points. The New Teacher, having cast doubt upon the veracity and importance of the Pledge of Allegiance, moves her attention to the object of that pledge, the flag itself. Flags are always symbolic. By definition, a flag is a symbol of the nation for which it stands, and thus nations create and codify rituals dictating how a flag should be treated, how to handle the flag, fly the flag, and salute the flag. Because the flag as physical object represents a political entity that is the nation-state, actions toward the flag are seen as an extension of one's feelings toward the nation. In leading the children to destroy their flag, the New Teacher betrays her true political project, which is to sway them to the objectives of the new regime.

At first the New Teacher seems to be an improvement over the old teacher because she is young and pretty and clean and promises the children food and new clothing and an educational atmosphere where they will be allowed to ask questions and to participate openly. All of these seem like improvements, and yet her actions are symbolic of the true goals of the new regime. First, she causes the children to doubt the authority of the old regime by rhetorically dismantling their faith in the Pledge of Allegiance and, by extension, the authorities that taught them to trust in the pledge. Then she causes the children to destroy the literal symbol of the old regime when they cut up the flag and throw the flagpole out the window. Finally, she undermines their belief in God by asking them to pray for something she knows a supernatural being cannot supply, only to surreptitiously supply it herself. She undermines their religious belief and uses that doubt to crack their trust in their parents by encouraging them to lie about no longer believing in God and to keep secrets from them. The New Teacher has, one by one, undermined all the symbols of authority the children know—their teacher, the pledge, the flag, God and family—and has done so in such a way as to harness the natural rebelliousness of children to win them over to her cause.

When Clavell published this story in the *Ladies' Home Journal* in 1963, the magazine received over 2,400 letters, most of them objecting to the story, outraged by what they perceived as its un-American message. Readers missed the satirical nature of the story—that it was not straightforward but was designed to expose what Clavell felt were the failings of the educational system and to express the general anxieties of the time about mind control and foreign invasion. Clavell distrusted teachers for the amount of influence they had on children. In order to express this distrust, he created a character who seems to be good and attractive and who uses what were at the time considered progressive educational techniques, like encouraging the children to ask questions. For readers who took the story at face value, all these qualities would have indicated that the New Teacher is better than the old teacher. Hence, they were outraged by the portrait of what they took to be a "good" teacher, who nonetheless leads the children into such subversive behavior. They missed the doubleness of meaning that is essential to satire. They missed that while the New Teacher *appears* to be a positive figure, her actions demonstrate that she is actually not a positive figure. Despite the social anxiety about the possibilities of foreign invasion and brainwashing, these readers missed the satirical nature of Clavell's story.

This is a danger inherent to satirical writing. Because it relies on the reader's abilities to interpret the doubleness of meaning, it can be misread and, on occasion, cause the sort of uproar that ensued upon Clavell's initial publication of the story. If there is a moral to Clavell's story, it is that one needs to develop and continue to hone one's critical thinking skills. Critical thinking skills allow us to recognize a satirical short story when we are presented with one, and Clavell seems to imply that it is critical thinking skills that will also allow a populace to avoid being turned, in a mere twenty-three minutes, to the cause of an invading force. In the handwritten endnote appended to the 1981 hardcover publication of the story, Clavell seems especially disturbed that his daughter was being taught that rote memorization was "learning" something. Learning, Clavell seems to imply in "The Children's Story," requires more than memorization; it requires learning both the literal and the allegorical meanings of words and also of symbols and stories. "The Children's Story" is a cautionary tale, one in which Clavell seeks to warn that critical thinking is the bulwark against demagoguery of all kinds.

Source: Charlotte Freeman, Critical Essay on "The Children's Story," in *Short Stories for Students*, Gale, Cengage Learning, 2017.

Peter Guttridge

In the following essay, Guttridge gives an overview of Clavell's accomplishments.

James Clavell claimed that his novels—rarely under 1,000 pages—were never plotted in advance. He would start writing and follow the story wherever it went, often expressing surprise in his interviews at twists in the plot which he said came as much of a surprise to him as to the reader.

"Check or you're dead" was one of the rules at Changi, the jail where Clavell spent four years of the Second World War as a prisoner-of-war of the Japanese, which he applied in turn to his writing. He went to infinite pains, often doing 20 drafts of the same page and spending days checking the smallest detail. He had strong views on writing. "The first time you write a novel you go into ecstasy with the purple prose—how the clouds look, what the sunset is like. All bullshit. What happens? Who does what to whom? That's all you need."

Although critics were often sniffy, James Clavell was a master storyteller whose success was unique: he wrote long, literate adventures set in a time and a place few people know much about and they all became best-sellers. *King Rat* (1962), *Taipan* (1966), *Shogun* (1975), *Noble House* (1981), *Whirlwind* (1986), *Gai-Jin* (1993): in a 40-year career his books sold some 21 million copies.

Clavell's character was formed by his wartime experiences at Changi. Born in Sydney, he was the son of Commander Richard Clavell RN, who was stationed in Australia to help establish the Royal Australian Navy. The family was posted back to England when James was nine months old. He was educated at Portsmouth Grammar School, and left at the outbreak of the war filled with notions of duty instilled by his family's long tradition of military service, and notions of heroism from reading Rider Haggard and other Empire writers. The war changed all that.

Clavell's eyesight kept him out of the Navy and the Air Force so he joined the Royal Artillery as a young captain. In 1941 the Japanese

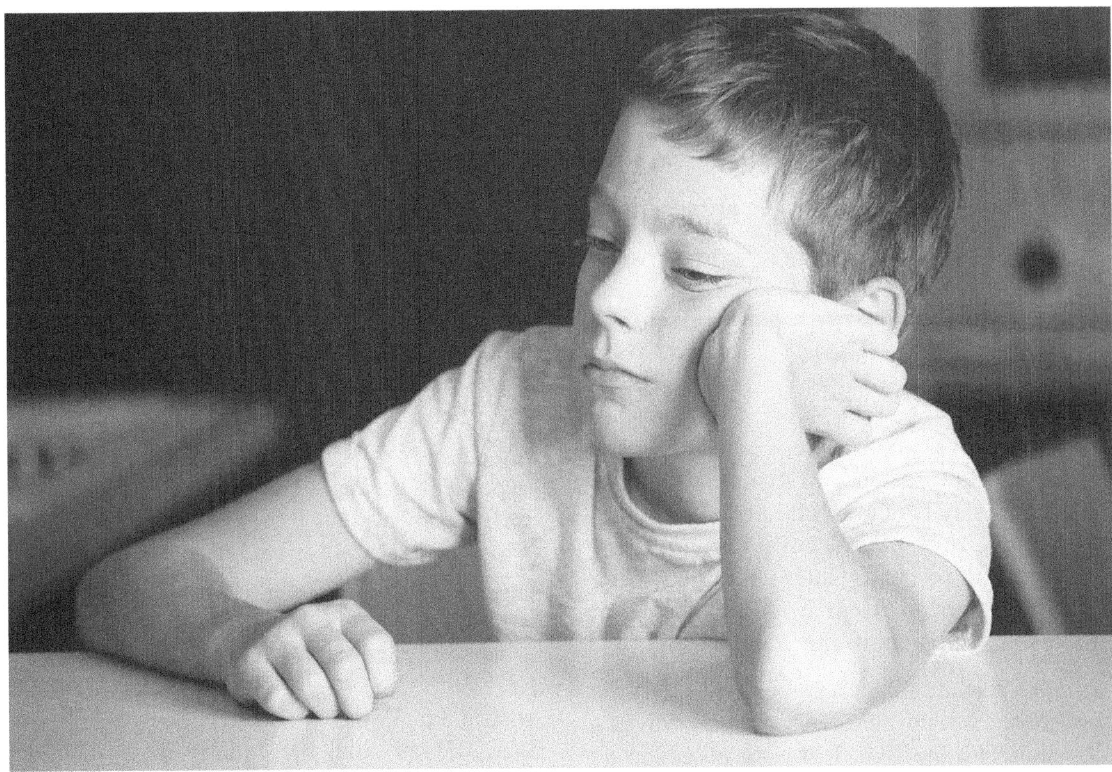

Only Johnny questions the new teacher's lessons, but in the end even he accepts the propaganda
(©Gladskikh Tatiana / Shutterstock.com)

captured him in Java and he was shipped to the hellish Changi jail in Singapore, where he remained until the end of the war. He was 18 years old. Only one in 15 men survived the malnutrition, disease and torture there. Clavell survived because, he said, he adopted an attitude in which he dominated the environment so that it could not destroy him. He never publicly discussed how his wartime experiences might have scarred him, but he was ruthless in ensuring that he kept total control of his extraordinary career.

At the end of the war he worked as a distributor, then in 1953 moved to Hollywood as a scriptwriter. Early success with the cult sci-fi film *The Fly* (1958) and the Rider Haggard B-movie adventure *Watusi* (1958) was followed by mainstream popular writing about men at war: *633 Squadron* (1963), the prisoner-of-war drama *The Great Escape* (1966). In 1959 he produced and directed—as well as wrote—*Five Gates to Hell*, a frenzied tale of American doctors and nurses snatched by Communist mercenaries in Vietnam. A year later he did the same for *Walk Like a Dragon*, a curious liberal western about a cowboy and a Chinese girl. His most successful film as a writer-director-producer (a "hyphenate") was the least likely: *To Sir with Love* (1966). Based on ER Braithwaite's autobiography, it was set in an east London secondary school with Sidney Poitier as a schoolteacher from British Guiana, coping with the likes of Judy Geeson and Lulu. Clavell followed it three years later with an underrated meditation on men at war, *The Last Valley*, starring Michael Caine as a ruthless mercenary in the Thirty Years War occupying a peaceful Alpine village.

By the time *The Last Valley* appeared, however, Clavell was already established as a best-selling novelist. A screenwriters' strike in 1960 left him idle for 12 weeks, and during this period he exorcised his prison-camp experience by writing *King Rat*, a novel set in Changi. It is an evocative account of the treatment of prisoners by the guards and focuses on the lives of an English prisoner (an RAF officer) and an American NCO (the King Rat of the title). Clavell's first draft was 850 pages long.

THE MAJORITY OF CLAVELL'S READERS ARE WOMEN AND HE THOUGHT MOST OF HIS BOOKS WERE SO POPULAR BECAUSE THEY FEATURE RUTHLESS, SUCCESSFUL WOMEN."

In working with his American publisher editing the novel line by line, Clavell reckoned he learned how to write. The first draft was finished in three months and the novel published in 1962. It became an immediate best-seller and three years later was filmed by Columbia starring George Segal, Denholm Elliott, James Fox and John Mills.

King Rat may have exorcised his wartime experiences, but nothing ever removed Clavell's obsession with the East. It was an obsession he inherited from his father, who had served in the Royal Navy in the China Station before the First World War. Clavell grew up listening to stories of adventures on the Yangtze river. His ancestors were adventurous too. The Clavell family traced itself back to Walter de Claville, an Armour Bearer for William the Conqueror.

Clavell turned his interest in the history of Anglo-Saxons in Asia into a series of best-selling novels whose popularity made him a very rich man. *Tai-Pan*, *Shogun* and *Noble House* were made into television mini-series, under Clavell's close supervision as producer. When *Shogun*, which chronicled the exploits of a British navigator in Japan in the early 1600s, was screened in 1980 starring Richard Chamberlain, it became the second highest rated mini-series in history with an audience of over 120 million. (*Shogun* the musical followed on Broadway in 1989.)

Clavell brooked no nonsense in his dealings with television companies. In the early Sixties he had turned down the chance to write the screenplay for the film of *King Rat* on the advice of two old pro scriptwriters. They told him if he wrote the script he would be a screenwriter who had written a book. If he didn't he would be a novelist and could therefore put a zero on his writing fee. When the same couple told him that producers like calling long distance, Clavell moved with his wife April to Vancouver to bring up their two daughters.

Clavell was tough on his publishers too. He eschewed advances and showed his publisher a novel only when it was completed. "I speculate," he explained. "They don't gamble with anything I do. I've got my own drop-dead money, so I write what I want at my own pace. When I finish it I let them read 200 pages. If they can't tell within 200 pages what it's about then they shouldn't be in the business." In 1986 his novel *Whirlwind* was auctioned for a record dollars 5m.

The majority of Clavell's readers are women and he thought most of his books were so popular because they feature ruthless, successful women.

Clavell had the look of a stern, choleric man and he could be chilly and distantly polite with people he didn't know. The huge success of his work made him a millionaire many times over and he and his wife had homes in the US, Austria and France, and travelled frequently in Asia. Clavell—like his wife—was a qualified pilot and they owned their own helicopters. But that was the extent of his extravagance. Later in life he said he trusted only his wife and his two daughters, Michaela and Holly.

James Clavell claimed to believe strongly in the contradictory notions of joss and karma. Joss—luck, God and the Devil mixed together—is something you can and can't control, but essentially you just have to accept it. Karma is preordained by what you did in previous lifetimes. Essentially, he thought, "The gods want to screw you up."

Clavell's most recent book, *Gai-Jin*, came out last year and became an international best-seller, but he was already working on another one. "There's no such thing as a retired writer," he once said. "We just go on and on."

Source: Peter Guttridge, "Obituary: James Clavell," in *Independent* (London, England), September 8, 1994.

SOURCES

Ahmed, Azam, and Julie Hirschfeld Davis, "U.S. and Cuba Reopen Long-Closed Embassies," in *New York Times*, July 20, 2015, http://www.nytimes.com/2015/07/21/world/americas/cuba-us-embassy-diplomatic-relations.html (accessed August 21, 2016).

"April 07, 1954: Eisenhower Gives Famous 'Domino Theory' Speech," History.com, http://www.history.com/

this-day-in-history/eisenhower-gives-famous-domino-theory-speech (accessed November 22, 2016).

Baldick, Chris, "Allegory," "Satire," and "Symbol," in *The Oxford Dictionary of Literary Terms*, Oxford University Press, 2009, pp. 7–8, 299, 326–27.

"The Birmingham Campaign (1963)," in *The King Encyclopedia*, http://kingencyclopedia.stanford.edu/encyclopedia/encyclopedia/enc_birmingham_campaign/ (accessed August 21, 2016).

Clavell, James, *The Children's Story*, Delacorte Press, 1981.

Cobb, Jelani, "The Matter of Black Lives," in *New Yorker*, March 14, 2014, http://www.newyorker.com/magazine/2016/03/14/where-is-black-lives-matter-headed (accessed August 21, 2016).

Fremont-Smith, Eliot, "Capture the Flag," in *Village Voice*, Vol. 26, No. 36, September 2, 1981, p. 37.

Grimes, William, "James Clavell, Best-Selling Storyteller of Far Eastern Epics, Is Dead at 69," in *New York Times*, September 8, 1994, http://www.nytimes.com/1994/09/08/obituaries/james-clavell-best-selling-storyteller-of-far-eastern-epics-is-dead-at-69.html (accessed August 21, 2016).

Guttridge, Peter, "Obituary: James Clavell," in *Independent* (London, England), September 8, 1994, http://www.independent.co.uk/news/people/obituary-james-clavell-1447652.html (accessed August 21, 2016).

Hartwell, Richard D., "Speaking My Mind: Don't Worry, It's Just Communist Propaganda," in *English Journal*, Vol. 94, No. 1, September 2004, pp. 19–20.

"John F. Kennedy Assassinated," History.com, http://www.history.com/this-day-in-history/john-f-kennedy-assassinated (accessed August 21, 2016).

Jones, Jeffery Owen, "The Man Who Wrote the Pledge of Allegiance," in *Smithsonian*, November 2003, http://www.smithsonianmag.com/history/the-man-who-wrote-the-pledge-of-allegiance-93907224/?all (accessed November 22, 2016).

Kornbluh, Peter, and Laurence Chang, "The Cuban Missile Crisis, 1962," National Security Archive website, October 1, 1998, http://nsarchive.gwu.edu/nsa/cuba_mis_cri/declass.htm (accessed August 21, 2016).

Levinson, Michael, "Donald Trump Is Full of Conspiracies—and Many Believe Him," in *Boston Globe*, June 30, 2016, https://www.bostonglobe.com/metro/2016/06/30/some-they-sound-crazy-but-trump-conspiracy-theories-resonate-with-wide-swath-public/7HFzyTzJAio6vn0QGGcTdO/story.html (accessed August 21, 2016).

Marshall, Kelli, "The Strange History behind the Pledge of Allegiance," in *Talking Points Memo*, September 15, 2015, http://talkingpointsmemo.com/cafe/strange-history-pledge-of-allegiance (accessed August 21, 2016).

Marx, Karl, "Critique of the Gotha Programme," in *Marx/Engels Selected Works*, Vol, 3, Progress Publishers, 1970, https://www.marxists.org/archive/marx/works/1875/gotha/ch01.htm (accessed August 21, 2016).

Trueman, C. N., "Changi POW Camp," History Learning Site, May 25, 2015, http://www.historylearningsite.co.uk/world-war-two/prisoners-of-war-in-ww2/changi-pow-camp/ (accessed August 21, 2016).

Wall, Wendy, "Anti-Communism in the 1950s," Gilder Lehrman Institute of American History website, http://www.gilderlehrman.org/history-by-era/fifties/essays/anti-communism-1950s (accessed August 21, 2016).

Weiner, Timothy, "Remembering Brainwashing," in *New York Times*, July 6, 2008, http://www.nytimes.com/2008/07/06/weekinreview/06weiner.html (accessed August 21, 2016).

Wright, Edmund, "Castro, Fidel," "Cold War," "Cuban Missile Crisis," and "Totalitarianism," in *Oxford Dictionary of World History*, 2nd ed., Oxford University Press, 2006, pp. 116, 139, 163, 641.

FURTHER READING

Clavell, James, *King Rat*, Little, Brown, 1962.
Clavell's first novel, *King Rat*, is the story of Peter Marlowe, a British prisoner of war in a Japanese internment camp, and his relationship with an American known as "King," who seeks to dominate not only the other prisoners but their captors as well. Loosely based on Clavell's experiences in the Changi camp near Singapore during World War II, this is the fourth chronological story in Clavell's Asian Saga.

———, *Tai-Pan*, Atheneum, 1966.
The second novel Clavell published, *Tai-Pan*, is also the second installment in his Asian Saga. This is the story of two traders, one European and one American, who move to Hong Kong in the wake of the First Opium War and establish great trading companies.

———, *Noble House*, Delacorte, 1981.
The fourth novel published in the Asian Saga, *Noble House* is the fifth chronological installment. Set in Hong Kong in 1936, this massive novel (at a thousand pages) spans a single week in the life of Ian Dunross, who seeks to save the "noble" Strauns trading house.

———, *Whirlwind*, William Morrow, 1986.
The fifth novel published in the Asian Saga, *Noble House* is the final chronological installment. Set in 1979 Iran in the wake of the Iranian Revolution, this is the story of a group of helicopter pilots from Strauns, their Iranian wives, and the escape they must make.

———, *Gai-Jin*, Delacorte, 1993.
The final novel published in the Asian Saga, *Gai-Jin* is the third chronological installment. The story takes place in Japan in the 1860s and tells the story of the establishment of

Strauns trading company and the difficulties that foreigners faced in the closed society that was Japan.

Morton, W. Scott, and J. Kenneth Olenik, *Japan: Its History and Culture*, McGraw-Hill, 2005.

This is a classic historical overview of Japan's history and culture, including its art, religion, and imperial court history. The book also covers the rich social, political, and economic life of Asia's wealthiest nation, including a section on Japan's economic challenges in the twenty-first century.

Spence, Jonathan, *The Search for Modern China*, 3rd ed., W. W. Norton, 2012.

Written in a narrative style that brings events to life, Spence covers the British attempts to subdue the Chinese with opium, the brutal Japanese occupation of World War II, the rise of Mao Zedong, and the devolution of the Chinese nation into chaos during the Cultural Revolution. With more than two hundred illustrations and a generous glossary that explains terms, this is an excellent single-volume guide to the period.

SUGGESTED SEARCH TERMS

James Clavell

James Clavell AND Asian Saga

The Children's Story AND Clavell

McCarthyism AND Cold War

House Un-American Activities Committee

Cultural Revolution AND China AND education

totalitarianism AND education

Pledge of Allegiance AND history

Cuban missile crisis

Defeat

KAY BOYLE

1941

One of the more prolific authors to emerge from the modernist hotbeds of New York City and Paris in the 1920s and 1930s, Kay Boyle garnered particular acclaim for her short stories. She published consistently in the most prestigious literary outlets of the day—including *Harper's*, the *Nation*, and the *Saturday Evening Post*—and earned several prizes and other honors with her short fiction.

Boyle earned the O. Henry Memorial Prize for the year's best short story for "Defeat," which was first published in the *New Yorker* on May 17, 1941. Boyle was living in the Alps region of France in the summer of 1940 when, in one of the earlier military actions of World War II, the German army invaded France and overran Paris in just six weeks, a shockingly quick defeat. The result was a German occupation across the north of France and all along the Atlantic coast, while a French puppet government operated out of the town of Vichy. This political background goes mostly unexplained in Boyle's story, but the essential details are made clear: France has been defeated, and the people's souls are bearing the burden. The story focuses on one returning soldier, a bus driver, and his own personal tale of the defeat of the nation's men and women alike. Boyle published the story in her collections *Thirty Stories* (1946) and *Fifty Stories* (1980), and it can also be found in *The Vintage Book of War Fiction* (2007).

Kay Boyle (©Library of Congress, Prints & Photographs Division, Reproduction number LC-USZ62-102458)

AUTHOR BIOGRAPHY

Katherine Evans Boyle was born in St. Paul, Minnesota, on February 19, 1902, to a then-affluent Irish immigrant family. In her childhood prior to World War I, they made several journeys to England and elsewhere in Europe. She was highly influenced by the self-assured women in her family, who instilled in her progressive attitudes toward art—such as through New York City's revolutionary, modernist 1913 Armory Show—and politics alike. By age fourteen, she was contributing verse to the likes of *Poetry* magazine and, with her mother's encouragement, holding firm against an editor's suggested revisions. After studying architecture at a conservatory in Cincinnati and the Ohio Mechanics Institute, she ended up graduating from a secretarial school and gaining work at *Vogue*, where her sister Joan was employed.

In 1922, while living in New York City, Boyle married Richard Brault, a French exchange student with an engineering degree, and they lived in poverty. But by 1923, Boyle was publishing verse in *Broom* and *Contact* and making connections with noted authors such as Edwin Arlington Robinson and Marianne Moore. When she and Brault moved to France, she was befriended by editors such as Robert McAlmon, Ernest Walsh, and Ethel Moorhead. Her marriage was interrupted by an affair with Walsh that took place after they had both become ill, she with bronchitis and he with tuberculosis. When Walsh died in 1926, Boyle was pregnant with a daughter. By 1928, Boyle had permanently left Brault to settle in Paris, where she joined a commune run by Raymond Duncan (brother of famed dancer Isadora Duncan). She had signed away her parental rights to her daughter to do so, but she eventually kidnapped her to get them both away. She was helped by a couple who ran the publishing house Black Sun Press; under that imprint, Boyle issued her first fiction collection, *Short Stories*, in 1929.

Around this time Boyle met expatriate artist Laurence Vail, whom she would have three daughters with and marry. Throughout the 1930s, Boyle was highly productive, writing poems, stories, essays, and novels. Her family moved to Austria in 1933, England in 1936, and then back to France and the Alpine village of Megève, where they stayed until 1941, the year "Defeat" was published in the *New Yorker*. Boyle was helping Jews and other refugees obtain US visas, but under the wartime pressure (the Alpine region would be occupied by Italy beginning in November 1942), Boyle's family just managed to secure travel to the United States. Settling in New York, Boyle left Vail over political differences—he was fatalistically content with fascism overrunning Europe—and in time married Joseph Franckenstein, an Austrian nobleman among those she had helped flee Europe, with whom she would have a son.

Boyle continued to write as a freelance contributor and correspondent for magazines, while Franckenstein worked for the US State Department, which took them to Germany.

They became suspected of having Communist ties, and in the fearful political atmosphere in the United States, Boyle's husband lost his job. It took nine years back in the United States for them to clear their names. Boyle continued to be at the forefront of historical events and social movements, becoming active in the 1960s in the civil rights movement as well as anti–Vietnam War protests in California. At various times Boyle taught in private schools and colleges, including as a creative writing instructor at San Francisco State University from around the time of Franckenstein's death in 1963 until 1979. She died in Mill Valley, California, on December 27, 1992.

PLOT SUMMARY

"Defeat" opens with a third-person narrator (that is, not part of the story), seemingly omniscient, relating the recent activity in France through June and July: defeated men, French soldiers who have abandoned their units or escaped from captivity at the hands of the Germans, have been trickling home in ones, twos, and threes, looking bedraggled, confused, and even anachronistic—like returning Confederate soldiers transplanted to the present day. Stories of the advancing German army are inflated to veritably mythical proportions: waves of blond young men without helmets sang their cheer even as their first waves were gunned down. As the French ran out of ammunition, the waves of Germans easily gained the victory. The French were terribly ill-equipped, as if carrying decades-old weaponry last used at the beginning of World War I. (By now, the story's setting of World War II is apparent; the specific year is 1940.) The returning soldiers almost invariably express feeling abandoned by their officers and dishonored as Frenchmen.

One man, a bus driver who returned to his former job, is not so defeatist, at least in conversation, saying very little about what happened during his service in the war. But on one occasion, while drinking with two traveling salesmen, he tells his own story about France's defeat. The salesmen express how they had pinned their hopes on the French troops' ability to hold the front line at various rivers—the Oise, the Seine, and the Loire—but the troops nonetheless retreated steadily south as the German troops advanced. One salesman wonders aloud why they did not retreat all the way to Senegal (then a French colony in West Africa).

The bus driver then begins relating what happened on the Fourteenth of July, which is Bastille Day, an important national holiday for France. In some towns in the unoccupied zone (the south and southeast), the people held symbolic funerals for the French nation that day, dressing all in black. The salesmen interject comments about soldiers having lost respect for their commanding officers and national customs. The bus driver continues, mentioning the flyers dropped by the "Boche" (a French epithet for the Germans) declaring death to Frenchmen and dancing for Frenchwomen on the Fourteenth of July. At the time, the bus driver scoffed.

He himself was in a prison camp near Rennes for three weeks but escaped on the evening of July 12. Along with a *copain* (friend), he traveled homeward by bicycle, riding all night. At eight the next morning, they came upon a house on the outskirts of a village. It was a schoolhouse, empty (for both the summer and the war) save for a schoolmistress devotedly sewing French flags, with bunting in the national colors draped around the room. They cautioned her about being caught and detained, but she dismissed their concern. Their uniforms would put them in danger if they were to be caught, so the woman went out to fetch them ordinary clothes, as well as food and wine. She instructed them to get out of their uniforms and drape themselves in the patriotic bunting while they waited for her. The bus driver recalls—or thinks he can recall—that later, while they were eating, he told the woman that a nation is not defeated until its women are.

After riding all that day, the bus driver and his friend reached a farmhouse, where a man rudely refused them food or quarters, pointing out that they would not have had Germans to worry about if the men had fought better. At the next farmhouse, they were fed and given space in a hayloft—but on the floor, not the comfortable hay. The next day, the *copain*'s bicycle tire went flat. They walked to a village, where, realizing what day it was—the Fourteenth—they were treated hospitably by a garage owner and given food and space to sleep in an upper-floor room overlooking the town square, where a dancing platform had been erected.

From his room, the bus driver mocked the Germans in the square that evening for thinking the Frenchwomen would join them. As the dance began, only well-dressed Germans, some with gloves, perhaps mildly anxious, occupied the floor and its entrances. Clusters of townspeople only lingered on the outskirts of the lighted dance area and beyond in the shadows. But in time—it must have been the banquet of food laid out, the bus driver imagines, what with the fruit tarts, chocolate, lemonade, and beer; or perhaps some of the women had had dresses they were just itching to wear; or perhaps, in their deprivation, the Germans' uniforms appealed to them after all. He trails off, leaving it unsaid that the French women, whom he had been so sure would refuse to surrender, danced with the German soldiers.

One of the salesmen offers, consolingly, that this was just one town, out of many in France. The bus driver agrees, but picks up his drink with tears in his eyes.

CHARACTERS

Bus Driver

The story's protagonist is in his twenties, short, graceful, dark, and handsome. He seems to live somewhere in the Alps region. The story revolves around his experience at the end of France's military effort in World War II, when France surrendered and many of its soldiers were in prison camps. Escaping from such a camp, the bus driver is greatly inspired by one woman who yet devotes herself to tending the national emblem of the flag—actually several flags and bunting. He thus puts his faith in Frenchwomen as the nation's saving grace, notwithstanding its military defeat. But the women of the village in which he finds himself on the Fourteenth of July, despite his hopes and expectations to the contrary, do dance with the triumphant Germans. From his manner after he tells the story, it is apparent that the sight broke his heart.

Copain

The bus driver's friend is as self-effacing as any secondary character in a short story could be. He does nothing of interest.

Garage Owner

The owner of the garage in the town in which the bus driver and his *copain* find themselves on the Fourteenth is a distinct contrast to the unfriendly peasant farmer they met previously. While the peasant turned them away with utter disdain, the garage owner is generous with food and drink on the national holiday, even though the German occupation is surely squeezing him economically, because the Germans have restricted the use of vehicles. The garage owner scoffs at how the French authorities, acting on behalf of Germany, have pleaded with people to meekly obey the regulations.

Peasant

A farmer referred to as a common peasant refuses to assist the bus driver and his friend with food and a place to sleep, saying Germans will come for milk the next day, find the escaped prisoners, and hold him responsible. He appears to be deliberately ungrateful for the soldiers' effort in the war, since that effort proved worthless, allowing a sudden German march down the countryside and the advent of occupation.

Schoolmistress

There is tension in the room when the bus driver and his friend first enter the schoolhouse where the teacher is fiercely maintaining the national colors. Even before speaking she seems well aware that they will not approve of her activities, considering how provocative the German officials might perceive them to be. Her dismissal of their concern might suggest two things: perhaps she has already learned how distressingly amiable the local officials are (as suggested by the dance) and does not fear that the Germans will act to prevent what is to them, at this point, a harmless patriotic gesture; or perhaps she believes that the boost in morale that the flags could provide the French people is more important than her personal safety.

Traveling Salesmen

The bus driver tells his story of defeat not to the people of the town in which he resides, the people he sees regularly and thus might reasonably open up to, but to two traveling salesmen. His revelations might be prompted simply by the stories the salesmen tell of what has happened in the places they have visited in their commercial travels; the bus driver shares his own story in a spirit of friendliness. Still, the fact that the bus driver opens up to these men alone, a couple of months after the experience, suggests that it is too painful for him to mention to people he will see regularly, and who thus, in sharing the knowledge with him, would recall it to his mind every time he sees them. In telling the story to two men he may never see again, the bus driver can be perceived as wrapping the memory up, as if in a package, and dispatching it out of his life—or trying to, at least. The salesmen help fuel the bus driver's anecdote with occasional comments, but it is apparent that the condolences offered by one of them at the end of the story—suggesting that the dancing represented only a single town—fail to boost the bus driver's spirits. The salesmen are nice enough, but it seems no consolations can dull his pain.

THEMES

War

The governing theme of "Defeat" is war—or more accurately, the end of war, specifically in the absence of victory. The story makes use of the idea that a nation's being at war becomes a state of mind, an awareness of instability that affects everyone regardless of the proximity of the actual fighting. This state of mind is in fact strikingly absent from the bus driver's tale, which takes place shortly after a ceasefire has been declared because of France's surrender. Historically, this armistice was signed on June 22 and took effect on June 25. Thus, when the bus driver was captured on June 17, the war was still going on; and in his mind it continued even through his weeks of imprisonment. After his escape (which might be seen as suspiciously easy), he slowly realizes that the war is quite simply over. He and his friend ride their bicycles all night on a main road in uniform and are not stopped once. Over the next two days, he sees no activity anywhere suggesting even civil resistance, never mind armed resistance.

One of Boyle's curious omissions in this story is any description of the bus driver's active war experiences. The reader is left unaware of, for example, how much death the protagonist saw, how many friends he lost, and whether he killed anyone himself. This knowledge gap effectively maintains the focus strictly on the bus driver's postwar experience: after he has escaped from the prison camp and discarded his uniform, it is as if the war never even happened: "The war was over for them; for this country the war was over." Boyle's repetition emphasizes the totality of the fact. France is in a state of defeat so complete that their former efforts to avert that defeat are no longer relevant to society as it persists. However, there remain some individuals who, like the garage owner, support the defeated soldiers regardless of the outcome, as well as those who, like the peasant, hold them responsible for the nation's failure.

Failure

It is clear that the majority of returning French soldiers hold no illusions as to what has taken place: the military has failed, and the nation has been overrun by what must thus be recognized as a superior force, that of Germany. It seems, based on Boyle's story, that there was something both inevitable and inexplicable about that failure, that defeat. In the descriptions of outdated military equipment, overburdened infantry, and criminally indifferent officers, there is a suggestion that the defeat was politically engineered. Perhaps French officials recognized that the German army would not be defeated without profound loss of life and great expense, potentially over the course of several years—and indeed the European war lasted six years. Is it cowardly to allow an entire nation to be overrun to avoid the unspeakable casualties that would result from trying to defend it? Some humanitarian strategists would argue that it is not; but for those trained under a military code, in which one is prepared to lay down one's life if it means advancing the army's objectives or saving lives, a failure to put up a fight is a failure in one's very purpose for existence. (The American reader might be inclined to compare France's military failure with the unquestionable success of the Allied landing in Normandy, when thousands of Americans and others precisely marched to their deaths on the beaches to help secure for the Allies an entry point into German-occupied French territory.) Based on Boyle's story, there is no question about the opinion of the common French soldier toward what France has allowed: it is an absolute shame.

TOPICS FOR FURTHER STUDY

- Select and read two other stories from Boyle's "French Group: 1939–1942" in *Thirty Stories* or the more extensive "French Group: 1939–1966" in *FiftyStories*. Then write an essay discussing whatever continuations or differences you notice in terms of historical events, themes, character types, nationalities, and so forth, and draw whatever conclusions you think you can about Boyle's overall personal perspective on France.
- Read the young-adult novel *For Freedom: The Story of a French Spy* (2005), by Kimberly Brubaker Bradley, about a teenage girl in Cherbourg, France, whose life is turned upside down when a bomb is dropped on her town in 1940. In an essay, discuss the merits of the novel and compare and contrast it with "Defeat," focusing on the message each story sends about female agency, that is, about girls' and women's ability to be responsible for themselves and take action.
- Create a website presenting an interactive representation of the bus driver's bicycle journey in "Defeat." He escapes from a prison near Rennes, in the northwest, and seems to be bicycling toward the Alps, as suggested by the setting established in the second paragraph. (Boyle was herself writing from that region.) Include a map tracing a route that he and his *copain* might have taken across the country. For each of the places he crosses along the way, link to at least one fact or anecdote from the World War II era relating to the location.
- The structure of "Defeat"—starting with broadly depicted scenes, then focusing on the bus driver as he talks with the salesmen, going back and forth in time, and then sharing episodes depending on brief conversations and vividly imagined scenes—seems to lend itself to a graphic-novel presentation. Create such an adaptation, which may be in black-and-white pencil drawings with relatively simple images, or in a more elaborate presentation, using close-ups, panoramas, and other artistic approaches as you see fit. Reproduce whatever snippets of narration and dialogue seem most important.
- Research the military actions taken during Germany's six-week defeat of France in World War II and write up your own strategic analysis, summarizing what took place and which strategic decisions proved crucial on both sides.
- Mature readers may consider the following topic. Read *Lysistrata* (411 BCE), by Aristophanes, about a cohort of Greek women who decide to try to end a war by denying their husbands sexual relations until peace has been declared. Then write an essay comparing and contrasting the gendered circumstances and perceptions represented in the play and in Boyle's "Defeat."

Shame

Once again Boyle uses the briefest repetition to reinforce the importance of a notion, as if the slightly varied wording accomplishes a slight shift in perspective, letting the full implications of the phrase stand out in relief: the elder French soldiers, in their defeat, are said to have remarked "in sober, part-embittered, part-vainglorious voices: 'I'm ashamed to be a Frenchman,' or 'I'm ashamed of being French today.'" Most people want to take pride in their home nation, especially when their own efforts are reflected in the nation's position. France's surrender to Germany is bad enough, but what is worse for the common soldier is that the surrender was utterly undignified—they never put up enough of a fight to be proud of.

The decorations put up for Bastille Day represent the people's quiet patriotism (©StockCube / Shutterstock.com)

The common soldier's inability to take pride in the French effort seems to be reflected in the bus driver's declining to ever speak about what happened—as if recalling everything simply causes him too much emotional pain: it injures his pride too greatly; he feels too acutely the national shame. Naturally, then, he craves some other aspect of French society in which to invest his wounded sense of pride. His happening upon the fiery schoolmistress gives him just the candidate he needs: womankind, those who have perhaps not contributed as directly to the war effort—not on the front lines—but who have played essential roles nonetheless, and, as the person of the schoolmistress suggests, who alone seem capable of sustaining the nation's morale, as if didactically. That the bus driver so heavily invests his sense of pride in the women of France makes it all the more painful for him when the women of the village, in the end, join the Germans—shamefully, as it seems—for a Fourteenth of July dance.

National Identity

National identity is the sort of thing many people take for granted. One can easily go through life occasionally singing the national anthem, seeing the national flag hung outside people's doors, and reading the news about national politics without feeling too personally invested in what takes place. Why should the actions of the select few—those elected to the highest government offices—reflect personally on any one individual? But the conversation shifts when war comes into play: now some people find themselves quite literally dying for their country, in doing their part (a part many others are not doing) to keep their fellow citizens safe. In an all-enveloping war, even the smallest towns and villages see a few men (and women, though far fewer in 1940 than today) go off to work and fight on behalf of their friends and family. Thus does national pride become so critical to the self-perception of the common soldier, the one who has quite literally invested his life in the nation's cause. Failure in the form of surrender is bad enough; an apparently shameful surrender is even worse. For the bus driver, when even the last part of his national pride is brought down—his faith in the patriotism of French women—his personal identity is shattered along with the terrible loss of his national identity.

STYLE

Modernism

Boyle was immersed in the modernist movement that swept literature through the 1910s, 1920s, and beyond. She was exposed in her youth to the works of modernist masters James Joyce and Gertrude Stein, she contributed to a number of magazines that were at the forefront of modernism, and she was personally acquainted with such literary greats as John Dos Passos, Marianne Moore, and William Carlos Williams. Boyle's modernism was especially reflected in the way she rejected standard narrative structure in many of her stories, such as by focusing on the lead-up to a dramatic event that is never actually described. Elizabeth S. Bell, in the *Dictionary of Literary Biography*, has noted that the narrative of "Defeat" has "more of a traditional plot than most of Boyle's stories," but the author's modernism is evident in other aspects.

One motivation for modernist originality was the way World War I, with its utterly unforeseen levels of carnage—millions were quite senselessly marched to slaughter—inverted people's understanding of the level of advancement that humanity had reached. The notion of the seemingly unstoppable advance of the goodness of civilization was suddenly overturned; the very industrial qualities that had helped push standards of living so far were now being used instead to wipe civilization out. Boyle emphasizes a sense of temporal dislocation in her curiously complex description of returning French soldiers seeming as out of place as Confederate soldiers—not merely in their own time, but as Confederate soldiers would seem if they were sent forward in time over seventy years and deposited in the French countryside. Having set out to join a modern war, it seems the returning soldiers ought to be representing "modern defeat," in a phrase of Boyle's that suggests perhaps mechanization, or detachment, or indifference—as if they should return with all they have experienced neatly categorized into identity cards marked "Defeated Soldier" and with a carefree, forward-looking, even ironic attitude toward life. To the contrary, the soldiers are devastated. It may be a modern world, but their existential pain in shameful collective defeat is age-old.

Fragmentation: History versus Myth

Along with the dismantling of people's conceptions of the modern world and the disruptions that technology was starting to cause, modernist literature is often characterized by a lament for fragmentation, for the way the fabric of people's relation to the greater world can be torn, perhaps irreparably. Fragmentation can be seen in "Defeat" especially in the way the two stories are told—the broader story of France's defeat, as told by an omniscient narrator, and the bus driver's personal story of his experience of that defeat, as framed within the broader narrative. (Such narrative framing techniques came into frequent use in the modernist era, for the way they could multiply the sense of a story.) The narrator's voice in the framing story comes across as effectively omniscient, knowing, for example, about the one and only time—"he told it only once"—that the bus driver has told his own story of defeat. But this omniscient narrator makes a point of simply presenting, without clarifying, the mythologizing accounts of what took place on the battlefields in France's defeat: "Legends or truth, the stories became indistinguishable in the mouths of the Frenchmen who returned," with the Germans described as "bright-haired, blond demigods" dressed like vacationers, singing like choirboys, and overawing like conquistadors. What actually took place on those battlefields, then, goes untold. For those who were not on the front lines, the story has been fragmented, becoming one of realism interrupted by something out of a folktale.

There is also a sense of narrative fragmentation in the bus driver's failure to say anything about the most important actions of the women in the village square on the night of the Fourteenth. He talks circles around exactly what happened, pondering what the women's motivations might have been and describing how they accepted chocolate, but only implying that they did the unthinkable—they danced. His most direct statement is, "perhaps once you got near enough to start eating and drinking, then the other thing just followed naturally afterward"—and even here the act of dancing is only called "the other thing," something unspeakable. His story is marked by a sort of linguistic black hole, an event about which no direct words can emerge, at least from him. With his listeners, this creates another knowledge gap, a hole in their understanding. This sort of blurring between the historical reality that took place and the ambiguous, even surreal sense produced through the communication of people's various impressions about that reality is the very foundation of myth.

COMPARE & CONTRAST

- **1940:** In May, the German army invades France and, gambling with risky tactics of abrupt advancement, manages to wring surrender and an armistice from the French in just six weeks. The defeat takes a devastating toll on the nation's psyche.

  Today: In view of French counterterrorist military operations in Syria and elsewhere, as well as perceived domestic discrimination against Muslims, the Islamic State (ISIS) has recently targeted French cities for major terrorist acts, including a massacre of twelve at the offices of humor magazine *Charlie Hebdo* in January 2015; the killing of 130 people at several sites in Paris, including the Bataclan theater, in November 2015; and a massacre of eighty-six people at a Bastille Day fireworks celebration in Nice in 2016. The nation has been psychologically reeling.

- **1940:** During the deprivation of wartime and the German occupation, travel by train and automobile is highly restricted in France, and bicycling across the entire country is a reasonable option.

  Today: Between highways, high-speed trains, and domestic airlines, French people are unlikely to be traveling long distances by bicycle unless they are participating in the Tour de France, the cross-country bicycle race that was first held in 1903.

- **1940:** French intellectual Simone de Beauvoir's groundbreaking feminist tract *The Second Sex* (1949) has yet to be published, and in fact women will not be able to either vote or hold political office in France until 1944. In this period, women hold few positions of power in society, leaving wartime decisions in the hands of men.

  Today: As of 2015, women hold approximately 25 percent of French parliamentary seats, a dramatic increase from 11 percent in 2000. France is still waiting for its first female president but did have a female prime minister, Édith Cresson, in 1991–1992.

HISTORICAL CONTEXT

France's Defeat in World War II

There is little debate among historians about the devastating nature of France's six-week defeat at the hands of Germany's military as World War II was steadily intensifying into the horror it would become. Sarah Fishman and Leonard V. Smith, in *France at War: Vichy and the Historians*, note the "crushing" nature of the German domination of the "dishonored and defeated Third Republic" and explain, "It would be difficult to overstate just how deeply the years of the Vichy regime and the German Occupation scarred the history of France." David Daiches, introducing Boyle's *Fifty Stories*, recalls firsthand "the shock of hearing of the abject French collapse in the face of Hitler's armies." Renowned historian Robert O. Paxton, in *Vichy France: Old Guard and New Order, 1940–1944*, goes further, declaring, "No one who lived through the French debacle of May–June 1940 ever quite got over the shock."

There is more room for ambiguity regarding the reasons for France's abrupt defeat. That is, the reasons are clearly many, but it is less clear which of them were the most important. Paxton, writing for publication in 1972, demonstrates a full grasp of the preceding scholarship as he makes a point of trying to set the record as straight as possible. At the time, politically motivated placement of blame produced a couple of contradictory accounts of the defeat: either politicians and officers affiliated with the political right bowed to pro-fascist leanings and fled to the rear, hopeful of holding

The multitudes of well-fed, well-equipped German soldiers demoralize the French (©Everett Historical / Shutterstock.com)

positions in the occupied state, and let Germany waltz in; or soldiers and dissidents affiliated with the political left betrayed the nation from the inside, with Communists presumed to be sympathizing with the USSR's Joseph Stalin (who was at the time the ally of Germany's Adolf Hitler). Both of these images stem more from rumor and propaganda than reality, even if they are partly founded in anecdotal accounts, and Paxton affirms that extremists at either end of the political spectrum were too few to affect the greater outcome.

A major factor was that France was still reeling from the effects of World War I, when out of some 8.4 million who served in the armed forces, 1.35 million were killed and 4.27 million were wounded. In Paxton's blunt words, the Great War "had made France a nation of old people and cripples." The mid-1930s were when France's military began feeling the effects of the low birth rate in 1914–1918, with the numbers of males becoming eligible to serve each year cut in half. France had a smaller population than Germany but was comparable in terms of military resources. However, with the addition of Austria's forces to Germany's, the situation for France looked grim. Some historians estimate that potential French deaths could have reached twenty-five million and led to the literal end of the French people.

Also weighing on people's minds was the possibility of the destruction of French infrastructure and monuments—Paris in ruins was an especially painful prospect—and the widespread scarring of the land. As Paxton notes, "There was . . . an instinctive shrinking from chaos that made war to the end against Germany simply unthinkable." When an announcement that France was seeking an armistice was broadcast over the radio on June 17, soldiers almost immediately laid down their arms, and civilians discouraged each other from resisting further. Indeed, some individuals who sought to stand firm anyway, like a tank officer who insisted on trying to hold bridges in Vierzon, were shot by their fellow Frenchmen, who hoped to avoid unnecessary massacres.

One can of course go deeper into the factors contributing to the French attitude toward war while Hitler threatened the continent, as many have, variously identifying cultural decadence, political stagnation, a middle-class sense of entitlement, consciousness of being technologically antiquated, and other factors. But ultimately such indirect factors are regarded as secondary. Paxton declines to lay the majority of the blame on any one aspect of the political or societal situations, favoring a straightforwardly strategic account regarding what took place on the battlefields:

> The most convincing studies of the campaign on both sides make it clear that the outcome is explicable in classical military terms: troops stretched too thinly along the Meuse facing the Ardennes, where the main German attack actually fell; slow communications, which hampered French realization of where the main German thrust lay; obsolete tactics which wasted excellent tanks and artillery in static line defense; and sagging morale.

However secure one might feel about the reasons behind it, the German defeat and occupation of France remains one of World War II's most curious episodes.

CRITICAL OVERVIEW

Boyle's body of work is very highly regarded. In the *Dictionary of Literary Biography*, Bell writes,

> Boyle was well known for her novels, poetry, and short fiction, but it is as a short-story writer that she excelled. . . . Noted as a stylist and as an architect of words, she received the accolades of peers and readers alike.

In her critical volume *Kay Boyle: A Study of the Short Fiction*, Bell comments that Boyle was "a premier stylist" and praises "her tireless exploration of the human face behind national and international political movements." Reviewing Boyle's *Fifty Stories* in 1980 in the *Christian Science Monitor*, Beth Ruby comments,

> All writers can be said to be "of their time and place." But Kay Boyle, in *Fifty Stories*, far outstrips the conventional understanding of that phrase. At her best, Boyle not only reflects those times, those places; she calls them into being and into question with the same stroke of the pen.

Ruby adds that "with quiet technical assurance, Boyle simply writes very well"; and that "power and delicacy . . . unite here in the stylistic equivalent of grace under pressure."

Reviewing *Thirty Stories* for the *Saturday Review* in 1946, Struthers Burt was effusive in his praise: "Miss Boyle is a storyteller, a superb one; by and large, the best in this country, and one of the best now living." He affirms that her status as such "emerges clearly" from these stories, all of which are "splendidly told." She is revealed even from her earliest work to be "an artist with a beautiful command of language, a unique gift for striking metaphor, granted as a rule only to poets, and a passionate, impelling drive." Her European stories, Burt notes, "have a sure touch; the touch of a master craftsman. A sure direction. They go places."

Reviewing *Thirty Stories* in the *New York Times Book Review*, Edith R. Mirrielees casually observes, "Each of her short-story collections thus far has enlarged her following. The present one can hardly fail to do the same." With that collection divided up into five sections based on time and geographical location, Mirrielees writes that the section "French Group: 1939–1942" is infused with "the rich savor of a special region" and is "the most consistently impressive. Here a France is built up which, whether a true France or not, has the feel of being true." Perhaps bearing "Defeat" in mind, Mirrielees concludes of the collection,

> What the stories push home is the high-heartedness and faith and daring, the relationship, thicker than blood, of those of all countries whose ideals are more precious to them than their safety. It is itself a high-hearted book.

In an introduction to *Critical Essays on Kay Boyle*, Marilyn Elkins affirms that Boyle merits classification "as among the best American short-story writers of the twentieth century."

CRITICISM

Michael Allen Holmes

Holmes is a writer with existential interests. In the following essay, he considers what the women's actions in the bus driver's tale in "Defeat" might be variously taken to signify.

"

ALL IN ALL, WHETHER INTENTIONALLY OR NOT, WITH A FEW BROAD STROKES OF THE BRUSH THE BUS DRIVER HAS PAINTED A PORTRAIT OF FRANCE'S WOMEN AS MATERIALISTIC, VAIN, SELF-ABSORBED, CALLOUS, CAPRICIOUS, AND PRACTICALLY TRAMPS."

Kay Boyle's short story "Defeat" is a gendered curiosity: the author has taken a sphere dominated by men—military activity in World War II—and extracted from a defeated Frenchman the belief that women, after all, must be France's saving grace, only for his belief to be dashed to pieces when he watches a Bastille Day dance where the Frenchwomen dance with the German soldiers. It is unclear whether and how the women can or should be judged for this action, either from the narrating bus driver's perspective or the reader's. This may be what Daiches is in part referring to, in his introduction to Boyle's *Fifty Stories*, when he notes that "Defeat" and the story "Effigy of War" derive power from "their illumination of some of the moral paradoxes at the center of experience." Without a doubt, Boyle was a progressively minded woman, greatly influenced by the strong female figures in her family, especially her mother and maternal grandmother. In a less permissive era than the present one, she divorced and remarried twice, had children out of wedlock, and even once experimented with collective child-raising in a commune (from which, admittedly, she bolted). Given this background, the background of an empowered woman, it is difficult to imagine that Boyle really means for the bus driver's conclusions about the women who participated in the Bastille Day dance to stand as the last word on the role of women in France's defeat.

That the bus driver is concerned primarily with the women who joined the dance that night is apparent from the trail of his thoughts over the course of his tale. He is pointedly inspired by the schoolmistress as a woman, and pointedly scoffs at the German expectation that the dance in the square will be a success, telling his friend, "They've only made one mistake so far, just one. . . . They haven't got the partners. That's what's going to be funny. That's what's going to be really funny." Curiously, one of Boyle's closest readers, Elizabeth S. Bell, author of *Kay Boyle: A Study of the Short Fiction*, sidesteps a gendered reading of "Defeat" in suggesting that, to the bus driver's dismay, "he sees the townswomen and men joining the Germans in merriment" at the dance. In fact, the driver's narration gives no indication that he saw any men joining the festivities. To the contrary, in telling his tale, after making a gender-neutral suggestion that eating and drinking could naturally lead to dancing, he slips into a discussion of the advantages of a nice dress without bothering to clarify until after the fact that his generic "you" is referring specifically to women (certainly not to the salesmen with whom he is speaking)—as if the Frenchwomen were the only ones who mattered that night; and he even suggests that any eligible Frenchmen were absent from the scene:

> Or maybe if you've had a dress a long time that you wanted to wear and you hadn't had the chance of putting it on and showing it off because all the men were away; I mean if you were a woman.

Not only are women the strict focus of the bus driver's interest, but he makes some rather uncharitable assumptions about what governs their behavior. This may be why Bell declines to investigate the gendered aspects of the story; on the surface, it seems to reflect poorly on the women. The bus driver continues:

> I worked it out that maybe the time comes when you want to put it on so badly that you put it on just the same whatever's happened, or maybe if you're one kind of woman any kind of uniform looks all right to you after a certain time. The music was good, it was first class.

This prolonged discussion of how a dress might be at the bottom of a woman's motives should certainly be considered in part symbolically. Earlier, of course, the bus driver and his friend were obliged to remove their uniforms and, for modesty's sake, clothe themselves in their nation's colors until the schoolmistress could return with more practical garments. The image of the two men wrapped in the flags effectively suggests both their vulnerability as

WHAT DO I READ NEXT?

- Some of Boyle's short fiction is set in France around World War II, and she has also written a novel, *Primer for Combat* (1942), specifically set in France in 1940, in the town of Pontcharra. In the form of a diary written by an American woman, it covers the hundred difficult days following the armistice (truce) and how the common French people coped with the situation.
- Famed French existentialist philosopher Jean-Paul Sartre addressed France's World War II defeat in a fiction trilogy titled *Les Chemins de la liberté*. The third novel, *La Mort dans l'âme* (1949), translated by Gerard Hopkins as *Iron in the Soul* (1951), is the one that depicts the devastation of the defeat itself.
- Paul Valéry was one of France's foremost literary figures at the time of the occupation; he was nominated for the Nobel Prize a dozen times. He died in 1945 at the age of seventy-three. Some of his writings are presented in English translation in *Selected Writings of Paul Valéry* (1964) and *Paul Valéry: An Anthology* (1977).
- One of the key modernist writers with whom Boyle became acquainted was the incomparable expatriate American Gertrude Stein, who endured the World War II occupation with her partner Alice B. Toklas by hiding out in the French countryside. Stein offers a modernist account of her experiences during both world wars in *Wars I Have Seen* (1945).
- An array of stories by France's literary masters—including Honoré de Balzac, Émile Zola, Gustave Flaubert, Guy de Maupassant, Albert Camus, and Simone de Beauvoir—is translated into English in *The Oxford Book of French Short Stories* (2002), edited by Elizabeth Fallaize.
- A trilogy of graphic novels suitable for young adults—*Resistance* (2010), *Defiance* (2011), and *Victory* (2012)—with text by Carla Jablonski and artwork by Leland Purvis, tell of three siblings living in the south of Vichy France and doing what they can to contribute to the resistance against the Nazi occupation.
- Poland was another nation subjected to humiliating circumstances—but with nearly ten times as many deaths as France—during World War II. Polish poet Tadeusz Borowski wrote a number of short stories about the war, with an English collection selected and translated by Barbara Vedder as *This Way for the Gas, Ladies and Gentleman* (1976).

---

defeated soldiers—left, by the surrender, as if naked and defenseless, clothed in nothing but their national identity as Frenchman—and their retention of the ideals they hold the national flag and colors to stand for. Yet this is utterly impractical: they cannot proceed through the town either as the residually proud, uniformed soldiers they were or as the idealistic but naked and vulnerable citizens they are now, swaddled in the blue, white, and red. Instead, they must reduce themselves to mere peasants, stripped of pride and self-worth. For women, then, in contrast, the idea of the special dress can represent a return to normalcy, or rather the best of normalcy, to the joys of daily life in the absence of war—and, notably, this is a sort of return to normalcy and joy unavailable to the average straight man unwilling to put on a dress and attend a social gathering; as presented, the pleasure does not seem to translate to a well-tailored suit.

While the idea of being clothed in particular ways is thematically important, there are greater narrative implications with regard to the women and the dresses. The bus driver leans on this one idea, the idea of the special dress, so completely that he creates an entire scenario explaining just why that special dress might be so appealing: because a woman wants to look and feel good; because after a certain period of time the desire to look and feel good is so overpowering that external circumstances become irrelevant; and because, for some women, at least, "any kind of uniform" looks good in the end, which is to say, the attention of the man inside the uniform is all that matters, and even an enemy can be an object of desire. Finally, with his mention of the "lads in uniform great big fellows handing out chocolates to all the girls," the bus driver ends his talk, unable to continue, the sensory delights of that particular dessert perhaps raising possibilities too disturbing to consider further. All in all, whether intentionally or not, with a few broad strokes of the brush the bus driver has painted a portrait of France's women as materialistic, vain, self-absorbed, callous, capricious, and practically tramps.

Surely, though, this cannot be the last word on the role of women in France's defeat—that of sealing Germany's victory by wearing those dresses that had gathered dust in the closet for too long, putting themselves on display for the blond victors (who are appealing enough, after all) and dancing the night away. Indeed, this idea is one that drives the bus driver to tears; it breaks his heart to think this was really what went through the Frenchwomen's minds when they attended that dance. (It is perhaps worth noting that ultimately some two hundred thousand children were born to French mothers and German fathers during the war, generally through consensual relationships; many such mothers and children suffered ridicule and social rejection later in French life.) On the one hand, Boyle's story is a straightforward lament for the fact of the defeat; the bus driver's tears represent the genuine sadness and despair felt by all patriotic French people at the sight of their country being so easily overrun by an invading force, one they were obliged to welcome, so to speak, in the end. But perhaps there is another layer to the story. The bus driver's idea of the women's state of mind seems so far removed from what the progressive and affirmative Boyle herself would have identified as the state of mind of France's women in the nation's defeat, that it seems the reader must reconsider the bus driver's lamentable conclusions.

One might, for example, conceive of the women's collective gesture—joining the dance with the Germans—as representing a deliberate rebuke of the men of France. Such a rebuke would not be unprecedented, considering how condescending the peasant farmer is to the returning soldiers, as if they were no better than shiftless hobos looking for handouts. From the politicians who wavered in the face of German aggression, to the officers who feared the destruction of the French army, to the intellectuals who feared the total annihilation of the French people, to the common soldiers who walked off the battlefields, men alone could be held responsible for France's defeat. And yet in that very formulation, the meaning of what the men of France accomplished becomes clear: they did at least prevent the catastrophic collapse of French society. As history shows, many of France's citizens were outright relieved at the cessation of hostilities, precluding the widespread damage to property and loss of life that they had so recently witnessed in the mindless slaughters of World War I, much of which took place in French territory. Indeed, it is hard to imagine that the women of the village could, like the ornery peasant farmer, be so ungrateful toward all the men who, in the end, acted with their families' and nation's best interests in mind.

One might instead, then, imagine that the women's gesture could be construed as somehow a positive one—a gesture not of defeat but of, say, resilience, or restoration, or reclamation. Consider how women of the time might have viewed the situation. The Germans had taken over the nation, occupying half of it and holding the remainder accountable to the puppet government at Vichy. The men were, in a word, defeated, whether straggling home haunted by the military humiliation or lingering in prison camps, as did some two million otherwise able-bodied soldiers. As the first half of Boyle's story suggests, those men who did find their way back home were too shocked by what had taken place to be capable of moving forward. As the narration relates, "they said: '*Nous avons été vendus*,' or, '*On nous a vendu*,' over and over until you could have made a popular song of these words and music of defeat." In translation, the soldiers are essentially saying, "We were sold out," and their shame is so strong that some do not even want to pay their respects to the war dead of the past in traditional Bastille Day ceremonies. In short, these men, compulsively now always looking backward, are unfit to lead France forward.

What, then, can the women do—in a time and place where gender roles remain relatively fixed, and power-wielding offices are outside the scope of even strong-willed and politically minded women? By and large, the women are not in a position to issue proclamations or lead initiatives—though, to be sure, some were in such positions. One anonymous woman writer in particular—writing on behalf of the collaborationist Vichy regime, it should be said—used her position to gesture toward the maintenance of restrictive gender roles in her vision of how women could help France heal. As cited by Miranda Pollard in her introduction to *Reign of Virtue: Mobilizing Gender in Vichy France*, this writer prefaced her thought with a saying: "'If everyone sweeps in front of her own door, the street will soon be clean.' Let's apply that to society and say that if each woman looks after, cleans and redoes her home, the fatherland will be beautiful." Pollard reads implications from this formulation:

> The rehabilitation of France after the worst defeat in its history is analogous to housework or spring-cleaning: women's work, unpaid labor, a responsibility and duty that is essential to sustain everyday life. Metaphorically, French men are rendered invisible: they are outside the great feminine business of cleaning up France.

The modern woman legitimately bristles at this formulation, which supposes that cleaning (i.e., cleaning up after men) is by default the responsibility of women; indeed, the Vichy regime was pro-Catholic and traditionalist, seeking to effectively keep women as well as everyone else "in their place" for the duration of the occupation. But Pollard implicitly brings out the merit of the formulation, in this historical instance: there was a special role to be filled—picking up the pieces and restoring morale after France's military defeat—and it seems, from consideration of Boyle's story, at least, that perhaps only the women were then capable of filling it. Certainly the task of standing the people of France back up on their collective feet would be too difficult for the elderly, too complicated for the young, and too demanding for those men who were too weak or disadvantaged to fight in the first place. The bus driver himself seems to realize that only the women can sustain the French people's morale when the schoolmistress, so fiercely devoted to her nation's flag and colors, inspires him to elevate women as the last remaining bastion of national pride. Mentally, he comes to depend on the stronghold that the undefeated women represent.

Finally, then, the reader might come to a satisfactory conclusion about what the women's seemingly fatal, or at least fatalistic, gesture—the gesture of dancing with the German men on France's independence day—might be seen to signify. There seem to have been roughly three choices with regard to how the French people under occupation could proceed. They could wallow in remorse and self-pity, as the men in Boyle's story are inclined to do, drained of that vigor that makes enduring the trials of everyday life possible—but to linger in such a state would represent a spiritual death, one that might never be recovered from. Or they could raise themselves in resistance, showing they still believe in an independent France with covert and guerrilla actions—but to do so would be to bring punishment on one's fellow citizens. Or, thirdly, they could endure the occupation with their pride and dignity intact—they could yet say that they have all done what they had to, what had to be done—sustaining morale through affirmations of the joy of being alive even while under the thumb of the occupiers. Above all, they could do *even what they inherently did not want to do*: they could cooperate with those whom they could only loathe at heart, the German soldiers, simply to ensure their own survival. Belligerent relations with those soldiers, after all, could only lead to animosity and harsh treatment.

What does it mean, then, for Frenchwomen to eat Germans' food and dance with German soldiers in France on July the Fourteenth? It perhaps indicates the persistence of French independence, even with those German soldiers stationed on the very doorsteps that they have so diligently sought to keep clean. The women did not need to *want* to dance with the Germans in order to do so; they only needed to want to make a gesture that would communicate something to everyone: to the Germans, a desire to respond well to reasonable civil expectations and maintain the peace; to the Frenchmen, a call to muster their energies and again become the ones with whom the women of France want

The defeated French soldiers come home slowly, riding bicycles and hitchhiking (©Sri J / Shutterstock.com)

to dance; and to all of France's citizens, a declaration that the soul can still be free, the soul can still dance, and one can still find joy in one's daily existence even in the wake of a tragedy. Life must go on, the people's attention must be returned from the past to the here and now, and spirits must be lifted—and Boyle perhaps means to say that it is women, exuding *joie de vivre* in their beautiful dresses, who can do the trick.

Source: Michael Allen Holmes, Critical Essay on "Defeat," in *Short Stories for Students*, Gale, Cengage Learning, 2017.

Richard C. Carpenter

In the following excerpt, Carpenter discusses whether Boyle's stories are pessimistic.

. . . Beyond technique, Miss Boyle's basic themes are also productive of suspense and intensity. Her fiction world is not a happy one: she deals with disease, war, perversion, cowardice, frustration. Her people are complex souls undergoing a variety of torments, prevented either by their own weaknesses or the devils of circumstance from living the rich and full lives which should be theirs. To make things worse, her people are not degraded but *potentially* fine and *potentially* happy. They are sensitive, courageous, artistic, profoundly emotional. We like them, usually, and would like to see them happy, but they are the beautiful and the damned. Miss Boyle achieves her characteristic force by showing us a vision of humanity in need of pity and understanding, a central idea that does not make for light reading but one which accounts for the realism and effectiveness we inescapably feel as we read through her work. While probably not the end result of a reasoned philosophy, it is a telling and significant attitude toward life that makes of her writing much more than a pretty toy or a tract. Miss Boyle is not simply *interested* in people; she is vitally *concerned* with people and profoundly moved to write about their struggles with themselves and with their dreams. She does not write just to tell a tale, to make money, to create a thing of beauty, even though these may sometimes be her motives; but, as she has said, she also writes "out of anger, out of compassion and grief . . . out of despair." This is truly the other side of the blade.

"MANY TALES ARE VITIATED BY MISS BOYLE'S INDISCRIMINATE TENDERNESS TOWARD THOSE WHO ARE THE VICTIMS OF WAR. HER BEST WORK IN THIS TYPE OF WRITING IS RATHER, THAT WHICH GROWS OUT OF INDIGNATION, THE FAILURE OF DEVOTION AND INTEGRITY."

From her earliest work we can see Miss Boyle working out this idea. *Plagued by the Nightingale* and *Year before Last* explore the relations between people whose happiness is shadowed by disease; *Gentlemen, I Address You Privately* is an analysis of perverted love. *Plagued by the Nightingale* is the story of an American girl who has married into a French family cursed with a hereditary disease which cripples the legs of the men. The conflict grows out of the insistence of the family, particularly Papa, that the young couple have a child, even though everyone knows the risk. A silent but bitter struggle, beneath the surface of an idyllic family life, is waged, with the family using the lever of promised money to weaken the son's resistance. The family loses, eventually, but the girl loses as well, for she leaves her husband, and her love, at the end. The novel is almost a parable, with Bridget and Nicholas—youth, beauty, and love—defeated by age and corruption, symbolized by the nature of the disease, a "rotting of the bone" as it is called. The corruption comes closer to home in her second novel, *Year before Last*, since Martin, the hero, is handsome, brave, sensitive, deeply in love, as well as tuberculous. He is, perhaps, a bit too much of these things and a trifle impossible, but he and his inamorata, Hannah, reiterate for us that the beautiful *are* often the damned. As we watch them flee across the south of France, with the hemorrhages becoming more frequent and deadly, we find our feeling of pity and our sense of irony steadily increasing until the inevitable death at the conclusion.

An interesting aspect of these novels is that they ought to be merely depressing instead of enthralling. However, through the poetic use of language and the method of implication and reticence, Miss Boyle lifts the story. Besides, because the reader creates the emotional tone for himself, as he gradually becomes aware of the situation, the essential tragedy is not sharply emphasized. The tale unfolds slowly, flower-like, so that we are almost able—almost, but not quite, like the characters themselves—to close our eyes on the worm i' the bud. The enervation of some of her later work is undoubtedly due to a partial abandonment of this method of implication for that of stream of consciousness and interior monologue where we are brought directly and explicitly into contact with the people's thoughts and emotions, usually in italics. In her weaker writing Miss Boyle tells us too much; in her better we float on a placid, shimmering current, all the time aware of the cold, black, rushing depths beneath.

Naturally, this method can be overdone, as it is in her third novel, *Gentlemen, I Address You Privately*, where we see everything through a glass most darkly, so much so that it is difficult to realize what the theme is. An analysis of the chiaroscuro, however, shows that all the characters are twisted in some way: the cast is composed of two homosexuals, two Lesbians, a prostitute, a fanatic, a sadist, and one fine woman starved for love. In general, love is perverted in this novel; the characters are lost souls, whirled through the darkness of their desires.

The tale comes to a flat and tasteless end, despite some tension in the last chapters, and its people are too much for us to swallow—possible perhaps, but hardly probable. Still, with all its frigidity and confusion, it somehow sticks in the mind, like a reflection in a distorting mirror, concentrating for us the pathos and irony of Miss Boyle's theme. It is, as well, the furthest advance she has made in the use of implication and memorable for that reason.

Throughout Miss Boyle's writings prior to the war we can see the same techniques, the same quivering emotion held in tight leash, the concern with the interrelations of personality, the same bitter brew. Though the short stories naturally play many variations, they show the same fundamental theme, not difficult to recognize once it has been analyzed.

In some stories the problem is pride, as in "Keep Your Pity," where the Wycherlys, impoverished Englishmen in the south of France, preserve appearances even beyond death. In others, such as "The White Horses of Vienna," it is the pathos of prejudice and misunderstanding. The young Jewish student-doctor, who has been called in to assist the injured Austrian Nazi, ought to be able to be a friend—he and the Austrian are really much alike, the Austrian with his worship of power and the Jew with his nostalgic idealism, his memory of the royal white horses of Vienna, "the relics of pride, the still unbroken vestiges of beauty bending their knees to the empty loge of royalty where there was no royalty any more." But of course they cannot be friends.

Other stories are tales of initiation, in which an innocent or unknowing character learns evil—as in "Black Boy," where a young white girl learns that she cannot have an innocent friendship with a black boy, at least not as far as her grandfather is concerned; or in *The Bridegroom's Body* (a novella), where Lady Glourie realizes that the young nurse who has come from the city has not been, as Lady Glourie suspected, in love with Lord Glourie or the farmer Panrandel but really with Lady Glourie herself. In "Natives Don't Cry" we see the beautifully low-keyed treatment of the real pathos in the old maid's life as the governess tries to pretend she is getting letters from her young man, when the mail was not delivered that day.

"Wedding Day," one of Miss Boyle's best, a light and delicate study of personal relations between brother and sister on her wedding day, does not force theme on our attention, but there is still the sense of loss, of youth left somewhere behind, forever. "Count Lothar's Heart" concerns itself with what has happened to a young man who has had a homosexual experience during the war and cannot get it out of his mind, his perversion symbolized by the swans of the Traunsee, emblems of passion. "One of Ours" studies through image and symbol the hidden feelings of a most proper Englishwoman who thinks a savage at an exposition is lusting after her—a projection of her desires, for he is really interested in the doll she is holding. The theme of distortion is carried out by her fascination with the savage's maleness as well as her fear of him.

It might be wondered whether or not Miss Boyle offers anything but utter blank and bitter pessimism with this constant iteration of the theme of a world out of joint. Indeed, it could be maintained that there is nothing else. A novel like *My Next Bride* (1934) leaves about as bad a taste in our mouths as anything we could find, with an American girl who deserves no evil falling into utter degradation through her love for another woman's husband. Perversely she becomes promiscuous rather than having her affair with Antony, making her pregnancy by some unknown especially fruitless. Probably the most unpleasant sequences Kay Boyle has ever written are to be found in the account of Victoria's attempts at abortion.

Yet the novel, *Monday Night* (1936), which has a protagonist who is repulsively dirty and possesses a nauseatingly mutilated ear, manages to distil something more positive from the flowers of evil. The contrast between the clean and the filthy, the innocent and the obscene, is implicit perhaps, but it is still there to provide a kind of counterpoint to the basic theme. In fact, this counterpoint may be seen running through many of her writings, indicating a corollary to the pessimism. A passage in "Count Lothar's Heart" symbolizes what this may be; speaking of the swans, she writes:

> Some of them had thrust the long stalks of their throats down into the deeper places before the falls and were seeking for refuse along the bottom. Nothing remained but the soft, flickering short peaks of their clean rumps and their leathery black elbows with the down blowing soft at the ebony bone. In such ecstasies of beauty were they seeking in the filth of lemon rinds and shells and garbage that had drifted down from the town, prodding the leaves and branches apart with their dark, lustful mouths.

Miss Boyle seems to be saying that the polarity between the beautiful and the ugly, the good and the bad, is central in our lives. Wilt, in *Monday Night*, disreputable and dirty, is yet a dreamer of beautiful dreams which he conveys to us in long monologues written in an incantatory style strongly reminiscent of Faulkner, who, Miss Boyle says, strongly influenced the book. Wilt ought to be a great writer, yet he is a seedy drunk. Miss Boyle is not telling us that he is going to triumph over himself; rather she is showing us that he cannot possibly do so: the fact that he and his friend never reach the goal they seek is the only logic that the underlying theme will permit the plot. Yet Wilt is somehow noble. He is giving himself to an ideal; the tale is almost an allegory, a *Pilgrim's Progress* of this modern world, where modern man fails of heaven as a goal but finds his soul in the quest itself. Here, as in other places, we can see Miss Boyle implying that devotion, integrity, and courage are the means by which we transcend our fate.

This implication is particularly evident in the tales since the war; dealing with social and political themes, they throw the contrast between what is and what ought to be into clearer light. In the backwash of a war-world, the need for undramatic devotion and integrity is particularly great. A number of tales since 1938 benefit from this larger context. There is less tendency toward attenuating the situation; the characters are often more believable, their suffering justified, their bravery less self-conscious, their defeat more real. It must be admitted that they transcend their fate but seldom. Many tales are vitiated by Miss Boyle's indiscriminate tenderness toward those who are the victims of war. Her best work in this type of writing is rather, that which grows out of indignation, the failure of devotion and integrity. "Defeat," which won the O. Henry Memorial Prize in 1941, shows this indignation combined effectively with tenderness, the indignation coming from the failure of the French girls to resist the German blandishments of food and dance music, the tenderness for the men who realize their country is defeated only when its women are defeated. . . .

Source: Richard C. Carpenter, "Kay Boyle," in *Critical Essays on Kay Boyle*, edited by Marilyn Elkins, G. K. Hall, 1997, pp. 91–95.

Elizabeth S. Bell

In the following excerpt, Bell characterizes the tales in Thirty Stories *as different from those in Boyle 's other collections.*

Thirty Stories (1946) is a significant departure from Boyle's earlier short story collections. Each of her three previous volumes contains either stories that appeared only in magazine or journal publications or those written specifically for that collection. As the circumstances under which Boyle lived changed, so did the tone and direction of the stories she wrote, published, and collected in these early volumes. In contrast, 14 of the stories in *Thirty Stories* come from these three earlier compilations and, instead of being labeled by the title of the original collection, are divided in this new volume into sections identified by time period and the country in which they were written. Three previously uncollected stories from the 1930s appear in this volume: "Ben" (*New Yorker*, 24 December 1938), "How Bridie's Girl Was Won" (*Harper's Magazine*, March 1936), and "The Herring Piece" (*New Yorker*, 10 April 1937). The remaining 13 stories, originally published in the early 1940s, are also collected for the first time. These stories, defined in the table of contents as the "French Group: 1939–1942" and the "American Group: 1942–1946," deal with events associated with World War II. Thus, as a collection *Thirty Stories* is a Janus of sorts, with a face looking consciously backward to well-known and highly respected fiction and one looking forward with fresh and timely new writings. This arrangement produces more than merely a group of short stories; it accomplishes a dual task.

> "THROUGH THE RELATIVELY BRIEF TIMESPAN OF THE STORY, BOYLE CONTRASTS REAL TIME WITH A SEEMINGLY MUCH LONGER EMOTIONAL TIME AS SHE EXPLORES THE GAP BETWEEN ONE MAN'S—AND ONE NATION'S—EXPECTATIONS OF HUMAN BEHAVIOR AND THE REALITY THAT HE—AND THE WORLD—HAVE TO FACE."

First, *Thirty Stories* represents a capsule view of Boyle's writing career and, consequently, her life and concerns. The re-collected stories range from portrayals of her family background and family members from whom she drew strength to glimpses of her life as a young writer in various parts of Europe, sometimes telling of her life with Ernest Walsh, the eccentrics and bohemians she knew, the lands she saw with Lawrence Vail, her shared concerns with Joseph Franckenstein, her life alone, and her life as a young mother traveling from Austria to England and back again. The stories plunge deeply into her emotional life and borrow details from the substance of her everyday existence to document the making of Kay Boyle, the journey of her life, with the forces that shaped her particular consciousness. Thus,

Thirty Stories becomes a retrospective of sorts for Boyle's career as writer.

Just as important, however, the volume documents some of the major periods of the twentieth century: the deceptively calm and secure years before the First World War, the unsettled and unstructured years of the 1920s in Europe, the strained and volatile years of the 1930s leading to the Second World War, and the war years themselves. The stories embody the journey Boyle saw our world embark on as the century took its shape.

Critical reception of the book was overwhelmingly favorable. Struthers Burt, writing for the *Saturday Review*, praises the collection, especially the European stories for their clarity and focus. He finds the selection of stories effective in showing the range of Boyle's writing. Edith R. Mirrielees, in the *New York Times Book Review*, mentions the commentary Boyle makes on the fractured world of the twentieth century. She recognizes Boyle's special place and voice in a time needing to be chronicled. Indeed, with few dissenting voices, in the opinions of most reviewers of *Thirty Stories*, Boyle demonstrated her mastery of form, content, and vision, and as the earlier pieces of the collection proved, she had been mastering them in individual works from virtually the beginning of her career.

The last two sections of *Thirty Stories* warrant attention, for they contain the previously uncollected stories that chronicle the progress of World War II as reflected in the periphery of the political and military spotlight. Boyle does not show her readers the literal battlegrounds or take them on reviews of troop movements, political conferences, treaty signings, or the like. Instead, she describes the lives and decisions of the misplaced—the foreigners on suddenly occupied soil, the prisoners of war, the resistance fighters whose lives depend on their being able to distinguish friend from foe, the everyday ordinary people riding out the air raids in dismal cellars, the new recruits, and the children who have seen or heard too much of war. The stories in the French section of the book and those of the American section have different personalities, different tempers, different realities.

FRANCE IN THE 1940S

The "French Group," the more extensive section of the two, contains a gamut of moods, beginning with Boyle's gently stinging indictment of misplaced civilian priorities in the ironically entitled "Major Engagement in Paris," originally published in *American Mercury* in 1940. Set during the war, but before France's fall to nazism or America's entry into the war, the story details the relationship between two women who have been friends for years. One of them, Mrs. Hodges, an American who has lived in Paris for 30 years, suddenly becomes much taken with toothpicks and, to the horror of her very proper friend Mrs. Peterson, uses them with glee in her favorite tea shop. Under pressure from Mrs. Hodges to try them out, a flustered Mrs. Peterson accidentally breaks two toothpicks against her teeth. Because of the resulting censure from Mrs. Hodges, Mrs. Peterson develops a mental block against the toothpicks, and when during an air raid, she must again confront both Mrs. Hodges and the dreaded toothpicks, she again fails to use them satisfactorily. Mrs. Hodges reacts in anger and promises never to think of anyone except herself again.

This story has been much misunderstood, as a review from the *San Francisco Chronicle* indicates. That reviewer sees the story as a discussion of senility, perhaps a nice character sketch of two old women no longer aware of the world around them. In fact, this story represents Boyle's mounting displeasure with civilian nonchalance in the face of war. For example, she lets Mrs. Hodges make a cavalier and disparaging comparison of "this war" with World War I in order to show a certain form of apathy too prevalent in 1940, an apathy born of the desire to look at the war as a personal inconvenience—if one had the privilege of distance from it. Boyle contrasts the triviality of "the battle of the toothpicks" with the larger battle surrounding them, as indicated by the tear gas cannisters the characters carry with them and the air raid that precipitates their final confrontation. The extent of the emotions spent in the confrontation between two friends is out of proportion to the issue involved. In the inappropriateness of their responses, Boyle establishes the fundamental conflict of the story.

Boyle returns to this theme in a more biting piece of nonfiction in "The Battle of the Sequins," published in the *Nation* (1944) and referring to the American public's concern for dwindling supplies of consumer goods at a time when the situation in Europe and other parts of the world was deteriorating rapidly. In this essay she again uses the language of battle to describe women fighting over sale items in a department store, as phantom faces from the jungles and battlefields of the real war look on accusingly. While the satirical mood of these two writings may appear at first glance to be light, the satire masks a deeper and darker irony leveled at the egocentrism of the human heart.

Despite its title, "Major Engagement in Paris" transcends its national setting, but other stories in the French section of this collection depend for their meanings on a specifically French setting and context. Boyle draws on the unexpectedly rapid invasion and defeat of France by Hitler in 1940 and the resulting establishment of a bitterly received collaborationist government at Vichy as backdrop to her stories. Some of her references to these events are oblique: for example, in several of these stories, she describes her characters' concern for crossing the Channel into England, although she does not specifically explain that they wish to join the Free French movement headed by Charles de Gaulle and fear official reprisals if they are caught in the attempt. In several stories, she alludes to the healthy Resistance in France and to the efforts of people of many nations to support it. And in several stories, she makes a distinction between those who arc French men and women by birth and those who are true French men and women by spirit, a distinction born of the contempt with which many French nationals held the Vichy government—and the French citizens who capitulated to Hitler without a fight—or the betrayal of their country. Thus, the stories depend for much of their power on the reader's knowledge of the undercurrents of anger, despair, defeatism, and courage that played across the face of France during the early 1940s.

The showcase story of this section, "Defeat," won the O. Henry Memorial Award for 1941 for its cogent and focused depiction of the disillusionment of one man who serves as a mirror for his nation. The story opens in the summer of 1940 with the return of soldiers who had served in the French army before its armistice with Nazi Germany. Boyle draws a subtle comparison between the disillusionment of these men who are "without victory" and the displacement that American Confederate soldiers must have felt when they returned to a home no longer as they remembered it. The returning Frenchmen explain their defeat through accounts of the superior forces and preparedness of strong young Germans, the outdated and poorly equipped French army, and the corresponding cowardice of the French leaders, many of whom were among the first to retreat. They testify to a shameful episode in French affairs and, in their retelling of the events witnessed, try to purge themselves of the outrage and perhaps guilt they feel.

In contrast, the protagonist of the story, a bus driver by trade, tells his story only once in the quiet atmosphere born of shared glasses of wine with two traveling salesmen, strangers—as if he could not bear to speak to friends of what he has seen. An escaped prisoner of war, he chronicles his travels through the French countryside, finding aid where he can from a courageous schoolmistress and generous farmer, but finding also an unexpected hostility from others who fear German reprisals and who blame the French army for its defeat. As he journeys, the bus driver encourages himself by focusing on the thought that France will never be defeated as long as its women remain strong, for he finds in the defiance he saw in the eyes of the schoolmistress a reminder of the France for which he fought.

His faith in his country, however, appears to be for naught. Throughout the country the German authorities have usurped the preparations being made for Bastille Day celebrations, and they urge the French to come join them in dancing and feasting. Concerning this insult to the spirit of France, the bus driver remains confident the Germans will celebrate alone. To his dismay, later that night, as he looks down on the village square from the window of the hayloft where he hides, he sees the townswomen and men joining the Germans in merriment. He tries to explain away what he has seen by blaming it on the vast display of food the Germans have provided, but at last he must comfort himself by the notion that he saw only one town. Even so, his tears indicate that he does not believe those events to be isolated.

Boyle uses three time settings, which are not chronological in the story: she begins in late June with the soldiers' return, then shifts forward in time—two months after the bus driver's return—to his confession, which takes us back again to July 14 and the events he witnessed. Although the events of the story span very little actual time, they represent a lifetime's journey into betrayal for the protagonist. Boyle suggests the depth of his disillusionment by the simple ploy of contrasting his hesitancy to speak of it with the openness and outspokenness of other returning soldiers. While they broadcast their shock and anger, his choice of confidants and the intimacy of conversation shared over wine point to a deep and abiding despair he cannot exorcise. Through the relatively brief timespan of the story, Boyle contrasts real time with a seemingly much longer emotional time as she explores the gap between one man's—and one nation's—expectations of human behavior and the reality that he—and the world—have to face. . . .

Source: Elizabeth S. Bell, "Recollections: *Thirty Stories*," in *Kay Boyle: A Study of the Short Fiction*, Twayne Publishers, 1992, pp. 44–48.

SOURCES

Allen, Felix, "Epicentre of Terror: Why Is France the Target of So Many Terrorist Atrocities?," in *Sun*, July 15, 2016, https://www.thesun.co.uk/news/1449033/why-is-france-the-target-of-so-many-terrorist-atrocities/ (accessed August 28, 2016).

Bell, Elizabeth S., "Kay Boyle," in *Dictionary of Literary Biography*, Vol. 86, *American Short-Story Writers, 1910–1945: First Series*, edited by Bobby Ellen Kimbel, Gale, 1989.

———, *Kay Boyle: A Study of the Short Fiction*, Twayne Publishers, 1992, pp. 3–85.

Boyle, Kay, "Defeat," in *Fifty Stories*, Doubleday, 1980, pp. 294–304.

Burt, Struthers, "The Mature Craft of Kay Boyle," in *Saturday Review*, November 30, 1946, p. 11, https://www.unz.org/Pub/SaturdayRev-1946nov30-00011?View=PDF (accessed August 26, 2016).

Carpenter, Richard C., "Kay Boyle," in *Critical Essays on Kay Boyle*, edited by Marilyn Elkins, G. K. Hall, 1997, pp. 89–95; originally published in *College English*, Vol. 15, No. 2, November 1953, pp. 81–87.

Daiches, David, Introduction to *Fifty Stories*, Doubleday, 1980, pp. 9–14.

Elkins, Marilyn, ed., Introduction to *Critical Essays on Kay Boyle*, G. K. Hall, 1997, pp. 1–2.

Fishman, Sarah, and Leonard V. Smith, Introduction to *France at War: Vichy and the Historians*, edited by Sarah Fishman, Laura Lee Downs, Ioannis Sinanoglou, Leonard V. Smith, and Robert Zaretsky, translated by David Lake, Berg, 2000, p. 1.

Holt, Patricia, "*PW* Interviews: Kay Boyle," in *Publishers Weekly*, Vol. 218, No. 16, October 17, 1980, pp. 8–9.

Krause, Suzanne, "The Forgotten Children of German-Occupied France," Deutsche Welle website, August 27, 2006, http://www.dw.com/en/the-forgotten-children-of-german-occupied-france/a-2145680 (accessed August 28, 2016).

Lambert, Caroline, "French Women in Politics: The Long Road to Parity," Brookings Institution website, May 1, 2001, https://www.brookings.edu/articles/french-women-in-politics-the-long-road-to-parity/ (accessed August 28, 2016).

Mirrielees, Edith R., "Stories to Remember," in *New York Times Book Review*, December 1, 1946, p. 9.

Pace, Eric, "Kay Boyle, 90, Writer of Novels and Stories, Dies," in *New York Times*, December 29, 1992, http://www.nytimes.com/1992/12/29/arts/kay-boyle-90-writer-of-novels-and-stories-dies.html (accessed August 26, 2016).

Paxton, Robert O., *Vichy France: Old Guard and New Order, 1940–1944*, Columbia University Press, 1982, pp. 3–24.

Pollard, Miranda, *Reign of Virtue: Mobilizing Gender in Vichy France*, University of Chicago Press, 1998, pp. 1–3.

"Proportion of Seats Held by Women in National Parliaments," World Bank website, http://data.worldbank.org/indicator/SG.GEN.PARL.ZS?locations=FR (accessed August 28, 2016).

Ruby, Beth, "Power and Delicacy from Kay Boyle," in *Christian Science Monitor*, November 10, 1980, http://www.csmonitor.com/1980/1110/111059.html (accessed August 26, 2016).

"WWI Casualty and Death Tables," PBS website, https://www.pbs.org/greatwar/resources/casdeath_pop.html (accessed August 27, 2016).

FURTHER READING

Moorehead, Caroline, *A Train in Winter: An Extraordinary Story of Women, Friendship, and Resistance in Occupied France*, HarperCollins, 2011.

For anyone wondering about the roles that women could play in the World War II era, this book tells the story of some 230 civilian French women—housewives, teachers, singers, and others—who did what they could for the resistance. As part of the broader tragedy, they were captured by the Gestapo and sent to Auschwitz; only forty-nine survived.

Peschanski, Denis, et al., *Collaboration and Resistance: Images of Life in Vichy France, 1940–1944*, translated by Lory Frankel, Harry N. Abrams, 2000.

Collecting photographs, newspaper clippings, leaflets, and other documents, Peschanski and his fellow contributors give readers the chance to delve into the time period and imagine what it was like for the people of France to endure Germany's occupation.

Schivelbusch, Wolfgang, *The Culture of Defeat: On National Trauma, Mourning, and Recovery*, translated by Jefferson Chase, Metropolitan Books, 2003.

German author Schivelbusch uses three case studies to consider defeat specifically in the context of war and the collective national psyche. France in World War II is not one of them, but two are highly relevant: France in the Franco-Prussian War in 1871 (with Prussia leading a German confederation) and Germany in World War I (setting the stage for World War II). The third is the Confederacy in the US Civil War.

Spanier, Sandra Whipple, *Kay Boyle: Artist and Activist*, Southern Illinois University Press, 1986.

Spanier's critical biography covers the breadth of Boyle's life and works, covering all the places and time periods that made her into one of the most significant American authors of the modernist era.

SUGGESTED SEARCH TERMS

Kay Boyle AND Defeat

Kay Boyle AND Thirty Stories OR Fifty Stories

Kay Boyle AND modernism

France AND American expatriate authors

France AND World War II defeat

France AND German occupation

1930s France AND fascism OR Communism

Vichy France AND collaboration

Kay Boyle AND Stein OR Hemingway OR Joyce

Greenleaf

FLANNERY O'CONNOR

1956

"Greenleaf" is a story by Flannery O'Connor, one of the best-known twentieth-century American short-story writers. The story was published in the *Kenyon Review* in the summer of 1956 and reprinted in *Prize Stories: The O. Henry Awards*, in 1957, as the first-prize story. It was reprinted again in 1965, in O'Connor's collection *Everything That Rises Must Converge*. In this tale, the protagonist is Mrs. May, a widow who runs an impoverished dairy farm in the South and lives with her two adult sons. The plot is simple: one of the bulls owned by her near neighbors escapes and gets into her milk herd. She summons her hired hand, Mr. Greenleaf, to round up the bull, but things go awry. It turns out there is a conflict of interest for Mr. Greenleaf, between his obligations to his landlord, Mrs. May, who resents him openly, and to the owners of the bull—his sons. With its southern setting, wry humor, religious symbolism, and sudden explosion of violence, "Greenleaf" might be seen as a typical O'Connor tale.

AUTHOR BIOGRAPHY

Mary Flannery O'Connor was born on March 25, 1925, in Savannah, Georgia, the only child of Edward F. O'Connor Jr. and Regina (Cline) O'Connor. The middle-class, Roman Catholic family moved to Milledgeville, in central

Flannery O'Connor (©Apic / Hulton Archive / Getty Images)

Georgia, in 1938. Only a couple of years later, in 1941, the father died of systemic lupus erythematosus, an autoimmune disease. In 1942, O'Connor attended Georgia State College for Women in Milledgeville, graduating in 1945 with a degree in social science. While still an undergraduate, she showed promise as a writer and also excelled as a cartoonist. She then attended the Writers' Workshop at what was then the State University of Iowa (now the University of Iowa), graduating with a master of fine arts in 1947. Her first published short story, "The Geranium," appeared in *Accent* in the summer of 1946. From that point on, her stories began appearing regularly in literary magazines such as the *Sewanee Review* and *Partisan Review*. In 1948, she spent several months living at Yaddo, the renowned artists' colony in Saratoga Springs, New York.

O'Connor lived briefly in New York City and also stayed with the poet and translator Robert Fitzgerald and his wife, Sally, in Ridgefield, Connecticut, from early 1949 to Christmas 1950. In early 1951, however, O'Connor was diagnosed with lupus, which forced her to return to the South, where she lived with her mother at Andalusia, their farm near Milledgeville.

In 1952, O'Connor published her first novel, *Wise Blood*. In 1954 and 1955, she won second prize in the O. Henry Awards for her short stories "The Life You Save May Be Your Own" and "A Circle in the Fire," respectively. Then in 1957, she won the O. Henry first prize for "Greenleaf," which had been published in the *Kenyon Review* in 1956.

Meanwhile, her first collection of stories, *A Good Man Is Hard to Find*, was published in 1955, to excellent reviews. In 1960, she published the novel *The Violent Bear It Away*. Three years later her story "Everything That Rises Must Converge" won the O. Henry first prize, and the following year, "Revelation" achieved the same distinction.

O'Connor's promising literary career was cut short. She died of lupus on August 3, 1964, in Milledgeville, at the age of thirty-nine. Her short-story collection *Everything That Rises Must Converge* was published posthumously in 1965, and *The Complete Stories of Flannery O'Connor* (1971) won the National Book Award.

PLOT SUMMARY

Mrs. May, a widow who owns a run-down dairy farm in the South, is awakened at night by the sound of a bull chewing the grass in front of the house. She looks out of the window, sees the bull, and realizes it is there because her tenant and employee, Mr. Greenleaf, left the lane gate open. She worries that the bull will soon be running around in her herd unless it is caught. She also knows that Mr. Greenleaf is likely still asleep in the tenant house half a mile down the road. She has a low opinion of his abilities so decides not to bother him.

The next day, Mrs. May informs the feckless Mr. Greenleaf of the stray bull and says she wants it penned up immediately. He tells her the bull has been loose for three days. Impatient, she tells him to deal with the matter. Then she goes into the dining room and watches her two sons, Scofield and Wesley, as they eat breakfast. Scofield tells her the stray bull belongs to Mr. Greenleaf's two sons, O.T. and E.T. Mrs. May is exasperated that Mr. Greenleaf did not know this (or pretended not to know). She worries about her sons because they are unmarried, and she does not trust them to marry

MEDIA ADAPTATIONS

- In 2010, Blackstone Audio issued an audio recording of O'Connor's stories titled *Everything That Rises Must Converge*. It includes "Greenleaf." The running time is nine hours, five minutes.

well, if they should decide to do so after she is dead, which is what Scofield says he will do.

This puts into Mrs. May's mind the notion that they might marry someone as bad as Mr. Greenleaf's wife, whom she despises because of her lower-class origins and because her five young children are always dirty. Mrs. May is contemptuous of her also because of the strange "prayer healing" that Mrs. Greenleaf often conducts outdoors, after burying a lot of newspaper cuttings containing news of tragedies and disasters in the world.

Mrs. May receives scant comfort from her other son, Wesley, who deliberately insults her. Mrs. May says she wishes that O.T. and E.T. were her sons, rather than the two she has, since they are much more successful and are both married with children. However, she does not like this thought and starts to cry. Wesley leaves the room.

Mrs. May goes outside, where she finds Mr. Greenleaf in the trench silo with a wheelbarrow. She berates him, saying he should be catching the bull, which must now be in her milk herd. She tells him the bull belongs to his sons, and he acts incredulous. She says she is going to drive over to O.T. and E.T. and tell them they must come for their bull that same day and urges Mr. Greenleaf again to get the bull. Within half an hour, she sees him on horseback following the bull down the dirt road that runs in front of the house.

By mid-morning, Mrs. May has driven to the home of O.T. and E.T. She honks on the horn and waits in the driveway. Some children come out and say that their parents are not at home. She drives down to the barn, hoping to find the man who works for the twins. Once there, she decides to look into the milking parlor that O.T. and E.T. have had built at great expense (with government assistance, she thinks). The farmhand is there, and Mrs. May gives him a written message to be delivered to O.T. and E.T. She also tells him that she wants their bull off her property that very day, and if O.T. and E.T. do not come and get it, she will get their father to shoot it. The employee says it is likely that his employers would just tell her to go ahead and shoot the bull.

That afternoon, Mrs. May sits at home waiting for the brothers to collect their bull, but they do not come. Mrs. May complains at supper to her sons that she is a victim, but as usual her sons offer her no sympathy. Instead, they tease her cruelly, and she runs out of the room. Wesley and Scofield fall to quarreling, and Mrs. May, rushing back into the room, finds Wesley lying on his back on the floor. She helps him to his feet, and he runs out of the door in pursuit of his brother.

Alerted by the commotion, Mr. Greenleaf knocks on the back door. He tells Mrs. May he will take the bull home tomorrow, but that does not satisfy Mrs. May. She complains about how badly she has been treated by O.T. and E.T. Had she been a man rather than a woman, she says, they would have come for the bull. Mr. Greenleaf immediately points out that she has two sons of her own, implying that they could have helped her.

At night, Mrs. May is again awoken by the sound of the bull munching on the grass. She realizes that Mr. Greenleaf has let it out. She looks out of the window and sees the bull.

At eleven o'clock the next morning, she drives to the barn, where Mr. Greenleaf is cleaning milk cans. She tells him to get his gun, saying that the bull is in the pasture with her cows. Mrs. May wants Mr. Greenleaf to drive the bull into an empty pasture and shoot it. She sits in her car as a reluctant Mr. Greenleaf gets his gun from the harness room and then gets into her car.

They reach the pasture, where the bull is grazing among the cows. Mrs. May tells Mr. Greenleaf to run the bull into the adjoining pasture. Mr. Greenleaf gets out of the car and reluctantly does as she has asked. He drives the bull out of the pasture and follows it at a leisurely pace. Mrs. May drives across the pasture, but when she reaches the gate, there is no sign of Mr. Greenleaf or the bull. She gets out and closes the gate, thinking that Mr. Greenleaf's plan is to lose the bull in the woods.

She drives to the center of the pasture, expecting soon to see Mr. Greenleaf emerge from the woods. She sits on the bumper of the car, waiting. Feeling sleepy, she closes her eyes. Ten minutes go by, but she hears no gunshot. She wonders for a moment whether the bull has gotten excited and gored Mr. Greenleaf. She honks on the horn several times and then sits on the bumper again.

The bull emerges from the tree line and gallops toward her. She calls out for Mr. Greenleaf, but he is nowhere to be seen. Meanwhile, the bull continues to race toward her, while she remains still, not quite comprehending what her eyes are telling her. The bull finally gores her, piercing her heart; a strange, contradictory expression appears on her face, like someone "whose sight has been suddenly restored but who finds the light unbearable." She sees Mr. Greenleaf approaching, and he shoots the bull four times through the eye. As the bull falls, it pulls Mrs. May forward onto its head, and she seems to be giving expression to another spiritual revelation.

CHARACTERS

Mr. Greenleaf

Mr. Greenleaf has been employed by Mrs. May for fifteen years to help on the farm. She regards him as lazy, incompetent, and lacking initiative. The only reason she has not fired him, as she conceives it, is because he would not be capable of finding another job. He and his wife have twin boys, O.T. and E.T., both of whom are married and live in the area. Mr. Greenleaf and his wife also have five daughters. When Mrs. May informs him of the escaped bull, he shows no urgency about the situation, leaving her frustrated and angry.

Mrs. Greenleaf

Mrs. Greenleaf is seen in a very negative light by Mrs. May, who thinks that the five young Greenleaf daughters are always dirty and that the yard looks like a trash heap. Mrs. Greenleaf conducts what she calls "prayer healing," muttering what to Mrs. May are unintelligible sounds over collections of newspaper reports of grisly crimes and accidents that she has buried in a hole in the ground. Mrs. Greenleaf is a contrast to Mrs. May in that she emphatically believes in the Christian religion and the power of Jesus to heal the world's hurts, whereas Mrs. May, although she says she approves of the proper expression of religion, does not actually believe that any of it is true.

O. T. and E. T. Greenleaf

O.T. and E.T. are the identical twin sons of the Greenleafs. They are always referred to together, as if they have no separate identities. They are hardworking and served overseas in the military during World War II, reaching the rank of sergeant. As a result, both became relatively cosmopolitan in outlook and married Frenchwomen. After the war, both brothers benefited from the GI Bill and studied agriculture at university. They live about two miles from the May farm in a house they built with help from the government. As military veterans who were wounded in combat, both receive government pensions. Each of the twins has three children. O.T. and E.T., who are ambitious and upwardly social mobile, are therefore contrasted with Mrs. May's sons, who are still unmarried and living with their mother. Also, O.T. and E.T., unlike Wesley and Scofield, get along very well together, according to their hired hand, and never quarrel.

Mrs. May

Mrs. May is a widow in her sixties who owns a dairy farm. She inherited it from her late husband, who was a businessman, not a farmer, but who happened to own the property. It was the only thing he had to leave her. Mrs. May has therefore faced an uphill battle in trying to make the farm work, having neither money nor experience. She is not a happy woman. She complains a lot about other people and thinks herself superior to them, but also regards herself as a victim. She is referred to as a "small woman with pale, near-sighted eyes and gray hair that rose on top like the crest of some disturbed bird."

Scofield May

Scofield May is the elder of Mrs. May's two sons. Thirty-six years old, he is unmarried and still lives with his mother and brother. He is quite different from his brother and is pursuing a career as an insurance salesman, selling insurance to African Americans because he thinks it is the most profitable form of insurance. He boasts about how good he is at his job. He also says he is not going to marry until his mother is dead. Then he will marry a farm girl and take over the farm. He served in the army for two years but did not rise above the rank of private. Neither Scofield nor his brother, Wesley, has ever learned anything about farming, so they are unable—and apparently unwilling—to offer their mother any assistance.

Wesley May

Wesley May is the younger of Mrs. May's two sons. She regards him as an intellectual, and he teaches at a university twenty miles away. He does not like his job, however, thinking that the university is second-rate and the students unintelligent. There seems to be nothing in his life that he actually enjoys. His mother worries about him because he is thin and nervous, and she thinks that eventually he may marry the wrong woman. Wesley and his brother do not like each other, and in one incident they get into an argument. It appears that Wesley is struck by Scofield, since Mrs. May discovers him lying on his back in the dining room.

The Negro

O. T. and E. T. Greenleaf employ a young African American man referred to in the story as "the Negro." Mrs. May gives him a note to pass on to his employers. He is the one who tells Mrs. May that O.T. and E.T. are very close to each other and never quarrel.

TOPICS FOR FURTHER STUDY

- Choose another story by O'Connor that you like, and write an essay in which you compare and contrast it with "Greenleaf."
- O'Connor writes with humor, but not everyone responds to it. Is there humor in "Greenleaf?" Explain the type of humor she employs. How does it work? Give a class presentation with some examples.
- O'Connor wrote from a Roman Catholic perspective, and a corresponding religious element is discernible in the story. In Christianity, one of the seven deadly sins is pride. Write an essay in which you describe Mrs. May's failings in terms of pride.
- Read *The Kissing Game: Short Stories* (2011), a collection of short stories for young adults by Aidan Chambers. Some of the stories contain moments in which a character experiences a sudden revelation. Choose one or two stories, and write an essay in which you compare and contrast them to "Greenleaf."
- Write a short story in which the protagonist attains some unexpected spiritual or religious revelation.
- Go to Easel.ly online and create an infographic for the life and work of Flannery O'Connor. Try to show the most important facts in a way that is easy to read and visually pleasing.

THEMES

Salvation

Although the ending of the story has a certain ambiguity, it is possible to argue that when the bull gores Mrs. May to death, she experiences something close to a spiritual awakening, which might also be thought of as salvation, a kind of liberation from the frustrations and unhappiness that she constantly experienced in life.

Mrs. May is presented throughout the story as a discontented woman who is constantly complaining about her lot. It seems that she was not able to choose her destiny in life. Her late husband was a businessman who left her the farm on his death, but he had never worked it himself, which left her in a difficult position, having to eke out a living in an unfamiliar occupation. Perpetually anxious and overworked, she has developed a sour view of life, constantly feeling put upon and having to deal with people she regards as her natural inferiors. When she speaks, she habitually makes a sound like a "restrained screech," which suggests her frustration and how it is building up inside her.

She is disappointed in her two sons, who are abusive to her at just about every chance they get and who offer her no support in the maintenance of the farm. She also resents them because she thinks they will not marry well after she is gone and their wives will ruin the property. She whispers to herself, "I work and slave, I struggle and sweat to keep this place for them and soon as I'm dead, they'll marry trash and bring it in here and ruin everything." Feeling vindictive, she even changes her will to ensure that her sons are not permitted to leave the property to their wives.

Mrs. May also complains about other people, especially Mr. and Mrs. Greenleaf. She regards the former, her hired hand for fifteen years, as virtually useless and the latter as disgusting. Her ire and contempt is aroused by Mrs. Greenleaf not only because she sees her as dirty but also because of the "prayer healing" Mrs. Greenleaf conducts over buried newspaper clips of the world's troubles. While Mrs. Greenleaf believes wholeheartedly in Jesus as the savior and calls on his name during these rituals, Mrs. May, while convincing herself that she has a "large respect for religion," does not actually believe that it contains any actual truth. She therefore feels completely superior to Mrs. Greenleaf. While grudgingly recognizing that the Greenleafs' sons have done well in the world, she still finds time to disparage their achievements as largely resulting from government assistance after the war. Nonetheless, she wants to take some credit for their success and makes a claim for her own contribution: "If the Greenleaf boys had risen in the world it was because she had given their father employment when no one else would have him."

Mrs. May is thus presented as an unhappy woman with a closed heart who does not enjoy good relations with anyone in her immediate environment. She seems unable to relate to others in a compassionate and understanding way. A Christian person might regard her as someone who is in need of the Lord, someone who needs to be saved from her own cynicism and despair. It is significant that Mrs. Greenleaf's cry, during one of her prayer rituals, "O Jesus, stab me in the heart!" annoys Mrs. May, who tells Mrs. Greenleaf, falling back into the dirt, that Jesus "would be *ashamed* of you." However, Mrs. Greenleaf is sympathetic to the world's pain and does what she can, in keeping with her religious beliefs, to heal it, or at least call upon God to heal it. She has managed to keep her heart open, in direct contrast to Mrs. May. This incident, and Mrs. Greenleaf's words, acquire greater significance at the end of the story, when Mrs. May's heart is indeed stabbed, not by Jesus but by the escaped bull.

The bull thus seems to have a symbolic significance that might indeed suggest Christ or some other unspecified god figure. At the beginning of the story, the bull is likened to "some patient god come down to woo her," which suggests that some mysterious religious process is unfolding. At the end, the bull's horn pierces Mrs. May's heart, as if the god has finally found his way to her. The bull's other horn "curved around her side and held her in an unbreakable grip," suggesting the embrace of the divine. As she dies, the expression on her face changes: "she had the look of a person whose sight has been suddenly restored but who finds the light unbearable." The wording suggests someone who has been granted a new spiritual vision of life, but who is not able to absorb or bear it. Finally, however, as Mr. Greenleaf arrives on the scene and shoots the bull, it sinks down, "pulling her forward on its head, so that she seemed . . . to be bent over whispering some last discovery into the animal's ear." It seems then that some final understanding of a spiritual nature has been granted to Mrs. May at the moment of her death.

Social Class

If the story has at one level a spiritual or religious significance, it is also a story about class conflict and the changes in the class structure that were taking place in the South in the decade following World War II. Mrs. May, impoverished though she may be, is nonetheless a landowner, and she looks down on the Greenleafs because they belong to a lower class. Even though the Greenleafs' sons, O.T. and E.T., have come up in the world and are now property owners as well, Mrs. May still looks down on them because of their humble origins. However, she is also aware of the social changes afoot; she knows that the twins' children will likely receive a good education and that the future belongs to them and those like them. She asks her sons, "in twenty years . . . do you know what those people will be?" She then

The story is set on a farm owned by the widow Mrs. May (©MaxyM / Shutterstock.com)

answers her own question: "*Society*." Seen in this light, the bull that kills Mrs. May does not have to possess any religious significance. After all, it belongs to the Greenleaf boys and shows how they are the new local powerhouses who will sweep away the older small landowners like Mrs. May, who are too weak and backward to resist them.

STYLE

Figurative Language

The bull has a "wreath across his horns" and is thus referred to as having a "crowned head," which puts in mind, for the Christian reader, the crown of thorns on the head of Christ. In a simile, the bull is likened to "an uncouth country suitor," suggesting the bull as lover, a suggestion that is also apparent in Mr. Greenleaf's comment near the end of the story, when the bull is grazing among the cows: "The gentleman is waiting on you."

At least two of the names of the characters may be meant symbolically, although only in an ironic sense. The name Wesley suggests John Wesley (1703–1791), the founder of Methodism in the eighteenth century. The name is ironic because Wesley in the story has no interest in religion and regards himself as an intellectual, in marked contrast to the emotionalism that Wesley produced in those who heard him preach and were converted. Scofield, in turn, was the name of a noted American biblical scholar and minister named Cyrus I. Scofield (1843–1921), whose notes and commentary on the scriptures appear in the Scofield Reference Bible, which first appeared in the early twentieth century and sold millions of copies in the decades leading up to the 1950s, when the story is set. Again, the name is likely used ironically, because Mrs. May's son Scofield, like his brother, has no interest in religion and is not a scholar but a businessman.

Foreshadowing

Foreshadowing in a work of literature occurs when an event takes place or something is mentioned that anticipates some other important event that takes place later. Foreshadowing therefore can act as a kind of warning or alert to the reader about what might happen in the future, as the story unfolds. In this story, the violent climax, when the bull gores Mrs. May, is foreshadowed by several thoughts and perceptions on the part of Mrs. May. For example, when she hears Mrs. Greenleaf calling out for Jesus during one of her healing and prayer sessions, "The sound was so piercing that she felt as if some violent unleashed force had broken out of the ground and was charging toward her." This anticipates the charging bull in the final scene. When Mr. Greenleaf gets his gun to shoot the bull and sits next to Mrs. May in the car, she thinks, "He'd like to shoot me instead of the bull," which hints at a violent climax, although not the one that actually occurs. Finally, while waiting for Mr. Greenleaf to shoot the bull but hearing no shot, Mrs. May wonders whether the bull "had turned on him and run him up against a tree and gored him." These references to violence and death foreshadow the ending of the story.

Point of View

The story is told by a limited third-person narrator from the point of view of Mrs. May. In other words, it is through Mrs. May's eyes that the reader views the events and characters. The narrator knows Mrs. May's thoughts, and the other characters are presented in a way that is colored by how Mrs. May sees them. They are revealed through their words and actions and Mrs. May's opinions about them, but the narration does not directly reveal their thoughts and states of mind. The other characters are thus presented to the reader in a rather negative light, because that is how Mrs. May thinks of them.

HISTORICAL CONTEXT

Southern Literature

O'Connor is known as a distinctively southern writer, and as such she was part of a well-established tradition. "Southern literature" refers to fiction that is written by southern writers and usually set in the US South. During the 1920s and 1930s, what is known as the Southern Renaissance produced many outstanding southern writers, including William Faulkner, with books such as *As I Lay Dying* (1930) and *Absalom, Absalom!* (1936), Allen Tate, Elizabeth Madox Roberts, Zora Neale Hurston, and Katherine Anne Porter. Such writers often examined southern history and culture, including the legacy of the past, such as defeat in the Civil War, and race relations. Religion was often a prominent factor, also. Faulkner used modernist techniques such as the stream-of-consciousness narrative.

During the 1950s, when O'Connor was most active, there were many southern writers, in addition to Faulkner and Porter, who continued to write about the South. The short stories of Eudora Welty are notable examples, as are the novels of Robert Penn Warren and Carson McCullers. Harper Lee's *To Kill a Mockingbird* (1960) is also a work of southern literature. In the case of O'Connor, most of her stories are set near her home in Milledgeville, Georgia, and in "Greenleaf," the setting, including the landscape and the infrastructure, was likely based on everyday sights in that area. The story is also notable for its use of southern dialect, in the speech of Mr. Greenleaf, and in general O'Connor's stories show a sharp ear for the patterns of speech, including syntax and diction, that were common in mid-Georgia at the time.

The South after World War II

In the decades before World War II, the South lagged behind other regions in the country in terms of material prosperity and other quality-of-life indicators. After the war, however, things began to change. Economic development and technological modernization came to the region, along with population growth, urbanization, and secularization. "Greenleaf," by showing the growth to prosperity of Mr. Greenleaf's two sons, shows one aspect of how the South was changing in the 1950s. The old South is represented by Mrs. May, but O.T. and E.T. represent the coming of a new, more prosperous order. For example, Mrs. May is, rather against her will, impressed by the new milking parlor that the Greenleaf sons have on their farm, which "had been built according to the latest specifications. . . . The

COMPARE & CONTRAST

- **1950s:** Religion plays a large role in the US South, strongly influencing its culture. Protestant denominations such as the Methodists, Presbyterians, and Baptists are the most prominent, but Roman Catholics are also fairly numerous. In the great social issue of the day, the civil rights movement, in general the churches are slow to support racial integration, and at first many reject it altogether.

  Today: Religion continues to be an important factor in southern life. According to a 2014 survey by the Pew Research Center, 62 percent of adults in the South say that religion is "very important" to them, while 21 percent say it is "somewhat important." The Roman Catholic Church reports that it is growing rapidly in the South, as measured by number of parishioners, especially in places such as Atlanta, Georgia; Charleston, South Carolina; Charlotte, North Carolina; and Little Rock, Arkansas.

- **1950s:** Although the explosion of significant works of literature by southern writers known as the Southern Renaissance belongs to earlier decades, writers from the South continue to make an impact on American literature. William Faulkner publishes the novels *A Fable* in 1954 and *The Town* in 1957. Tennessee Williams's play *Cat on a Hot Tin Roof* is produced in 1955, and Robert Penn Warren publishes the novel *Band of Angels* (1955) and the poetry collection *Promises* (1957).

  Today: Distinctively southern literature still features prominently in the American literary landscape. Jesmyn Ward wins the National Book Award for her 2011 novel *Salvage the Bones*, set in Mississippi at the time of Hurricane Katrina in 2005. T. Geronimo Johnson publishes his first novel, *Hold It until It Hurts* (2012), which becomes a finalist for the PEN/Faulkner Award in 2013. Part of Johnson's story is set in New Orleans, where he was born.

- **1950s:** The modern civil rights movement begins. At the start of the decade, Georgia, like other southern states, is racially segregated, but after the 1954 Supreme Court ruling in *Brown v. Board of Education* declares that such segregation in schools is unconstitutional, the process of desegregation begins. However, in Georgia and other states, desegregation faces fierce opposition from many white people. Some even believe that schools should be closed rather than racially integrated.

  Today: Not all the gains of the civil rights movement regarding desegregation are being preserved in the South. For example, because many judges no longer support court-ordered integration, many African American and Latino students attend schools in which they form the majority, and funding is not necessarily equal.

---

milk ran in pipes from the machines to the milk house" and went untouched by human hands. It would have cost Mrs. May thousands of dollars to install such machinery, and it was far beyond her means. Despite changes such as this, as noted by historian Charles Reagan Wilson in his article "Religion and the New South," the South after the war

> retained a self-consciousness promoted by new national acceptance of cultural identities of all shapes, by appreciation of southern cultural traditions, by a concern for tourism, by nostalgia, and by the functionality of southern organizations within a national federalist framework.

The Greenleaf sons own a bull, which breaks free and gores Mrs. May (©ABB Photo / Shutterstock.com)

CRITICAL OVERVIEW

"Greenleaf" has attracted a fair amount of attention from scholars of O'Connor's work. In 1965, shortly after O'Connor's death, Louise Y. Gossett, in "The Test by Fire: Flannery O'Connor," noted that the bull "is the ancient symbol of sex" and that "behind him stand his owners, the Greenleaf sons—and the host of those with animal energy who will devour the effete and unproductive like Mrs. May's sons." Mrs. May's death "comes in a lurid rite of spring. . . . The violence welds together the hatred of the sons for the mother and the vulgar pride of the mother." In *Flannery O'Connor*, Dorothy Walters discusses the means by which Mrs. May dies as "a familiar imaginative archetype. Renaissance writers often cast the abstract concept of death in the role of the insistent suitor." Walters notes that in the work of Sigmund Freud, there are "affinities of Eros with Thanatos, the warring life-death impulses that constantly struggle for ascendency."

In *The Flannery O'Connor Companion*, James A. Grimshaw Jr. discusses the ambiguity with which the story ends. "Does Mrs. May accept her moment of grace?" he asks. He acknowledges that it is impossible to know for sure but suggests that

> we are at least comforted by the fact that her moment came, regardless of her choice, because in believing that we can share in the faith that our moment will also come, even in an unexpected and violent way.

Suzanne Morrow Paulson, in *Flannery O'Connor: A Study of the Short Fiction*, discusses the story in terms of "male/female antagonisms," as seen in the rivalry between Mrs. May and Mr. Greenleaf and between Mrs. May and her sons. In fact, "all of the characters in this story interrelate by aggressively competing," the destructive effects of which are apparent at the end of the story: "Mr. Greenleaf seeks revenge because this castrating woman emasculated him when she ordered him to shoot his sons' bull.'" Carol Schloss, in *Flannery O'Connor's Dark Comedies: The Limits of Inference*, also comments on the ending of the story, writing that it

> dramatizes . . . the protagonist's encounter with what represents her fears. . . . Mrs. May is the victim of irrational force, overcome by it even as she fantasizes about subduing her antagonist, whom she still perceives to be the Greenleaf family.

CRITICISM

Bryan Aubrey

Aubrey holds a PhD in English. In the following essay, he analyzes the spiritual and psychological themes of Flannery O'Connor's "Greenleaf."

Flannery O'Connor's story "Greenleaf" resonates on several different levels, including the spiritual and psychological. One salient fact about O'Connor was her staunch Catholicism. She wrote in her 1957 essay "The Fiction Writer and His Country," as quoted by Dorothy Walters in *Flannery O'Connor*:

> I see from the standpoint of Christian orthodoxy. This means for me the meaning of life is centered in our Redemption by Christ and what I see in the world I see in its relation to that.

> "THE UNSPOKEN LINES OF BATTLE BETWEEN THEM MOVE QUICKLY TO THE STORY'S CLIMAX. MRS. MAY EXPECTS TO TRIUMPH, FULLY BELIEVING THAT MR. GREENLEAF WILL FOLLOW HER INSTRUCTIONS TO SHOOT THE BULL, EVEN THOUGH THE ANIMAL BELONGS TO HIS TWO SONS."

O'Connor's personal religious beliefs carried over into her fiction, which often shows characters unexpectedly, and in unusual ways, coming to some new spiritual understanding. In an April 1958 letter to her correspondent Betty Hester published in O'Connor's collected letters, *The Habit of Being*, O'Connor writes, "All good stories are about conversion, about a character's changing." Such a change results from "the action of grace," and O'Connor adds: "All my stories are about the action of grace on a character who is not very willing to support it."

That comment, written a little over two years after O'Connor wrote "Greenleaf," serves as an apt explanation of the story's meaning. In "Greenleaf," the protagonist, Mrs. May, is presented as a character badly in need of the touch of divine grace. She complains endlessly about her life and always feels put upon. She feels superior to others and despises the earthy expression of religious faith that Mrs. Greenleaf enacts in her prayer rituals. Mrs. May has rigid ideas and thinks that the only place for the word *Jesus*—which Mrs. Greenleaf is in the habit of uttering during her rituals—is within the four walls of a church. Despite this, however, Mrs. May thinks of herself as "a good Christian woman with a large respect for religion, though she did not, of course, believe any of it was true." This suggests that she thinks of the church as an institution that has a social value in that it keeps people respectable and upholds the proper order of things—in which she is on a higher plane than the Greenleafs, for example—but has little to offer beyond that. As for Mrs. May's belief that she is a Christian, it would be hard to find in the story a single moment in which she expresses a thought or performs an action that the average person might regard as ideally Christian. Such a character, in Flannery O'Connor's world, may well be heading for a reckoning, whether she likes it or not, and indeed, that is exactly what happens.

O'Connor offers an ironic clue to what might be awaiting Mrs. May when, exasperated by her sons' lack of interest in the escaped bull, she wants to say, "You'll find out one of these days . . . what *Reality* is when it's too late!" Of course, it is not the sons who discover Reality with a capital *R* but Mrs. Greenleaf, when she dies after being gored by the bull and is granted some kind of unspecified revelation. Irony is apparent also in her thought, directed at her sons soon after her statement quoted above, that "They needn't think I'm going to die any time soon . . . I'll die when I get good and ready." Not only will the latter statement be recognized by Christians of all stripes as a very un-Christian thought—because it is God, not the individual, who decides such things—but it will also be undermined by Mrs. May's actual fate. When the bull gores her, she is anything but good and ready—quite the reverse, in fact, which shows that her belief that she is in control of her life—and death—is just an illusion.

Enlightenment of some kind comes to Mrs. May, however, regardless of her own foolishness, stubbornness, and lack of belief. As one of the bull's horns pierces her heart and the other curls around her side like the grip of a lover, she "had the look of a person whose sight has been suddenly restored but who finds the light unbearable." Although this description is somewhat ambiguous, it suggests a soul newly admitted to the heavenly realms being dazzled by the pure light of the divine, so unlike anything it has witnessed or experienced on Earth. In the next paragraph, which concludes the story, there is a suggestion that Mrs. May may have begun to grasp the significance of what has happened to her. As the bull sinks down after being shot by Mr. Greenleaf, it pulls Mrs. May onto its head, making it seem as if she is "bent over whispering some last discovery into the animal's ear."

If this process represents a kind of spiritual redemption for poor Mrs. May, it by no means exhausts the interest of the story, which also works at a psychological level, quite apart from

WHAT DO I READ NEXT?

- "Revelation" is a story by O'Connor published in her 1965 collection *Everything That Rises Must Converge.* Like "Greenleaf," it features a female protagonist, Ruby Turpin, who considers herself superior to other people. Just like Mrs. May in "Greenleaf," at the end of the story, Ruby Turpin receives an unexpected spiritual revelation, although unlike Mrs. May, she does not have to pay for it with her life.
- Like O'Connor, Eudora Welty was a writer of short stories set in the South. "Moon Lake" was published in Welty's 1949 collection *The Golden Apples* and was republished in *The Collected Stories of Eudora Welty* in 1980. Set in Mississippi, the story focuses on the relationships between three girls at summer camp and explores the themes of identity and belonging.
- Twentieth-century southern writer Carson McCullers published her novel *The Member of the Wedding* in 1946. It is a coming-of-age story set in a small town in Georgia. The protagonist is a twelve-year-old tomboy.
- *Flannery: The Life of Flannery O'Connor* (2009) is an authoritative biography by Brad Gooch that frequently connects events in O'Connor's life with her fiction.
- Katherine Anne Porter's *The Old Order: Stories of the South* (1955) contains nine short stories and a short novel, all set in the South from the late nineteenth century to the early twentieth century. The stories give a picture of life in the South at the time when Porter was growing up. Many of the stories show the continuing effects of racial discrimination and also offer a critique of the patriarchal social structure.
- Although she no longer lives in the South, African American author ZZ Packer, who was raised in Atlanta and Louisville, considers herself a southerner. Her short-story collection *Drinking Coffee Elsewhere* (2003) was widely acclaimed.
- *New Stories from the South: The Year's Best, 2008*, edited by ZZ Packer, is a wide-ranging collection of twenty stories from contemporary southern writers.
- *Sixteen: Short Stories by Outstanding Writers for Young Adults* (1985), edited by Donald R. Gallo, contains sixteen stories that cover a wide range of situations and emotions. The collection is organized thematically, under such topics as friendships, love, decisions, and families. Robert Lipsyte and Richard Peck are among the well-known writers who contribute stories.

any spiritual or religious implications. At the psychological level, the story presents a conflict in which the female is set against the male and the employer against her employee, and the apparently powerless (the male employee) ends up winning the day against his female antagonist. This is the conflict between Mrs. May and Mr. Greenleaf, in which Mrs. May appears to hold most of the aces—or at least one would think so, since she is the landowning employer—while Mr. Greenleaf indulges in a kind of passive aggressiveness toward her that perhaps prevents him, at least in his own eyes, from being too emasculated by the subordinate position he occupies.

Mrs. May holds Mr. Greenleaf in contempt as a lazy worker who lacks initiative and is tricky to deal with. He never looks her in the face if he can avoid it. When she confronts him about the escaped bull, he looks down at his feet while informing her that the bull has been loose for three days. He tried penning it up, but it escaped. Mrs. May responds in a peremptory manner, demanding that he take care of the situation and remove the bull. All the time,

Mr. Greenleaf never even looks at her. He pretends not to know who the bull belongs to, but when Mrs. May finds out from her sons that the bull belongs to Mr. Greenleaf's sons, O.T. and E.T., she knows that Mr. Greenleaf must have been aware of it.

When she next encounters him, he is working in the trench silo. Mrs. May reminds him that he is supposed to be taking care of the situation regarding the bull, but he replies that he cannot do two things at once. He also denies that he knew the bull belonged to his sons. Later, she sees the bull walking slowly down the dirt road in front of the house, with Mr. Greenleaf following it on horseback. She remarks that the bull is certainly a Greenleaf bull, likely referring to her belief that it is a poor specimen, but her remark will later acquire more significance.

Mrs. May and Mr. Greenleaf seem frequently to engage in a kind of verbal sparring in which Mr. Greenleaf often compares Mrs. May's sons unfavorably to his own. His sons are married with children and are successful in the world; in contrast, her sons are unmarried and avoid taking responsibility for anything. The way Mrs. May sees it, "he never lost an opportunity of letting her see by his expression or some simple gesture, that he held the two of them [her sons] in infinite contempt." This seems to be his way of compensating for the subordinate position he occupies in relation to Mrs. May, which likely irks him. For her part, she seems to know intuitively that he is hostile to her and is therefore wary of him.

In one incident, when Mr. Greenleaf taps on the back door just after Mrs. May has been upset by the scuffle between her sons, "All her resources returned in full strength as if she had only needed to be challenged by the devil himself to regain them." The reference to the devil might perhaps be passed over as not especially significant until, later in that same scene, Mr. Greenleaf, "quick as a snake striking," takes another dig at the uselessness of her two sons, this time in reference to the fact that they have made no effort to catch the bull. The successive references to devil and snake suggest a Christian symbolism, in which the snake is the tempter of Eve in the Garden of Eden, as recorded in the book of Genesis. The snake is often taken to be an embodiment of Satan, known for his power to deceive. Mrs. May immediately looks down at Mr. Greenleaf's

Mrs. May hires Mr. Greenleaf to work her land because neither of her sons are interested in farm work *(©jabiru / Shutterstock.com)*

"dark crafty face," a description that acquires a sinister quality in light of the symbolism.

The unspoken lines of battle between them move quickly to the story's climax. Mrs. May expects to triumph, fully believing that Mr. Greenleaf will follow her instructions to shoot the bull, even though the animal belongs to his two sons. For a while it looks as if the problem is going to be solved on her terms, some delay notwithstanding. Mrs. May remains aware of Mr. Greenleaf's hostility to her—"He'd like to shoot me instead of the bull," she thinks to herself—but she believes she is in control of the situation. In that, she is quite mistaken, and the bull charges her and gores her to death. Leaving aside any possible religious symbolism associated with the bull, as it heads straight for Mrs. May at a gallop, it might be seen as an expression of the full power of masculine energy—associated with the Greenleaf family perhaps—which is finally asserting itself against its female tormentor. At one level, Mrs. May

"

IN ALL OF THESE STORIES, THE DOMINANCE OF MASCULINE VALUES, STEREOTYPICALLY DEFINED, RESULTS IN AN ATTACK ON THE MOTHER, A FRAGMENTED FAMILY, AND A FAILURE TO CONTINUE THE ONGOING CHAIN OF HUMAN DEVELOPMENT."

may have found some kind of spiritual salvation, but at another, she is roundly defeated by Mr. Greenleaf and his family, who represent the more virile new order of things in the neighborhood, condemning the proud but powerless Mrs. May to an ignominious death.

Source: Bryan Aubrey, Critical Essay on "Greenleaf," in *Short Stories for Students*, Gale, Cengage Learning, 2017.

Suzanne Morrow Paulson

In the following excerpt, Paulson examines the male/female conflict in "Greenleaf."

. . . There is only one other story that *primarily* focuses on male/female antagonisms, sex-related differences, and mother figures affected by the dominant male culture. One of the most aggressive of the widowed mothers in O'Connor's canon is Mrs. May, the protagonist of "Greenleaf"; this story draws on sex-related stereotypes as they appear in myth. Thus, before pursuing this line of the author's thought as it relates to myth, we need to address the author's comments about the influence of myth in her work. Asals notes that O'Connor once said, "I never think in terms of fable or myth. Those things are far removed from anything that I know when I write." And yet in a 1962 interview, she refers to the Bible as our "sacred history and our mythic background," and in her essays she declares that "It takes a story to make a story. It takes a story of mythic dimensions, one which belongs to everybody" (*MM*). Asals points out that Eliot and Joyce, authors O'Connor admired and studied, brought myth to literature. And we learn from the letters that, as the author puts it, "The only good things I read when I was a child were the Greek and Roman myths" (*Letters*).

The plot of "Greenleaf" exploits the mythical male/female dichotomy by presenting the rivalry between Mrs. May and Mr. Greenleaf—and the rivalry between Mrs. May and her sons. Mr. Greenleaf appears to represent male potency: his phallic nature is emphasized in the figure of his sons' bull, which he allows to run loose in Mrs. May's herd—his way of asserting power over his female employer and of establishing his own territory. The bull is described as "squirrel-colored, with jutting hips and long light horns . . . a Greenleaf bull if I ever saw one" (*CS*), as Mrs. May puts it. The sexual connotations of Greenleaf's phallic bull is further reinforced when the hired hand looks "with approval at the bull's rump." Moreover, Greenleaf has five daughters and twin sons (representing self-procreative power, as previously mentioned). Greenleaf's sons married French wives and produced three children each. On the other hand, Mrs. May has only two unmarried sons who still live with their mother. Mr. Greenleaf's sons represent male power; Mrs. May's sons represent female impotence and passivity as they function in the world—male aggression when they attack their mother at home.

But Mrs. May herself matches Mr. Greenleaf in her masculine characteristics. When challenged by her sons, she holds "her back stiff as a rake handle" (*CS*)—a phallic image also suggesting her abrasive nature. She carries "a long stick" when walking in the woods "in case she saw a snake" (*CS*). In fact, this unfeminine but female farm manager ironically uses her femininity as an excuse for not being more successful in exacting obedience from her hired male hand: she complains to Mr. Greenleaf that his sons do not comply with her wishes because she is a woman ("They didn't come because I'm a woman. . . . You can get away with anything when you're dealing with a woman," *CS*). The competition between Mrs. May and Mr. Greenleaf results in a power struggle that reveals the violence of the male, materialistic world suggested by both characters—perhaps especially by Mrs. May as she takes over the powerful male role of her dead husband.

In the first incident of the story, the Greenleaf boys' bull appears in the middle of the night beneath Mrs. May's bedroom window and disturbs her sleep. The release of a bull and the construction of the temple at the place of his slaughter was a common ritual of ancient times. The sociologist Mircea Eliade explains this ritual as an attempt to eliminate chaos, discover the real, and organize space by centering himself in the world—choosing a place and then constructing a city in order to found the world. The release of a bull, then, represents a means of staking out a territory, sanctifying space, and creating cosmos.

Mr. Greenleaf operates on such a primitive level in his aim to organize his world in Mrs. May's space. Repeatedly, he is depicted as walking "on the perimeter of some invisible circle" (*CS*, *CS*); he is primitive and confined to the circle of self. This circle implies his narcissism; "circling" also connotes the hunter's attitude toward his prey. Greenleaf strives to increase his power, to enlarge his "territory," and to center himself in the world—thus ritualistically eliminating chaos by superimposing his own order on reality. The pursuit of material territory and the inability to transcend self indicate primitive natures in O'Connor's view. Both Mr. Greenleaf and Mrs. May's ambitions are regressive and profane. In fact, Mrs. May's fear of being eaten—which is suggested in a dream caused by the bull's munching on the hedge outside her window—suggests a regression to the oral stage of infancy, when the infant compulsively takes in the world through the mouth. Mrs. May dreams that something was "eating her and the boys and . . . eating everything until nothing was left but the Greenleafs on a little island all their own in the middle of what had been her place" (*CS*). The relevance here of territorial claims, possessiveness, and competitiveness coincides with what one expects of the narcissistic self—both Mrs. May and Mr. Greenleaf. That the bull intrudes "like some patient god come down to woo her" and "to tear at the hedge" (*CS*) again suggests myth (violence to women; for example, the rape of Europa) as well as the conflict between male and female forces, the spiritual and the bestial.

Some critics see Christ in the image of "the hedge-wreath" that the "god" wears, and this reference is perhaps suggested elsewhere in the story when Mrs. May perceives Mrs. Greenleaf's shrieks of "Jesus" as "some violent unleashed force. . . charging toward her" (*CS*). But what is clear is the primitive nature of both Mr. and Mrs. Greenleaf's behavior—their distance from the Catholic world. Likewise, Mrs. May wants to become her own God, to be self-creative rather than God's creature. Her "primitive" fear of being eaten by the bull reverses what occurs in Dionysian rites wherein the worshippers rend and devour a live bull.

What at first seems a simple contest of wills between a male farm hand and a female farm manager takes on a complex of allusions relating to primitive ritual and to life-death/male-female iconography found in myth. "Greenleaf" and "May" ironically suggest regeneration. "Green" is the color of the resurrection; spring is the season of regeneration. And yet Greenleaf's character is paradoxical (essentially, he murders Mrs. May), suggesting the death-life oxymoron of Picasso's Minotaur, the surrealist depiction of a mythical god holding a knife formed as a leaf.

Without Christianity's promise of the resurrection, human beings regress to self-destructive, primitive practices. Mrs. Greenleaf's peculiar ritual of burying tragic newspaper clippings enables her to believe she controls death. The self-preservation instinct is prominent in the competition between Mr. Greenleaf and Mrs. May—competition that intensifies when they vie for superiority in terms of their offspring. Constantly critical of Wesley and Scofield (Mrs. May's unassertive, bachelor sons), Mr. Greenleaf accuses them of being lazy, and he asserts that his own sons are superior to them. Similarly, Mrs. May accuses O.T. and E.T. (eat/devouring) of lacking pride, when in fact she herself represents prideful self-assertion. She even presumes to control death and says, "I'll die when I get good and ready" (*CS*). The replacement of religious faith by American ideals of resourcefulness, hard work, and possessiveness causes Mrs. May to be "near-sighted" (*CS*), obsessed with acquisitive struggles for material success measured by the success of her offspring and the size of her property.

Mrs. May's other self in fact becomes her property. Thinking of the praise bestowed by her friends who admire her success at managing a farm, she identifies with what she has achieved in the material world: "When she looked out any window in her house, she saw the reflection of her own character" (*CS*). This is the portrait of an egoistic self projecting an identity on the whole world to extend the boundaries of the self (cf. Mrs. Shortley's character in "The Displaced Person"). Mrs. May prides herself on marrying a businessman, and she berates Greenleaf for not having "the initiative to steal" (*CS*). Jealous that both of Greenleaf's sons managed to gain the rank of sergeant in the service, Mrs. May laments the fact that Scofield was only a Private First Class and Wesley's heart condition exempted him altogether.

Especially significant is the fact that Mrs. May worries over the potential of her sons to secure wives. Obviously, neither son has progressed far enough in his development to acknowledge the feminine side of the self and to relate constructively to the opposite sex. Scofield is an overly differentiated male in his pursuit of success defined by acquiring material goods. He exploits Negroes by selling them insurance they probably do not need. And the hate-filled intellectual schoolteacher, Wesley, obviously directs his rage toward the female elements of his life: we are told that he "didn't like nice girls. . . . he hated living with his mother" (*CS*), declaring openly to her, "I wouldn't milk a cow to save your soul from hell" (*CS*). He "snarls" at his mother and belittles her respect for religion—ridiculing her by comparing her to Mrs. Greenleaf ("Why don't you do something practical, Woman? Why don't you pray for me like Mrs. Greenleaf would?" [*CS*]).

In sum, Mr. Greenleaf compares his sons to Mrs. May's in order to taunt his female employer; Mrs. May compares E.T. and O.T. to her sons in order to belittle her own offspring. Following the example of their mother, Scofield and Wesley then compare their mother to Mrs. Greenleaf—thus belittling the one who supports them. Moreover, they bicker and brawl between themselves. All of the characters in this story interrelate by aggressively competing.

The destructiveness of this kind of behavior is suggested by the violent ending of the story when Mrs. May is impaled on the horns of the Greenleaf bull, while Mr. Greenleaf more than likely passively observes the disaster (cf. the death of Guizac in the "The Displaced Person"). The hired hand appears too late, killing the bull only after it has brought Mrs. May to the ground. Mr. Greenleaf seeks revenge because this castrating woman emasculated him when she ordered him to shoot his sons' bull and then gloated over her own phallic power—over controlling "the gun between his knees" (*CS*). Mrs. May's "sacrifice" represents Mr. Greenleaf's triumph over space and time. He aggressively centers himself in the cosmos. His subtle aggression against Mrs. May is prefigured by the "crash as if he had kicked something out of his way" as he enters the harness room to get the gun. He responds to the order to shoot the bull by "violently" wiping his hands and "violently" getting into the car. Mrs. May realizes then that "he'd like to shoot [her] instead of the bull" (*CS*). His complicity in Mrs. May's death is again suggested when we are told that she surmises her hired hand is "loitering in the woods" (*CS*).

Most important, Mr. Greenleaf's complicity in Mrs. May's death is subtly indicated by a repetition of circling images at the end—images clearly associated with Greenleaf earlier in the story. He "circles" the car as they set out after the bull. He "circles" the gate and the hill (*CS*) before he allows his escape. And while Mrs. May waits for Mr. Greenleaf and the bull to reappear, she expects to see Mr. Greenleaf emerge "from the circle of trees" (*CS*). The "green arena" of the pasture where Mrs. May dies is "encircled" by woods (*CS*). Greenleaf approaches her mortally wounded body as if "on the outside of some invisible circle" (*CS*).

The "last discovery" of Mrs. May is made through "the quake in the huge body" of the bull (*CS*), a body defining the physicality and violence of human secular life and the destructiveness of male/female antagonisms. Self-sacrifice rather than self-assertion, affiliation with others rather than competition, the capacity to love others (especially those of the opposite sex), and a capacity for tenderness rather than aggression are necessary in order to achieve wholeness of self and harmony within the family.

In all of these stories, the dominance of masculine values, stereotypically defined, results in an attack on the mother, a fragmented family, and a failure to continue the ongoing chain of human development. Some of these concerns continue in the next group of stories, but in a broader context, encompassing social contexts and community.

Source: Suzanne Morrow Paulson, "The Short Fiction: A Critical Analysis," in *Flannery O'Connor: A Study of the Short Fiction*, Twayne, 1988, pp. 40–45.

SOURCES

Beale, Stephen, "Protestant South Becoming a New Catholic Stronghold," in *National Catholic Register*, May 11, 2013, http://www.ncregister.com/daily-news/

protestant-south-becoming-a-new-catholic-stronghold/ (accessed August 15, 2016).

Bruinius, Harry, "Why Southern Writers Still Captivate, 55 Years after 'To Kill a Mockingbird,'" in *Christian Science Monitor*, July 5, 2015, http://www.csmonitor.com/USA/Society/2015/0705/Why-Southern-writers-still-captivate-55-years-after-To-Kill-a-Mockingbird (accessed August 15, 2016).

Gordon, Sarah, "Flannery O'Connor," in *New Georgia Encyclopedia*, 2015, http://www.georgiaencyclopedia.org/articles/arts-culture/flannery-oconnor-1925-1964 (accessed August 14, 2016).

Gossett, Louise Y., "The Test by Fire: Flannery O'Connor," in *The Critical Response to Flannery O'Connor*, by Douglas Robillard Jr., Praeger, 2004, p. 80.

Grimshaw, James A., Jr., *The Flannery O'Connor Companion*, Greenwood Press, 1981, p. 54.

Hannah-Jones, Nikole, "Resegregation in the American South," in *Atlantic*, April 16, 2014, http://www.amren.com/news/2014/04/resegregation-in-the-american-south/ (accessed August 15, 2016).

Kirk, Connie Ann, *Critical Companion to Flannery O'Connor*, Facts on File, 2008, p. 80.

O'Connor, Flannery, "Greenleaf," in *The Complete Stories of Flannery O'Connor*, Farrar, Straus and Giroux, 1971.

———, *The Habit of Being: Letters*, edited by Sally Fitzgerald, Farrar, Straus, Giroux, 1979, p. 275.

Paulson, Suzanne Morrow, in *Flannery O'Connor: A Study of the Short Fiction*, Twayne, 1988, pp. 40, 44.

Schloss, Carol, *Flannery O'Connor's Dark Comedies: The Limits of Inference*, Louisiana State University Press, 1980, p. 72.

Walters, Dorothy, *Flannery O'Connor*, Twayne, 1973, pp. 18, 139.

Wilson, Charles Reagan, "Religion and the New South," in *Southern Spaces*, March 16, 2004, https://southernspaces.org/2004/overview-religion-and-us-south (accessed August 15, 2016).

FURTHER READING

Coles, Robert, *Flannery O'Connor's South*, Louisiana State University Press, 1980.

Coles examines the religious, social, and intellectual milieu in which O'Connor wrote her stories.

Schiff, Jonathan, "'That's a Greenleaf Bull': Totemism and Exogamy in Flannery O'Connor's 'Greenleaf,'" in *English Language Notes*, Vol. 33, No. 3, March 1995, pp. 69–76.

Schiff argues that O'Connor used Sigmund Freud's book *Totem and Taboo* as a direct source for the story.

Sexton, Mark S., "'Blessed Insurance': An Examination of Flannery O'Connor's 'Greenleaf,'" in *Flannery O'Connor Bulletin*, Vol. 19, 1990, pp. 38–43.

Sexton examines the issue of Mrs. May's insurance coverage in the story, suggesting it has a thematic and structural importance.

Whitt, Margaret Earley, *Understanding Flannery O'Connor*, University of South Carolina Press, 1995.

This is a straightforward, readable analysis of O'Connor's major works, and it includes a section on "Greenleaf."

SUGGESTED SEARCH TERMS

Flannery O'Connor

O'Connor AND Greenleaf

O'Connor AND redemption

Southern Renaissance

southern literature

bull AND symbolism

Greenleaf AND symbolism

religion and the South

The House behind a Weeping Cherry

HA JIN

2008

In Ha Jin's short story "The House behind a Weeping Cherry," first published in the *New Yorker* in 2008 and later collected in *A Good Fall* (2009), the pressures of immigrant life are illustrated through the story of Wanren, an unassuming man who believes in hard work and decency, and Huong, an undocumented immigrant who must work as a prostitute to pay back her debt to the gangster who smuggled her into the United States. After Wanren takes the job of chauffeuring Huong and the other prostitutes who share a house in Flushing, Queens, New York, a budding romance takes on high stakes. Their dreams cannot take flight while they are bound by debt and financial responsibility to their families overseas, so Huong and Wanren have a mind to break themselves free, never to be seen again. Narrated with the simple yet evocative language that earned Jin the 1999 National Book Award for his novel *Waiting*, "The House behind a Weeping Cherry" cleverly uses two characters caught in an unsustainable situation to express the profound complications of Chinese immigrant life in America.

AUTHOR BIOGRAPHY

Jin was born in Liaoning Province, China, on February 21, 1956, as Xuefei Jin, later using the name Ha Jin as a pen name. Jin came of age at

Ha Jin *(©Ulf Andersen / Getty Images Entertainment / Getty Images)*

the height of Mao Zedong's Cultural Revolution, and his mother was harassed because of her wealthy background. Jin witnessed soldiers burning his father's collection of books in a bonfire on their front lawn. He attended boarding school for two years, starting at the age of seven, until the schools were abruptly shut down, and then joined the Little Red Guard. He enlisted in the People's Liberation Army just before he turned fourteen, lying about his age in his enthusiasm to leave home. Stationed on the Russian border, he discovered a translated copy of *War and Peace*, by Leo Tolstoy, which sparked an interest not only in literature but also in the lives of people outside of Communist China. After being discharged from the army at the age of nineteen, Jin worked as a telegraph operator until the country's schools were reopened in 1977.

He first attended Heilongjiang University, where he majored in English. Learning the language was challenging physically as well as intellectually, leaving Jin with a sore throat and mouth. He earned his master's degree in American literature from Shandong University before moving to the United States in 1985 to pursue a doctorate at Brandeis University, near Boston, Massachusetts. His wife and son were forced to stay behind in China as an incentive for Jin to return to the country; however, after developing a painful (but temporary) stomach problem, he persuaded the Chinese government to let his wife join him in the United States to look after his health, leaving their son behind in China with family. Though he intended to return to China, Jin could not support the government's actions during the Tiananmen Square massacre in 1989. Jin arranged for his son to join him and his wife in the United States, and he has yet to return to his homeland.

Jin's first collection of poetry, *Between Silences*, was published in 1990. That year, he was accepted into the creative writing program at Boston University. After graduation, he began to teach, first at Boston University and then at Emory University in Atlanta, Georgia, before returning to Boston. His first short-story collection, *Ocean of Words* (1996), was awarded the PEN/Hemingway Prize. His second collection, *Under the Red Flag* (1997), won the Flannery

O'Connor Award for Short Fiction. In 1999, his novel *Waiting* won the National Book Award, joining a very short list of books by nonnative English speakers to win the prestigious prize. Both *Waiting* and his 2004 novel *War Trash* won the PEN/Faulkner Award. In 2005, he was named a fellow of the American Academy of Arts and Sciences. His 2009 collection *A Good Fall*, in which "The House behind a Weeping Cherry" is published, was well received by critics. The short story itself was first published in 2008 in *The New Yorker*. Jin writes almost exclusively in the English language, and many of his works are banned in China.

PLOT SUMMARY

This summary follows the *New Yorker* version of "The House behind a Weeping Cherry," which is available online. This version is narrated in the first person by Wanren, a Chinese immigrant to the United States; in *A Good Fall*, the narrator's name is Wanping.

After Wanren's roommate moves out of their rented quarters, Wanren worries he will need to find a more inexpensive place to live. He likes the house he lives in, though, which features an immense cherry tree in the yard that blooms prettily and attracts songbirds. Near the downtown neighborhood of Flushing, in Queens, New York, the house is close to Wanren's place of employment at a garment factory. Before his roommate left, Wanren paid three hundred dollars a month for half of the room. He cannot afford to pay any more than that, though he anticipates that his landlady, Mrs. Chen, will expect him to cover his roommate's half, too.

The roommate left in objection to the fact that the house is secretly a brothel and the three female tenants are working prostitutes. Though this fact makes Wanren uncomfortable as well, he is fond of the women and lonely after immigrating to New York City by himself. Of the three women, he most admires Huong, a Vietnamese-speaking, ethnically Chinese woman in her early twenties.

Mrs. Chen approaches Wanren to discuss the rent now that his roommate is gone. She offers him a position as a chauffeur for the three prostitutes. Wanren is suspicious, not entirely trusting Mrs. Chen. She assures him the job will be painless: driving the women to hotels and homes in Queens and Brooklyn a few times a week. In exchange, he will continue to rent the room at three hundred dollars a month and can eat free meals with the women. Wanren agrees. He looks forward to the feeling of driving again. It has been months since he was last behind the wheel.

Though he knows he will be participating in the illegal activities of the brothel, Wanren understands that people will do anything to survive: "I, too, was selling myself. Every weekday I stood at the table ironing. . . . It was sultry in the basement, where the air-conditioner was at least ten years old, inefficient, and whined loudly." He finds it hard to believe that he works in a sweatshop that makes clothes for high-end boutiques in Manhattan, considering it the ultimate disappointment of his life. He had hoped to attend college but cannot pass the required test of English proficiency, no matter how hard he studies. He saves his money to send home to China so that his little brother can afford veterinary school.

The brothel has no official name, though Wanren once discovered a newspaper ad for the women that listed the house phone number. Huong, Nana, and Lili—a college student—are all originally from China, though Huong was raised in Vietnam by her Chinese parents. Lili answers the phone because her English is best. Though Mrs. Chen seems to run the brothel's day-to-day business, the women answer to a gangster called the Croc.

Wanren enjoys eating dinner with the women with the exception of Lili, who seems to think little of him. The women tease him about being single. A man named Mr. Han calls, requesting a girl to come to his hotel room. Lili tells Huong to go, so Wanren drives her. Waiting outside the hotel, Wanren laments the fact that Huong must make money as a prostitute. Like Wanren, she sends money home to her family. As an illegal alien, she cannot go to school, though she is smart as well as multilingual. He worries about her safety and wishes he could date her, but he cannot offer much—he is plain, gangly, and poor—and, besides, he considers her career too shameful. Huong returns to the car and gives Wanren ten dollars for driving her. She complains that Mr. Han is a government official and asked her for a receipt.

Around the dinner table, Wanren and the women discuss the men who call. Wanren's opinion of them has changed over time. He used to consider them all bad men but feels more sympathetic after hearing the women share the various reasons that their customers have sought out a prostitute's company: "I could see that some of them were nothing but wrecks with serious personal problems that they didn't know how to handle." Wanren helps Nana kick a belligerent man out of the house one night after he refuses to leave, after which the women treat him more warmly than ever. Even Lili begins to thaw. Wanren feels uncomfortable, however, because he does not want to be a part of their illicit world.

In late July, Wanren comes down with the flu. When he falls at work, too weak to even walk across the factory floor, Jimmy Choi, his foreman, tells him to go home—his coworkers, Marc and Danny, can cover his shift. He misses dinner, staying in bed instead. Huong brings him a glass of orange juice before devoting herself to work that night. Miserable and alone, Wanren misses home: "Such a feeling hadn't visited me for a long time—I had always managed to suppress my homesickness so that I would make it through my daily routine." Huong returns after working with a bowl of cabbage soup she cooked herself, knowing that the soup is a staple of the province where Wanren grew up in China. When Lili tells Huong she has an outcall, Huong says she must stay and take care of Wanren. Lili reluctantly agrees to go instead.

Wanren tells Huong not to refrain from working because of him. She tells him not to be foolish and gives him aspirin and vitamin C. She checks on him throughout the night, until he finally falls asleep. The next morning his fever has broken.

A week later, a few of the sewing workers leave the factory where Wanren works. Most of these workers are Chinese, and they are allowed to set their own schedules. The boss, Mr. Fuh, even provides health-care benefits for his employees. Wanren brings a flyer about the open positions at the factory home to show the women. He promises to help them get jobs there if they would like. Nana scoffs at how little the sewing workers make, only three hundred dollars a week, and tells Wanren the job is not for her. Huong asks if there are illegal aliens working there. Wanren says yes. She laments the fact that she never learned to sew, but Wanren assures her it is an easy skill to learn. There are even three-week sewing classes offered downtown for a few hundred dollars. Huong wants to go, but she owes too enormous of a debt to the Croc.

That night, Huong and Wanren meet under the cherry tree to discuss their future. Wanren asks her to quit so that they can be together. She wishes she could, but she still owes the Croc eighteen thousand dollars in payment for smuggling her into the United States, which she pays off in installments of two thousand dollars a month. They cannot make enough money together to pay the installments without Huong remaining a prostitute, though she wants to escape the work.

They talk for an hour, examining the situation from all angles. Huong is so excited about Wanren's help that he wonders if he is jumping into their relationship too fast. Yet he has a vision of her "in a white cottage stirring a pot with a large ladle while humming a song—outside, children's voices were rising and falling." He tells her they should meet the Croc in person to see if he is willing to compromise for them. They part for the night, fearing that the other women will inform Mrs. Chen of their budding relationship if they are discovered plotting together.

They travel to the Croc's headquarters inside a large warehouse on Thirty-second Avenue filled with boxes of textiles and shoes. The Croc is sitting in an office smoking a cigar. Huong introduces Wanren as her boyfriend before asking if she can lower her payments from two thousand a month to thirteen hundred. The Croc says no. She asks if fifteen hundred would be acceptable. He says no. She lies, telling him she has a medical condition and can no longer do the same work. He is immovable on the payments. Wanren says they only need a short amount of time, but the Croc does not care. He has never given an extension to anyone before, and he does not intend to start now. He tells Huong that she knows what they will do if she does not make her payments. Huong looks at Wanren with tears in her eyes. They thank the Croc for his time and leave the warehouse together.

On the way home, they talk about the consequences of not paying. The Asian Mafia is brutal, with stories circulating frequently about the horrific punishments dealt to those who cross them. Not only could they injure or kill people in the United States, but they could also hurt a person's family using their connections in China and Vietnam. Wanren is not certain that the Croc is in the Mafia, but he is without a doubt a powerful gang member with a wide reach.

After dinner, Wanren goes to Huong's room to suggest they simply leave New York and move somewhere else in the United States under false names. Huong is worried the Croc will go after her parents if she runs, but Wanren encourages her to think of herself first. Huong tells him they will never forgive her for running away. Wanren counters that they apparently value her only for the money she sends and do not care how she suffers in America. Finally, Huong agrees. They will leave as soon as possible.

Huong has two thousand dollars, and Wanren has fourteen hundred in a savings account. He withdraws the money, feeling regret that he will not be able to contact his family to explain his disappearance: "To my family, I would be as good as dead. In this place, we had no choice but to take loss as necessity." Huong packs their belongings in secret, and they have a strained final dinner with Nana and Lili, who do not know that they are about to run. Wanren regrets not being able to get his three hundred dollar deposit back from Mrs. Chen as well as not saying goodbye to his coworkers, but there is no other way. That night, after Nana and Lili have gone to bed, Wanren and Huong leave the house with one bag each and do not look back.

CHARACTERS

Belligerent Man

The belligerent man is a customer who refuses to leave the house, shouting at Nana until Wanren comes and makes him leave. After this incident, the women treat Wanren with more respect.

Mrs. Chen

Mrs. Chen is the landlady who runs a brothel out of the house where Wanren lives. He distrusts her, believing her to be a smooth-talker. She is an immigrant from the Chinese province of Fujian.

Jimmy Choi

Jimmy Choi is Wanren's foreman at the garment factory. He sends Wanren home when he is sick with the flu. He is a broad-shouldered man, forty-five years old.

The Croc

The Croc is the owner of the brothel. He also runs a gambling den, owns a warehouse full of textiles and shoes that serves as his headquarters, and works as a "coyote," a smuggler of illegal immigrants into the United States. He smuggled Huong into the country, for which she still owes him eighteen thousand dollars. When she asks for his help with payments, he is unwilling to negotiate and reminds her what will happen if she does not pay: she or her family in Vietnam will be attacked. He may or may not be a member of the Asian Mafia, but Wanren is certain he is in a gang of some kind, if not its leader.

Danny

Danny is Wanren's coworker at the garment factory.

Mr. Fuh

Mr. Fuh is the boss at the garment factory. He speaks English well, offers health insurance, and allows his employees to have flexible schedules as long as their work gets done on time.

Mr. Han

Mr. Han calls the brothel requesting a Thai prostitute. Huong is chosen to go, as she can pass as Thai more easily than Nana or Lili can. Mr. Han is an official from Beijing who asks Huong for a receipt—a problematic request for someone in an illegal trade.

Huong

Huong is a prostitute in her early twenties who lives in the house where Wanren lives. She was born to Chinese parents living in Vietnam, and she was smuggled illegally to the United States with the help of the Croc. She pays him two thousand dollars a month and still owes him eighteen thousand dollars. Because she is an illegal immigrant, she cannot attend school to better her situation. Huong can speak Vietnamese, Chinese, and English. She is attracted to Wanren's sensitive and unassuming nature and agrees to run away from New York with him.

Huong's Parents

Huong's parents migrated to Cholon, Vietnam, from China thirty years ago. They paid fifteen percent of the Croc's fee to smuggle their daughter to the United States. She sends money home to them in addition to paying the remainder of her debt to the Croc. By running away, Huong puts her parents in danger of retribution from the Croc and his connections in Vietnam.

Dr. Liang

Dr. Liang is an herbalist who works at Sun Garden Herbs. Wanren swears by him and sends Huong there when she is sick.

Lili

Lili is a prostitute who lives in the house where Wanren lives. A college student, Lili speaks English the best out of the three women, so she answers the phone when men call the brothel. At first she pays little attention to Wanren, but after he helps kick a belligerent man out of the house, Lili treats him with more respect. Wanren senses that Nana and Huong do not care for Lili. She is originally from Shanghai.

Marc

Marc is Wanren's coworker at the garment factory.

Nana

Nana is a prostitute who lives in the house where Wanren lives. She is originally from Hong Kong. After Wanren helps her kick a belligerent man out of the house, she is especially nice to him. When he offers to get her a job at the garment factory, she says the money is not good enough to draw her away from prostitution.

Owner

The owner of the garment factory where Wanren works is a Taiwanese man who had been a professor before immigrating to the United States.

Wanren

Wanren is a Chinese immigrant in his late twenties who works as a presser at a garment factory. He lives in a house that doubles as a brothel and works as the women's chauffeur. He does not approve of the nature of their work, but he understands the necessity of doing whatever it takes to survive in the United States. While he finds Lili to be rude and condescending, he has a soft spot for Huong, whom he gradually comes to adore. He asks her to quit her work so that they can be together. She agrees, but they must first escape her debts to the Croc. When this proves impossible, Wanren suggests they make a run for it, fleeing to elsewhere in the United States and taking on assumed names. Wanren has trouble mastering the English language, which prevents him from pursuing his education. He is unassuming and well liked by those around him. He regrets leaving his job and cutting ties with his family in China without an explanation.

Wanren's Brother

Wanren's younger brother was accepted to veterinary school in China. Wanren sends home money for his tuition.

Wanren's Parents

Wanren regrets that after he leaves New York City, he will never be able to explain to his parents why he disappeared.

Wanren's Roommate

Wanren's roommate moves out after he discovers that the women in the house are prostitutes.

THEMES

Hope

Though they are beset on all sides by troubles, Wanren and Huong do not lose hope. It is this unshakable spirit that makes their decision to run from New York admirable. Wanren has faced the disappointment of settling for life as a sweatshop employee instead of pursuing his education. Huong is so deeply in debt that she has no choice but to work as a prostitute; without a green card, she cannot find good work. Yet they are not paralyzed by their circumstances. Instead, both characters chase what they want—each other and a life of freedom—with an inexhaustible sense of hope. To pack one bag and leave, exchanging a stable life for an uncertain one, is an act of courage that requires deep wells of hope and the emotional strength necessary to face the unknow n. Huong and Wanren do not give up in their flight from their families, Mrs. Chen, and the Croc; instead, they

TOPICS FOR FURTHER STUDY

- Read Jean Kwok's young-adult novel *Girl in Translation* (2010). What role does money play in the novel? How do Chang and her mother's financial struggles compare to the struggles of Huong and Wanren? How does each story depict life as a sweatshop worker? Write an essay in which you compare and contrast the two works' representations of immigrant poverty.
- Research online to find another Asian American author or poet who interests you. Read a novel or a short story or poetry collection by your chosen author and create a PowerPoint presentation that includes a brief biography, summary of the work, and discussion of the work's main themes and style. Include relevant photos and a slide with a list of your sources.
- Create a blog in which you focus on the experience of another immigrant group coming to the United States. In a minimum of five posts, explore the most recent immigration data available on the group, the major factors leading to their immigration, the major challenges they face in the United States, famous immigrants from the group and what they have contributed to American society, and a summary of a work of literature written about that group. Include photos and links to relevant articles in your posts. Free blog space is available at Blogger.
- What is the symbolic significance of Jin's short story's title? Write an essay in which you explore the title's meaning, explaining how it contributes to the story's overall plot, mood, themes, characters, style, and other aspects of the narrative.

leap off the edge of their known world hand in hand, as immigrants still new to the country and without the support of their families. Whether or not their hope for a better life will be fulfilled is a mystery that the author leaves open. However, they are headed away from the circumstances that could bind them forever to a mundane life, and so the reader, too, cannot help but see them off with sympathy and hope for only the best.

Isolation

Wanren's social isolation leads him not only to live in a brothel but also to accept the job of chauffeur for the prostitutes. He is immensely lonely, having arrived in America alone and friendless. After his roommate moves out, he has no one but the women of the brothel to keep him company in the hours between work and sleep. The women are lonely as well—none of them seem to be close friends, despite the intimacy of their living arrangements. Each of the characters is too concerned with making ends meet, supporting her family overseas, and paying off debt to have time to socialize freely. In addition, the women's line of work makes them unappealing as girlfriends, while Wanren's lack of resources makes him an ineligible bachelor. The isolation of the house and its residents is represented by the cherry tree, which hides the house from view, appropriately enough for the secret activity that takes place there. When Wanren and Huong cast off their lives as lonely, drifting souls, they leave the lonely cherry tree behind them as they walk away from the house toward a future together.

Money

Nothing looms larger over the narrative of "The House behind a Weeping Cherry" than money, which informs every decision the characters make. No matter who they are—from Nana to the Croc—they always need more money for themselves or their families. Wanren finds himself in financial trouble at the start of the story. He takes the job as a chauffeur because of his need to make rent, works at the sweatshop even when he is delirious with the flu because he is scared of losing out on his wages, and considers himself unworthy of a girlfriend because he is poor. Huong is trapped in the life of a prostitute because of her debts, which are insurmountable for a person with no green card and no hope of finding a well-paying job. Nana, too, cannot leave prostitution for a career as a garment worker, and Lili must keep her job in order to pay her way through school. Entrapped by their financial needs, Huong's and Wanren's lives are stunted, and they cannot

The protagonist, Wanren, has recently immigrated from China (©arek_malang / Shutterstock.com)

reach their true potential as immigrants in the United States. Only by removing themselves from their situation entirely, which entails the extreme but necessary reality of losing contact with their families overseas forever, do the protagonists escape the money trap into which they were forced as new immigrants at the mercy of the established Chinese immigrant community and Asian Mafia. By setting themselves free of financial obligations, they are able to face the future as a couple rather than two lonely souls struggling to stay afloat.

STYLE

Episodes

"The House behind a Weeping Cherry" is an episodic narrative. An episode is a short, often self-contained scene that is related to a larger narrative arc. The episodes each contribute an important detail to the story's main plot. For example, the first episode of the story is Mrs. Chen's offer of a job to Wanren and his acceptance. The second episode is much shorter, describing the three women and their work. The third is a scene around the dinner table with Wanren and the women. Each of these episodes adds new information and advances the plot toward Wanren and Huong's decision to run away together, but each represents a contained moment in time.

Suspense

Suspense in a narrative is created through the buildup of tension toward a specific event. By using suspense, an author holds a reader's attention through the desire to see the tension resolved. Jin uses suspense in the final episodes of "The House behind a Weeping Cherry" as Wanren and Huong search for a way to be together. With each option that is tested and fails, the suspense climbs higher. By sending his characters into the path of a dangerous man in the character of the Croc, Jin manipulates his readers' feelings of sympathy for the protagonists into fear for their lives. The suspense of this story is never resolved, as it would be in a more traditional narrative. Instead, readers are left wondering whether Wanren and Huong will survive and prosper on their own or be tracked down by the Croc and punished for attempting to flee from debt.

HISTORICAL CONTEXT

Chinese Immigration

Chinese immigration to the United States can be divided into two main periods. The first wave of immigrants arrived between 1850 and the 1880s. The second wave began in 1965 and continues to this day. Beginning in 1850, Chinese immigrants driven from their country by political and economic instability began to arrive in the United States in search of financial opportunities. Approximately three hundred thousand Chinese immigrants moved to the United States between 1850 and 1889. They built railroads, worked in garment factories, mined for gold, and worked as field hands, seeking out temporary positions where little previous experience was required and Chinese workers were accepted. While about half of these immigrants returned home with their

Huong owes money to a gangster, so she and Wanren run away together (©wavebreakmedia / Shutterstock.com)

earnings, prejudice and discrimination against the remaining Chinese immigrant population grew rapidly. In 1882, the US Congress passed the Chinese Exclusion Act in response to growing resentment against Chinese immigrants. The first of its kind in US history, the act barred Chinese people already living in the United States from becoming citizens and forbade the future immigration of Chinese laborers. In 1888, the Scott Act extended these restrictions by forbidding Chinese residents to return to the United States if they left the country temporarily.

The Chinese Exclusion Act was repealed in 1943 in an attempt to improve the diplomatic relationship between China and America during World War II, but the second wave of immigration did not begin until 1965, when the Immigration and Nationality Act was signed into law. The act provided an easier path for non-European immigrants to enter the United States. In 1978, the Chinese government lifted a ban on emigration to other countries, and the number of Chinese immigrants to the United States rose significantly: from 299,000 in 1980 to 536,000 in 1990. Today, Chinese immigrants make up the largest foreign-born student population in American colleges and universities. Compared with other immigrant groups, Chinese immigrants tend to be better educated, have a higher income, and are more often employed. About 21 percent of Chinese immigrants in the United States today live in the state of New York.

Immigrant Poverty in the United States

Immigrants to the United States face a variety of challenges in establishing financial stability. In 2010, over one-quarter of the nation's 46.2 million people living in poverty were immigrants. Immigrants are less likely to be insured or to own a home, and they make less in yearly wages than American-born citizens, no matter how many years they have lived in the United States. While Chinese immigrants are more likely to have a higher income than other immigrant groups, they also suffer a poverty rate similar to immigrant groups of other nations. As of 2012, 19 percent of Chinese immigrants lived in poverty, as compared with 15 percent of American-born citizens. Like Wanren, many Chinese immigrants struggle to master the

English language. They are both less likely to speak English at home and less likely to report proficiency in using English than other immigrant groups. While Chinese immigrants have a high rate of success at gaining citizenship, as of 2012 an estimated 210,000 were living illegally in the United States.

CRITICAL OVERVIEW

A Good Fall debuted to positive reviews, with critics praising "The House behind a Weeping Cherry" in particular for its depiction of the deleterious effect of debt on the dreams of newly arrived Chinese immigrants. Julie Wittes Schlack states in "Bitter, Humorous Tales of Chinese Immigrants" for Boston.com: "Jin's protagonists are caught between the financial needs of the families they've left behind and the demands of keeping themselves afloat . . . between the false and real promises of freedom." Both Wanren and Huong send money home to their families regularly despite their dismal financial situations.

Breaking this sense of indebtedness to their families forms a major obstacle in the couples' plans to escape from their unhappy lives in New York. Clayton Moore, in "Chinese Emigré Ha Jin's Stories Reflect Daily Life of Exiles," for the *Denver Post*, is especially impressed by the global scale Jin condenses into the minute details of the immigrants' everyday struggles, calling *A Good Fall* "a collection that spans the universe of the immigration experience through the microcosm of a single community . . . capturing both the daily grind and the little victories of life among exiles and refugees." Wanren and Huong's brave leap to freedom illustrates the powerful constraints on an immigrant's life, including family expectations, loneliness, debts, and issues of language.

In "Ha Jin on the Immigrant Life" for *BookPage*, Robert Weibezahl finds that Jin's trademark narrative style matches his subject matter: "Jin writes with a direct, unfussy style that captures the odd cadences of these lives lived in translation." It is fitting that the story of a humble man who cannot pass his English language test is told honestly, without embellished language. The honesty of the language reflects the sincerity of Wanren's wish to succeed.

In a review of the collection for *SFGate*, Fan Wu appreciates the depth, realism, and relatability of Jin's characters, praising Jin's "prowess to study and reveal, often with heartfelt humor, the compromised and damaged heart and soul, and the impact of time and history on ordinary people." Huong's ensnarement by the Croc is all the more horrible because, despite knowing she could be something more, she is resigned to her fate. Since she entered the country illegally, her own fate is out of her control.

Colm Toibin, in "Exiles from Themselves" for the *New York Times*, summarizes the intellectual and emotional appeal of Jin's collection of Chinese immigrant tales, paying tribute to the way these stories "dramatize lives in which hope has been crushed rather than abandoned, in which the struggle to find a place to live becomes as much a daily battle within the self as it is with society." For Wanren and Huong, the cost of becoming free and independent Americans is the severance of all ties with their former lives as immigrants.

CRITICISM

Amy L. Miller

Miller is a graduate of the University of Cincinnati. In the following essay, she examines how Jin uses Wanren and Huong's victory against their economic constraints in "The House behind a Weeping Cherry" to explore the universal struggles of immigrant life.

In Jin's "The House behind a Weeping Cherry," the struggle of a man and woman toward achieving the American dream of financial stability, family, and home ownership is made particularly difficult by their unique circumstances. They are not born-and-raised Americans but are recently arrived Chinese immigrants. Huong is an illegal alien, and Wanren cannot master the English language. Yet their desires are the same as those of any young couple striking out on their own: the freedom to love each other and the hope of avoiding economic peril. Jin's characters take on a universality through their familiar desires, transforming the mundane details of their everyday lives—working, eating, sleeping—into an immigrant origin story with broad appeal. Wanren and Huong are not just any pair of lovers but

WHAT DO I READ NEXT?

- In Gene Luen Yang's young-adult graphic novel *American Born Chinese* (2007), three characters balance school, family, friends, and cultures as they search for an identity all their own: the folk hero the Monkey King, who struggles to gain fame; Jin Wang, the only Asian American in his new school; and the fully assimilated Danny, who is embarrassed by his painfully stereotypically Chinese cousin, Chin-Kee. The three plots crash together with unexpected and delightful results in this award-winning work.
- Jin's *Waiting* (1999), winner of the National Book Award and PEN/Faulkner Award, tells the story of Lin Kong, who, unable to divorce his traditional and provincial wife Shuyu, waits eighteen years to be with the woman he loves, a nurse named Manna Wu. Set against the backdrop of Communist China, the novel's exploration of individuality within a collectivist society makes it a remarkable allegory of the national political crisis running parallel to the drama of the ill-fated lovers.
- Jhumpa Lahiri's Pulitzer Prize–winning short story collection *The Interpreter of Maladies* (1999) follows the lives of Indian immigrants to the United States as they attempt to preserve their identity and culture in an unfamiliar landscape.
- Peter Kwong's *The New Chinatown* (1996) explores crime inside America's urban Chinatowns, with a particular focus on how the isolation of Chinese American communities provides an environment vulnerable to organized crime and corruption.
- Henry Park of Chang-rae Lee's novel *Native Speaker* (1995) feels alienated from American society after a long struggle to master the English language. Mourning the death of his son and separated from his wife, he struggles to keep himself emotionally distant from his job when he is assigned to spy on a Korean American politician.
- In Gish Jen's *Typical American* (1991), the Chang family find themselves calling the United States home after the 1949 Chinese Communist Revolution. They are reluctant at first to adapt to the new culture, but they soon find themselves wrapped up in chasing the elusive American dream. Ralph, Teresa, and Helen become typical Americans as they cease to think as a family and begin to follow their own desires, with hilarious and sometimes heartbreaking results.
- In Amy Tan's *The Joy Luck Club* (1989), four women, all Chinese immigrants living in San Francisco in 1949, meet to play mahjong, eat dim sum, and share the stories of their lives growing up in China, the struggles of their families, and their hopes for their daughters' futures in the United States.

---

archetypical lovers of a kind, mythical figures who escape the clutches of money to live free in the open American landscape. Because they never lose faith in each other, they find their way out of the maze of debts, bills, and rent and are never seen again. In this way, Jin's characters straddle their Chinese and American identities to represent a global concept of freedom and become larger than life.

In an interview with the *Paris Review*, Jin noted the difference between an immigrant and an exile: "An exile has a significant past: he often lives in the past . . . but an immigrant gets to start from scratch. The past is not essential. He formulates his own frame of reference." Jin shows Wanren actively suppressing his memories of home in order to make it through the day without giving in to homesickness. His

> "STARTING OVER IN A NEW COUNTRY IS NOT DEPICTED AS EASY, AS THE CHARACTERS MUST FIGHT THEIR DESIRE FOR COMFORTS THAT SIMPLY ARE NOT AVAILABLE. THEY ARE ALONE, WITHOUT OLD FRIENDS OR FAMILY. THEY MUST LOOK OUT FOR THEMSELVES."

love for Huong solidifies when she makes him soup from his home province. Starting over in a new country is not depicted as easy, as the characters must fight their desire for comforts that simply are not available. They are alone, without old friends or family. They must look out for themselves. This level of vigilance takes an emotional, physical, and mental toll, and economic strain pressurizes the situation further. Both Wanren and Huong are expected to send money home to their families in China, yet neither has money to spare. Wanren cannot pay more than three hundred dollars in rent without going broke, while Huong pays an exorbitant two thousand dollars a month to the Croc, with eighteen thousand more to go before she is free of debt. The need to send money back home puts them at a disadvantage, as they have no leisure time, no money with which to indulge themselves, and no hobbies outside of work. The characters are seen at their most relaxed around the dinner table, and Wanren enjoys driving Mrs. Chen's car, but each of these pleasures is circumscribed by employment and money: driving is Wanren's job, taken out of desperation, and the women could be called away from the table at any moment by a client. The need for money leaves little time for Wanren and Huong to develop their new identities as Chinese Americans; instead it is their drive to survive that becomes their immigrant identity.

Toibin writes of the characters' narrow horizons in their new country: "Their emotional universe has become as circumscribed as their physical surroundings. Once inhabitants of a sprawling and familiar culture, they are now confined to a few rooms, a few streets." Symbolizing their isolation is the weeping cherry tree itself, a representative of the Chinese heritage of the tenants that hides their activities from public view. Their low profile as immigrants allows the brothel to remain in operation, while Huong, too, slips under the radar as an illegal alien by way of her illegal occupation. The cherry tree attracts Wanren to the house, and it is under the cherry tree that he and Huong discuss their relationship. When they leave the house, it is the cherry tree they leave behind: "The weeping cherry blurred in the haze, its crown edgeless, like a small hill." The house and its cherry tree, in the isolated lives of the couple, have become representative of their ties to China. By leaving their connections to their homeland, they leave their lives as new immigrants and embark on their lives as Americans—hitting the open road with no safety net in place if their risky decision should fail.

Wanren and Huong are not satisfied with their lonely and repetitive lives, especially not after their attraction to one another becomes clear. But as long as they are financially bound to their jobs and families, they are not free to pursue the desires of their hearts. Toibin comments that Jin "writes about money as if it were the opposite of love, and he manages to be unsettlingly precise and convincing in conveying what poverty feels like, what it does to relationships." When Wanren and Huong choose to run away, for example, they sacrifice their relationships with their families. Not only can they never speak to their families again, but they must live with the knowledge that their actions may have brought punishment down on their loved ones. Yet in order to run away, Wanren must convince Huong that her family is the enemy, milking her for money from their home in China while she suffers in the United States alone.

Old debts are the antagonist of Wanren and Huong's new love as well. Wanren grows suspicious of Huong's eagerness to be helped out of her situation in a rare moment of distrust, exemplifying not only his learned state of vigilance as an immigrant but the way in which money works its way between lovers and friends. Wanren's distrust is not unfounded, as Huong is both younger and in a far worse financial situation than himself, but as is appropriate in a universal tale of love conquering money, his rising doubt is replaced by a sudden, calming vision of the American dream: Huong stirring a pot happily in the kitchen of a white

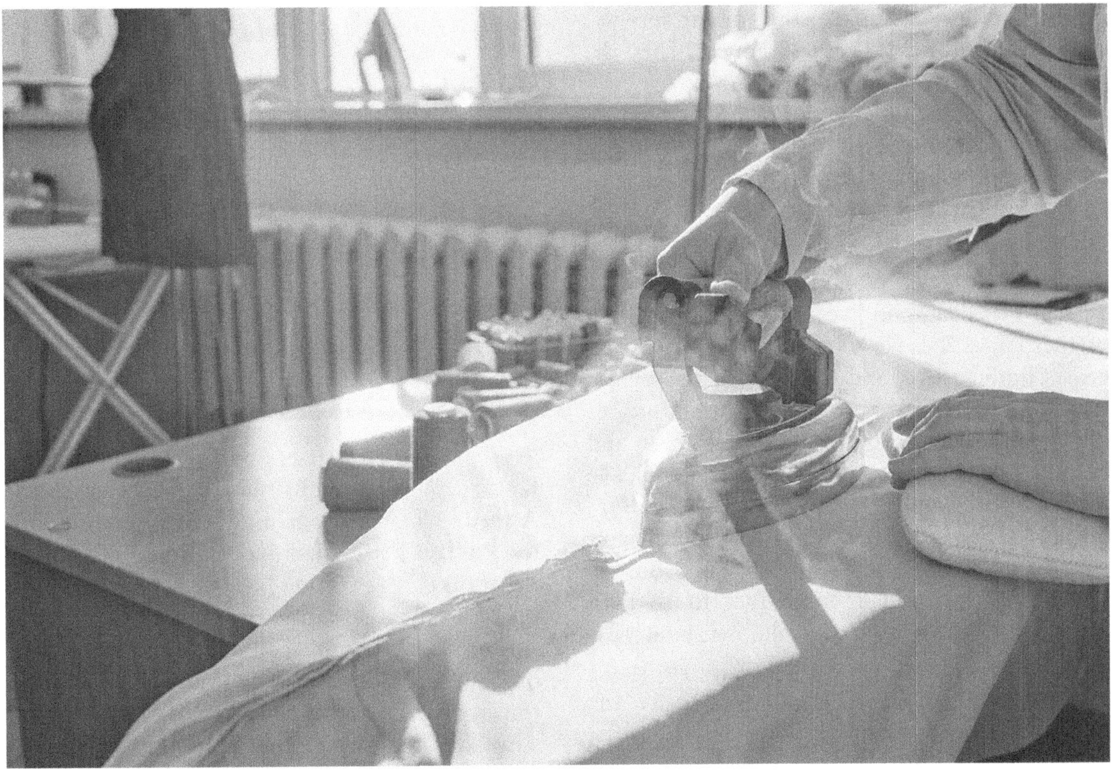

Wanren works ironing clothes in a factory (©Lumen Photos / Shutterstock.com)

cottage as their children play outside. Toibin writes: "They are people beginning in America, creating a new self in a new country." These characters become representative of larger forces; they are "small in their hopes and experiences but large in their implications." Although the path from their life in New York to the fulfillment of Wanren's dream is unclear, it is immediately clear that it will take courage to get there. Wanren and Huong become larger than life in their willingness to plunge into the unknown together. Jin's narrative pulls away before the outcome of their tale is known, but the story's message is clear. Rather than live out their lives in the lonely pursuit of money, Wanren and Huong choose love and risk, disappearing into the American fabric and ending their isolation as immigrants. Wu writes: "[Jin's] characters, regardless of their miseries and misfortunes, are eager to negotiate with the threatening situation and to take advantage of the newly discovered freedom in America at all levels—financially, politically, socially and psychologically."

The economic forces in the life of the couple—Mrs. Chen, the garment factory, the brothel, the Croc, and their respective families—have led to their meeting each other as tenants of the house behind the weeping cherry, but these same factors work to prevent the success of their love. Toibin writes: "These characters are subject to unusual pressures as they try to fulfill their destinies. One of the greatest is that they find themselves trapped in a land of hope." Both let their desires run wild. For Huong to wish for a boyfriend is an unrealistic fantasy, and Lili and Nana tease her frequently for the way she dotes on Wanren as if they were dating. Wanren, meanwhile, does not consider either himself or Huong worthy of a relationship. He is too poor, while she is, in his opinion, degrading herself. However, he jumps at the chance to leave everything behind with her at his side. Though they are well fed, sheltered, and employed in New York, their stable lives are limited ones. Until meeting each other, they did not realize just how small their lives are—small enough to choke their dreams, leaving no room to wriggle loose. The Croc offers no leniency on the monthly payments of Huong's debt, while Wanren works two jobs just to make ends meet—and one of those jobs makes him an accomplice to criminal activity. This is not the life he envisioned when he moved to the United States to pursue his education. Huong, too, did not expect to be so deeply in debt upon arrival that she would have to take extreme measures simply to avoid violent retribution from a sinister gang.

"The House behind a Weeping Cherry" turns the struggles of Huong and Wanren to escape their dead-end lives into a universal tale of desperate people choosing hope, lonely hearts finding love, and the poor discovering a wealth outside of money. New immigrants to the United States without support, Wanren and Huong find a family in each other and leave their Chinese families, coworkers, and culture behind. They join the hunt for the elusive American dream, turning their backs on the weeping cherry tree, in an effort to find an identity all their own in an unknown land.

Source: Amy L. Miller, Critical Essay on "The House behind a Weeping Cherry," in *Short Stories for Students*, Gale, Cengage Learning, 2017.

Steven G. Yao

In the following excerpt, Yao discusses Jin in the context of Asian American literature.

Having come to America in 1985 to pursue graduate study in English literature at Brandeis University, Ha Jin (pen name of Jin Xuefei [. . .]) has achieved considerable renown as a writer of specifically Chinese descent in the United States. He has earned that notoriety mainly for his fictional prose narratives about life in the People's Republic of China, particularly during the tumultuous period of the Cultural Revolution (1966–76). His first collection of short stories, *Ocean of Words*, for example, won the PEN/Hemingway Award in 1996, while his second volume, *Under the Red Flag*, garnered the Flannery O'Connor Award for Short Fiction from the University of Georgia Press in 1997. Most notably, his second novel, *Waiting*, earned the National Book Award and the PEN/Faulkner Award in 1999. Since that highly visible and significant success, Jin has published two additional short story collections, *The Bridegroom: Stories* (2000) and *A Good Fall: Stories* (2009), as well as three novels, *The Crazed* (2002), *War Trash* (2004), and *A Free Life* (2007), all to consistent acclaim. In fact, *War Trash*, which relates the travails of a soldier in the Chinese People's Volunteer Army captured by opposition forces during the Korean War, brought another PEN/Faulkner Award, while also gaining a nomination for the Pulitzer Prize. Such recognitions, along with the frankly astonishing pace of his literary production, together arguably make Ha Jin the single most accomplished contemporary writer of Chinese descent working in the United States today, at least as gauged by the measures of successful commercial publication and acknowledgment from the dominant American cultural establishment. Indeed, such renown has even led to opportunities within other artistic arenas. Thus, in collaboration with acclaimed Chinese composer Tan Dun, Jin co-wrote the English-language libretto for the recent opera, *The First Emperor*, which debuted at the Metropolitan Opera in New York City on December 21, 2006, with no less than Plácido Domingo singing the title role.

"YET, LIKE THE ANGEL ISLAND POETS WHO ARE HIS CO-ETHNIC PREDECESSORS, JIN ADVANCES HIS OWN POETICS OF SPECIFICALLY CHINESE CULTURAL IDENTITY PARTLY AS A RESULT OF AND IN TRAUMATIZED RESPONSE TO THE EXPERIENCE OF IMMIGRATION TO THE UNITED STATES."

Ironically, perhaps, his recent foray into the more socially rarefied domain of opera libretti represents something of a return to generic origins. For alongside his remarkable accomplishments in prose, Ha Jin has also published over the last two decades or so three books of verse, an output that matches the levels of production by all the contemporary Chinese American poets examined in this study, with the notable exception of John Yau. In fact, Ha Jin actually began his writing career in English specifically as a poet. Appearing a full six years before his inaugural, prize-winning short story collection, *Ocean of Words*, Jin's first substantial publication in the United States was a book of verse titled *Between Silences* (1990), brought out by the University of Chicago Press in its Phoenix Poets series. And his second volume of poems, *Facing Shadows*, appeared in 1996, the same year that *Ocean of Words* was published.

Moreover, even as he began to write and then came quickly to achieve steadily expanding notice for his prose fiction, Jin continued to produce verse, with a third book of poems, *Wreckage*, seeing publication in 2001, fully two years after he won the National Book Award for *Waiting*. To be sure, given the general lack of interest in verse within contemporary American (literary) culture more broadly, it comes as no surprise either that Jin would take up prose narrative following his initial, poetic debut, or that his considerable reputation has derived almost entirely from his already substantial and still-growing body of fiction. Even so, within the trajectory of his individual career, poetry stands out as the avenue by which he first emerged as a writer in English, as well as a steadily maintained practice over the course of his development thus far.

Accordingly, then, Ha Jin's efforts as a poet offer a unique vantage on both the logic and the broader stakes of his overall accomplishment as a writer of Asian (and specifically Chinese) descent in the United States. In this chapter I want to consider through the distinctive lens of his verse the significance, as well as the specific ideological functioning, of Ha Jin's project as a writer within the context of our current regime of American liberal multiculturalism. More particularly, I think through the structural irony or contradiction that underwrites his entire body of work, which sets forth in English the terms for an explicitly named "Chinese" ethnic and cultural subjectivity. By doing so, I seek to understand the reasons behind his meteoric rise to prominence during the decade of the 1990s. Crucially, this period witnessed the reemergence of "China" and "the Chinese" as both political and looming economic threats to continued American global dominance. For at that point in recent U.S. political history, mainland China stood out as at once the largest remaining socialist nation after the collapse of the Soviet Union and as an emerging economic competitor of the United States, an apparent trend forebodingly punctuated by the return of Hong Kong to the People's Republic in 1997. The political, governmental, and media hysteria surrounding both the campaign finance scandal involving John Huang in 1996 and the woeful miscarriage of the Wen Ho Lee spy case beginning in 1999 testify at once to the intensity and the pervasiveness of this perceived threat. Ha Jin's linguistically transparent depictions of Chinese "humanity" struggling within and against the restrictions of a totalitarian communist state apparatus first appeared and subsequently came to enjoy steadily increasing acclaim, then, in the wake of the end of the cold war and immediately before radical Islam gained temporary ascendancy as the most pressing threat to global "American interests" following the events of September 11, 2001.

Curiously, despite all the positive notice that Ha Jin has received from mainstream readerships in the United States and elsewhere, critics of Asian American literature and culture have for the most part remained conspicuously quiet on the matter of his accomplishments. Such comparative neglect contrasts with the steady and abundant attention already paid to other contemporary American writers of Asian descent in the United States who have also enjoyed the approbation of the dominant American literary establishment, including writers such as Maxine Hong Kingston, Gish Jen, Chang-rae Lee, as well as even Theresa Hak Kyung Cha. A number of factors have contributed to this collective reticence. Most immediately, perhaps, as a relatively recent and adult immigrant to the United States from the People's Republic of China, Jin occupies a social location that deviates from prevailing conceptions of "Asian American" ethnic identity which have historically privileged American-born citizens of various Asian cultural heritages, or at least those who arrived to this country from different parts of Asia at a fairly young age. Such an emphasis has resulted in the great incidence of *Bildungsroman* narratives of individual minority subject formation within the established Asian American literary canon. Hence, Jin's biography departs from the familiar patterns of recognition for Asian American ethnic and cultural identity. In addition, he writes about subjects and events that fall outside the conventional scope of interests animating the great majority of literary production by "Asian Americans" with their focus on the articulation of minority experiential and cultural "difference" in the United States through the treatment of themes such as the travails of immigration, simultaneous alienation from both a heritage cultural tradition and the values of dominant (i.e., "white") American society, intergenerational conflict, and so forth. Thus, in his narratives as well Jin has been seen to operate outside the sanctioned boundaries of Asian American studies in its current formation. Contributing to his neglect further still, the basic simplicity of his realist style has worked to make any extended historical or cultural explication seem largely superfluous. And finally, the depth and breadth of the mainstream acclaim that he enjoys has apparently obviated any need for cultural advocacy or ideological recuperation.

Yet, like the Angel Island poets who are his co-ethnic predecessors, Jin advances his own poetics of specifically Chinese cultural identity partly as a result of and in traumatized response to the experience of immigration to the United States. Of course, he has done so under a markedly changed set of geopolitical, economic, and social conditions both domestically and internationally. Some sense of the magnitude of those changes can be gleaned from the stark disparities in theme and operative language, as well as reception, of the poetry by these writers. Still, Jin's work represents the latest in a long line of expressly transpacific literary production to achieve visibility across the broader American cultural landscape. And as such, notwithstanding existing methodological biases within Asian American literary studies, it fits squarely within the historical poetics of Chinese/American verse that I have been tracing in this study. Indeed, Jin's achievement underscores the need to continue expanding the notion of "Asian American" beyond the conceptual boundaries of national citizenship and the referential domain of the United States to better account for the current variety of signification ventured in contemporary cultural production by people of Asian descent in the United States. For his work and its spectacular success among mainstream audiences together illustrate the extent to which both the dynamic process of immigration itself and the variously distinctive feats of cultural representation to which that process gives rise together continue to inform and reshape the evolving contours of the category of "Asian American" itself. At the same time, precisely the renown that Jin has achieved for his depictions of Chinese identity under the conditions of a totalitarian political regime indicates that his work also reveals something about the role that notions of specifically Chinese "difference" continue to play within the dominant American cultural imaginary.

Seeking in just this manner to challenge the established limits of Asian American studies, a very few critics have addressed Jin's work, navigating the issue of his "foreign" political identity and subject matter in various ways. Rey Chow, for example, has situated his accomplishment within an expressly international context by discussing the negative reaction in the People's Republic of China to a proposed translation of Jin's National Book Award–winning novel, *Waiting*. More interested in the contemporary logic of ethnicity as such, however, she abstains from ever actually discussing the content of the work itself. Instead, she explains the accusations of cultural treachery and betrayal leveled at Jin by his fellow Chinese nationals, theorizing them in terms of what she calls postcolonial "ethnic *ressentiment*." Elaborating on "the unbearable lightness of postcolonial, postmodern ethnicity," she explains this phenomenon as the "psychic structure of a reaction to injustice created by the coercive and unequal encounter with the white world, a reaction that, in the course of postcoloniality, ends up directing rancor toward certain members of one's own ethnic group—that ends up, as it were, ethnically profiling, shaming, and scapegoating these members." For all its insight into the dynamics of ethnicity as a contemporary global phenomenon, her assessment declines to interrogate either the logic or the domestic stakes of the National Book Award itself, thereby neglecting to consider the cultural meaning of Jin's transpacific literary production within the ideological and social environment of the United States, the site for the original composition, publication, primary readership, and subsequent cultural endorsement of both his prose and verse. Consequently, her model ignores the possibility of a substantive critique developed in relation to the intertwined contexts of American liberal multiculturalism and the literary history of "minority" (and especially ethnic "Chinese") expression in English. . . .

Source: Steven G. Yao, "'A Voice from China': Ha Jin and the Cultural Politics of Antisocialist Realism," in *Foreign Accents: Chinese American Verse from Exclusion to Postethnicity*, Oxford University Press, 2010, pp. 109–13.

SOURCES

Batalova, Jeanna, and Kate Hooper, "Chinese Immigrants in the United States," Migration Policy Institute website, January 28, 2015, http://www.migrationpolicy.org/article/chinese-immigrants-united-states (accessed August 1, 2016).

"Chinese Immigration and the Chinese Exclusion Acts," US Department of State: Office of the Historian website, https://history.state.gov/milestones/1866-1898/chinese-immigration (accessed August 1, 2016).

Fay, Sarah, "Ha Jin, the Art of Fiction No. 202," in *Paris Review*, No. 191, Winter 2009, http://www.theparisreview.org/interviews/5991/the-art-of-fiction-no-202-ha-jin (accessed July 20, 2016).

Garner, Dwight, "Ha Jin's Cultural Revolution," in *New York Times*, February 6, 2000, http://www.nytimes.com/2000/02/06/magazine/ha-jin-s-cultural-revolution.html (accessed July 20, 2016).

"Ha Jin," Boston University website, http://www.bu.edu/creativewriting/people/faculty/ha-jin/ (accessed July 20, 2016).

"Ha Jin," Poetry Foundation website, https://www.poetryfoundation.org/poems-and-poets/poets/detail/ha-jin (accessed June 20, 2016).

"Immigrants in the United States: A Profile of America's Foreign-Born Population," Center for Immigration Studies website, http://cis.org/node/3876 (accessed August 1, 2016).

Jin, Ha, "The House behind a Weeping Cherry," in *New Yorker*, April 7, 2008, http://www.newyorker.com/magazine/2008/04/07/the-house-behind-a-weeping-cherry (accessed June 15, 2016).

Moore, Clayton, "Chinese Emigré Ha Jin's Stories Reflect Daily Life of Exiles," in *Denver Post*, December 10, 2009, http://www.denverpost.com/2009/12/10/book-review-chinese-emigre-ha-jins-stories-reflect-daily-life-of-exiles/ (accessed July 20, 2016).

Schlack, Julie Wittes, "Bitter, Humorous Tales of Chinese Immigrants," Boston.com, January 9, 2010, http://archive.boston.com/ae/books/articles/2010/01/09/author_ha_jin_spins_tales_of_immigrant_experience/ (accessed July 20, 2016).

Toibin, Colm, "Exiles from Themselves," in *New York Times*, December 31, 2009, http://www.nytimes.com/2010/01/03/books/review/Toibin-t.html (accessed July 20, 2016).

Weibezahl, Robert, "*A Good Fall: Stories*: Ha Jin on the Immigrant Life," in *BookPage*, December 2009, https://bookpage.com/reviews/6245-ha-jin-good-fall-stories#.V7LWUyMrK_U (accessed June 20, 2016).

Wu, Fan, "*A Good Fall* by Ha Jin," in *SFGate*, December 13, 2009, http://www.sfgate.com/books/article/A-Good-Fall-by-Ha-Jin-3207282.php (accessed July 20, 2016).

FURTHER READING

Jin, Ha, *Ocean of Words*, Vintage, 1998.

Jin's first short-story collection, originally published in 1996, draws on his experiences in the People's Liberation Army on the freezing border between Russia and China. As the soldiers entertain themselves, learn from each other, and make do with little food and without the comfort of family, the collectivist nature of Chinese society is explored with heartwarming and heartbreaking results.

Kwong, Peter, and Dusanka Miscevic, *Chinese Americans: The Immigrant Experience*, Universe, 2000.

This volume combines high-quality black-and-white photographs with text that tells the long and complex history of Chinese immigration to the United States. Exploring the ways in which Chinese immigrants have maintained their identity and traditions while gaining a foothold in American society, *Chinese Americans* also considers the ways this group has been treated in comparison with immigrants from other nations arriving at the same times.

Lee, Erika, *The Making of Asian America: A History*, Simon & Schuster, 2016.

The Making of Asian America traces the history of Asian immigration to the United States from the sixteenth century to the present day, with a focus on the contributions of Asians to American society as well as the changing national attitude toward the Asian and Asian American populations, from the incarceration of Japanese in internment camps in World War II to the rise of Asians as the "model minority," and the drawbacks of this perception.

Seligman, Scott D., *Tong Wars: The Untold Story of Vice, Money, and Murder in New York's Chinatown*, Viking, 2016.

Seligman's history of violence and corruption in New York City's Chinatown covers thirty years of war between rival gangs, police, and reformers attempting to clean up the streets.

SUGGESTED SEARCH TERMS

Ha Jin

The House behind a Weeping Cherry

Ha Jin AND The House behind a Weeping Cherry

Ha Jin AND A Good Fall

A Good Fall AND The House behind a Weeping Cherry

The House behind a Weeping Cherry AND short story

A Good Fall AND immigration

A Good Fall AND Chinese American literature

Just Before the War with the Eskimos

J. D. SALINGER

1948

"Just Before the War with the Eskimos" is a short story by J. D. Salinger that first saw the light of day in the *New Yorker* on June 5, 1948. It was one of Salinger's early successes, appearing three years before his novel *The Catcher in the Rye*—one of the most famous books ever published—and helping break a long series of early rejections. The story contains mildly and self-consciously profane dialogue and a temperamental young-adult character who finds herself at a turning point in life. These and other elements are early appearances of some of the hallmarks of Salinger's fiction.

The plot is threadbare. Over the course of a late morning in New York City, fifteen-year-old Ginnie Mannox quarrels with her friend Selena Graff, has a lengthy but wandering conversation with Selena's eccentric older brother Franklin at the Graffs' apartment, meets Franklin's equally eccentric friend Eric, and leaves. But the deceptively simple plot, moved forward for the most part by conversation, masks the story's subtle complexities. Salinger's depiction of the shifting relationships between these four young adults and his treatment of Ginnie's sudden maturation leave the story open to multiple interpretations: it has been analyzed as a critique of youth culture, a Christian allegory, and a love story.

The story was the third by Salinger to appear in the *New Yorker*. It won an O. Henry Award

J.D. Salinger (©Bettmann / Getty Images)

one year after its publication and was anthologized twice, first in his 1953 collection *Nine Stories* and then in the anthology *Manhattan: Stories from the Heart of a Great City* in 1954.

AUTHOR BIOGRAPHY

Jerome David Salinger was born on January 1, 1919, in Manhattan. Throughout his childhood Salinger showed a flair for writing and the stage, pursuits his father disdained. Poor academic performance led to an expulsion from one school and dropping out of college, and in 1937 his father sent him to travel across Europe, hoping Salinger would develop a taste for the import business which had enriched the family. But he remained firm in his creative interests, and his father reluctantly reenrolled him in college to study writing.

In 1940 Salinger published his first short story, "The Young Folks," in *Story* magazine. Over the following year and a half all but one of his stories were turned down by everyone he submitted them to. World War II had begun a year earlier, and while the United States had so far remained uninvolved, Salinger, with no other means of support, attempted to enlist in the US Army. To his disappointment he was rejected because of a heart irregularity.

Salinger's dedication to writing finally paid off in 1941 when he published stories in both *Collier's* and *Esquire*. The *New Yorker* accepted "Slight Rebellion off Madison," whose protagonist, Holden Caulfield, would later become one of modern literature's most famous teenagers, but the attack on Pearl Harbor in December led the magazine to suspend publication of the story indefinitely.

Salinger's gloom was relieved when the army relaxed its standards and accepted him for service. He took part in major combat operations, and these were eye-opening and traumatic. In 1944 he participated in the invasion of Normandy, the Battle of Hürtgen Forest, and the Battle of the Bulge, all scenes of terrible carnage. The war features both obliquely and directly in several short stories, and he remarked once to his daughter, Margaret, as she relates in her memoir *Dream Catcher*, "You never really get the smell of burning flesh out of your nose entirely. No matter how long you live."

After recuperating from the war, Salinger plunged himself into writing, and this time his efforts were rewarded. "Slight Rebellion off Madison" finally appeared in the *New Yorker* in December 1946, followed by "A Perfect Day for Bananafish" in January 1947. Quirky, discomfiting, and unexpectedly bleak, this story brought him immediate acclaim and, though many subsequent stories would still be rejected, it opened the doors of the publishing world. "Just Before the War with the Eskimos," published in 1948, and other short fiction followed.

In 1949 Salinger undertook what would become his most famous work, and one of the best known in the English language: *The Catcher in the Rye*. The novel, which follows sixteen-year-old Holden Caulfield as he wanders through New York City after expulsion from a private school, was a best seller for over two years and has remained in print ever since its publication in 1951.

After the success of *The Catcher in the Rye*, Salinger began a slow but steady withdrawal from public life and published ever more rarely. He became an adherent of Hinduism and explored a number of esoteric spiritual and medicinal practices. A new family could not prevent his increasing alienation from society, and his marriage did not survive it; neither did his professional life as a writer. Salinger published three more books before abandoning the publishing world altogether, though he continued to write with as much discipline as before. In his later years he brought a number of lawsuits against people for unauthorized use of his work and violations of his privacy, and his zeal for seclusion is well illustrated by an incident in 1992 in which he hid in the remains of his house after a major fire to avoid questions from a journalist.

Salinger died of natural causes on January 27, 2010, at the age of ninety-one.

PLOT SUMMARY

Fifteen-year-old Ginnie Mannox and her friend Selena Graff are taking a taxi home after a game of tennis on Manhattan's East Side. In an opening exposition, the reader learns that Ginnie regards Selena as "the biggest drip" at school, though she appreciates Selena's providing an apparently limitless supply of tennis balls (her father is somehow involved in their manufacture); Ginnie is also stewing over the fact that, after each cab ride from the last four games of tennis they have played, Selena, who is the first to be dropped off, has left the cab without offering to help pay the fare.

Ginnie brings the matter up with Selena, who first feigns surprise, then protests that the tennis balls she donates to their games should even the score. Ginnie insists that because Mr. Graff makes tennis balls, Selena sacrifices nothing to bring them, and that Selena should pay for her half of the last four cab fares home. When Selena asks for some extra time to come up with the money, Ginnie tells her that she needs the money that night for a movie.

The girls ride to Selena's house in angry silence. Selena exits the cab, leaving Ginnie to pay the entire fare again. Ginnie follows her into the apartment building where the Graffs live and informs her of the new total she is owed. Selena now claims that her mother is ill ("She virtually has pneumonia") and she is reluctant to disturb her for the money. Ginnie responds that she is not to blame for Mrs. Graff's health.

Ginnie waits in the living room while Selena, after a final angry protest, goes to collect the fare. Alone, Ginnie mentally redecorates the "altogether hideous room—expensive but cheesy."

Her brief solitude is interrupted by Franklin, Selena's brother, whose voice precedes his appearance ("*Eric? That you?*"). Noisy, stooping, narrow-chested, and dressed in pajamas, Franklin informs her that he has just cut his "goddam finger," and the rest of his dialogue is marked by an absurd overuse of mild blasphemies. After they introduce themselves, he tells Ginnie that he knows her sister, referring to her as a snob. Ginnie briefly defends her sister before admitting to herself that Franklin's observations are actually somewhat interesting. When she informs him that her sister is getting married in a month, Franklin expresses pity for the fiancé.

He returns abruptly to the topic of his injured finger, and she advises him on its treatment, suggesting iodine and urging him not to touch it. In response, Franklin asks her if she would like the uneaten half of a chicken sandwich in his room. She politely refuses, explaining that her mother will be upset if she is not hungry for lunch. Then he offers a glass of milk. When Ginnie refuses this offer as well, he abruptly changes course and asks who her sister's fiancé is. Over the course of their back-and-forth (during which he expresses further contempt for both parties), Franklin scratches skin ailments on his legs, smokes a bent cigarette in a dramatic "French" style, and curses with enthusiastic carelessness.

Franklin complains that he wrote Ginnie's sister eight times and that she never wrote back. When Ginnie explains that he should have phoned, he says that he was in Ohio, not, he further clarifies, for college ("Quit") or the Army ("Ticker," meaning that he was rejected for service due to a heart condition), but for work in an airplane factory. She asks if he enjoyed the work, and is interested enough in him that his sarcastic response ("I just *adore* airplanes. They're so *cute*") fails to offend her.

Then, changing course again, he announces, "We're gonna fight the Eskimos next. . . .This time all the old guys're gonna go. Guys around sixty." Ginnie tells him that this age requirement will prevent him from serving, which seems to hurt his feelings, though he simply agrees with her.

Abruptly, he informs her that someone is coming to pick him up and asks her to tell the visitor that he is shaving to get ready. He leaves, then returns almost immediately with the chicken sandwich half, urging it on her so fervently that she gives up and takes it. After making sure she takes a bite, he leaves the room once and for all.

A few seconds later the visitor, Eric, arrives. He sits down, rubs his eyes, and exclaims, "This has been the most horrible morning of my entire life." When Selena presses him for details, he proceeds to describe his experiences living with a poor writer whom he had welcomed into his apartment. After months of leaving messes everywhere, the writer effectively robbed the apartment and left.

Like Franklin, Eric is adept at changing course in a conversation. He breaks off the tale of his horrible morning to (in rapid succession) exclaim over the quality of Ginnie's camel-hair polo coat and ask where she got it; ask what time of year her mother goes to Nassau; ask her name and association with Franklin's sister; bemoan the amount of dog hair on his clothes; and announce his intention to be on time for a showing that afternoon of Jean Cocteau's 1946 film *Beauty and the Beast*. Ginnie also discovers that he, too, worked at the airplane factory in Ohio.

At that moment Selena returns with the money she owes Ginnie. Ginnie quickly refuses the money, acknowledging that providing tennis balls is enough after all. Before Selena has a chance to make sense of this change in Ginnie's attitude, Ginnie asks her to walk with her to the front door, where she asks if Selena is busy that evening and suggests she might drop by for a visit. Selena, baffled, agrees. Waiting outside the elevator door, Ginnie inquires about Franklin. Selena tells her that he recently quit his job and that their father wants him to go to college, but he is unwilling because he is "too old" (twenty-four).

Outside the building Ginnie reaches into her purse and finds the unfinished half of Franklin's sandwich. She almost discards it, then puts it in her coat pocket, recalling a time a few years before when it took her "three days to dispose of the Easter chick she had found dead on the sawdust in the bottom of her wastebasket."

CHARACTERS

Eric

Eric is a friend of Franklin's who comes to the Graff apartment to pick Franklin up and bring him to a screening of Jean Cocteau's *Beauty and the Beast*. While Franklin gets ready, Eric and Ginnie embark on a conversation. In his early thirties, Eric is somewhat nondescript physically, but he makes up for this with a combination of hyperbole, worldliness, and breathless affectation.

He dominates their conversation with a long and self-absorbed preamble about his experiences that morning: his housemate, a penniless writer whom Eric took in out of pity months before and whose filthy habits made the apartment a constant mess, has robbed Eric and disappeared. Once this introduction is over, Eric's conversational style is revealed to be as erratic as his friend Franklin's, jumping from one topic to another with little or no warning. The effect is one of restlessness and discontinuity, but it keeps Ginnie interested, and his self-absorption yields midway to a series of questions about Ginnie herself.

In general, Eric is more a caricature than a three-dimensional character, and the overall impression is not necessarily a positive one. His speaking style is theatrical in the extreme. It is rendered with frequent italics, meant to indicate a highly exaggerated emphasis on certain words, and utilizes florid rhetoric. This quality, in combination with his appreciation for the quality of Ginnie's coat and elliptical reference to some unstated drama with the male housemate who just robbed him, has suggested to some critics that Eric is gay. But his sexuality is not otherwise focused on and seems to make no particular impression on Ginnie.

The topics they discuss in the living room do not serve to move the plot forward, or to reveal much about Eric beyond his essential manner and style. On the face of it, the entire episode seems merely to introduce another odd character to Ginnie in the space of a few minutes (since immediately before his appearance Ginnie has had a similarly peculiar conversation with Franklin). But both encounters serve to move her beyond the comforts of her own previously limited world so that she can engage with the wider one.

Franklin Graff

Franklin, Selena's brother, comes into the living room while Ginnie is waiting for Selena to collect money owed for cab fare. He is "the funniest-looking boy, or man—it was hard to tell which he was—she had ever seen." Hair disheveled, barefoot, and still in his pajamas, Franklin launches immediately into a discussion of his injured finger, which he has cut while rummaging in a wastebasket "fulla razor blades." His obsessive focus on it suggests that the injury is "obviously for him the true and only focal point in the room." After they introduce themselves, their conversation proceeds to follow a strange but interesting course, full of detours; his peculiar observations arouse in Ginnie everything from disdain to fascination.

Franklin is unattractive, even somewhat repulsive in his manner ("She watched him scratch his ankle till it was red. When he began to scratch off a minor skin eruption on his calf with his fingernail, she stopped watching"). His fundamental character is that of a child trapped in a man's body, strangely direct and unguarded about some things and self-conscious about others. Franklin's dialogue is littered with *goddam*s to an extreme, effort-filled extent, reminiscent of a teenager's clumsy attempts to ape maturity. On the other hand, his ostentatious smoking style is "not part of the sofa vaudeville of a showoff but, rather, the private, exposed achievement of a young man who, at one time or another, might have tried shaving himself left-handed." And he is totally oblivious to social norms, for example scratching the skin on his legs with enthusiasm in front of his sister's teenaged friend. The overall impression is one of almost intimately unpleasant physicality coupled with a good dose of mental chaos.

And yet Ginnie, despite her careful attempts to appear disinterested or annoyed, is captivated by him. Though he is clearly a social misfit, a twenty-four-year-old still living in his parents' apartment, trapped in an adolescent stage of emotional development and with an uncertain future, Franklin is the catalyst for Ginnie's own sudden growing up. Despite his extreme awkwardness, he of all four characters is the most sympathetic. He comes across as almost desperate in his efforts to establish a connection with Ginnie, as his responses to even the slightest demonstrations of warmth reveal: her admonition that he stop touching his cut finger reduces him from childlike antagonism to instant obedience, and he is so grateful for her other suggestions that he offers her the uneaten half of a chicken sandwich, a gesture that is no less generous and heartfelt for its absurdity. In fact it may represent the limits of his ability to express gratitude, and it has a transformative effect on her own life.

Selena Graff

Selena, Ginnie's friend, is the least fleshed-out character in the story, although it is through her that Ginnie meets Franklin and Eric and experiences a change in her relation to the world at large. Her role is otherwise minimal. Selena routinely leaves Ginnie to pay the cab fare when they finish their tennis games, and Ginnie, who has been dwelling on this and regards Selena as a "drip" in any case, demands recompense. The demand causes an at-least momentary rift in their already marginal friendship.

Ginnie does not have much respect for Selena. Selena is for some reason reluctant to pay back the cab fare; her father is involved at some level in the manufacture of tennis balls; the Graff apartment is decorated, Ginnie feels, in an "expensive but cheesy" way, kept by a maid "with whom Selena didn't seem to be on speaking terms"—and these utterly incidental details are the only ones Salinger offers the reader about her, aside from the offense she takes at Ginnie's demand and the apparent lie about her mother being too ill to disturb for the money. Indeed, she vanishes from the story after three pages, returning only at the very end.

As there is little about Selena to inspire curiosity, anything of interest must be inferred, such as the reason behind her reluctance to come up with the money she owes: she may be stingy, the family may have fallen on hard times despite the apartment's expensive furnishings, et cetera. Her name, certainly, is almost an epithet suggestive of good breeding and high lineage—*Selena* derives from Selene, a goddess of Greek mythology, and *Graff* is a term for German nobility—but she remains a flat character.

And yet the very lack of detail about Selena works in the story's favor. At its heart, "Just Before the War with the Eskimos" is about Ginnie's relationship with the world at large. Selena is too generic to provide plausible reasons for Ginnie's disdain, which, in the absence of any decent excuse, looks like what it is: the harsh judgmentalism of a girl cut off from real human connection. At the story's end, Ginnie buries the hatchet with Selena, although the reconciliation seems tactical, simply a way for Ginnie to continue talking with Franklin. Despite this, Selena's role has been fulfilled, and Ginnie is more open to the world than she was before entering the Graff apartment.

Ginnie Mannox

Ginnie, the protagonist of the story, is a fifteen-year-old student at Miss Basehoar's, a school in New York City "abounding with fair-sized drips." She applies this term particularly to her classmate Selena, with whom she has been playing tennis on Saturdays. Selena has helped with cab fare only once, and the story opens as Ginnie abruptly demands compensation from her.

Ginnie's attitude toward her classmate is one of contempt, and since she considers Selena one drip among many, the reader can infer a broader contempt for the world around her. Nevertheless, they have a standing weekly tennis date, maintained at least partly because Selena provides a limitless supply of tennis balls. Not only does Ginnie look down her nose at her classmate, then, but she is willing to tolerate Selena if she can be of advantage to her in some way. These two qualities, which Salinger establishes within the first paragraph, suggest an unpleasant young person walled off from others, unable to establish meaningful connections, and the story hinges on the breaking down of that wall.

While waiting in the living room for Selena to return with her share of the cab fare, Ginnie encounters Selena's brother Franklin, and over the next few minutes their conversation triggers a transformation in her. Franklin starts things off with an offensive remark about Ginnie's sister; this provokes a briefly antagonistic back-and-forth, during which she is secretly intrigued, and the dynamic changes for the better when she advises him about his injured finger.

Like her, Franklin is something of a social outsider. Ginnie, however, is adept at social niceties and at hiding her distance from others. Franklin is truer to his inner self, and seems to crave contact—he virtually lunges into a dialogue with her, and once she has had time to digest his peculiar appearance, his juvenile self-absorption, his odd history, and his awkward gratitude for her willingness to talk with him, she warms up in a way which would have been impossible for her earlier.

All that remains is for her to meet his flamboyant visitor, Eric. It may be that Eric's relationship to Franklin makes Ginnie reconsider her relationship with Selena, or that his posturing reminds her of her own. In any case, Ginnie seems to recognize that these encounters have real value, and at the story's end, she is eager to pursue another one.

THEMES

Outsiders

Franklin, obviously, is the story's clearest embodiment of this theme. Salinger never bothers specifying the reasons for Franklin's behavior, but he certainly strikes Ginnie as odd (as his sister later remarks, "Isn't he a character?"). He is still in his pajamas, though it is the middle of the day; he appears not to have shaved for several days; his hair is a mess; and he is strangely childlike—self-involved, temperamental, and disarmingly candid with his opinions.

Franklin is no hermit. He reveals that he tried to enlist in the army but was turned away due to a heart condition. He also tells Ginnie that he was employed at an airplane factory in Ohio for three years, and his sister says that their father wants him to "go back" to college, meaning that he was enrolled at some point. He also has a friend, Eric, coming to take him out to a movie, and he is clearly desperate to make a connection with Ginnie from the instant they meet.

But his efforts to engage her are awkward in the extreme, hardly the kind that would meet a positive response in most people, and one could be forgiven for imagining he might be somewhat mentally ill. His future as a member of society does not seem to hold much promise. The story's success turns on the fact that, against the odds, his efforts to connect with Ginnie are successful. This says as much about Ginnie as it does about Franklin. Though she seems far more engaged with the world than he is, she has isolated herself from it, regarding even Selena, her supposed friend, as a secret object of contempt. It has taken another outsider to reach her.

TOPICS FOR FURTHER STUDY

- Does Franklin Graff suffer from mental illness of some kind, or is he unwilling to engage with society on society's terms for sound reasons of his own? In a blog post to share with classmates, write an informal psychological assessment of Franklin in which you play the role of psychologist, analyze his behavior, and determine whether he might be mentally ill. Refer to http://psychcentral.com/disorders/ for a list of mental issues. Standard psychological assessments consist of testing and interviews; you will be limited to passive observation (i.e., of his behavior as depicted by Salinger). The group Physicians for Human Rights recommends starting "at the beginning of the interview, with the very first contact. The individual's overall appearance and manner of dress . . . signs of anxiety or emotional distress, numbness or over-excitement, moments of emotional intensity, startled responses, posture and bodily expression . . . can give important clues about the personal history and psychological functioning of an individual." What course of treatment would you recommend for him, if any?

- "Just Before the War with the Eskimos" is fundamentally about breaking through social and emotional barriers to establish connection. A contemporary novel exploring the same issue is *The Astonishing Adventures of Fanboy and Goth Girl* (2006), by Barry Lyga. Write an essay comparing Salinger's short story and Lyga's novel. Focus on the differences between Salinger's 1940s-era treatment of young adults and Lyga's contemporary one. Offer specific examples with regard to social issues, writing styles, treatment of characters, use of profanity, and other potentially controversial elements. How did the social environments of the two periods in which these authors wrote affect their writing itself?

- Franklin is a social misfit—an outsider. The *Oxford English Dictionary* defines the term *outsider* as "A person who does not belong to a particular group," "A person who is not accepted by or who is isolated from society," and "A competitor, applicant, etc., thought to have little chance of success." Many different people and populations have been considered outsiders by society; some become famous and successful in their own right (like certain artists, musicians, and scientists), while others remain marginalized their entire lives (including, for example, some members of the homeless population). Write an essay in which you choose an outsider, either someone known to you or someone known to society at large, and compare him or her to Franklin. What, precisely, marks Franklin as an outsider? Research your chosen subject's personal demeanor via interviews or a biography. Are there any similarities to Franklin?

- One of the story's more startling moments is the exchange from which it derives its title, when Franklin informs Ginnie about an upcoming war with the Eskimos. Write a short story about an older version of Franklin attempting to sign up to fight in this peculiar war, from the recruiter's point of view. Keep in mind the way Franklin describes it to Ginnie: no one on the American side can fight in this war unless they are older ("around sixty"), and combat will be limited to a few hours a day ("Just give 'em shorter hours is all"). Also recall his heart condition. Is Franklin's older self simply playing an antiwar prank on the recruiter, is he suffering from a delusional disorder, or is there some other dynamic at work? Write the story in your own style, but maintain Salinger's tone: comic yet sympathetic to Franklin and those around him. Most importantly, make use of Salinger's overarching theme: the effort to break through social barriers and connect with others.

High school students Selena Graff and Ginnie Mannox argue over Selena's habit of never paying for their shared taxi *(©Wittayayut / Shutterstock.com)*

Buried within the story is another emblem of outsiders and the effort to connect. Eric, Franklin's visitor, is taking him out to see *Beauty and the Beast*. The eponymous Beast of this French fairy tale lives in isolation; Beauty, the daughter of a merchant, takes up residence in his castle and comes to love him as a friend, later transforming his corpse with her tears into a prince, whom she marries. One should not assume that Salinger is suggesting the possibility of romantic love between Franklin and Ginnie, but the essential parallel of connecting with an outsider is clear enough.

Coming of Age

Salinger is best known for his novel *The Catcher in the Rye*, a classic coming-of-age tale, and many of his stories feature a protagonist making the transition from childhood to maturity. Ginnie is introduced to the reader as an overly judgmental fifteen-year-old, and the story's chief pleasure lies in watching Franklin's candor catch her off guard and relax her defenses. While the story is told from Ginnie's point of view, only occasionally does Salinger allow the reader into Ginnie's mind. For the most part, the transformation in her character is glimpsed through her responses to Franklin's odd conversational gambits; it is only at the story's end that the extent of this transformation is made clear, and even then nothing is overstated.

Where Franklin's peculiar demeanor might provoke indifference or estrangement in many, Ginnie is moved, even fascinated. Her anger with his sister at the story's outset, while merited to a degree, is coupled with an unappealing disdain: Selena is, in her eyes, a "drip" living in an "altogether hideous" apartment. By contrast, once her strange encounter with Franklin is near its end, she is acutely aware of the possibly negative impact her words may have on him ("without meaning anything but the truth, yet knowing before the statement was completely out that she was saying the wrong thing"). And when he offers her the uneaten half of a chicken sandwich, a gesture of generosity quirky at best, she offers only token resistance before accepting it and even having the good grace to take a bite, though she "swallowed with difficulty."

The exchange has altered her attitude toward not only Franklin but his sister as well. While not going so far as to offer an apology, Ginnie is markedly warm to Selena, even surprisingly so, and it is clear that their relationship has changed for the better. While Salinger's treatment of the coming-of-age theme is mild and subtle here, it lies at the story's heart.

STYLE

Colloquialism

One of Salinger's most recognizable traits as a writer is his use of colloquialism, that is, language used in casual conversation but not in formal, written communication. Franklin, especially, is liberal in his use of colloquial speech. "Christ, I'm bleedin' to death," he tells Ginnie. "Stick around. I may need a goddam transfusion." Casual language in dialogue, common in literature, is most frequently used to lend authenticity to characters' speech. Here, however, Salinger uses it to reveal something deeper about Franklin himself. His heavy dependence on the word "goddam" and other colloquialisms might be intended to convey maturity, or perhaps he is attempting to encourage informality; either way, he is self-conscious in the extreme. Franklin's verbal efforts veer into the realm of absurdity when he asks Ginnie, "Jeat jet?" He clarifies for her: "Jeat lunch yet? . . . Aren'tcha hungry?"

Point of View

The story is told from a limited third-person point of view: it consists solely of Ginnie Mannox's impressions and thoughts, but as related by an external narrator. Typically this point of view is used to explore not just the world of the story through a particular character's eyes, but the interior environment of that character. Salinger allows his readers generous access to Ginnie's thoughts and opinions for the first few pages, enough to give a sense of her identity: she is young, passionate in her opinions, and judgmental. Once Franklin appears, however, Ginnie's interior life recedes into the background until it is virtually invisible. Only three times in the course of their conversation does Salinger record her very brief mental responses to Franklin's offensive, strange, fascinating, or pathetic statements, and she is given no time in the narration to mull over their conversation before Eric appears. After this point, Salinger writes nothing of her interior life except for a brief memory at the story's conclusion; the reader is left alone to interpret Ginnie's actions and statements. It is an interesting and unusual use of the third person.

Symbolism

Much has been written about the story's most famous symbol, which Salinger saves for the story's final lines. Ginnie prepares to throw away the sandwich half which Franklin has given her, then reconsiders and puts it back in her pocket. "A few years before, it had taken her three days to dispose of the Easter chick she had found dead on the sawdust in the bottom of her wastebasket." The Easter chick has been interpreted by several critics as part of a larger Christian parable in this story, with Franklin as a Christ figure and the sandwich half representing Christian communion. This interpretation is tempting, of course, but hardly the only one: the Easter chick and the sandwich have proven to be fertile ground for the imaginations of readers.

Other images in the story yield symbolic meaning as well. The airplane factory in which Franklin worked could represent how ill suited he is to earthbound pursuits. *Beauty and the Beast*, as mentioned earlier, is obviously symbolic of the changing dynamic between Franklin and Ginnie.

HISTORICAL CONTEXT

Mid-Twentieth-Century America

In 1948, following World War II, which had ended three years earlier, the United States was widely recognized as the leading world power. Its economy, especially, was in robust shape, unlike those of most other countries that had participated in the war and which had been devastated to varying degrees. Weapons production had employed millions and lifted America out of the Great Depression; women, particularly, were now a major part of the workforce, and while they would continue to face employment difficulties, overall the cultural status of

COMPARE & CONTRAST

- **1948:** The first volume of the Kinsey Reports, *Sexual Behavior in the Human Male*, is published (to be followed five years later by *Sexuality in the Human Female*) and meets with immediate controversy. It initiates a radical change in the way America views and discusses gender and sexuality.

  Today: Societal views on sexuality and gender are again changing rapidly, with, for example, liberals championing greater freedoms and protection for transgender people, while conservatives, who regard these changes as endangering society, enact laws limiting them.

- **1948:** In psychology, Bertram Forer discovers what is dubbed the Forer effect: the tendency of people to believe that a general personality description applies to them in particular. The effect is used to explain people's beliefs in astrology and similar pseudosciences.

  Today: The validity of the concept of ego depletion, whereby acts of willpower are said to lead to mental exhaustion, based on experiments repeated hundreds of times by scientists, is questioned by a major study—part of a series of long-accepted scientific theories' proofs abruptly failing to be repeated in laboratories.

- **1948:** On March 8, in a case involving the son of an atheist being ostracized in school for not attending voluntary religious classes, the Supreme Court rules that religious instruction in public schools violates the Constitution of the United States.

  Today: Across the nation, a heated debate about the merits and disadvantages of the public school system leads many states to begin privatizing local school systems, diverting public funds to private schools; the results themselves are hotly debated.

---

women had been transformed in a radical and lasting way.

Likewise, African Americans saw changes in their cultural and economic positions. The pressures of war production had spurred many employers to hire black Americans, and their performance in the armed forces prompted President Harry S. Truman to sign Executive Order 9981, ending racial discrimination in the military. There were cultural troubles as well, however. Racial segregation and a lack of civil rights for African Americans would remain a reality across the United States for years, and Asian American communities, especially Japanese Americans, who had suffered terribly during the war, still faced significant hardships.

The Soviet Union was regarded as a growing threat to American security, and the political arena in Washington was convulsed by the extreme anti-Soviet efforts of Senator Joseph McCarthy and the House Un-American Activities Committee, whose fearmongering led to the blacklisting of actors in Hollywood, a generally antagonistic mood toward social radicals, and other "Red Scare" repercussions. Two years after the appearance of "Just Before the War with the Eskimos," for example, Congress would pass the Internal Security Act, curtailing civil liberties in the name of protecting America. Much of the act was eventually repealed, but its passage made clear how vulnerable civil liberties were. The Cold War had begun, triggering an arms race, placing America's world supremacy in jeopardy, and initiating decades of geopolitical angst as the United States and Russia played chess on a global stage.

For the most part, though, the mood at home was defiantly cheerful. The war effort had required multiple small daily sacrifices on the part of average Americans, from food rationing and limited gasoline for cars and

Franklin shares his chicken sandwich with Ginnie while waiting for his friend Eric to show up, and then Ginnie leaves the house with the sandwich still in her hand (©Sergey Peterman / Shutterstock.com)

trucks to inferior materials used for clothing. Following its victories and the war's end, America embraced an optimism and a readiness to indulge. Domestic car production had halted completely during the war; now cars returned to the domestic market bigger and more luxurious than ever before. Fashion, on the other hand, which had embraced billowy contours in the immediate cultural aftermath of the war, turned to looks of spare elegance, and the revealing bikini made its first appearance on American beaches. The music of Bing Crosby and Frank Sinatra, brimming with self-confidence, was everywhere.

Salinger was writing against a backdrop of major changes in American literature. The year he wrote this short story saw the publication of Norman Mailer's *The Naked and the Dead*, a grimly realistic novel based on Mailer's experiences fighting in the Philippines during World War II. His focus on the dehumanization of soldiers and other impacts of war made the novel a best seller for years. Two years earlier, in 1946, Robert Penn Warren had written and published *All the King's Men*, a novel about the dark side of American politics, showcasing a crooked politician's rise to the office of governor. The literature of this period was beginning to reckon with the underside of politics and culture, warts and all.

This year also saw the introduction of the term "Beat generation." The term *beat*, originating in the African American community as a synonym for "tired" or "beaten down," was applied to a new generation of disaffected youth in New York who refused to conform to societal norms. The best-known voices of this generation—Allen Ginsberg, Jack Kerouac, William S. Burroughs, and others—were getting to know one another in New York before, during, and after 1948 and incubating a literary and cultural movement that would fundamentally change American society, testing its tolerance for cultural dissent and prefiguring the radical movements of the 1960s.

CRITICAL OVERVIEW

"Just Before the War with the Eskimos" is generally well regarded by critics. It has not garnered the attention of Salinger's best-known stories, and most direct references to the story are in scholarly essays rather than reviews, but reviewers enthused about the entire collection in which the story was first anthologized, *Nine Stories*. Eudora Welty, in the *New York Times* in 1953, praised Salinger's writing as "original, first rate, serious and beautiful," and wrote that the collection

> starts with innocence: from there it can penetrate a full range of relationships, follow the spirit's private adventure, inquire into grave problems gravely—into life and death and human vulnerability and into the occasional mystical experience where age does not, after a point, any longer apply.

It is a testament to the power of Salinger's fiction that reviewers continue to mention it six decades later. Joe Gross, writing in the *Austin American-Statesman* in 2010, calls the entire collection "dazzling" and this particular story "touching." Also in 2010, Leo Robson, in a review for the *New Statesman*, identifies "Just Before the War with the Eskimos" as representative of a "terrific" collection "characterised by Salinger's minute observations about his characters' speech, thought and behaviour."

Scholars, by and large admiring of the story, point out more specific qualities in their books and essays. Kenneth Slawenski calls this particular story "an allegory rich in metaphor and symbolism." Ihab Hassan, writing about the self-conscious loss of innocence in Salinger's fiction, writes that "it is this helpless sense of *shame* that pieces like 'Just Before the War with the Eskimos' . . . dramatize so fastidiously." James Lundquist calls it "one of his most muted stories." Warren French, however, writes that "it suffers from mechanical plotting and from the imposition on the basic story of obvious symbolism uncharacteristic of Salinger's work." He also raises the issue of Salinger's portrait of Eric, an effeminate caricature, and points out that "homosexuality is one subject that excites great confusion and bitter resentment the few times it is even hinted at in Salinger's writings."

In an interview in the *Paris Review*, John Updike, another giant of American literature, acknowledges his literary debt to Salinger, saying,

> I learned a lot from Salinger's short stories; he did remove the short narrative from the wise-guy, slice-of-life stories of the thirties and forties. Like most innovative artists, he made new room for shapelessness, for life as it is lived. I'm thinking of a story like "Just Before the War with the Eskimos."

CRITICISM

William Rosencrans

Rosencrans is a writer and copy editor. In the following essay, he discusses literary technique in "Just Before the War with the Eskimos," focusing on Salinger's use of allusions to signal his narrow-minded heroine's coming of age.

Salinger's protagonists tend to wear their hearts on their sleeves. They have no time for society's dishonesties, its empty social gestures and endless compromises. The same holds true for his writing: it is known for a certain heartfelt sincerity, and never more so than when he is dealing with the theme that made him famous—the collision of young people with the adult world. The pleasure in reading Salinger often consists of the unpredictable dynamism of these collisions. Holden Caulfield of *The Catcher in the Rye* pinballs across New York City in a state of extraordinary mental tumult; Seymour Glass, in "A Perfect Day for Bananafish," is prey to strange and unnerving impulses, almost pedophilic and tragically suicidal. Ginnie Mannox, the fifteen-year-old heroine of "Just Before the War with the Eskimos," is another excellent example of the classic Salinger youth perched over the abyss of adulthood.

Unlike the rest of Salinger's coming-of-age protagonists, however, Ginnie starts off unaware of her quandary, and what makes this story stand out from Salinger's other writings is the process by which her eyes are opened to her place in the world. Essentially, she experiences what philosophers might call a

" NORMAL SOCIAL BARRIERS ARE APPARENTLY NONEXISTENT FOR FRANKLIN, AND HIS IGNORANCE OF THOSE BARRIERS LEAVES GINNIE OPEN TO THE TRUE AIMS OF THE STORY: TO RECOGNIZE THE LIMITS OF HER WORLD AND POINT OF VIEW, AND TO BEGIN EXPANDING THEM."

phenomenological awakening. After being treated to a series of teasingly brief glimpses into other people's lives, she recognizes herself as a single point of view, a limited perspective on the world, and realizes that other people, too, constitute single points of view; her appreciation of the broader world as rich and complex leads to a life-changing epiphany, all in a living room in New York City.

The story begins with a description of Ginnie and Selena's return from a tennis match, the fifth Saturday match in a row. The only other details Salinger offers about Ginnie's life are a mention of one of her family dinners and the fact that she is in school; these three details conjure a sense of circumscribed routine, of life limited by schedules and small social horizons. What remain are her impressions, opinions, and judgments about Selena's life and character, and they are, fittingly, small-minded. Salinger drops hints about Ginnie's personality that suggest something deeper: though her opinions occupy a fairly limited mental landscape, she is engagingly passionate about them, and his physical description of her ("At fifteen, Ginnie was about five feet nine in her 9-B tennis shoes, and as she entered the lobby, her self-conscious, rubber-soled awkwardness lent her a dangerous amateur quality") is both amusing and suggestive of the potential for change. Still, she occupies her small world with little curiosity, and once she is in Selena's apartment, waiting for her friend to come up with cab fare, she proceeds to dismantle this new world with gusto, "mentally rearranging furniture, throwing out table lamps, removing artificial flowers. In her opinion, it was an altogether hideous room—expensive but cheesy." There seems to be little room in her mind for anything but the confines she is accustomed to.

The rest of the story consists of two unexpected encounters, the first with Selena's brother Franklin and the second with his friend Eric. Over the course of the conversations she has with these young men, she is offered a succession of hints about the world beyond the one she has grown up in, and these hints, as much as the engaging aspects of Franklin's off-kilter mental state, are the catalysts for her sudden maturation.

Franklin is a disarming presence. Tall, stooped, in his pajamas and unshaven, his physicality is both repulsive and weirdly compelling. He has just cut his finger on a used razor blade while digging in a wastebasket, and obsesses over this for several pages. It is a curiously intimate topic for a conversation with a stranger, especially a young woman in 1948, but Ginnie is a captive audience and in short order finds herself offering medical advice, which he responds to with the gratitude and obedience of a child, though he is (we learn at the story's end) twenty-four. In the course of their conversation she watches him scratch at a red eruption on the skin of his ankle and is offered a half-eaten chicken sandwich. Normal social barriers are apparently nonexistent for Franklin, and his ignorance of those barriers leaves Ginnie open to the true aims of the story: to recognize the limits of her world and point of view, and to begin expanding them.

Franklin tosses the details of his life at her almost carelessly. After their introductions, he tells her that her sister is a snob, and when she responds angrily he steps up the tenor of his insults. Only later in their conversation does Ginnie remember to return to this topic, and he reveals that he wrote Ginnie's sister eight times without receiving a response. Ginnie never has the opportunity to learn what the story is behind these letters. It has been assumed, inevitably, by some critics that they were love letters, but given his peculiar personality they may simply have been efforts at establishing a friendship. Regardless, an unexplored world lies behind these very brief remarks, a small window through which Ginnie can peak at the terra incognita that his own life contains.

Their dialogue is full of these little windows. When she asks why he never called after his letters went unanswered, he tells her he was

WHAT DO I READ NEXT?

- In 1961 Salinger followed *Nine Stories* with *Franny and Zooey*, a novella and short story under a single cover, describing members of the Glass family, a fictional clan Salinger wrote about often. The book received mixed reviews but was a success with readers.
- *The Catcher in the Rye*, a novel published by Salinger in 1951, is perhaps the most famous exploration of teen angst and alienation ever written. This iconic tale has been banned more frequently than any other book in American public schools; it is simultaneously one of the most taught.
- For another classic coming-of-age story, readers can turn to *I Know Why the Caged Bird Sings* (1969), an autobiography by Maya Angelou. This tale of a young African American woman confronts challenging topics such as racism and rape and, like *The Catcher in the Rye*, has occasionally been the target of censorship.
- Sherman Alexie's *The Absolutely True Diary of a Part-Time Indian* (2007) tackles coming-of-age from a Native American perspective in a twenty-first-century setting. Reviewers praised its balance of humor and gritty realism.
- Salinger's daughter, Margaret Salinger, wrote about her childhood in the Salinger household in her autobiography, *Dream Catcher* (2000). Few knew the reclusive author as well as his daughter, and she offers an extremely personal portrait of him.
- *The Prime of Life: A History of Modern Adulthood* (2015), by Stephen Mintz, is a nonfiction work offering a historical perspective on the transition from adolescence to adulthood, detailing the basic cultural components of adulthood that have persisted over time and describing how the details have changed.
- In *Outsiders: A Collection of Fiction and Non-fiction* (2007), Roy Blatchford has gathered essays, poetry, fiction, and journalism about those who stand outside society. Divided into four sections—"Fictional Outsiders," "Heroes and Heroines," "Moving Places, Moving Lives," and "Feeling Different"—the collection includes texts by Harper Lee and others.

in Ohio. College? "Nope. Quit." Again, there is a whole story hidden behind those two words, one left for Ginnie to mull over later (as she no doubt will, given the interest she expresses in his background while saying goodbye to Selena). Army? "Nope. . . . Ticker." Here he offers the briefest explanation ("I had rheumatic fever when I was a kid") before Ginnie herself, fascinated, turns the topic back to Ohio. What was he doing there? "Working in a goddam airplane factory."

No sooner does she attempt to open that particular window a little wider than he directs his attention out of the real window in the apartment living room, surveying the street below. Here he offers her a truly intriguing glimpse into his inner life, asserting that the next war will be fought against the Eskimos, and that the armed forces for this war will consist of old men with reduced fighting hours. Is he being funny? Is he delusional? Again, there is no time for Ginnie to get to the bottom of things. Having delivered this odd little prophecy, he leaves to prepare for an unnamed visitor. He returns with a sandwich, which readers have analyzed endlessly; but whatever its deeper meaning, Franklin has already accomplished Salinger's goal. The boundaries of Ginnie's world are cracking, and by the end of the story they will lie in pieces.

Selena returns with the money she owes, but Ginnie will not take it *(©This Is Me / Shutterstock.com)*

Her next encounter repeats this same process, but in an absurdly accelerated fashion. Eric enters the living room with perfect timing, seconds after Franklin's exit, lending the story a comically theatrical touch. Eric is drawn in exceedingly broad literary strokes and is more a caricature than a fully fleshed-out character, and his presumed homosexuality, given Salinger's literary unease around the topic, is perhaps intended as a strike against him. Here again, however, his primary role is to offer Ginnie glimpses of a wider world.

The story's dominant literary device is on full display during this encounter. "This has been the most horrible morning of my entire life," he announces, in response to Ginnie's curiosity adding, "Oh. . . . It's too long a story." Ginnie probes again, and he tells her that after generously sharing his apartment with a writer for months, he has discovered that the young man robbed him and left. The brief tale is littered with little hints of other stories. The writer in question had a life of his own: he hailed from Altoona, Pennsylvania; Eric introduced him to theatrical producers, so evidently he was a playwright. Eric specifically mentions that this young man left the apartment cluttered with "*radishes*, and whatnot." The emphasis on radishes suggests a specific incident, as well. Virtually every sentence contains a detail with a larger story behind it lying just out of Ginnie's reach.

After a brief detour on the topic of camel's hair coats, he asks if Ginnie is "the famous *Maxine* that Selena talks about." But, in keeping with Salinger's technique, the topic of the mysterious Maxine is abandoned immediately after its introduction.

Eric ends with a series of references to the history of his friendship with Franklin. He has arrived to take Franklin to see *Beauty and the Beast*; during the war, Franklin took him to see distinctly lowbrow fare ("gangster pictures, Western pictures, *musicals*"), and Eric, too, worked at the airplane factory. They have known each other, then, for some time. But, as with Franklin's letters to Ginnie's sister, nothing can be gleaned from these details with certainty. Some read a homosexual affair into his friendship with Eric, but it is safer simply to acknowledge yet another long and unknowable story here, a sign of the infinite stories the world has to offer.

In a painting, aspects of the scene suggesting a story are referred to as anecdotal details. There is no literary term for "brief allusions to backstories." The term for a story within a story is *metadiagesis*, whose root word, *diagesis*, means simply "narrative" but is derived from a Greek verb which means "guiding through." While this term is not exactly appropriate here, since Ginnie is offered numerous hints at backstories rather than the stories themselves, they do serve to "guide her through" her limitations.

Selena enters the room, ending Ginnie's encounter with Eric, but by this time her transformation has been accomplished. There has yet been no outward evidence of it (save her acceptance of a distinctly unappetizing sandwich half from Franklin, accepted so as not to cause offense); but Salinger signifies this transformation with a startling change in her attitude toward Selena, whom she held in such withering disdain at the story's outset. It may well be that she is merely using Selena to stay in contact with Franklin; the reader must be content to infer.

Most scholarship on this story grapples with the last line: "A few years before, it had taken her three days to dispose of the Easter chick she had found dead on the sawdust in the bottom of her wastebasket." The story is rich with symbolism and worth symbolic analysis. But the technique Salinger uses is equal in depth to his symbolism, and even the symbol of that Easter chick is an example of this literary technique: it suggests a world beyond the pages of the story which the reader, limited like Ginnie to his or her own experience of the world, can only wonder at.

Source: William Rosencrans, Critical Essay on "Just Before the War with the Eskimos," in *Short Stories for Students*, Gale, Cengage Learning, 2017.

John Wenke

In the following excerpt, Wenke examines the collection Nine Stories *as a whole.*

With the 31 January 1948 publication of "A Perfect Day for Bananafish" Salinger initiated a practice that would continue for 15 years: the publication of his short fiction in periodicals would be followed by hardback (and then paperback) collections. Had Salinger drawn his line a month earlier, *Ten Stories* would have included "The Inverted Forest." We have nine stories rather than eleven or

"HOWEVER FRIGHTENING, THE WORLD MUST REMAIN OPEN. IT IS FROM THIS PERSPECTIVE, THEN, THAT SALINGER OFFERS A SEQUENCE OF TALES THAT EXCITE, EVEN AS THEY FRUSTRATE, THE ACTIVITY OF READING."

twelve because Salinger did not collect "A Girl I Knew" and "Blue Melody," both of which appeared after "A Perfect Day." Clearly, Salinger chose the stories he wished to stand on.

Once collected, these nine stories lost their vagrant, and separate, existences as periodical pieces and became part of a sequence. Each story assumes a relationship with its companion pieces. But how does one approach a collection? Does one see the stories as constituting a version of the novel? Are they merely stories that the author admired enough to collect? What is the cumulative effect of disparate tales on related themes?

Such questions have invited vexed critical inquiry into matters of theme and genre. Warren French, for example, argues for what he calls a short story cycle with a "progression based upon the slow and painful achievement of spiritual enlightenment" (1988, 63–64). French sees the stories as parts of an ordered thematic continuum with a beginning, middle, and end. James E. Miller, Jr., finds alienation to be Salinger's dominant theme, giving "the volume a singleness of impact which belies its multiplicity." Without question, *Nine Stories* resonates with those thematic complexes which animate the uncollected stories. For example, Salinger explores the conflict between the innocent, if problematic, world of children and the decadent, sterile world of adulthood ("A Perfect Day," "Uncle Wiggily in Connecticut," "The Laughing Man," "Down at the Dinghy," "For Esmé—with Love and Squalor"); the alienation of a postadolescent youth not yet initiated into manhood ("Just before the War with the Eskimos," "The Laughing Man," "De Daumier-Smith's Blue Period"); the ravages of war as a source of psychological breakdown ("A Perfect Day," "For Esmé"); and the use of cryptic fables and self-reflexive fiction-making ("A Perfect Day," "The Laughing Man"). Revealing his preoccupation with human beings living in the aftermath of some fall from a once-saving grace, Salinger presents in *every* story some version of a lost idyll, lost innocence, lost past, or lost opportunity. Indeed Salinger's characters frequently seem like posthumous survivors of a better world. It is also possible to view *Nine Stories* as being unified by Salinger's devotion to characters who belong to a recognizable socioeconomic world. They are white upper-middle-class residents of New York City or the surrounding suburbs. If Salinger's characters are on vacation, as they are in "A Perfect Day," "Down at the Dinghy," and "Teddy," or at war, as Sergeant X is in "For Esmé," then they are only temporarily displaced.

The presence of related themes, characters, and settings does not settle the issue of genre, the matter of what happens when one puts distinctive short stories together in the same book. On what aesthetic ground does one stand? Regardless of the reaches of critical ingenuity, *Nine Stories* can be classed neither as a novel nor as a serial story, nor, I submit, as reflecting an intelligible thematic organization with a beginning, middle, and end. The primary danger of pursuing self-contained artistic unity as a desirable critical goal derives from privileging the problematic New Critical axiom that successful works of literary art possess demonstrably coherent and cohesive structures. Second, applying such an axiom to a collection of stories presupposes that there is such a thing as The Novel (there are only multiple versions of novelized form) and that The Novel is the standard form to which modern prose fiction aspires. Once one points out that *Nine Stories* begins with the account of Seymour Glass's suicide and ends with Teddy's probable, though unconfirmed, death, one has little to go on regarding plot.

Nine Stories, as a whole, has its generic analogue not in well-wrought novels but in those fictional domains which create the context for establishing interconnections yet steadfastly refuse to impose the fiction of completed wholeness. As a collection, *Nine Stories* should be classed with such modernist works as James Joyce's *Dubliners*; Sherwood Anderson's *Winesburg, Ohio*; Ernest Hemingway's *In Our Time*; William Faulkner's *Go Down, Moses*; and Eudora Welty's *The Golden Apples*. Contemporary collections that suggest relationships but deny narrative completion can be found in John Barth's *Lost in the Funhouse*, Susan Minot's *Monkeys*, Lee K. Abbott's *Strangers in Paradise*, and Richard Ford's *Rock Springs*. Barth presents a series of self-reflexive, ingenious narrative frames; Minot's Vincent family, living north of Boston, provides the focus for nine teasingly short stories; Abbott depicts the doings of hell-raisers, desperadoes, obsessives, and loners in the country-club desertlands of Deming, New Mexico; Ford explores the monotones of assorted Montana lowlifes who grope toward the wisdom that is sadness. Like *Nine Stories*, these works evoke the presence of an encompassing fictional world where characters in one tale would be (and sometimes are) at home in another. What is crucial is that the authors refuse to impose the fiction of closure. Instead they celebrate the entanglement of many loose ends. Rather than supporting the notion of unity and resolution, these collections, and *Nine Stories* in particular, raise possibilities but frustrate hopes for full disclosure. The tales tend to conclude with open-ended suggestion and sometimes even epiphany. What always looms is the blank space between stories.

One has intimations of a larger, more complex world operating beyond the confines of the present narrative. For example, in *Nine Stories* four members of the Glass family appear or are mentioned: Seymour in "A Perfect Day," Walt in "Uncle Wiggily," and Boo Boo and Webb (presumably Buddy) in "Down at the Dinghy." Questions arise that are never addressed. What, for instance, is the significance of Lionel's attachment to the late Seymour's diving goggles in "Down at the Dinghy"? Is it a mere detail? Does it make Boo Boo afraid that Lionel might eventually share his uncle's fate? The appearance of family members in separate stories suggests a complex ongoing life that remains unreported. These connected stories—as in Joyce, Salinger, Ford—attempt to render life as a series of loose-fitting fragments. The encompassing form—suggested by titles that are matter-of-fact (*Nine Stories*), geographical (*Dubliners*, *Rock Springs*), or symbolic (*Strangers in Paradise*)—identify the perimeters within which the juxtaposition of related themes or characters will deny aesthetic closure.

The famous epigraph to *Nine Stories*—"We know the sound of two hands clapping. / But what is the sound of one hand clapping?"—provides access to Salinger's mysterious and open-ended narratives. The epigraph is a Zen koan, an epigrammatic form designed to eclipse the pursuit of solutions through logic and rationality. Its prominent placement has invited speculation regarding the relationship between Eastern thought and these stories about urbane Americans, especially insofar as Eastern philosophy offers a religious and experiential alternative to materialistic America. As James Lundquist remarks, "The word *Zen* means thinking, meditation, to see, to contemplate." A koan offers an intense focus for this meditative process. Salinger's epigraph seems to be a riddle that has no solution per se: Is silence the sound of one hand clapping? Is it the sound a tree makes when it falls in the forest with no one there to hear? In focusing meditation, any koan releases the tranquil play of mind. Ostensibly, the koan presents a riddle; actually, it constitutes an approach to experience: intuitive rather than rational, poetic rather than empirical, connotative rather than denotative. A koan opens one's being to the impress of intuition, which achieves its most conscious expression through the experience of epiphany. Many of the nine stories turn on a character's apparently stunning realization. Often the character achieves such insight in response to some physical object: the intoxicated Eloise in "Uncle Wiggily" weeps over her daughter's eyeglasses; Sergeant X begins to regain his faculties after unwrapping the gift from Esmé. Such moments of awakening have their counterpoint in more cryptic endings usually characterized by odd, disjunctive events. At the end of "Just before the War," Ginnie decides to keep Franklin's chicken sandwich, an act that presumably has something to do with the fact that it once took her three days to dispose of a dead Easter chick. Booper's scream at the end of "Teddy" suggests (but does not confirm) that she, as Teddy had predicted, shoved him into an empty swimming pool.

At issue is Salinger's insistence on interpretive openness, an antidote, as it were, to Holden Caulfield's rigid and prescribed reading of the world. Holden views himself, for example, as a self-proclaimed Messiah, a catcher of children who might otherwise tumble off "some crazy cliff" (*Catcher*). His realization that he has to let the children fall constitutes an acceptance of random cause and effect. However frightening, the world must remain open. It is from this perspective, then, that Salinger offers a sequence of tales that excite, even as they frustrate, the activity of reading. . . .

Source: John Wenke, "The Short Fiction: *Nine Stories*," in *J. D. Salinger: A Study of the Short Fiction*, Twayne, 1991, pp. 31–34.

SOURCES

French, Warren, *J. D. Salinger*, Twayne Publishers, 1963, pp. 87–89.

Gross, Joe, "More to Salinger Than the Genius in the Rye," in *Austin American-Statesman*, January 28, 2010, http://www.statesman.com/news/news/national/more-to-salinger-than-the-genius-in-the-rye/nRhjh/ (accessed July 8, 2016).

Gwynn, Frederick L., and Blotner, Joseph, "All His Faculties Intact: The Classic Period (1948–1951)," in *The Fiction of J. D. Salinger*, University of Pittsburgh Press, 1958, pp. 23–24.

Hamilton, Ian, *In Search of J. D. Salinger*, Random House, 1988, p. 113.

Hassan, Ihab, "The Rare Quixotic Gesture," in *Salinger: A Critical and Personal Portrait*, edited by Henry Anatole Grunwald, Harper & Brothers, 1962, p. 146.

Lundquist, James, *J. D. Salinger*, Frederick Ungar Publishing, 1979, pp. 90–92.

Robson, Leo, "To Have and to Holden," in *New Statesman*, February 4, 2010, http://www.newstatesman.com/books/2010/02/salinger-holden-rye-catcher (accessed July 16, 2016).

Salinger, J. D., "Just Before the War with the Eskimos," in *Nine Stories*, Little, Brown, 1953, pp. 57–82.

Salinger, Margaret A., *Dream Catcher: A Memoir*, Washington Square Press, 2000, p. 55.

Samuels, Charles Thomas, "John Updike: The Art of Fiction No. 43," in *Paris Review*, No. 45, Winter 1968, http://www.theparisreview.org/interviews/4219/the-art-of-fiction-no-43-john-updike (accessed July 3, 2016).

Slawenski, Kenneth, *J. D. Salinger: A Life*, Random House, 2010, pp. 170–71, 249.

FURTHER READING

Baxter, Kent, *The Modern Age: Turn-of-the-Century American Culture and the Invention of Adolescence*, University of Alabama Press, 2008.

This book examines the ways in which America has conceived of the notion of adolescence itself, analyzing it as a cultural invention in response to specific anxieties present in American society. Among other accomplishments, *The Modern Age* forces a useful reevaluation of the very concept of coming-of-age novels, especially as written in the very cultural environment Baxter critiques.

Foertsch, Jacqueline, *American Culture in the 1940s*, Edinburgh University Press, 2008.

Foertsch's book provides an overview of American culture across the decade in which Salinger first began publishing, covering literature, film, music, pop culture, politics, and much else. The book is a valuable companion piece to "Just Before the War with the Eskimos," placing the story's teenage protagonist in cultural context.

Grunwald, Henry Anatole, ed., *Salinger: A Critical and Personal Portrait*, Harper & Brothers, 1962.

This collection of critical essays brings together John Updike, Alfred Kazin, Arthur Mizener, and two dozen other writers whose essays range from the scholarly to the subjective. The negative tone in some of the essays will come as a surprise to many readers, but it remains the best-known collection of literary criticism on Salinger.

Slawenski, Kenneth, *J. D. Salinger: A Life*, Random House, 2010.

Salinger was notorious for his fierce love of privacy, which posed an obvious difficulty for his biographers. Slawenski's book succeeds in assembling a complete and in-depth portrait, uncovering hitherto unknown details about his life. Reviewers especially praised the book's treatment of Salinger's experiences as a soldier in World War II.

Trites, Roberta Seelinger, *Disturbing the Universe: Power and Repression in Adolescent Literature*, University of Iowa Press, 2000.

Trites explores the ways in which adolescents are both liberated and oppressed as they come of age in young-adult literature, especially in contemporary novels. An in-depth analysis making use of literary theory via thinkers like Jacques Lacan and Michel Foucault, the book is challenging but has been well received by critics and readers.

SUGGESTED SEARCH TERMS

Just Before the War with the Eskimos

Salinger AND coming of age

Salinger AND war

Salinger AND symbolism

adolescence

adolescence AND adulthood

outsider AND society

outsider AND society AND fiction

Kindred Spirits

ALICE WALKER

1985

Alice Walker's short story "Kindred Spirits," first published in *Esquire* in 1985 and later collected in *The Way Forward Is with a Broken Heart* in 2000, reveals the hidden fault lines in the life of a newly divorced writer coming to terms with the loss of her grandfather. With the realization that her family resents her for using their lives as fodder for her stories, Rosa reels with the sudden knowledge that she is a human recording device—taking in details and never forgetting—as cold and hard as a camera's armored body. Winner of the 1986 O. Henry Award, "Kindred Spirits" explores family dynamics, love, heartbreak, the scars of racial segregation, and pollution, both physical and spiritual.

AUTHOR BIOGRAPHY

Walker was born in Eatonton, Georgia, on February 9, 1944, the last of Minnie Lou Tallulah Grant and Willie Lee Walker's eight children. Walker was blinded in her right eye in 1952 after one of her brothers shot her with a BB gun by accident. The injury to her eye caused scar tissue to form, making Walker self-conscious of her appearance. She turned inward, writing down her thoughts and feelings as poetry to escape the daily torment of bullies. Though she was homecoming queen and valedictorian, Walker remained devoted

Alice Walker (©Peter Kramer / Getty Images Entertainment / Getty Images)

to solitude, reading and writing throughout high school. She first attended Spelman College, in Atlanta, before transferring to Sarah Lawrence College, outside New York City, graduating with a bachelor's degree in 1965. A political activist, she returned to Georgia to participate in the civil rights movement, registering black voters in Liberty County. In Jackson, Mississippi, she met a Jewish civil rights leader named Melvyn Rosenman Leventhal, whom she married on March 17, 1967. They became the first married interracial couple in the state and had a daughter, Rebecca, in 1969.

Walker published her first novel, *The Third Life of Grange Copeland*, in 1970. In 1973, she uncovered the unmarked grave of Zora Neale Hurston, and in 1975 her article in *Ms.* magazine, "In Search of Zora Neale Hurston," was responsible for reviving academic interest in the forgotten literary legend. Her second novel, *Meridian*, was published in 1976. That same year, Walker and her husband divorced, prompting her move to California.

In 1982, Walker published *The Color Purple*, securing her place in American literary history and skyrocketing her to international fame. Walker became the first African American woman to win the Pulitzer Prize for Fiction as well as the National Book Award, both awarded to her in 1983. In 1985, the novel was adapted into a film by Steven Spielberg, starring Whoopi Goldberg. Also in 1985, "Kindred Spirits" was published in *Esquire*; it earned the O. Henry Award in 1986.

Walker was awarded an honorary degree from the California Institute of the Arts in 1995. The American Humanist Organization named Walker "Humanist of the Year" in 1997. In 2000, "Kindred Spirits" was published as part of Walker's collection *The Way Forward Is with a Broken Heart*. In 2005, a musical production of *The Color Purple*, which ran until 2008, debuted at Broadway Theatre in New York City, earning a Tony Award for best leading actress in a musical in 2006. The musical's revival in 2015 also earned a Tony Award for best leading actress in a musical as well as the award for best revival of a musical. Walker was inducted into the Georgia Writers Hall of Fame in 2001 and the California Hall of Fame in 2006. One hundred twenty-two boxes of her papers are collected at Emory University's Stuart A. Rose Manuscript, Archives, and Rare Book Library. An active voice in global human rights campaigns, Walker received the Domestic Human Rights Award from Global Exchange in 2007 and the LennonOno Grant for Peace award in 2010. She has taught African American and women's studies at Brandeis University, the University of California at Berkeley, the University of Massachusetts at Boston, Wellesley College, and Yale University.

PLOT SUMMARY

On a plane with her sister, Rosa cannot find the courage to admit how grateful she is to have Barbara's company or how scared she would be if she had to make the trip alone. Instead, the two sisters make small talk. Rosa gazes out the window at the clouds, thinking of how the trip is months too late but nevertheless sentimental. She is visiting her aunt's house, where her grandfather died.

She has traveled the world this summer, making stops in Cyprus, Greece, and Jamaica. Following her divorce from her husband, Ivan, she has felt as if she has no home. She left him with their house in Park Slope (Brooklyn), their car, and even the cat. Their child has been away at summer camp. Rosa has trouble sleeping; when she does sleep, she has cold, empty dreams filled with static. She eats spaghetti and shrimp, always listening to the jazz station on the radio with "her heart in her mouth."

Barbara asks after Ivan. She liked her brother-in-law and wishes he had not disappeared so thoroughly from their lives after the divorce. Rosa and Ivan were an interracial couple, and Ivan "sunk back into the white world so completely that even a Christmas card was too much trouble to send people who had come to love him." He lives with a Jewish woman now, which, Rosa realizes, explains why he has not sent any Christmas cards. Barbara asks what the woman is like. Rosa answers that she is kind, good-looking, and loves him, though in fact she is guessing, having only met Ivan's new girlfriend once. But she hopes this is true. The woman, Sheila, moved into the house Rosa shared with Ivan only a week after Rosa left it. Ivan's family seems to like Sheila, especially his mother. Once, after Rosa borrowed the car (though the car, in reality, belonged to her), she returned to the house to find a party inside and her former mother-in-law and Sheila blocking the front gate so that she could not enter. They seemed happy to unite against her.

Rosa tells herself that she does not care because she is free. She walked away from that scene, her high-heel boots' clicking on the sidewalk like the sound of freedom. She calmed the beating of her heart down by sheer will—but at night awoke to find her heart still thumping, "rattling and crackling." Barbara tells Rosa that their mother misses Ivan. Rosa knows this is true, but her mother could not understand that Ivan was guilty of not caring about her the way she cared about him. When the mother suffered a series of strokes following the divorce, Ivan never called to ask if she was okay.

The plane begins to land in Miami. Barbara and Rosa switch seats so that Barbara may watch the landing. Rosa has traveled so frequently in the past months that she no longer cares to watch the descent. The trip to Cyprus had tested her patience. In Nicosia the temperature had reached 120 degrees. She visited refugee camps and spoke to a Socialist family whose son had been assassinated by mistake at a rally after standing beside a party leader. His father openly wept for the loss of his only son, wishing he had many more. Afterward Rosa traveled to Greece, where Athens was hot beyond belief and the Parthenon was disappointingly small in real life.

At the airport, Barbara and Rosa look with the eyes of those who once knew segregation: "Their formative years had been lived under racist restrictions so pervasive that wherever they traveled in the world they expected . . . to encounter some, if only symbolic, racial barrier." Rosa spots it: an advertisement on which a white couple dances to a black band while a black waiter and chef smile happily at them. A tall woman in a blue cotton dress meets them at the airport: Barbara and Rosa's aunt Lily. Barbara hugs Aunt Lily in a happy greeting. Rosa lets herself be hugged next, inhaling the perfume and thinking how her aunt is always changing. Rosa remembers as a child being impressed by Aunt Lily's power compared with her husband, who always seemed the less dominant partner in their relationship. She thinks about how Aunt Lily in all her neatness and perfect posture was once oppressed under segregation, banned from trying on a dress at the department store or eating at a nice restaurant or even drinking at the same fountain as a white person. Aunt Lily drives them to her house in her enormous brown station wagon. Barbara sits in the front seat, as she is both older than Rosa and closer to their aunt. Rosa watches the scenery pass, thinking of the city's sewage problems that trouble the otherwise beautiful canals.

They are greeted by five of Aunt Lily's seven foster children, as well as a young woman named Raymyna Ann, who was once fostered by Aunt Lily but now shares the house with her, helping to care for the others. After losing her baby son, Aunt Lily had seemed for years to not care for children, making her generosity toward these children a surprise. Though she is not physically affectionate, there is always food on the table, clean sheets, and hot baths. That night, Aunt Lily appears in Rosa's bedroom door to ask her not to smoke in the house. Rosa puts her cigarette out but reminds Aunt Lily she used to be a smoker, too. Aunt Lily says that was just a lie her mother told

Rosa, and Rosa realizes from her tone that Aunt Lily does not like her mother. That night, unable to sleep, she wonders why. She also wonders why Ivan does not like her anymore, after living with her and loving her for over ten years. She does not understand how, as soon as the divorce was settled, Ivan no longer seemed to care about her at all. She thought the marriage was perfect. It was only the divorce that was bad, and losing Ivan's friendship was the worst part of all.

Two weeks after their divorce, Rosa was hospitalized for surgery. Ivan did not call or send a note. Years later, he would explain to Rosa that Sheila would not have liked it. By then, Sheila would be his wife, and they would have a large family together. The next morning while the children are away at school, Barbara combs and braids Aunt Lily's hair while Rosa watches. Raymyna does household chores and fetches them water. She will soon be married, with a house of her own. Though Rosa does not react outwardly to this news, she is secretly surprised that anyone would get married, now that she has divorced. She feels no happiness at the idea of another poor black woman getting married and starting a family. Then she chastises herself for such a cynical attitude. When she was married, she loved it. She loved her family, too.

The women go sightseeing that afternoon. Rosa cannot stop thinking of the pollution in the area, too distracted to admire any of the natural beauty she sees: "In their attempt to hog it away from the poor, the black and the local in general, the beachfront 'developers' had erected massive boxlike hotels that blocked the view of the water." Only those rich enough, Rosa reflects bitterly, can walk on the eroded beaches. That night at dinner Rosa explains why she did not come to her grandfather's funeral. She had received the news just before leaving for Cyprus and regretted traveling away from rather than toward the funeral, but she found that she could not stop. She had spent too much time and energy planning her trip. Also, she could not bear to see her family so soon after the divorce from Ivan. Barbara and Aunt Lily let her speak. They do not know where Cyprus is or the political situation there, which does not surprise Rosa. She explains about the Socialist man whose son died and how he seemed to care nothing for his surviving daughters. She tells them that women have little value there.

Aunt Lily tells her nieces that after her mother died she brought her father, their grandfather, home to live with her. She told him there was to be no smoking or drinking in the house. Rosa remembers how her grandfather had always smoked cigars. She liked the smell. Aunt Lily goes on to say she banned card playing, noise, and complaining as well. Rosa knows that her brothers and sisters had visited him, but she had felt afraid. Yet in pictures he seemed so happy: "A deeply silent man with those odd peaceful eyes—she did not know, and she was confident her aunt didn't, what he really thought about anything." Rosa does not understand Aunt Lily's restrictions on him, as he seemed happiest when left alone. Rosa believes and hopes that he liked her, though he never said he did. He never gave her more than fifteen cents, but he paid for Barbara's trade-school education after her father refused to do so. Rosa cannot decide what it is that made her turn her back on his funeral. She had no excuse and knew that at the time.

That night, she looks at her own face in the mirror. She sees similarities between her grandfather and herself. She looks the way he did when he was spiritually and physically exhausted: "It was there in her eyes. So clearly. The look of abandonment. Of having no support. Of loneliness so severe every minute was a chant against self-destruction."

She massages her sister's shoulders before bed, feeling as if they are strangers without a meaningful connection. She used to visit Barbara when she was attending college. She was there when Barbara's husband beat her and locked them both out of the house. She had stood nearby while Barbara gave the police her report, though Rosa was embarrassed that something so gauche could be happening in their well-respected family. Rosa watched Barbara suffer from her husband's beatings for years, until Rosa wanted to kill him just to free her sister. More than anything, she was disappointed in Barbara for her life choices that made her seem a polluted version of the sister Rosa had grown up beside.

Barbara's helplessness disturbed Rosa, but so did her own inaction. She had once defended her sister from their father with a butcher knife, but she had never gotten between Barbara and her husband with similar ferocity. The incident with their father had come as a result of Barbara's refusal to attend the funeral of a church elder because she wanted to go to her little brother's grammar-school graduation instead. Their father had slapped her, and Rosa had stepped between them with the knife. She could have killed him if she were stronger. Rosa considers what her life would have been like if she had killed him. Thinking of Barbara standing up to their father on that day, Rosa cries. Barbara had attended the funeral with makeup covering the handprint on her cheek.

She was too young then to understand how her life would change. Rosa holds on to this as a reason she did not interfere later, hearing Barbara and her husband fight. She could not kill him as an adult, knowing the consequences of such an action. In her inaction, she became silent like her grandfather, hiding how her guilt tainted her feelings of love for Barbara. She equates silence with her powerlessness and disappointment. Though he had grown up in the South in the early twentieth century, her grandfather rarely mentioned his past. Instead, he complained so bitterly about his wife, Rosa's grandmother, that the family began to dislike her as well. However, after she died, the house they shared seemed empty and cold.

Aunt Lily gives her nieces their grandfather's remaining possessions. Barbara receives his trunk. Rosa is given his shaving mirror. They split his collection of handkerchiefs. The only items left are two hats, a brown and a gray fedora. Rosa tries one on and adores how she looks like her grandfather in it. She cannot believe how much she loves him despite his stinginess and cruelty toward their grandmother. But he was also a beautiful person: "Peaceful, mystical almost in his silences and calm, and she realized he was imprinted on her heart just that way. It really did not seem fair." To keep herself from crying, she asks Aunt Lily what her father was like when he was a boy. Aunt Lily looks at her with open hatred and tells her she should have asked him when he was alive. Without Barbara, who has gone to the bathroom, Rosa starts to cry. Aunt Lily is unaffected, telling Rosa not to use her as a character in her work and to leave her father out as well.

Rosa flees the room. She walks in on Barbara in the bathroom, forgetting that they are full-grown adults who do not invade each other's privacy. She remembers how she had thrown a handful of sand at a white man who had nearly run Barbara, their cousin, and herself over with his car. The man confronted her, but Barbara told the man that Rosa had not thrown any sand. He drove off angry. From this, Rosa learned that Barbara could get her out of any trouble, even trouble caused by an angry white man who was mad at a little girl.

However, the way Barbara looks at Rosa in the bathroom tells her that Barbara overheard and agrees with Aunt Lily. Rosa is a known snoop and has embarrassed her family in writing before. Rosa is like a meter that records every word said to her, rather than like a person who listens and cares. Rosa cannot help herself: "She could no more stop the meter running than she could stop her breath." Suddenly, she laughs, realizing that her grandfather was the same way. Though he did not write, she is sure he composed stories in his thoughts, during the long silences he favored. Rather than share them and embarrass others as Rosa did, he kept his stories private. On the plane home, she sits with one of his hats on her head and the other in her lap, thinking that she and her grandfather were kindred spirits. She has uncovered their mysterious connection.

She thinks of Ivan, who she once thought was her kindred spirit. She realizes that maybe Ivan is simply a bad person—his every action is not worth plumbing for meaning. She feels as if her life could not get any worse. She has not looked at Barbara since meeting her eyes in the bathroom. She knows that she will never see Aunt Lily again or attend her funeral. She thinks, too, that she will never write about her. She strokes the felt of the hat in her lap. Her reflection in the shaving mirror tells her that she is at the very end of her rope emotionally. She thinks she might slide away into silence and find happiness there, but just as she is about to disconnect from the world completely, Barbara puts the other hat on and takes Rosa's hand.

CHARACTERS

Barbara

Barbara is Rosa's older sister. She is forty-one years old. Her husband is abusive, but she continually forgives him. Rosa is ashamed of the kind of foul language Barbara uses during fights with her husband. Their father once slapped Barbara, and Rosa stepped in to defend her with a butcher knife. Barbara once stood up to an angry white man who was mad at Rosa for throwing dirt at his car. Barbara is well liked by Aunt Lily and shares her opinion that Rosa snoops too much in their family history, embarrassing them when her stories are published. However, she puts on one of their grandfather's hats at the end of the story and takes Rosa's hand to show her that she is still loved.

Barbara's Husband

Barbara's husband is abusive toward her. Though Rosa has been present for many of their fights, she has never attempted to intervene, but she wishes she could kill him.

Charlie

Charlie was Aunt Lily's husband, now deceased. He gave the impression of being the weaker partner in their relationship.

Cousin

Barbara and Rosa's cousin is with them the day the white man almost hits the girls with his car as they walk on the side of the road.

Father

Rosa and Barbara's father, who has died, was abusive. Aunt Lily is protective of his memory when Rosa asks what he was like as a little boy. She tells Rosa not to write about her father's life.

Grandfather

Rosa feels connected to her grandfather while visiting the house where he was living when he died. Though he was cruel to his grandmother and stingy with his money, Rosa remembers his long silences as having an admirable, deep quality. She realizes that he was like her—an observer detached from the world around him. Rosa did not attend his funeral.

Grandmother

Rosa and Barbara's grandmother was treated poorly by her husband, who believed she was not intelligent and spread this belief among their extended family. However, after her death the house where they lived seemed cold and empty.

Ivan

Ivan is Rosa's ex-husband. A white man, he was never fully accepted by Rosa's extended family, though Barbara and Rosa's mother adored him. After the divorce he became emotionally distanced from Rosa. One week after they divorced, his new girlfriend, Sheila, moved into the house he had shared with Rosa. Rosa and Ivan have a child together.

Ivan's Mother

Ivan's mother likes Sheila more than Rosa. She and Sheila bar Rosa from entering the house where Rosa once lived with Ivan.

Aunt Lily

Aunt Lily is Rosa and Barbara's aunt on their father's side. She is neat and upright in all things that she does. When her husband, Charlie, was alive, she was the dominant partner in their relationship. After she lost a baby son, she seemed to dislike children during Rosa's childhood. However, she has seven foster children when Rosa visits her as an adult. After her mother died, Aunt Lily took her father into her home. He died while he was living at her house. Aunt Lily has strict rules for the people who stay with her, including her own father, who was not allowed to smoke, drink, play cards, or make noise. Aunt Lily likes Barbara but feels contempt for Rosa. She sees Rosa as a snoop who feels no shame at exposing their family's secrets through her writing. She demands that Rosa never use her life in one of her stories.

Mama

Mama is Barbara and Rosa's mother. Aunt Lily does not like her, though Barbara does not know why. She dotes on Ivan and has recently suffered a series of strokes.

Man

The man almost hits Barbara, Rosa, and their cousin as they walk down a dirt road when they are young. When Rosa throws dirt at his car, he pulls over and gets out to confront her. However, Barbara stands up for her sister in the face of his anger, and he drives away.

Raymyna Ann

Raymyna was once a foster child of Aunt Lily's. Now grown, she lives with Lily to help with the children. However, she is to be married in a few weeks and will have a house of her own.

Rosa

Rosa is a thirty-five-year-old writer recently divorced from her husband, Ivan. She has a cool and detached personality because she is a practiced observer of the world around her. However, owing to her fragile emotional state following the divorce, her observations are tainted by cynicism and negativity. She has a child at summer camp and a sister, Barbara, whom she loves dearly but feels disconnected from emotionally. She is heartbroken by the fact that her ex-husband did not contact her after her recent surgery or after her mother's series of strokes. She is concerned with pollution, not only in the canals of Miami but also in people. For example, she sees Barbara as a polluted version of her former self.

She is especially interested in life under segregation, which she experienced as a child and under which her older relatives lived for much of their lives. She can no longer sleep through the night, a victim of racing thoughts as she tries to piece together the mysteries of her divorce. She traveled the world after moving out of the house she shared with Ivan, though it came at the cost of missing her grandfather's funeral. Once at her Aunt Lily's house, however, she feels a strong connection to his memory, even if he was often cruel and unsympathetic. After Aunt Lily rejects her, exposing a family prejudice against Rosa because of her writing, Rosa realizes that her grandfather was an observer too. She thinks she looks like her grandfather and enjoys wearing his hats. They carry a similar look of exhaustion in their eyes. Barbara saves her at the last moment from her downward spiral, becoming the living kindred spirit Rosa feels she lacks.

Rosa's Child

Rosa's child is away at summer camp. Ivan is the child's father.

Sheila

Sheila, a friendly Jewish woman, is at first Ivan's new girlfriend. She becomes Ivan's wife, and they have children together.

Socialist Father

The father of a boy who was shot at a Socialist rally mourns the loss of his son. He wishes he had more sons, tormented by the fact that he has only daughters left.

Socialist Son

The only son of a Socialist family in Cyprus is accidentally assassinated at a rally while standing next to a Socialist leader.

THEMES

Bereavement

In "Kindred Spirits," Rosa mourns not only the loss of her grandfather but also the loss of her husband and former life as a married woman. She skips her grandfather's funeral, only to return full of regret to the house where he died. She has only her memories of her grandfather left, just as she has been unexpectedly left with only her memories of her husband. Ivan will no longer speak to her, and she left the house they shared with few of her possessions. She mourns the loss of their friendship, struggling to understand how he has lost his once powerful feelings toward her. At the same time she mourns her grandfather, wondering why she feels such a strong connection to him after his death when they had not been close while he was alive. While the other members of her family were capable of mourning appropriately by attending his funeral, Rosa—embarking on a postdivorce world tour—founds that she could not face her family twice-bereaved, when many had not seen her since the divorce. After Aunt Lily rejects her, Rosa mourns her own life—lonely and disconnected without a kindred spirit to understand her troubles. As she begins to succumb to her grief once and for all, Barbara saves her sister by volunteering to be her kindred spirit and her shoulder to cry on until she has the strength again to bear the heavy weight of her losses.

Family

Family is a central theme in this story, as Rosa feels isolated from her relatives as well as her family by marriage following her recent divorce. Aunts, grandparents, mothers, fathers, siblings, in-laws, and children all play an important role in the story as Rosa remembers the relationships of her past that have led to her current state of despair. Ivan's family is more welcoming to his new girlfriend than they were to Rosa, while Rosa's family still cares for Ivan despite what Rosa believes are his obvious flaws. Rosa, Ivan,

TOPICS FOR FURTHER STUDY

- Read Sharon G. Flake's young-adult novel *The Skin I'm In* (1998). What comparison can you draw between the women of "Kindred Spirits" and Mrs. Saunders, Maleeka, and Maleeka's mother? How is mourning depicted in the novel versus the short story? Write an essay in which you compare and contrast the two works with special focus on the protagonists.
- Research the history of interracial marriage online. How long has interracial marriage been legal in the United States? What Supreme Court case is responsible for overturning earlier laws against interracial marriage? What were the details of the case and the positions of the justices? How were interracial couples punished or discriminated against under the law before the Supreme Court declared their marriages legal? Write a few paragraphs answering these questions in preparation for a class discussion. Be sure to note your sources at the bottom of the page.
- Create a blog in which you explore the history of racial segregation in the United States. In a minimum of five posts, define and explain segregation, Jim Crow laws, and either *Plessy v. Ferguson* or *Brown v. Board of Education*. Dedicate at least one post to exploring one of the specific aspects of segregation mentioned in "Kindred Spirits"—for example, the establishment of separate water fountains for blacks and whites or segregated restaurants. Include links to relevant articles as well as photos or videos you find relevant to your definitions. Free blogspace is available at Blogger.
- Read Walker's short story "To My Young Husband," which precedes "Kindred Spirits" in *The Way Forward Is with a Broken Heart*. How are the two stories related? What are the similarities and differences between Tatala and Rosa? How is interracial marriage represented in each work? Write an essay in which you discuss the way in which the two stories complement and complicate each other through the similarities and differences in their major themes and characters.

---

and their child are all currently separated from one another, with Ivan in New York, Rosa in Florida, and their child at summer camp. Rosa's relatives represent a tangled web of connections and betrayals, from Aunt Lily and Barbara's easy friendship to Barbara's abusive husband and father. Aunt Lily's dislike of their mother is revealed, as are a reflection on the child she lost and her newfound love of fostering children. Rosa's love of her grandfather is a focal point of the story, contrasted by her grandfather's cruelty toward Rosa's grandmother and the devastating realization that Rosa is considered a family embarrassment—revealing too many of their secrets in her work as a writer. Without any family to whom she feels a close connection, Rosa is cut adrift, finding an anchor in Barbara at the last possible moment before sinking into emotional oblivion.

Observation

Rosa is a practiced observer of the world around her, a trait necessary for her job as a writer. However, the recent setbacks in her life have caused her observations to be tainted with cynicism and bitterness. She observes the selfishness in people, the decay and pollution of her surroundings, and the emptiness of her own life. Become a misanthrope, she cannot react to the news of Raymyna's upcoming marriage with anything but pity and doubt, and judges her aunt for fostering children who share her dark complexion as if surrogate-parenting seven children were not an impressively selfless feat but a

The story is set in Florida (©fotomak / Shutterstock.com)

self-serving one. Rosa finds the bad in everything she sees, unaware that her family has caught on to her negative attitude. So inward facing are her thoughts that Aunt Lily's reprimand of her habit of spilling family secrets in her writing comes as a surprise, and the fact that Barbara feels the same seems to Rosa like a slap in the face. Yet Rosa finds solace in the knowledge that her grandfather, too, was an observer. The only difference between their quiet natures is that her grandfather did not write his observations down. The camaraderie Rosa feels with him represents her first step toward healing her broken heart and adjusting her sour attitude toward the world.

STYLE

Interior Monologue

An interior monologue is the stream of private thoughts of a character in a narrative: the feelings, opinions, and memories experienced exclusively in the character's thoughts during a story's action. Rosa's interior monologue is prominent throughout "Kindred Spirits." For example, while massaging Barbara's shoulders she remembers the history of domestic abuse she has observed, judges Barbara as a polluted version of her younger self, and reflects on how they have drifted apart as sisters. All of this takes place during the action of the massage, but none of these memories or conflicted emotions are spoken aloud. The act of the massage, in fact, contrasts with Rosa's interior monologue, as it is an example of the sisters' physical closeness. Rosa's interior monologue provides the majority of the information in the story, as she sits up at night unable to sleep, thinking of her past, or finds herself more interested in a memory than in the action occurring in front of her eyes. As a writer and an observer, she is inwardly focused. Appropriately, the narrative depicts her thinking process more than her active socialization.

Symbol

Rosa's grandfather's pair of hats symbolizes the concept of kindred spirits. A symbol is something that is used to represent a separate, unrelated thing, whether a person, place, or abstract concept. Rosa finds herself instantly enamored of the pair of hats, seeing her resemblance to her grandfather when she wears one hat as further proof of their subtle similarities. The problem for Rosa is that there are two hats,

COMPARE & CONTRAST

- **1985:** The conflict in Cyprus remains at a standstill as talks between Turkish Cypriot leader Rauf Denktash and Spyros Kyprianou, president of Cyprus, fail to result in an agreement between sides in the conflict between Cypriot's hardliners and the breakaway Turkish state.

  Today: Beginning in 2014, new progress toward a peaceful resolution of the Cyprus conflict begins, with the sides releasing a joint declaration in which they proclaim the current situation unsatisfactory and agree to work together toward a solution.

- **1985:** Integration of public schools in the United States reaches an all-time high, with black students in formerly all-white schools in the American South making up 44 percent of the student population.

  Today: The process of integration has reversed since its highs in the mid- to late 1980s, with southern schools reporting an average black student population of 23 percent in otherwise white schools.

- **1985:** Of the 51,114 married couples in the United States, a total of 762 are interracial.

  Today: The number of interracial couples rises each year, as does the national opinion of interracial marriages, with 37 percent of Americans in 2014 agreeing that interracial marriage has a positive effect on society.

and she can wear only one—symbolizing her loneliness following her divorce. She had thought Ivan was her kindred spirit, but this notion proved false when he fell out of love with her. Her grandfather, who she is sure is her kindred spirit, is no longer alive. Rosa is then left with one hat on her head and one in her lap as she grieves for herself on the plane ride home from Miami. When Barbara puts on the other hat, she is symbolically taking the role of Rosa's kindred spirit, offering her sister unconditional love.

HISTORICAL CONTEXT

Conflict in Cyprus

Cyprus is an island in the Mediterranean Sea in which two ethnic groups, the Greek and Turkish Cypriots, live in conflict. Under British rule of the island from 1878 to 1960, each group instructed their school-aged children to identify as either "Greek" or "Turk," rather than as citizens of Cyprus. As a result, much ingrained prejudice exists between the two cultures, which live separately from each other. Cyprus became independent from British rule in 1960, ratifying a complicated constitution that allowed power to be shared between the Greek and Turkish Cypriots. It soon became clear, however, that neither side would cooperate.

By 1963 conditions had deteriorated to the point that the president of Cyprus, Archbishop Markarios, threatened to change the constitution. This resulted in the formation of the Green Line through the city of Nicosia, dividing the island in two between its Greek and Turkish populations. This action prompted Turkey to threaten to intervene militarily on the Turkish Cypriots' behalf in 1964. Though the Turkish government was persuaded to stand down, relations worsened in the following years. On July 20, 1974, Turkey invaded the island, creating over 250,000 Greek Cypriot refugees. Greek Cypriots countered this attack by ethnically cleansing Turkish Cypriots from their population. In all, over 6,000 lives were lost during the invasion, and 1,500 people are considered missing to this day. The United Nations oversaw a population exchange of surviving members of the ethnic groups caught on opposite sides of the Green Line, but little

Aunt Lily runs a foster home, creating a family for the children in her care (©pixelheadphoto digitalskillet / Shutterstock.com)

forward progress has been made in the conflict since 1974 despite multiple attempts to reach a conclusion at UN-sponsored peace talks.

Segregation

Racial segregation in the United States took the form of a series of laws restricting the rights of African American citizens following the end of the Civil War. After a short period of relative equality immediately following the war, from the late 1880s until the Civil Rights Act of 1964 African Americans found themselves at the mercy of laws that separated them from the white population. Called Jim Crow laws, they included the establishment of separate hospitals, schools, cemeteries, public bathrooms, water fountains, and more for black and white citizens. In addition, blacks were forced to sit at the back of public buses, on the balcony in movie theaters, and in a separate section at restaurants, if they were allowed inside at all. When the Supreme Court ruled in favor of "separate but equal" facilities in *Plessy v. Ferguson* in 1896, segregation became entrenched in American society, affecting not only the American South but the northern states as well. "Separate but equal" rarely meant equal in practice, as government funding seldom focused on maintaining or upgrading black facilities. In addition, measures were passed to prevent blacks from voting, though this was a constitutional right extended to them under the Fourteenth and Fifteenth Amendments.

Public opinion of segregation began to sour following World War II, after the unthinkable tragedy of the Holocaust made Americans reconsider their own racist practices. In *Brown v. Board of Education* in 1954, the Supreme Court reversed their previous ruling in *Plessy v. Ferguson*, declaring the "separate but equal" practices of segregation to be unconstitutional, but the everyday realities of racial segregation took much longer to uproot. The civil rights movement, led by Martin Luther King Jr., began that year with a mission to restore equal rights to long oppressed African Americans. The Civil Rights Act of 1964 outlawed discrimination based on race at work, in schools, and in public facilities, but, as seen in "Kindred Spirits," the scars of the nation's segregated past continue to haunt the African American population. Rosa herself shares the name of famous civil rights activist Rosa Parks, whose refusal to move to the back of a bus for a white passenger sparked national protests against segregation.

CRITICAL OVERVIEW

"Kindred Spirits" was hailed as a success both in its 1985 publication in *Esquire* and as a part of the 2000 collection *The Way Forward Is with a Broken Heart*. A *Publishers Weekly* critic writes in praise of the emotional, spiritual, and thematic range of Walker's narratives in a review of the collection: "Infusing her intimate tales with grace and humor, Walker probes hidden corners of the human experience, at once questioning and acknowledging sexual, racial, and cultural rifts."

The short story won the prestigious O. Henry Award for short fiction in 1986. Christopher Benfey writes of that year's finalists for the *New York Times*: "Since most of these stories hinge on what happens to family ties in the face of extreme experience, it is fitting that first prize was awarded to . . . 'Kindred Spirits,' which recounts a family's resentment." Ed Piacentino is fascinated by Rosa's reaction to her divorce—one of slow implosion rather than explosion—in his essay "Reconciliation with Family in Alice Walker's 'Kindred Spirits,'" for *Southern Quarterly*: "Rosa, divorced, out of love and out of sync with her family, prefers to be alone, aloof, in short, to be principally an unobtrusive observer of rather than participant in the lives of others."

A *Kirkus Reviews* writer admires Walker's ability to infuse her stories with the perspective of a wide range of characters, some autobiographical, some purely fictional, but each with their own motivations: "Many voices are heard here, and whether they preach or praise, coo or condemn, they all come from one heart." In her review for *BookPage*, Kelly Koepke finds Walker's representation of the slow healing process following heartbreak to be as realistic as it is moving. She writes with admiration that each of the stories depicts a moment of sudden clarity: "Many times this clarity is won with consequences both painful and joyful. We are reminded that life is fragile, but that with love, we can move forward and heal our wounded souls."

"HER RETURN TO AUNT LILY'S HOUSE TO MOURN HER GRANDFATHER'S DEATH MARKS ROSA'S RETURN TO LIFE. THIS CONFRONTATION RUBS RAW WOUNDS, HOWEVER, AND PUSHES ROSA, AT LONG LAST, TO HER BREAKING POINT."

CRITICISM

Amy L. Miller

Miller is a graduate of the University of Cincinnati. In the following essay, she examines the state of Rosa's closest relationships as she reaches a point of crisis in Walker's "Kindred Spirits."

In Walker's "Kindred Spirits," Rosa struggles beneath the combined weight of her failed relationships. Her father and grandfather are dead, her sister and aunt disapprove of her choices, and her ex-husband waited just one week following their divorce before moving his new girlfriend into the house they once shared. Disconnected from humanity and drowning in misery, Rosa turns her back on a world that seems to have turned its back on her, leaving the country and her family behind as she tours impoverished and beleaguered nations. Whatever distraction she attempts, she cannot outrun her own sleepless nights or the guilt brought on by her decision to skip her grandfather's funeral. Her return to Aunt Lily's house to mourn her grandfather's death marks Rosa's return to life. This confrontation rubs raw wounds, however, and pushes Rosa, at long last, to her breaking point. Though Rosa feels she is a victim of injustice, she must accept her own cruel treatment of others before she is saved from loneliness.

The most pressing of Rosa's recent misfortunes is her divorce from her husband, Ivan, who—to Rosa's shock—avoids contact with both her and her family following their separation. Rosa feels she has the right to remain friends with Ivan, but Ivan actively avoids her: "The most horrible thing of all was losing Ivan's friendship and comradely support, which he

WHAT DO I READ NEXT?

- In Jacqueline Woodson's young-adult novel *Locomotion* (2010), Lonnie must start a new life after the death of his parents and separation from his sister, who is sent to live with another family. Yet he learns to love his tough foster mother, Miss Edna, and copes with his grief through poetry.
- In *Making Whiteness: The Culture of Segregation in the South, 1890–1940* (1999), Grace Elizabeth Hale examines how white southerners deliberately created segregation as a system of oppression to prevent newly freed African American citizens from gaining cultural power equal to their own.
- Walker's *The Color Purple* (1982), winner of the National Book Award and Pulitzer Prize for Fiction, tells the story of Celie, an uneducated black woman so beaten and abused by the men in her life that she has lost all confidence, and the unlikely love she finds with her husband's mistress, Shug Avery, which leads Celie back to herself.
- In Yaa Gyasi's *Homecoming* (2016), two half sisters from Ghana are separated by the British slave trade, one married to a slaver and one imprisoned beneath their castle, only to have their ancestors reunited after three hundred years of war, oppression, escape, and freedom.
- Jean Toomer's *Cane* (1923) combines poetry and prose to paint a portrait of black lives in the American South in the Jim Crow era. Cited by Walker as a major influence in her artistic development, *Cane* effortlessly shifts form and style without losing sight of the beauty and tragedy of its subject.
- Langston Hughes's short-story collection *The Ways of White Folks* (1934) examines the clash of cultures between whites and blacks in segregated America and the ways in which prejudice shapes perception on either side of a racial divide.
- Flannery O'Connor's short-story collection *A Good Man Is Hard to Find* (1953) depicts the American South in rural, gothic glory, from poverty to peacocks, murderers to grandmothers who always know what is best.
- Zora Neale Hurston's *Their Eyes Were Watching God* (1937) asks how powerful a woman can be when she throws off society's yoke of expectations. Janie Crawford is the beautiful but cold wife of the mayor of Eatonville until her passionate love for Tea Cake unlocks the secrets of her heart, causing a scandal in her small-town community.
- Toni Morrison's Pulitzer Prize–winning novel *Beloved* (1987) tells the story of Sethe, a woman haunted by the specter of slavery in the form of the restless spirit of her dead daughter. Ostracized by her community for her desperate act of motherly love, Sethe must fight her past if she wishes to have a future.

---

yanked out of her reach with a vengeance that sent her reeling." Lying to herself, Rosa believes that her decision to leave their house, car, and cat with Ivan shows strength, but they merely serve as excuses for Rosa to check up on her ex, until the day she borrows the car, only to find upon her return her former mother-in-law and Ivan's new girlfriend united in their disapproval of her presence at the house. Rosa's trip around the world is another example of the kind of false progress she has made since the divorce. Through her travels she runs away from her friends and family rather than facing them in the height of her shame. Piacentino writes:

> Rosa, while celebrating her sense of freedom, is actually distraught and disillusioned. . . . In pain, mostly emotional, unable to sleep, having lost much of her former sense of compassion, extremely cynical, Rosa [is] a single mother suffering a mental crisis.

The pain and panic Rosa has masked seep into her attitude and taint her perception until the world she observes is harsh, the people selfish, and the land poisoned by pollution. As for her own life's bleakness, she blames exterior rather than interior forces, as yet unaware how her behavior has gradually pushed those closest to her away.

Sharan Gibson writes in her review of *The Way Forward Is with a Broken Heart* for the *Houston Chronicle*: "Walker's women have learned to protect the self in hostile environments." Rosa, faced with attending her grandfather's funeral alone or disappearing from her family's lives for the summer, chooses to vanish. She knows that both Barbara and their mother dote on Ivan, making them poor companions for Rosa's heartbreak. Many other members of her family never understood Rosa's interracial relationship, making the thought of awkward hypothetical conversations she might be forced to endure a distressing prospect. She flees to protect her fragile emotions, but—with no one to draw out the truth of her vulnerability—turns too drastically inward, losing her empathy for others. When she hears the news of Raymyna's marriage, "she could not easily comprehend anyone getting married, now that she no longer was, but it was impossible for her to feel happy at the prospect of yet another poor black woman marrying." This attitude is shockingly harsh, so much so that even Rosa chastises herself afterward for being too cynical. Yet as cynical as she has become since the divorce, Rosa is naïve in her inability to recognize that others are observing her just as she observes them, casting judgments based on such behavior as hearing of a coming marriage impassively, without even a smile for the bride. Piacentino writes: "Overwhelmed by her personal torment and angst, she has become bitterly judgmental, uncompromising, and unreservedly incapable of recognizing and applauding good when she sees it."

Aunt Lily stands in direct opposition to Rosa. Rosa thinks upon first seeing her at the airport: "It's me . . . my old self." But the resemblance between them stops short at the superficial. Throughout her stay, Rosa interprets Aunt Lily's actions to reflect a self-righteous attitude. For example, she observes that Aunt Lily's seven foster children all share her exact complexion, as if her taking in orphans was more a vanity project than an act of charity. She finds Aunt Lily's no smoking or drinking rules to be oppressive and, in her grandfather's case, uncalled for, as if Aunt Lily has no right as hostess to set ground rules inside her own home. Aunt Lily reciprocates Rosa's dislike—hinting that she did not like Rosa's mother and refusing to share her memories of Rosa's father owing to Rosa's reputation as the family sneak. Gibson comments: "Writing that cannibalizes family history is tricky. . . . To the others, the writer is always snooping about the family's business and distorting things in ways that make them shudder." As Barbara's reaction confirms, Aunt Lily is right to distrust Rosa. Considering that Rosa herself remembers her father as a "raving madman," her sudden interest in his childhood is suspect. In fact, she pursues this line of questioning only to distract herself from her conflicted emotions toward her grandfather, not out of any feeling of love for her father. Rosa's question about her father's past may come out of nowhere, but Aunt Lily serves it back to her with vicious precision—making her feelings toward Rosa absolutely clear. Aunt Lily does not feel pity for Rosa, no matter how she weeps, because Rosa has ostracized herself from the family through monetizing their secrets.

This rejection comes on the heels of Rosa's revelation that she and her grandfather share an innate ability to observe without forgetting. Having considered herself alone in this trait before the visit to Aunt Lily's, Rosa struggles to understand why it is she shares such a powerful connection to a man with whom she rarely interacted and who she knows was at times cruel and miserable. To understand their connection she must understand how she, too, can be cruel and miserable company. Piacentino writes: "Like her grandfather, Rosa is silent, powerless, introspective, and has only tenuous connections with others in her family." When she draws this conclusion at last, Rosa takes her first step toward healing her broken heart. She has found that Ivan was not her only kindred spirit in the world, learning of her grandfather. Both men, however, are out of reach, with Ivan enveloped in his new life with Sheila and her grandfather dead. Confronted by the judgment of her family in Barbara and Aunt Lily's unsympathetic opinions, she begins her final collapse inward, feeling "in the very wreckage of her life." At this moment, Barbara reaches out to save her floundering sister.

Rosa and her sister Barbara visit their Aunt Lily (©Jami Rae / Shutterstock.com)

Piacentino writes:

> Love . . . is a state of caring and connection realized when one shows the courage and willingness to confront and accept the broader notion of home . . . by venturing out to that which may seem strange, intimidating, . . . or even misunderstood.

By her sister's side, Barbara, too, has made observations. She sees her sister's emotional struggles and knows, when she bursts into the bathroom crying, that Rosa's hard shell has finally broken. Though she agrees with Aunt Lily, with whom she gets along well, that Rosa's behavior as a writer alienates her from the family's love, she still loves her sister. A victim of abuse from both her husband and father, Barbara certainly must sense the deep heartbreak in her sister. But Rosa considers Barbara a polluted version of her girlhood self and an embarrassment to the family through her abusive marriage. Whether Barbara knows of Rosa's low opinion of her, the need to comfort overpowers her need to keep her distance, and she extends a hand to Rosa at the exact moment of her greatest crisis. Rosa, who has begun to understand through her grandfather's memory the personal price she will pay for her cool observations, clings to Barbara as her last hope at a human connection. Having decided to cut Aunt Lily from her life, her sister represents all Rosa has left. When Barbara places their grandfather's other hat on her head, she unconsciously demonstrates to Rosa that every person has two sides. One cannot be cold or cruel at all times. For example, though Rosa remembers her grandfather as stingy, she also acknowledges that he paid for Barbara's trade-school education when their father refused to do it. Finding a balance between observation and experience will be for Rosa like balancing both hats on her head, but with Barbara's love to lean on she may yet find her way through heartbreak.

"Kindred Spirits" explores the crisis that follows after family ties snap, leaving Rosa grasping for ends always pulled out of reach. Though she stands with the ruin of her life all around her, Rosa finds the first connection of her new life as a divorcée in her similarities to her grandfather. With the next fragile connection she forges with her sister, Rosa climbs onto the path toward a healthier attitude and a happier life.

> "IT IS A COMMONPLACE OF WALKER CRITICISM THAT SHE IS MORE SYMPATHETIC TOWARD HER BLACK MALE CHARACTERS AS THEY GROW OLDER. HER IMAGES OF YOUNG BLACK MALE BRUTALITY TOWARD WOMEN ARE NOT SURPRISING; VIOLENCE WAS A FACT OF LIFE IN EATONTON IN GENERAL AND IN HER OWN FAMILY IN PARTICULAR."

Source: Amy L. Miller, Critical Essay on "Kindred Spirits," in *Short Stories for Students*, Gale, Cengage Learning, 2017.

Donna Haisty Winchell

In the following excerpt, Winchell describes people and events in Walker's life that may have influenced her work.

. . . SEEDS OF POSSIBILITY

Part of Walker's understanding of herself as woman and as artist comes from her awareness that she is linked across continents and through generations with women who have exercised their creativity despite the racism and sexism that would deny its expression. In *In Search of Our Mothers' Gardens* (1983), she wrote, "To be an artist and a black woman, even today, lowers our status in many respects, rather than raises it: and yet, artists we will be" (*Gardens*). Walker's art thus far includes four novels, two essay collections, five poetry books, and two short-story collections.

In the essay "In Search of Our Mothers' Gardens," she questions with awed respect how her female ancestors kept alive their creativity during times when even teaching a black man or woman how to read and write was illegal. She writes of mothers and grandmothers who were "driven to a numb and bleeding madness by the springs of creativity in them for which there was no release. . . . Creators, who lived lives of spiritual waste, because they were so rich in spirituality—which is the basis of Art—that the strain of enduring their unused and unwanted talent drove them insane" (*Gardens*). Like the anonymous black woman whose quilt of extraordinary beauty hangs in the Smithsonian Institution, these women expressed their creativity through whatever meager materials society allowed them and "waited for a day when the unknown thing that was in them would be made known; but guessed, somehow in their darkness, that on the day of their revelation they would be long dead" (*Gardens*). Walker mourns the gifts that were stifled within the artists of the past, but her essay goes on to celebrate the future. Many a sculptor, singer, poet, and painter may have died unknown, but the possibility of art did not die. Rather, in the absence of material goods, it became a legacy passed down from mother to daughter: "And so our mothers and grandmothers have, more often than not anonymously, handed on the creative spark, the seed of the flower they themselves never hoped to see: or like a sealed letter they could not plainly read" (*Gardens*).

"In Search of Our Mothers' Gardens" records Walker's discovery of her mother's art form. In the essay Walker draws her imagery from the impressive garden that was her mother's particular means of keeping the creative seed alive wherever the Walkers went as they lived the unsettled life of the Georgia sharecropper. Little in Minnie Tallulah (Lou) Walker's background prepared her for the life of an artist. Minnie Lou ran away from home to marry at 17 and by 20 had two children and another on the way. When Alice was born in Eatonton, Georgia, on 9 February 1944—the first time her parents were able to pay the midwife cash rather than making the usual payment, a pig—she was eighth, last, and unplanned.

Walker's mother's family had lived in Georgia so long that no one remembered how or when they first came there. Walker does know, however, that her father's great-great-grandmother, Mrs. Mary Poole, came as a slave on foot from Virginia, carrying a baby on each hip, a trek that Walker commemorates by keeping her maiden name. Walker points out that, having buried generations of family in the red clay of central Georgia, surely a portion was theirs, yet even the land her father's grandfather managed to buy after the Civil War was taken from him following Reconstruction (*Gardens*).

There is no sentimentality in Walker's recollections of Southern country life: "I can recall that I hated it, generally. The hard work in the fields, the shabby houses, the evil greedy men who worked my father to death and almost broke the courage of that strong woman, my mother" (*Gardens*).

Her mother refused to be broken, though, and came home from the fields each day to plant and prune more than 50 different varieties of plants. She covered the holes in the walls of their run-down sharecroppers' cabins with flowers. Walker writes, "Because of her creativity with her flowers, even my memories of poverty are seen through a screen of blooms—sunflowers, petunias, roses, dahlias, forsythia, spirea, delphiniums, verbena . . . and on and on" (*Gardens*). In her garden Mrs. Walker is an artist at work: "I notice that it is only when my mother is working in her flowers that she is radiant, almost to the point of being invisible—except as Creator: hand and eye. She is involved in work her soul must have. Ordering the universe in the image of her personal conception of Beauty. Her face, as she prepares the Art that is her gift, is a legacy of respect she leaves to me, for all that illuminates and cherishes life. She handed down respect for the possibilities—and the will to grasp them" (*Gardens*).

Minnie Lou Walker knew that possibility was, in part, tied to education. On behalf of her eight children, she fought for the education she knew was essential if they were ever to escape the sharecropping system, the vicious cycle that kept many a black family perpetually in debt and perpetually on the move. Walker saw her mother's quick, violent temper "only a few times a year, when she battled with the white landlord who had the misfortune to suggest that her children did not need to go to school" (*Gardens*). In the essay, Walker pays tribute to her mother and others of her generation.

At a time when there was not even a high school in Eatonton, one of Walker's sisters, described as "a brilliant, studious girl," became "one of those Negro wonders—who collected scholarships like trading stamps and wandered all over the world" (*Gardens*). Walker herself started school at four when her mother could no longer take her to the fields, and she went on to become her high school's valedictorian.

An accident when Alice was eight, however, helped determine the form her artistic flowering would take. Up to that time Alice had been a precocious child, giving Easter speeches in starched dresses and patent leather shoes and smugly declaring at two and a half, "I'm the prettiest." As she writes, "*It was great fun being cute. But then, one day, it ended*" (*Gardens*). Her self-confidence ended when she and two of her older brothers were playing cowboys and Indians. A shot from a brother's BB gun injured her right eye leaving it blind and scarred. After the accident she lowered her eyes from the curious stares of others, and for six years she did not raise her head.

From the time of the accident, she writes in "From an Interview," she "daydreamed—not of fairy tales—but of falling on swords, of putting guns to my heart or head, or of slashing my wrists with a razor" (*Gardens*). She felt ugly and disfigured. Out of her isolation, however, grew her art: "I believe . . . that it was from this period—from my solitary, lonely position, the position of an outcast—that I began really to see people and things, really to notice relationships and to learn to be patient enough to care about how they turned out. I no longer felt like the little girl I was. I felt old, and because I felt I was unpleasant to look at, filled with shame. I retreated into solitude, and read stories and began to write poems" (*Gardens*).

Mrs. Walker had the wisdom to recognize that Alice had a special gift more valuable than physical beauty. As Mary Helen Washington explains in "Alice Walker: Her Mother's Gifts," a 1982 article based on an interview with Walker, Walker's mother granted her "permission" to be a writer; someone less perceptive might have deemed a sharecropper's cabin in Georgia an odd place to raise a poet. Even when Mrs. Walker was working in the fields or in white women's kitchens and Alice was the only daughter still living at home, Mrs. Walker excused Alice from household chores, respecting her right—and her need—to sit and read.

Washington discusses three gifts Walker's mother bought on layaway out of less than $20 a week she made as a domestic. The first, when her daughter was 15 or 16, was a sewing machine so that Walker could make her own clothes, and as Walker explains, "The message about independence and self-sufficiency was clear." The second was a suitcase, "as nice a one as anyone in Eatonton had ever had. That suitcase gave me permission to travel and part of the joy in going very far from home was the message of that suitcase." The third was a typewriter. "If that wasn't saying, 'Go write your ass off,' I don't know what you need" (Washington).

When Walker was offered a scholarship to Spelman College in Atlanta, the ladies of the Methodist church collected $75 to bless her on her way.

HARVEST OF DESPAIR

Walker's father, however, feared the world into which they sent his daughter. For Willie Lee Walker education was something to be feared because of the barrier it placed between him and his children. "And why not?" Walker asks. "Though he risked his life and livelihood to vote more than once, nothing changed in his world. Cotton prices continued low. Dairying was hard. White men and women continued to run things, badly. In his whole life my father never had a vacation. . . . Education merely seemed to make his children more critical of him" (*Living*). Walker's experiences at Spelman and then later at Sarah Lawrence in New York, to which she transferred after two and a half years, seem to have confirmed his fears. In "My Father's Country Is the Poor," Walker writes of how her "always tenuous" relationship with her father virtually ended when she left for Spelman: "This brilliant man—great at mathematics, unbeatable at storytelling, but unschooled beyond the primary grades—found the manners of his suddenly middle-class (by virtue of being in college) daughter a barrier to easy contact, if not actually frightening. I found it painful to expose my thoughts in language that to him obscured more than it revealed" (*Gardens*).

It is a commonplace of Walker criticism that she is more sympathetic toward her black male characters as they grow older. Her images of young black male brutality toward women are not surprising; violence was a fact of life in Eatonton in general and in her own family in particular. In an interview with David Bradley, Walker recalls, "I knew both my grandfathers, and they were just doting, indulgent, sweet old men. I just loved them both and they were crazy about me. However, as young men, middle-aged men, they were . . . brutal. One grandfather knocked my grandmother out of a window. He beat one of his children so severely that the child had epilepsy. Just a horrible, horrible man. But when I knew him, he was a sensitive, wonderful man." Asked if her father would have eventually been like her grandfather, Walker replies wistfully, "Oh, he had it in him to be." Unfortunately, although Walker and her father never discussed her works, she feels that as he grew older he became more like some of her worst characters (*Living*). She never saw him mellow into the benevolent old man each of her grandfathers had become.

In the afterword to the 1988 edition of *The Third Life of Grange Copeland*, her fictional portrayal of domestic brutality, she writes, "In my immediate family too there was violence. Its roots seemed always to be embedded in my father's need to dominate my mother and their children and in her resistance (and ours), verbal and physical, to any such domination." In Alice's eyes, his sexist attitudes made him a failure as the male role model he should have been. When his middle daughter, Ruth, showed an interest in boys, he beat her and locked her in her room; he told her never to come home if she found herself pregnant. At the same time, he expected his sons to experiment with sex. Also failures as role models were the four of Walker's five brothers still living at home during the years Walker was old enough to remember: "I desperately needed my father and brothers to give me male models I could respect, because white men (for example; being particularly handy in this sort of comparison)—whether in films or in person—offered man as dominator, as killer, and always as hypocrite. My father failed because he copied the hypocrisy. And my brothers—except for one—never understood they must represent half the world to me, as I must represent the other half to them" (*Gardens*).

As Walker herself grew older, she came to understand more fully what made her father what he was. Looking back during the course of a May 1989 *Life* interview with Gregory Jaynes, Walker explains that when her father was 11, his mother was murdered on the way home from church "by a man whose advances she had spurned" and that he "was just crazed by this early pain." Because her sister Ruth resembled his dead mother, "he rejected her and missed no opportunity that I ever saw to put her down" (*Living*).

In "Brothers and Sisters" Walker explains that she understood and forgave her father only when she studied women's liberation ideology. From it she learned that his sexism was merely an imitation of the society in which he lived (*Gardens*). Willie Lee Walker never had the chance for escape that his youngest daughter had. Analyzing her relationship with her father in the 1984 essay "Father," she expresses her love for what he might have been but adds, "Knowing now, at forty, what it takes out of body and spirit to go and how much more to stay, and having learned, too, by now, some of the pitiful confusions in behavior caused by ignorance and pain, I love you no less for what you were" (*Living*). In "My Father's Country Is the Poor," she looks back on the day she boarded the bus for Spelman, leaving him standing beside the lonely Georgia highway. She writes, "I moved—blinded by tears of guilt and relief—ever farther and farther away; until, by the time of his death, all I understood, *truly*, of my father's life, was how few of its possibilities he had realized, how relatively little of its possible grandeur I had known" (*Gardens*). Walker feels she has achieved reconciliation with her father only since his death.

One of Walker's most successful stories, "A Sudden Trip Home in the Spring," is a fictional portrayal of a young black woman's response to the death of her father. The character, Sarah Davis, *feels* as alienated from her father as Walker felt from hers. Word of her father's death back home in Georgia reaches Sarah at her prestigious girls' school in New York. One of only two black girls at Cresselton, she is studying art on a scholarship. (There were six black students at Sarah Lawrence when Walker was enrolled.) As far as her art is concerned, Sarah faces two problems: At Cresselton, she lives in a world where there are no faces like her own, save one, to serve as her models. She also finds herself incapable of drawing or painting black men because she cannot "bear to trace defeat onto blank pages" (*GW*).

Like Walker, Sarah feels that she and her father have stopped speaking the same language. She blames him for her mother's death; he protests that constantly following the crops, moving from one ramshackle shack to another, killed her. He, like Walker's father, had his violent moments. After his death, Sarah wonders, "Did it matter now that often he had threatened their lives with the rage of his despair? That once he had spanked the crying baby violently, who later died of something else altogether . . . and that the next day they moved? She answers, No . . . I don't think it does" (*GW*). She can say so, however, only after her trip south for the funeral.

Sarah draws on her reading about black novelist Richard Wright's experiences with his father to try to decide for herself what a child owes a father after his death. One of her classmates at Cresselton tells her that a strong man does not need a father. The implication is that neither does a strong woman. Sarah realizes, however, that her father is her link to generations of her family, that he is, as Sarah puts it, "one faulty door in a house of many ancient rooms. Was that one faulty door to shut [her] off forever from the rest of the house?" (*GW*).

At her father's funeral, Sarah realizes she has seen defeat in black men's faces only because she has always seen them against a background of white. Standing at her father's grave, looking at her grandfather out of the corner of her eye, Sarah thinks, "*It is strange . . . that I never thought to paint him like this, simply as he stands; without anonymous meaningless people hovering beyond his profile; his face turned brownly against the light*. The defeat that had frightened her in the faces of black men was the defeat of black forever defined by white" (*GW*). At her father's grave Sarah discovers where one's definition of self should come from: "But that defeat was nowhere on her grandfather's face. He stood like a rock, outwardly calm, the comfort and support of the Davis family. The family alone defined him, and he was not about to let them down" (*GW*). When Sarah realizes she can indeed capture such strength on canvas, her grandfather tells her to capture him in stone instead. Sarah knows finally that in pursuing her art she will be saying "NO with capital letters" to the system that killed her mother and broke her father's spirit.

Sarah finds the "doors" to the house of her heritage in her grandfather and in her brother. If in Walker's own life there is a counterpart to the brother who wraps Sarah in his arms and encourages her to get the education her parents would have wanted for her, it is her oldest brother, Fred, who left home to live and work on his own when Walker was still quite small. (In "Brothers and Sisters" she calls him Jason.) Not until their father's funeral did she meet this older brother again.

In "A Sudden Trip," Sarah and her grandfather are the only ones who do not shed a tear at Sarah's father's funeral. At Willie Lee Walker's, Fred and Alice alone were dry-eyed. Leaving the grave, Fred introduced himself, taking her in his arms and saying, "You don't ever have to walk alone." Walker thought in response, "One out of five ain't *too* bad" (*Gardens*). . . .

Source: Donna Haisty Winchell, "Survival, Literal and Literary," in *Alice Walker*, Twayne, 1992, pp. 2–9.

SOURCES

"Alice Walker," Poetry Foundation website, https://www.poetryfoundation.org/poems-and-poets/poets/detail/alice-walker (accessed July 22, 2016).

Aulph, Rebecca, "Alice Walker through the Years," in *Deep South*, February 11, 2013, http://deepsouthmag.com/2013/02/11/alice-walker-through-the-years/ (accessed July 22, 2016).

Benfey, Christopher, "In Short: Fiction," in *New York Times*, April 27, 1986, http://www.nytimes.com/1986/04/27/books/in-short-fiction-972686.html (accessed July 22, 2016).

Billingsley, Sarah, Review of *The Way Forward Is with a Broken Heart*, in *Pittsburgh Post-Gazette*, December 10, 2000, http://old.post-gazette.com/books/reviews/20001210review647.asp (accessed July 22, 2016).

Boddy, Kasia, "Broken-Hearted Nation," in *Guardian* (London, England), March 2, 2001, https://www.theguardian.com/books/2001/mar/03/fiction.reviews3 (accessed July 22, 2016).

Britt, Donna, "Alice Walker, the Inner Mysteries Unraveled: The Author Focusing on Nature and Self in Her Temple," in *Washington Post*, May 8, 1989, https://www.washingtonpost.com/news/arts-and-entertainment/wp/2016/03/29/in-1989-alice-walker-had-so-much-wisdom-about-love-literary-success-and-hair-care/ (accessed July 22, 2016).

Childress, Sarah, "A Return to School Segregation in America?," PBS website, July 2, 2014, http://www.pbs.org/wgbh/frontline/article/a-return-to-school-segregation-in-america/ (accessed August 2, 2016).

Gibson, Sharan, Review of *The Way Forward Is with a Broken Heart*, in *Houston Chronicle*, December 31, 2000, http://www.chron.com/life/article/The-Way-Forward-is-With-a-Broken-Heart-by-Alice-2018945.php (accessed July 22, 2016).

Hannah-Jones, Nikole, "Choosing a School for My Daughter in a Segregated City," in *New York Times*, June 9, 2016, http://www.nytimes.com/2016/06/12/magazine/choosing-a-school-for-my-daughter-in-a-segregated-city.html?_r=0 (accessed August 2, 2016).

Hensinger, Shane, "The History of the Cyprus Conflict: A Background with Peacebuilding Strategies," in *Daily Kos*, February 20, 2010, http://www.dailykos.com/story/2010/2/20/839037/- (accessed August 2, 2016).

"Interracial Married Couples: 1960 to Present," US Census Bureau website, http://www.census.gov/population/socdemo/ms-la/tabms-3.txt (accessed August 2, 2016).

Kaloudis, George Stergiou, "Cyprus: The Unresolved Conflict," University of Pennsylvania website, https://www.stwing.upenn.edu/~durduran/dergi/kaloul.htm (accessed August 2, 2016).

Koepke, Kelly, Review of *The Way Forward Is with a Broken Heart*, in *BookPage*, October 2000, https://bookpage.com/reviews/1558-alice-walker-way-forward-with-broken-heart#.V6sBYSMrK_U (accessed July 22, 2016).

Lawson, Steven F., "Segregation," National Humanities Center website, May 2010, http://nationalhumanitiescenter.org/tserve/freedom/1865-1917/essays/segregation.htm (accessed August 2, 2016).

Padilla, Natasha, "Alice Walker Bio, Selected Awards, Honors & Works," Thirteen website, http://www.thirteen.org/13pressroom/files/2014/01/AM-Alice-Walker-bio-awards-works.pdf (accessed July 22, 2016).

Piacentino, Ed, "Reconciliation with Family in Alice Walker's 'Kindred Spirits,'" in *Southern Quarterly*, Vol. 46, No. 1, Fall 2008, pp. 91–99.

Review of *The Way Forward Is with a Broken Heart*, in *Kirkus Reviews*, September 1, 2000, https://www.kirkusreviews.com/book-reviews/alice-walker/the-way-forward-is-with-a-broken-heart/ (accessed July 22, 2016).

Review of *The Way Forward Is with a Broken Heart*, in *Publishers Weekly*, October 2, 2000, http://www.publishersweekly.com/978-0-679-45587-5 (accessed July 22, 2016).

Smith, Helena, "Cyprus Peace Talks Raise Hopes of an End to a Conflict That Has Haunted Europe," in *Guardian* (London, England), May 14, 2015, https://www.theguardian.com/world/2015/may/14/cyprus-peace-talks-raise-hopes-end-conflict-haunted-europe (accessed August 2, 2016).

"Timeline: Cyprus," BBC website, December 13, 2011, http://news.bbc.co.uk/2/hi/europe/1021835.stm (accessed August 2, 2016).

Walker, Alice, "Kindred Spirits," in *The Way Forward Is with a Broken Heart*, Random House, 2000, pp. 52–68.

Wang, Wendy, "Interracial Marriage: Who Is 'Marrying Out'?," Pew Research Center website, June 12, 2015, http://www.pewresearch.org/fact-tank/2015/06/12/interracial-marriage-who-is-marrying-out/ (accessed August 2, 2016).

Whitted, Qiana, "Alice Walker," in *Georgia Encyclopedia*, August 12, 2014, http://www.georgiaencyclopedia.org/articles/arts-culture/alice-walker-b-1944 (accessed July 22, 2016).

FURTHER READING

Allen, Tuzyline Jita, *Womanist & Feminist Aesthetics: A Comparative Review*, Ohio University Press, 1995.

This collection of essays on Walker's theory of womanism examines the distinction between womanism and feminism as well as the importance of providing black women with a distinct form of feminism separate from that of white women, while keeping hearts and minds open toward cooperation between the groups.

Bambara, Toni Cade, *The Black Woman: An Anthology*, Washington Square Press, 2005.

First published in 1970, this anthology includes the work of leading African American women artists, including Walker, Nikki Giovanni, Grace Lee Boggs, Audre Lorde, Ann Cook, Joyce Green, Frances Beale, Maude White Katz, and many more.

Massey, Douglas S., and Nancy A. Denton, *American Apartheid: Segregation and the Making of the Underclass*, Harvard University Press, 1993.

American Apartheid presents evidence suggesting that, though overtly racist Jim Crow laws were abolished decades ago, segregation continues in a more insidious form through the isolation of African American urban communities.

Walker, Alice, *In Search of Our Mothers' Gardens: Womanist Prose*, Mariner Books, 2003.

Walker's nonfiction collection includes essays on political activism, authors, motherhood, *The Color Purple*, and civil rights movement leaders and a recounting of the childhood injury that left her blind in one eye, as well as her thoughts on womanism and feminism.

SUGGESTED SEARCH TERMS

Alice Walker

Alice Walker AND Kindred Spirits

Alice Walker AND The Way Forward Is with a Broken Heart

Alice Walker AND Kindred Spirits AND family

family dynamics AND African American literature

Cyprus AND civil war

segregation AND history

interracial marriage AND United States

The Man in the Black Suit

STEPHEN KING

1994

"The Man in the Black Suit" is a short framed narrative by Stephen King, inspired by the story of a friend's grandfather. It is also a tribute to Nathaniel Hawthorne's short story "Young Goodman Brown," according to the author. First published in the *New Yorker* on October 31, 1994, the tale went on to earn the O. Henry Prize in 1996 and was published in King's collection *Six Stories* in 1997. Told in the first person, a style that is common in King's work, this psychological thriller explores the childhood memory of a ninety-year-old man and how it continues to haunt him. A chance encounter with the devil at the age of nine introduces a supernatural theme. The memory forces the narrator to examine his fear while exploring the ideas of isolation, death, and faith. "The Man in the Black Suit" is also available in King's collection *Everything's Eventual: 14 Dark Tales*, published in 2002.

AUTHOR BIOGRAPHY

Stephen Edwin King was born in Portland, Maine, on September 21, 1947, the second son of Ruth and Donald King. Donald abandoned his wife and two sons when King was two years old. He was raised by his mother but lived with different relatives for a time after his parents' separation. The family moved to Durham,

Stephen King (©Featureflash Photo Agency / Shutterstock.com)

Maine, in 1958, where they remained for eight years. King attended the University of Maine, where he wrote for the school paper. During this time, he began writing and selling short stories. He graduated in 1970 with a BA in English and became certified to teach. The next year, he married Tabitha Spruce, with whom he has three children. Early in their relationship, he worked as a laborer and teacher while he wrote fiction.

In 1974, King published the novel *Carrie.* That same year, he began work on *The Shining.* His second book, *Salem's Lot*, appeared in 1975, and *The Shining* followed in 1977. Other popular horror novels included *Firestarter* in 1980, *Cujo* in 1981, and *It* in 1986. King also began writing under the name Richard Bachman, publishing *Rage* in 1977, *The Long Walk* in 1979, and *Roadwork* in 1981. Although he is known for horror, King never limited himself to that genre. The novella *Rita Hayworth and Shawshank Redemption*, for example, was included in 1982's *Different Seasons* and tells the story of a man wrongfully convicted of murder. At the beginning of his career, King published frequently.

Many of King's books and stories have been adapted for films, television series, and plays. The first film adaptation, *Carrie*, was released in 1976, and a Broadway musical was produced in 1988. Stanley Kubrick produced and directed the horror classic *The Shining* in 1980. *Pet Sematary* followed in 1989. Films of his work were not limited to his horror or supernatural fiction. *The Shawshank Redemption*, for example, was nominated for seven Academy Awards, including Best Picture, after its 1994 release. In 1994, the *New Yorker* published "The Man in the Black Suit." The short story won the O. Henry Award in 1996 and appeared in *Six Stories* in 1997.

In 1999, the distracted driver of a minivan struck the author while he was walking on the shoulder of the road, and the injuries King sustained slowed the pace of his work. He announced in 2002 that he planned to stop writing, but he has remained a prolific author, earning a National Book Award in 2003. King has published over fifty novels and two hundred short stories. One story line, however, has spanned most of the author's career—the Dark Tower series. *The Gunslinger*, the first volume, was published in 1982 and the eighth volume, *The Wind through the Keyhole*, in 2012. The series is so popular that it has also been created in comic form, and a movie is scheduled for release in 2017. Along with writing, King has collaborated on a musical play and played in the band Rock Bottom Remainders. As of 2016, he had homes in Bangor and Lovell, Maine, and in Sarasota, Florida.

PLOT SUMMARY

"The Man in the Black Suit" is told in the first person. The narrator, Gary, is ninety and lives in a nursing home. He has trouble with his memory, but meeting the man in the black suit is clear in his memory and still terrifies him. Gary writes the story in a journal to help remove it from his mind.

In 1914, Gary is nine years old and lives in the rural town of Motton, Maine, where the farms are spread out so that people do not see each other often. The area is surrounded by

MEDIA ADAPTATIONS

- *The Man in the Black Suit: 4 Dark Tales* is an audio collection of four King stories that features "The Man in the Black Suit." Read by John Cullum, Peter Gerety, and Becky Ann Baker, the album was released by Simon & Schuster Audio on CD in 2014 and is also available for download. The run time is three hours and forty minutes.

woods, and Gary says that there is a history of ghosts there. His brother, Dan, was killed by a bee sting the year before. His mother, Loretta, refuses to accept that an allergy to bees caused his death. She stopped going to church when one of the members mentioned that her relative died the same way.

On the day that Gary will meet the man in the black suit, his father gives him permission to go fishing after finishing his chores. His father makes him promise not to go beyond the split in Castle Stream. He also makes the same promise to his mother, who looks nervous about his going to the stream alone. Gary remembers how his father wept and covered his brother's body with his shirt the day he died. He again promises his mother not to go beyond the fork in the stream.

The family dog, Candy Bill, follows Gary as he completes his chores. When Gary leaves to go fishing, however, the dog barks and refuses to come with him. Gary's mother reminds him to follow his father's instructions as he is walking away. Gary stops at two or more places to fish. At one point, he catches a nineteen-inch trout, cleans it, and puts it in his creel (a container used to carry fish). Finally, he wanders to where the stream splits. Gary catches one more fish and falls asleep while waiting for another.

Gary wakes up when he feels a pull at his line. He discovers that there is a bee sitting on his nose, and it refuses to leave. He is terrified of dying like his brother, even though he has been stung by bees in the past. Gary hears the sound of hands clapping together, and the bee falls dead onto his lap. Gary tries to pull in the fish, but his line snaps. When Gary looks toward the sound, he sees a man in a black three-piece suit. The man is pale with black hair and eyes that are orange flames. The sight of him causes Gary to wet himself. Gary knows that he is not human but hopes that pretending not to notice will protect him.

The man tells Gary that he saved him from the bee and asks if they are well met, which is an archaic greeting. The man approaches, and Gary smells sulfur. The man does not crush or touch any grass as he walks, and he has long, clawed fingers. Gary knows that the man is the devil and is certain that he will die, but the fear paralyzes him. Gary asks the man not to harm him, but the man only jokes about Gary's being unable to control his bladder and throws himself back on the grass to laugh. Gary is most afraid of what the devil will do to him *after* he dies.

The man tells Gary that Loretta, his mother, is dead. He gives gruesome details about how she died of a bee sting. Pausing, he abruptly kills a leaping fish by pointing at it. He concludes that Gary's mother is the one responsible for Dan's death because she carried the allergy he inherited. Gary gives in and accepts that his mother is dead.

The man says that he is hungry and plans on eating Gary. He tells Gary to be grateful because his father would abuse him without Gary's mother in their lives. He also adds that everyone who is murdered goes to heaven. Gary gives the man the nineteen-inch fish that he caught, and he swallows it whole like a shark. The fish begins to cook as it enters the man's mouth. The man starts to cry tears of blood, and the image spurs Gary to run. The man in the black suit chases Gary, and Gary throws his fishing pole at him. When Gary is finally out of breath and too tired to keep going, he discovers that the man is no longer following him on the road. Gary feels that the man is watching him in the woods.

He sees his father in the road; he has his fishing gear with him to join Gary. The two run toward each other, and a crying Gary says that the man told him his mother is dead. His father tells Gary that he just saw his mother and that she is alive. His father is furious that someone lied to Gary but asks if it could have been a dream. He walks toward the river to get Gary's rod and creel, but Gary persuades his father to take him home first, so that he can see his mother. As they walk home, Gary tells him that he caught a fish. At home, Gary kisses his mother, and his father tells her that he had a nightmare. His father asks Gary if he wants to come with him to retrieve the fishing gear, and Gary realizes that he wants Gary to face his fear.

Gary brings the family Bible with him when they return to the stream. The grass where the man had fallen back laughing is now yellow and dead. Gary holds the Bible out in front of him while his father goes down to the bank. He smells the area and brings back the now empty creel. Heat has also damaged the ground near the rod. His father wonders why the creel is empty, because Gary told him that he had caught a fish. Gary says that the man must have eaten the other fish out of his creel. His father throws the creel away into the stream and tells Gary not to say anything about its being missing to his mother unless she asks. She never asks.

Now an old man, Gary believes that he escaped the devil out of sheer luck, not because God protected him. He tries to convince himself that he has been a good person. He even persuaded his mother to return to church. Gary also knows that he did nothing at the age of nine to deserve seeing the man in the black suit. He fears the man's return and wonders if he is still ravenous.

CHARACTERS

Albion

See Dad

Candy Bill

Candy Bill is the family dog. A black Scottie, he is Gary's constant companion, following him everywhere. He refuses, however, to follow Gary fishing the day that he meets the man in the black suit. The dog barks at Gary as he leaves.

Dad

Gary calls his father Dad. Dad covers Dan's body with his shirt before bringing his son home, where he cries and swears. He is a farmer and promises Gary that he can go fishing after completing his chores on the farm. He warns Gary, however, not to go beyond where the stream splits. Later, he attempts to rationalize Gary's meeting the man in the black suit by blaming it on a dream, but he is apparently startled by what he finds when they return to the stream for Gary's rod and creel. He throws the creel into the stream and warns Gary never to mention it to his mother.

Dan

Dan is Gary's older brother, who died the year before Gary met the man in the black suit. Dan died from an allergic reaction to a bee sting, and the family is deeply affected by the loss. Gary has nightmares, and his mother refuses to accept the cause of his death.

Devil

See Man in the Black Suit

Gary

Gary is ninety years old when he writes about meeting the man in the black suit as a nine-year-old boy. Dan, his older brother, died of a bee sting the year before the encounter, and Gary has had nightmares since his death. Gary promises not to go beyond the split in the stream, but he does go to where the stream forks, where he meets the man in the black suit. Gary narrowly escapes the inhuman monster intent on eating him. At the age of ninety, he is still afraid of seeing the man again.

Loretta

See Mother

Man in the Black Suit

Gary identifies the man in the black suit as the devil. He kills a bee on Gary's nose with a clap before approaching the boy. His eyes are flames, and his fingers have claws. He has a twisted sense of humor and makes jokes about Gary. He lies to the boy about his mother's death to convince Gary that he does not want to live. The man plans on eating Gary, but his eating Gary's fish gives the boy a chance to escape. He chases Gary for a while and suddenly vanishes. Gary still fears his return.

Mother

Gary's mother is still grieving the loss of Dan and remains protective of Gary. She refuses to believe that Dan died from a bee sting, and she stopped going to church after a woman mentioned that her uncle died the same way. She is uncomfortable with Gary's fishing alone, but she allows it as long as he promises to obey his father and not go past the split in the stream.

Mama Sweet

Mama Sweet is a member of the same church Gary's family attends. Her uncle died of an allergic reaction to a bee sting. When she tells Gary's mother that her family member died the same way Dan did, Loretta becomes incensed. Gary's mother does not believe that a bee could have killed her son, and she stops going to church so that she does not have to see Mama Sweet again.

THEMES

Isolation

Isolation is a continuing theme in "The Man in the Black Suit." Gary's childhood home is a farm in New England. It seems ideal in its beauty and provides the family with independence. The independence of the farming community, however, also creates great social isolation. Neighbors do not see each other often, and in the winter families rarely leave their homes. The extreme isolation has negative consequences. There is the physical risk of not being able to reach necessary medical care. There are also psychological risks. For example, a father murdered his family over the winter because he had "a headful of bad ideas."

The danger of isolation is evident in Gary's life. Gary chooses to go fishing by himself, despite knowing the risk that comes with being alone. His mother is uncomfortable about Gary's leaving on his own, but she ignores her instincts and allows him to go. Even Gary's dog is unwilling to follow him the day he meets the man in the black suit. The isolation of Gary's situation is the first clue to the extreme danger he is in on his journey.

Death

Death is a part of Gary's life throughout the story. He begins the story as an elderly man who knows death is near. As he explains his childhood encounter with the man in the black suit, Gary recalls the death of his brother and how it affected his family. His father wept and swore, and his mother refused to face the reality

TOPICS FOR FURTHER STUDY

- Read *Level Up* (2011), by Gene Luen Yang. This young-adult graphic novel is the story of Dennis Ouyang. When he fails college after his father's death, angels appear to help him achieve his goals. Create your own comic where Gary and Dennis meet. They can meet at any age and in any scenario. What do they have in common? Would they be able to help each other? Draw or use a computer to create your comic and share it with the class.
- Research the history of horror in literature. When did it begin, and how has it evolved over time? Create a web page that provides an overview of the history and famous individuals. Focus most of your discussion on American authors, and include a link for King.
- Read "Young Goodman Brown" (1835), by Nathaniel Hawthorne, which King says partially inspired "The Man in the Black Suit." Hawthorne tells the story of a young man who is tempted by the devil and loses his faith in his community and all that he loves. Compare and contrast the two tales in an essay. How are the themes, style, settings, and characters similar, and how are they different?
- Break into small groups and research local myths and urban legends. Together, choose a myth or legend and create a short, one-act play based on it. Record the group acting out the play and upload it using EDPuzzle.
- Research rural America in the 1910s and write a report. Consider what life on a farm was like and how the culture and demographics were changing. What were some commonly held traditions or beliefs, such as dowsing? Share your paper with the class and discuss your findings together. Use Easel.ly to organize information and create useful graphics for your presentation.

As an old man, Gary fears he will no longer be able to outrun the man in the suit if he meets him again
(©Nuno Monteiro / Shutterstock.com)

that a bee could cause his death. She left the church, and Gary had nightmares.

As the story progresses, it is clear that Gary fears death, when a bee lands on his nose. Gary has been stung by bees before, but the idea comes to him that it is the same bee that killed his brother: "This was a special bee, a devil-bee, and it had come back to finish the other of Albion and Loretta's two boys." It is not until the man in the black suit appears that Gary faces the reality of his own death. The man does not just threaten Gary's life; he also torments him by saying that Gary's mother is dead. Although Gary escapes death at the hands of the man in the black suit, he is waiting for the man's return and his death. His terror, however, goes beyond the fear of death to what will happen to him after he dies.

Supernatural

Like many of King's stories, "The Man in the Black Suit" blends supernatural elements with everyday activities. The simple act of fishing leads to a meeting with the man in the black suit, an encounter that haunts Gary until the end of his life. The most obvious supernatural character is the devil. He can kill with the clap of a hand or the point of a finger. He has fiery eyes and claws for fingers, and he smells of sulfur and leaves dead grass and flowers in his wake. All of these are demonic signs. The man, however, is not the only supernatural aspect of the story.

When Gary describes his childhood, he recalls a man who killed his family and claimed that "the ghosts made him do it." The woods around his home were "dark long places full of moose and mosquitoes, snakes and secrets. In those days there were ghosts everywhere." He also remembers a local man who practiced dowsing, which is a supernatural method of finding water using a divining rod. King hints that there is a collective fear of supernatural evil in the woods. Both of his parents warn Gary against going beyond the split in the creek when he has permission to go fishing on his own. Gary chooses to push his boundaries, however, and he goes all the way up to where the stream splits. By making this decision, he places himself in the path of the man in the black suit.

Faith

Faith is an important topic in "The Man in the Black Suit." Gary's family struggles with faith after losing Dan. They have more faith in the potential for evil than good, which is why his parents want him to avoid the split in the stream. They do not want to lose another son. His mother has stopped going to church, and his father took God's name in vain, suggesting that they blame God for not protecting their family. Gary loses faith in both logic and religion when the bee remains on his nose. Although he understands that the bee that stung his brother is dead and that he has had no reactions to bee stings in the past, Gary still believes that the bee is a source of evil and the same one that killed Dan.

When Gary meets the man in the black suit, he does not place his faith in his religious upbringing. He believes the words of the devil and barely escapes with his life. As an old man waiting for death, Gary confesses that he still does not have faith in God. Gary lives in fear because of the devil's words. He feels that it was "*just* luck" that saved him from the man in the black suit when he was a child, and he is concerned that his luck has run out and that the devil will return.

STYLE

Point of View

"The Man in the Black Suit" is told from the first-person point of view, like many of King's narratives. Gary is the ninety-year-old narrator who explains his present situation and tells a story that takes place in his childhood. The first-person perspective provides insight into Gary's thoughts and feelings in the present as well as the past. For example, Gary explains how he felt the man in the black suit watching him from the woods after he escaped. He also shares that he can still hear the devil's voice when he is an old man, and Gary is afraid that the man will one day return.

Narrative

"The Man in the Black Suit" is not a simple narrative. It functions as a framework narrative. As William Harmon explains in *A Handbook to Literature*, a framework is "a story inside a story." Gary begins the narrative as a ninety-year-old man in a nursing home, where he tells another story. He explains that he is writing about this memory because he does not want it. As he puts it, "What you write down sometimes leaves you forever." He tells the story of meeting the man in the black suit and the terror of coming face to face with the devil. He ends the narrative in the present as he shares his lingering doubt in his faith as well as his fear of the man's return.

Symbolism

The use of symbolism is widely recognized in King's work. A symbol, according to M. H. Abrams in *A Glossary of Literary Terms*, is "a word or phrase that signifies an object or event which in its turn signifies something . . . beyond itself." For example, bees are symbols of death in "The Man in the Black Suit." Dan is killed by a bee, and Gary fears that the bee on his nose will kill him. He also accepts the man's lie that his mother is dead because he hears that a bee killed her.

HISTORICAL CONTEXT

America in the 1990s and Supernatural Entertainment

Human cultures have always been drawn to the supernatural, so it should not be surprising that the supernatural is embedded in American popular culture. In the 1990s, when King wrote "The Man in the Black Suit," the way people viewed the supernatural was evolving. For example, television shows based on the supernatural were becoming more realistic, as Lawrence R. Samuel points out in *Supernatural America: A Cultural History*.

The 1990s was a decade of change. After the weak economy of the 1980s, there was a "sustained period of expansion that, as of mid-2000, was the third longest since World War II," according to the *Encyclopedia of the Nations*. The decade, however, was not without its share of tragedies. Linnie Blake, writing in "Vampires, Mad Scientists and the Unquiet Dead," argues that the deadly confrontation between the family of Randy Weaver and federal agents at Ruby Ridge, Idaho, in 1992; the Waco, Texas, siege of the Branch Davidians religious group in 1993; and the bombing of the Oklahoma City Alfred P. Murrah Federal

COMPARE & CONTRAST

- **1910s:** The decade sees growth in the overall economy and a rise in the middle class. This economic growth extends to rural farming communities. Minority farmers and day laborers do not benefit as much financially.

  1990s: The United States experiences an economic increase that improves the lives of many Americans in the middle class. The economic boom does not affect everyone equally, and many minorities do not experience the same gains.

  Today: The US economy is not entirely recovered after the 2008 economic crash. CBS News reports that the middle class is in decline, and the majority of Americans believe that it is harder to remain part of the middle class now than it was twenty-five years ago.

- **1910s:** The rural population begins to decline. Many people choose to move to urban areas to pursue industrial jobs. Day laborers and African Americans who do not profit well in the countryside are more likely to relocate.

  1990s: The farming population continues to decrease in the 1980s owing to an agricultural recession. By 1993, only 1.7 percent of the population works on farms, according to the *Monthly Labor Review*.

  Today: The population growth in rural areas is lower than that in cities, but the population in rural counties remains stable between 2014 and 2015. The slight change indicates that the massive population loss over the past decades may be slowing.

- **1910s:** Gothic fiction and supernatural tales are familiar and established in American fiction, from early legends to the works of the nineteenth-century author Edgar Allan Poe. Henry James, Edith Wharton, and Ambrose Bierce are early twentieth-century authors who continue the gothic tradition.

  1990s: Violent tragedies, such as the standoff in Waco, Texas, and the bombing of the Oklahoma City federal building, change society. Supernatural entertainment, especially in film, becomes more realistic and reflects the insecurities of the time.

  Today: Supernatural, horror, and fantasy are well-established genres in popular culture. Television shows such as *Game of Thrones* and *American Horror Story* are mainstream entertainment, and movies based on comic books and hero myths are commercial successes.

Building in 1995 collectively provided the ideal societal backdrop for gothic, supernatural shows.

The Ruby Ridge incident began as a standoff that occurred when Randy Weaver failed to appear in court on a weapons charge. According to *Encyclopædia Britannica*: "Marshals assessed that Weaver and his family were likely to resist violently if confronted directly, so plans for a stealth operation were drawn up." The situation became violent after the family dog found the marshals. After the marshals killed Weaver's son and lost one of their own, help from the FBI was requested. An FBI sniper shot Weaver as well as his wife and a friend inside the cabin. The shots were later declared unconstitutional.

Much like the Ruby Ridge incident, the Waco siege involved a confrontation with the government. The Bureau of Alcohol, Tobacco, and Firearms (ATF) obtained a warrant to search the compound of the Branch Davidian sect, led by David Koresh, in 1993. The compound housed his followers, including women and children. A shootout ensued on February 28, 1993, resulting in a standoff. On April 19,

Gary falls asleep while fishing one day (©Sergey Nivens / Shutterstock.com)

1993, the FBI and ATF were authorized to use tear gas. According to *Frontline*, the Davidians were warned to exit before agents sprayed the tear gas. After the gas had been used, three fires broke out in the compound, killing over eighty people.

On April 19, 1995, the Alfred P. Murrah Federal Building in Oklahoma City was destroyed by a bomb, killing 168 men, women, and children and wounding over 500. Timothy McVeigh and Terry Nichols were arrested for the crime. According to John Philip Jenkins in the *Encyclopædia Britannica*, "McVeigh claimed that the building in Oklahoma City was targeted to avenge the more than 70 deaths at Waco." These tragedies changed America, and Blake points out that "a range of gothic programmes addressed themselves to the climate of conspiratorial secrecy and social malaise that dominated popular perceptions." Television shows such as *The X-Files* (1993–2002, 2016–) and *American Gothic* (1995–1996) explored the supernatural as well as the dangers of trusting authority. Other popular shows with supernatural themes in the 1990s included *Highlander: The Series* (1992–1998), *Buffy the Vampire Slayer* (1997–2003), *Angel* (1999–2004), *Charmed* (1998–2006), and remakes of the classic program *The Outer Limits* (1995–2002).

Rural America in the 1910s

"The Man in the Black Suit" takes place in 1914 in rural Maine. Life in rural America was very different from life in the cities. The rural population in New England fell in the early twentieth century. As Alexander E. Cance points out in "The Decline of the Rural Population in New England," the New England soil was found to be difficult to farm, causing an exodus that began in the nineteenth century. The number of people moving to the cities increased, but "the period was one of the few truly affluent times in modern rural America," according to David Blanke in *The 1910s*. Blanke lists improvement in fertilizers, machines, and the global market as reasons for the increased production.

The financial strength of rural America would last until the end of World War I, which officially began the same year that Gary met the man in the black suit. The United States, however, did not enter the conflict until 1917. Gary's family appears to benefit from the current economic development. They own their farm and seem to be financially stable. Still, they are hard workers, including Gary, who has to complete his chores before taking any leisure time. The growth of farming income, however, was limited to commercial farm owners. Day laborers and African American farmers did not benefit, and many of them left rural life to find work in the cities.

CRITICAL OVERVIEW

King quickly became a commercial success, but the respect of literary critics was not forthcoming. Even when reviews were positive, many people did not consider horror, suspense, or science fiction to be genuine literature. The *Kirkus Reviews* assessment of *Carrie* reports, "King handles his first novel with considerable accomplishment and very little hokum." This first novel provided King with financial security and secured his reputation as a horror writer. His reputation continued with the success of *Salem's Lot* and *The Shining*, which were praised as great works of horror fiction. *Kirkus Reviews*, for example, describes *The Shining* as "back-prickling indeed despite the reader's unwillingness at being mercilessly manipulated."

King's versatility and talent as an author, however, were not always appreciated. In his *New York Times* review of *Misery*, for example, John Katzenbach points out that the author's popularity and reputation keep his work from being taken seriously. "Success has a way of diminishing value and obscuring actual worth. The numbers attached to a book (one million copies first printing, $400,000 promotional budget) gain more attention than the words the book contains." King's skill as a literary author was affirmed when he won the O. Henry Award for "The Man in the Black Suit" in 1996. Although blind submissions determine the winners, Cindy Dyson points out in "Biography of Stephen King," "Some of his competitors for the award have voiced dissatisfaction with a winner who scoffs the literary establishment."

In 2003, King won the National Book Foundation's Medal for Distinguished Contribution to American Letters, after decades of success. The literary world was outraged. As David D. Kirkpatrick says in the *New York Times*, "Very little of Mr. King's work would qualify as literary fiction." He quotes Harold Bloom's displeasure with the selection: "That they could believe that there is any literary value there or any aesthetic accomplishment or signs of an inventive human intelligence is simply a testimony to their own idiocy."

King's writing remains popular, and critics have continued to argue over the literary merits of his writing. His work has been adapted for films, television shows, plays, and comics. The length of King's career has given him the time to show his range as an artist as well as to complete any unfinished stories. *Doctor Sleep*, published in 2013, for example, continues the story of the main character in *The Shining*. Erik Spanberg's review of the book for the *Christian Science Monitor* comes to this conclusion: "After more than 50 novels, every one a strong seller, reviewers now recognize that King endures on the basis of more than just blood and guts, though he still relishes those moments, too." While some critics will always refuse to accept King's accomplishments simply because of the genre of his books, he has managed to earn the respect of others and the love of the public.

CRITICISM

April Paris

Paris is a freelance writer with a degree in classical literature and a background in academic writing. In the following essay, she argues that Gary does not survive his encounter with the devil unscathed and that his past still affects his present in "The Man in the Black Suit."

The connection between the past and the present in "The Man in the Black Suit" reveals how the narrator remains emotionally trapped in the terror of his childhood. Despite his physical escape from the devil when he was nine years old, Gary did not leave behind the psychological effects of the encounter. The incident remains with him, fueling his doubt, loss of faith, and fear. As Gary waits for his coming death at the age of ninety, he cannot escape the sense of impending doom. By focusing his attention on evil, he proves that he never stopped believing the man in the black suit.

> "DESPITE HIS PHYSICAL ESCAPE FROM THE DEVIL WHEN HE WAS NINE YEARS OLD, GARY DOES NOT LEAVE BEHIND THE PSYCHOLOGICAL EFFECTS OF THE ENCOUNTER. THE INCIDENT REMAINS WITH HIM, FUELING HIS DOUBT, LOSS OF FAITH, AND FEAR."

In *Six Stories*, as quoted by Stephen Spignesi in *The Essential Stephen King*, the author says that there is "a long New England tradition of stories which dealt with meeting the devil in the woods." He goes on to explain that these encounters are religious tests. Viewing the meeting as a spiritual test gives it new meaning. The faith of both Gary and his family has been shaken. They are traumatized by the unexpected death of Dan, Gary's older brother, to a bee sting. Each one mourns in a different way, and they do not express the same trust in God they once had. Gary has nightmares about his brother, and his mother leaves the church because she refuses to believe that her son was killed by something as simple as a bee sting. Gary's father shows emotion only when he carries Gary's body back to the family home, but it seems that he blames God for the tragedy. Gary recalls, "It was the only time I ever heard my dad take the savior's name in vain." Another clue to the family's wavering faith is the ribbon his mother wove into his father's creel. The ribbon reads, "DEDICATED TO JESUS." The ribbon is a symbol of the religious conviction that his mother had, a belief that she expected her family to share. Gary, however, makes it very clear that the ribbon was placed on the creel before Dan died.

Gary's religious upbringing allows him to easily recognize the man in the black suit as the devil when he sees him on the bank of Castle Stream. The man in the black suit has the trademarks of the Christian view of the devil. He smells of sulfur and has eyes of flame. The sulfur and the fire are associated with Hell, the domain of the devil. Although Gary sees the man in the black suit for who he is, his fear clouds his judgment. As R. Mac Jones says in "Replacing People and Reinforcing Family in Stephen King's 'The Man in the Black Suit,'" "The Devil the rhetorician, rather than the Devil the preternatural predator, turns a young boy's feeble attempts at argumentation into an occasion to generate fear and despair." He remembers that the devil lies and that one name for the devil is the father of lies, but he still accepts what the man in the black suit says as true.

One confirmed lie that the man in the black suit tells Gary is that his mother is dead. Gary calls the man a liar to his face but confesses that "on some level I believed him completely." With this belief, the man in the black suit has taken hold of Gary's mind. The lie about his mother's death is quickly disproved when Gary sees her again. The other statements, however, are not so easy to discern as lies. He claims that Dan died because his mother had the same allergy to bees and passed the sensitivity on to her son. The devil blames the mother for the son's death, which Gary accepts in the moment. He also makes other suspicious claims. For example, the devil says that murder victims go to heaven and that Gary will never be able to escape him. When Gary first runs away, it seems possible that he will not escape, but the devil vanishes without any explanation. The boy, however, still feels that the man is watching him from the woods.

Jones points out that the man in the black suit's failure to kill and eat Gary when he had the chance is "telling." His inability to capture Gary when he runs also hints at the idea that physically consuming the nine-year-old is not his primary goal. After all, he killed a bee with a clap and a fish with a snap. He could easily have immobilized or destroyed a child from a distance. Instead, he chooses to torment Gary mentally and emotionally in order to shatter his faith once and for all. The devil is preying on the boy's weakness, a weakness that the man in the black suit did not have to create.

Gary's fear of death and belief in supernatural evil are evident before he ever sees the devil. When he wakes up with a bee on his nose, Gary is terrified that it will kill him. He knows that bee stings have never bothered him in the past, but the fear remains. In his mind, it is the same bee that killed his brother, "a devil-bee": "Now the bee had returned, and now it would kill me." In Gary's mind, the life of his innocent brother was not extinguished by a random

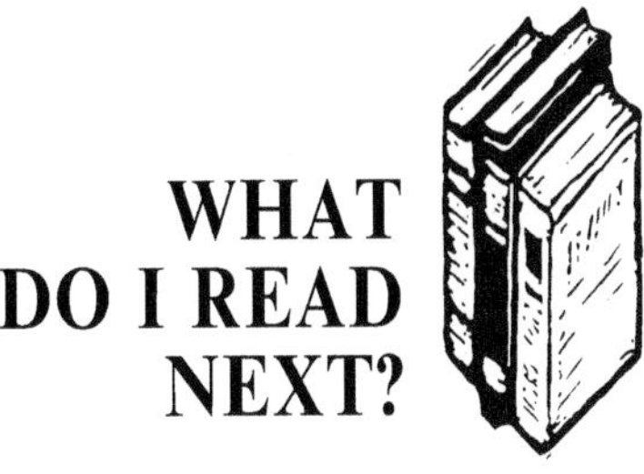

WHAT DO I READ NEXT?

- Published in 2005, *America in the 1910s*, by Jim Callan, gives an overview of the decade and setting of "The Man in the Black Suit." The young-adult nonfiction text is a useful introduction to the decade.
- *On Writing: A Memoir of the Craft*, written by King, is both an autobiography and a writing tutorial. Published in 2000 and reissued in a tenth-anniversary edition in 2010, the book provides valuable insight for anyone who wants to better understand King's life and work.
- *Horror: A Literary History*, by Xavier Aldana Reyes, was published in 2016. Reyes examines the history of horror fiction for the past 250 years and explains the literary merit of supernatural fiction.
- *The Icarus Girl* (2005) is Helen Oyeyemi's first novel and has been compared to King's work. Somewhat based on Nigerian mythology, the story is about an eight-year-old girl who makes a new friend while visiting family in Nigeria, only to discover her friend is not what she seems.
- Published in 2008, *The Graveyard Book*, by Neil Gaiman, earned the Newbery Medal. This story of a boy raised by ghosts reverses the traditional views of which creatures are good and which are evil.
- King's novel *The Eyes of the Dragon*, published in 1987, is a fantasy story and a classic tale of good and evil. The book is a departure from his horror and shows the author's versatility.

accident but by a terrifying evil. God failed to save Dan from death, and Gary is sure that he will not save him either. After the bee dies, Gary turns from an irrational fear of a supernatural death to a very rational terror. Meeting the man in the black suit merely confirms Gary's previous suspicion that God will not protect him.

His encounter with the man in the black suit takes on symbolic meaning. Gary is fishing, and the devil calls him "fisherboy." Fish and fishing are symbolic in the Christian tradition. As Peter Maser points out in the *Encyclopedia of Christianity*, "The church fathers developed the following train of thought: believers as fish, Christ as fisherman, Christ as fish." Gary as a young fisherman becomes a Christ figure tempted by the devil. As the man in the black suit threatens to eat Gary, the boy gives him the nineteen-inch fish that he caught earlier. He sacrifices his prize catch, another Christ symbol, which finally gives him the opportunity to escape as the man in the black suit is preoccupied with eating the fish. While watching the devil eat his fish, Gary can overcome the paralyzing fear that has been holding him by the stream and runs.

Escaping the man in the black suit does not end Gary's fear. He carries the family Bible back with him to retrieve his creel with his father. He holds it in front of him like a shield. The Bible, however, offers him no relief. "I don't know if I had the sense of being watched that time or not; I was too scared to have a sense of anything," Gary explains. For much of his life, Gary represses his introduction to the devil, but it does not stop the incident from haunting him as he reviews his life.

In "Rising like Old Corpses: Stephen King and the Horrors of Time-Past," Leonard G. Heldreth points out a common element in King's work: "Throughout the novels and short stories, past-time escapes and intrudes into the present, corrupting the current moment with old values, outgrown beliefs, and long suppressed fears." At the end of his life, a ninety-year-old Gary is no longer able to hide his doubt or his terror. As he recalls the events over the decades, the voice of the man in the black suit is what he hears the loudest. He can

> hear that voice drop even lower, into ranges which are inhuman. Big fish! It whispers in tones of hushed greed, and all the truths of the moral world fall to ruin before its hunger.

Gary is no longer able to run away from the devil, and part of his past self remains with him in the present. Heldreth notes, "The past must be permanently escaped—even the past self must be escaped—if the future is to achieve realization." Unfortunately for Gary, his escape was only physical. The doubting and terrified

Gary is frightened by the bee because his brother recently died from an allergic reaction to a bee sting
(©irin-k / Shutterstock.com)

child remained hidden away and now demands to be heard. None of Gary's good works in life give him any confidence in his future. Not even his ability to talk his mother into returning to the church can make Gary feel that he will have divine protection in this life or the next. He fears the return of the devil after leading a moral life, because he had lived a good life when he first met the man in the black suit, yet it did not protect him.

The faith that Gary began to lose in the past is still broken in the present. He is disappointed that God did not intervene to save him from the devil. As he says, "I feel more and more strongly that my escaping him was my luck—*just* luck." The adult Gary is able to believe that evil will come for him when his life comes to an end. As a child, the devil said to him, "You can't get away, fisherboy!" Just like the boy from the past, Gary still fears that the promises of the man in the black suit will come true. He is also terrified of what awaits if the devil did tell him the truth.

Source: April Paris, Critical Essay on "The Man in the Black Suit," in *Short Stories for Students*, Gale, Cengage Learning, 2017.

SOURCES

Abrams, M. H., "Symbol," in *A Glossary of Literary Terms*, Harcourt Brace College Publishers, 1999, pp. 311–14.

"The Author," Stephen King website, http://stephenking.com/the_author.html (accessed August 21, 2016).

Beahm, George, *The Stephen King Companion*, Thomas Dunne Books, 2015.

Blake, Linnie, "Vampires, Mad Scientists and the Unquiet Dead," in *The Gothic in Contemporary Literature and Popular Culture: Pop Goth*, edited by Justin D. Edwards and Agnieszka Soltysik Monnet, Routledge, 2012, pp. 39–40.

Blanke, David, *The 1910s*, Greenwood Press, 2002, p. 5.

Cance, Alexander E., "The Decline of the Rural Population in New England," in *Publications of the American Statistical Association*, Vol. 13, No. 97, March 1912, pp. 96–101.

Dyson, Cindy, "Biography of Stephen King," in *Bloom's BioCritiques: Stephen King*, edited by Harold Bloom, Chelsea House Publishers, 2002, p. 39.

Harmon, William, "Framework-Story," in *A Handbook to Literature*, Prentice Hall, 2003, p. 219.

Heldreth, Leonard G., "Rising like Old Corpses: Stephen King and the Horrors of Time-Past," in *Journal of the Fantastic in the Arts*, Vol. 2, No. 1, Spring 1989, pp. 5–13.

Ilg, Randy E., "The Changing Face of Farm Employment," in *Monthly Labor Review*, April 1995, pp. 3–12.

Jenkins, John Philip, "Oklahoma City Bombing," in *Encyclopædia Britannica*, https://www.britannica.com/event/Oklahoma-City-bombing (accessed August 21, 2016).

Jones, R. Mac, "Replacing People and Reinforcing Family in Stephen King's 'The Man in the Black Suit,'" in *Revenant*, Vol. 1, No. 1, Winter 2015, pp. 23–34, http://www.revenantjournal.com/contents/replacing-people-and-reinforcing-family-in-stephen-kings-the-man-in-the-black-suit-2/#sthash.CfYtlt75.dpbs (accessed August 21, 2016).

Katzenbach, John, "Summer Reading: Sheldon Gets the Ax," in *New York Times*, May 31, 1987, https://www.nytimes.com/books/97/03/09/lifetimes/kin-r-misery.html (accessed August 21, 2016).

King, Stephen, "The Man in the Black Suit," in *Everything's Eventual: 14 Dark Tales*, Scribner, 2002, pp. 45–70.

Kirkpatrick, David D., "A Literary Reward for Stephen King," in *New York Times*, September 15, 2003, http://www.nytimes.com/2003/09/15/books/a-literary-award-for-stephen-king (accessed August 21, 2016).

Maser, Peter, "Fish," in *Encyclopedia of Christianity*, edited by Erwin Falbush, Geoffrey W. Bromily, and David Barrett, William B. Eerdmans Publishing, 2001, p. 321.

Picchi, Aimee, "7 Signs You're Dropping Out of the Middle Class," CBS News website, http://www.cbsnews.com/media/7-signs-youre-dropping-out-of-the-middle-class/ (accessed August 21, 2016).

"Population and Migration," US Department of Agriculture website, http://www.ers.usda.gov/topics/rural-economy-population/population-migration.aspx (accessed August 21, 2016).

Review of *Carrie*, in *Kirkus Reviews*, April 1, 1974, https://www.kirkusreviews.com/book-reviews/stephen-king/carrie/ (accessed August 21, 2016).

Review of *The Shining*, in *Kirkus Reviews*, January 1, 1976, https://www.kirkusreviews.com/book-reviews/stephen-king/the-shining/ (accessed August 21, 2016).

"Ruby Ridge Incident," in *Encyclopædia Britannica*, https://www.britannica.com/event/Ruby-Ridge-incident (accessed August 21, 2016).

Samuel, Lawrence R., *Supernatural America: A Cultural History*, Praeger, 2011, p. 144.

Spanberg, Erik, Review of *Doctor Sleep*, in *Christian Science Monitor*, September 27, 2013.

Spignesi, Stephen J., *The Essential Stephen King*, New Page Books, 2001, p. 135.

"United States—Economy," in *Encyclopedia of the Nations*, http://www.nationsencyclopedia.com/Americas/United-States-ECONOMY.html (accessed August 21, 2016).

"Waco: The Inside Story—Chronology of the Siege," PBS website, http://www.pbs.org/wgbh/pages/frontline/waco/timeline5.html (accessed August 21, 2016).

FURTHER READING

Derks, Scott, *This Is Who We Were: In the 1910s*, Grey House Publishing, 2014.

Derks blends personal interviews with the history and economy of the decade. The interviews provide a personal view of events and create a better understanding of the time.

Held, Jacob M., ed., *Stephen King and Philosophy*, Rowman & Littlefield, 2016.

This critical view of King's work examines the author's understanding of human natures and fears. The volume will help readers gain greater insight into King's fiction.

Ochoa, George, *America in the 1990s*, Facts on File, 2005.

This nonfiction text was developed for young adults. It provides information about the culture as well as the history of the time period when "The Man in the Black Suit" was written.

Sears, John, *Stephen King's Gothic*, University of Wales Press, 2001.

Sears looks at the gothic influence on King's fiction. The analysis will benefit anyone who desires a greater understanding of the author's work.

Spignesi, Stephen J., *The Complete Stephen King Encyclopedia: The Definitive Guide to the Works of America's Master of Horror*, Contemporary Books, 1991.

This encyclopedia of King's early works is a basic reference manual. The text is beneficial for researchers who have various levels of expertise.

SUGGESTED SEARCH TERMS

Stephen King AND biography

Stephen King AND criticism

Stephen King AND short stories

United States AND 1910s

Stephen King AND The Man in the Dark Suit

supernatural literature AND American culture

1990s AND American culture

devil AND American literature

María Concepción

KATHERINE ANNE PORTER

1922

Short-story master Katherine Anne Porter traveled extensively in her lifetime, both in the United States and all over the world. Her travels, especially her long trips in Mexico in a time of political turmoil, often influenced her work, such as with "María Concepción," which is set in a small Mexican town. This story was first published in *Century* magazine in 1922 and was also included in Porter's first collection, *Flowering Judas and Other Stories*, which debuted in 1930. "María Concepción" highlights dark emotions—betrayal and violent jealousy—which Porter undoubtedly witnessed during her stays in Mexico during a lengthy and bloody revolution. However, the story also offers themes of community and loyalty, resulting in an interesting mix of the many facets of human behavior, good and bad.

AUTHOR BIOGRAPHY

The fourth of five children, Porter was born on May 15, 1890, in Indian Creek, Texas, to Harrison Boone Porter and Mary Alice Jones. When Porter was two years old, her mother died in childbirth. Her father took the children to live with his own mother. After Porter's grandmother passed away in 1901, she spent the remainder of her school years in convent

María Concepción is pregnant when she discovers that her husband, Juan, has been unfaithful
(©K3S / Shutterstock.com)

schools in Texas and Louisiana. She was always a voracious reader.

When Porter was sixteen years old, she ran away from school and eloped with John Henry Koontz. The marriage was never very successful. Some biographers believe that her husband was abusive, and all agree that the two were not compatible. He was often away from home, and the solitude allowed Porter time for writing. She published her first poem, "Texas by the Gulf of Mexico," in 1912. In 1914 she moved to Chicago, hoping for a career on the stage, and spent a few years acting, singing, and working as a secretary to pay the bills. She had several whirlwind romances, divorcing Koontz and then marrying and divorcing twice more. After a period spent in a sanatorium for ill health, Porter found a job as a society writer for the *Fort Worth Critic*, followed by a position with the *Rocky Mountain News* in Denver, Colorado, writing book reviews and some news items.

The 1920s were formative for Porter as a writer. She moved to Greenwich Village, in New York City, and began focusing on writing fiction. She studied art and traveled a lot, often to Mexico. Her travels influenced her writing, as can be seen in her first published story, "María Concepción," which appeared in *Century* magazine in 1922. She continued to write short stories, often publishing in smaller, less popular magazines, where she retained more control over editing; this was important to her because of her perfectionist approach to her work.

Flowering Judas and Other Stories, Porter's first collection, which includes "María Concepción," was published in 1930. Although critical reception was favorable, it was only a modest success in terms of sales. Porter broadened her travels, heading to Europe with Eugene Pressly, who was sent to Switzerland and Paris for his work with the American Foreign Service. Porter and Pressly married in 1933. The marriage lasted five years, and upon her divorce, Porter almost immediately married Albert Erskine. The couple were separated within two years, though they did not formally divorce until 1942.

Porter's second short-fiction collection, *Pale Horse, Pale Rider*, was published in 1939, followed by *The Leaning Tower and Other Stories* in 1944. *Ship of Fools*, Porter's only novel, came out in 1962 and was an instant success. After the book's publication, Porter wrote infrequently, but her *Collected Stories* (1964) received both the Pulitzer Prize and the National Book Award.

In the late 1970s, Porter experienced several major strokes. She went into decline, requiring constant nursing care until her death on September 18, 1980, in Silver Spring, Maryland.

MEDIA ADAPTATIONS

- In 1999, Blackstone Audio released an audiobook of *The Collected Stories of Katherine Anne Porter*, which includes the works that originally appeared in *Flowering Judas*, *Pale Horse, Pale Rider*, and *The Leaning Tower*. The recording, available online, runs two hours and forty-nine minutes and is narrated by Siobhan McKenna.
- Jane Whynaught reads the stories in *Flowering Judas* in a 1986 recording. Because the recording is only available on audiocassette, it is difficult to find.

PLOT SUMMARY

The story opens with María Concepción making her way down a rural road. Because she is barefoot, she walks in the center to avoid the cactus needles clustered at the edges. Over one shoulder, she carries tethered chickens that she will later sell at the town market. With the other arm, she totes a basket with lunch for her husband and his boss. Her upright posture and the serene look in her eyes give her an appearance of ease and confidence. She is pregnant but carries the weight of her growing belly well. She has been married to her husband, Juan Villegas, for almost a year. They are both just eighteen years old. Because she is proud, María Concepción paid for an official marriage license and an in-church ceremony rather than getting married behind the church, as most people do.

María Concepción passes a small house belonging to Lupe the medicine woman and her goddaughter, María Rosa, who keeps bees. Getting a craving for "a fresh crust of honey," María Concepción looks to see if María Rosa is there and hears her flirting with a man. As María Concepción watches, she realizes that the man is her own husband, Juan. Shocked, she walks away in a daze, continuing her errand of bringing lunch to her husband's work site.

Juan's boss, an Anglo archaeologist named Givens, asks María Concepción to kill and dress a chicken for his meal. He is taken aback by her efficiency in beheading the bird. She asks about Juan, and Givens assumes that he will be back at work soon. María Concepción leaves for the market.

As the day passes, María Concepción finds her anger at Juan waning, but her resentment against María Rosa grows. Juan does not come home that night, instead running away to war—presumably joining one of the rebel forces of the Mexican Revolution. María Rosa goes with him, marching with the women who cook and scavenge for the soldiers.

María Concepción shows no emotion at Juan's departure. She does not even cry when her baby is born and dies after only four days. Lupe the medicine woman visits, but María Concepción sends her away rudely.

Juan and María Rosa are gone for a year. María Concepción continues to go to church and to take her wares to market. Lupe struggles to take care of the bees without María Rosa. The people of the town admire María Concepción even more than they already did for bearing up so well under so much grief. However, María Concepción grows thin and bitter. She avoids speaking to the other women in the town, though they feel great sympathy for her.

When Juan grows tired of fighting, he returns to the village one morning at daybreak with María Rosa, who is pregnant. Because he deserted his military duties, he is arrested by military police. After they take him away, explaining that he will be shot as punishment, María Rosa collapses hysterically. She is taken to Lupe's house, which has fallen into disrepair because Lupe is too old and arthritic to maintain it. María Rosa gives birth to Juan's son.

Later in the morning, the captain at the military barracks recognizes Juan and informs Givens, his friend, that Givens's workman is under threat of execution. The captain releases Juan to Givens, who warns Juan that he might one day be too late to rescue him. He also warns Juan to be more careful about how he treats María Concepción, because all is not well. Juan heads into town to celebrate his release, not thinking to visit María Rosa until almost noon. He finally approaches her home and sees her with their son. Though he is overcome with emotion, he says nothing and returns to town for more celebrating.

When Juan leaves town later, now very drunk, he goes to the house he shared with María Concepción. He attempts to beat her, but she stands her ground. He gives up and goes to sleep. María Concepción readies her chickens as if to go to market, but when she leaves the house, she is overcome by her grief and sits tensely in the shade.

Juan wakes up and sees María Concepción in the doorway of their house. She carries her knife in her hand, and he fears she will kill him, but she throws aside the knife, which is covered in blood. She approaches on hands and knees and whispers to Juan. He is horrified but quickly decides to help María Concepción. He washes the knife and instructs her to change her clothes and cook for him, pretending that everything is normal.

As María Concepción and Juan eat their dinner, policemen from the village arrive with the news that María Rosa has been killed. Likely the reader has already assumed that when María Concepción was whispering to Juan, she was confessing to having killed her rival. The policemen take María Concepción and Juan with them to María Rosa's house.

María Rosa's body has been prepared for burial and rests in a coffin with candles at its head. María Concepción is not afraid to look at the body. Lupe explains the morning's events to the policemen, but the details of her story are vague. The police also question Juan and María Concepción, who claim that she went to the market as usual. The neighbors support María Concepción, telling the policemen, "She is a woman of good reputation among us, and María Rosa was not." A woman named Soledad lies about seeing María Concepción in the market that day. The police are convinced of María Concepción's guilt, but there is no evidence, so they leave, apologizing for their intrusion.

María Concepción takes up María Rosa's baby, claiming him as her own. An exhausted Juan follows her home, collapses onto the floor, and goes to sleep. María Concepción milks a goat to feed the baby. She holds him on her lap and, though very sleepy, feels an odd contentment.

CHARACTERS

Anita

Anita is a young mother in the town who speaks in María Concepción's favor when the gendarmes are questioning her about María Rosa's murder.

Captain

The captain is the local military authority. When he recognizes Juan, he sends word to Givens and releases Juan to his custody as a favor.

Givens

Givens is the archaeologist, seemingly American. Many of the men in the village, including Juan, work for Givens, "helping him to uncover the lost city of their ancestors." Givens's face is burned and wrinkled from spending so much time in the sun. When Juan is arrested, Givens comes to speak to the captain to get him released from the military prison, saving him from being shot for desertion. He warns Juan that he might not always be able to get away with his irresponsible behavior.

Lupe

Lupe, the medicine woman, is María Rosa's godmother. She makes herbal remedies and charms for the people of the town. After María Rosa runs away with Juan, Lupe, an old woman "hard in the joints," struggles to do all of her work without help, and the beehives suffer. It is Lupe who hears María Rosa's murderer running away and discovers the body.

María Concepción Manríquez

María Concepción is just past eighteen and has been married to Juan for nearly a year. Among the townspeople, she has "a good reputation with the neighbors as an energetic religious woman who could drive a bargain to the end." For Juan's boss, Givens, "Her grand manner sometimes reminded him of royalty in exile." When Juan runs away with María Rosa, María Concepción changes. She is fiercely angry and deeply sad, and the intense emotion seems to consume her. She is pregnant at the start of the story, but the baby dies a few days after its birth while Juan is still away. She becomes even more quiet and withdrawn from day-to-day life in the village. Still, after María Rosa's murder, María Concepción is protected by the women of the town, including María Rosa's godmother, Lupe. Once it is clear that the gendarmes have no evidence to convict her of killing María Rosa, María Concepción takes Juan's baby with María Rosa as her own.

María Rosa

María Rosa is fifteen years old when Juan starts flirting with her. To Juan, she is like "honey" to a bee. He likes her because, as he tells Givens, "she is just a girl with whom I do as I please," unlike María Concepción, who is a stronger personality; the latter would not put up with Juan slapping her and telling her to be quiet. María Rosa has Juan's child, the birth seemingly brought on early by the shock of seeing Juan arrested for desertion. Soon after the baby is born, María Rosa is killed.

Old Man

When the gendarmes suspect that María Concepción is the murderer, among the many female supporters is one "toothless old man" who speaks up for her.

Soledad

Soledad is one of the townspeople who protects María Concepción from the police. She lies, claiming she saw María Concepción in the market on the day of María Rosa's death.

Juan de Dios Villegas

Juan has been married to María Concepción for almost a year. He is eighteen years old and works at Givens's archaeological dig site. Though still a newlywed, Juan is often unfaithful to María Concepción. Givens teases that his wife will catch him one day, but Juan just "laugh[s] with immense pleasure." Juan cheats on María Concepción with María Rosa and runs away to join the military. Later, he deserts his post and returns home to María Concepción as if he has nothing to apologize for. After María Concepción kills María Rosa, Juan covers for her, telling the police that they were home together at the time of the murder. Juan unquestioningly accepts María Concepción's adoption of his son with María Rosa.

THEMES

Jealousy

In "María Concepción," Porter offers a detailed portrayal of the hurt and anger tied up with the feeling of jealousy. When María Concepción first sees Juan with María Rosa, she "did not stir nor breathe for some seconds. Her forehead was cold, and yet boiling water seemed to be pouring slowly along her spine." She feels as if she "burned all over . . . , as if a layer of tiny fig-cactus bristles, as cruel as spun glass, had crawled under her skin." The initial shock of Juan's betrayal fades, leaving "a dark empty feeling." María Concepción wants "to sit down quietly and wait for her death, but not until she had cut the throats of her man and that girl who were laughing and kissing under the cornstalks." The intensity of María Concepción's jealousy obsesses her, making it impossible for her to register any other emotion. For example, she shows almost no emotion when her baby dies four days after it is born. She becomes "gaunt, as if something were gnawing her away inside," as if her jealousy consumes her.

In addition to showing the deep pain of jealousy, Porter shows that jealousy is not a rational feeling. Logically, María Concepción has more reason to be angry with Juan, because he is her husband. He promised to be faithful when he married her, so he broke that promise, whereas María Rosa owes María Concepción nothing. However, in the hours after she first saw Juan cheating, María Concepción's "anger against him died, and her anger against María Rosa grew." Perhaps because she loves him, she finds it easier to forgive him, though his offense against her was much greater.

Moral Ambiguity

"María Concepción" is not a story with a clear moral. One does not finish reading with the sense that Porter was attempting either to condemn the conduct of any of the characters or to hold them up as examples of how people should

TOPICS FOR FURTHER STUDY

- The setting of "María Concepción," a village in Mexico, is drawn from Porter's frequent travels there. Read the story again, paying particular attention to the descriptions of the setting. Draw a few of the scenes, and then present your artwork to your class, explaining why you included specific elements in your drawings.
- Porter's stories often reveal the darker side of human nature. Working with a partner or small group, find summaries of six to eight other short stories, by Porter or other authors, that similarly show elements that appear in "María Concepción," such as infidelity, jealousy, lying, and murderous rage. Then find an equal number of short stories that show the positive side of human behavior, perhaps with themes like love, heroism, and self-sacrifice. Use these stories as the basis of an online database of short fiction. Include links to the stories if they are available online, as well as a summary of each tale. Invite your classmates to comment on the stories you have selected and contribute their own suggestions for the database.
- Pick a scene from "María Concepción" and write it from the close first-person point of view of one of the characters, to give deep insight into his or her reactions to the events portrayed. For example, you could write from the perspective of María Rosa upon returning to the town and seeing Juan arrested for desertion. Is she afraid for Juan? Or only worried about supporting herself and her unborn child without him? Or your narration could closely follow María Concepción's point of view when Juan wakes to find her with the knife in her hand. What is she thinking? What does she say to explain what has happened? Does she feel any guilt? Share your scene with your class.
- Read E. Lockhart's 2014 young-adult novel *We Were Liars*, which centers on teenage protagonist Cadence and the summer two years earlier that she cannot remember. Cadence's surfacing memories reveal the dark story of a crime of passion with deadly consequences. Write an essay that compares Lockhart's portrayal of the darker side of human nature with that of Porter in "María Concepción." Do Lockhart and Porter want readers to understand why the crimes were committed, at least to some degree? Do the authors hope readers will feel compassion for the perpetrators? Or that readers will condemn their actions? Use examples from both texts to support your argument.

behave. Few would argue that Juan's behavior is acceptable: cheating on his wife, abandoning her when she is pregnant with his child, and then deserting his post in the military. María Rosa's actions are also far from exemplary: enticing a married man away from his wife and leaving her old, arthritic godmother, Lupe, without help at home. María Rosa dies for her transgressions, but Juan's behavior goes largely unpunished. Juan's boss, Givens, gets him released from prison after he has been arrested for desertion, and María Concepción accepts him into their home without question when he returns.

There is nothing in the tale to suggest that bad behavior will be punished and good behavior rewarded. Indeed, the worst crime of all, murder, is enacted completely without consequences. Rather, after María Concepción commits murder, everyone protects her, though her guilt is obvious. The townspeople think well of María Concepción and continue to do so, in spite of her crime. In contrast, people judge Juan for his infidelity and have no sympathy

Juan is having an affair with María Rosa, who is only fifteen years old *(©Paul Matthew Photography / Shutterstock.com)*

for any sadness he may feel over the death of his lover. Apparently, the town disapproves of Juan and María Rosa's adultery more than they condemn the vengeance by María Concepción.

With the morally ambiguous conclusion of the story, Porter is providing a realistic depiction of life. Bad deeds do indeed go unpunished, and often people react to crimes based on their emotions—like the townspeople who sympathize with María Concepción—rather than their intellect or their understanding of the law.

STYLE

Foreshadowing

The pastoral opening of "María Concepción" does not give the reader a sense of the violence that will appear later in the story. As María Concepción carries lunch to her husband, Juan, and his boss, Givens, Porter describes the "instinctive serenity" that "softened her black eyes." However, Porter quickly offers a few details that hint at the potential for violence under María Concepción's calm exterior. Her neighbors see her as "an energetic religious woman," but after seeing Juan with María Rosa, María Concepción displays her capacity for violence in killing the chicken for Givens's meal. She "swiftly drew her knife across its throat, twisting the head off with the casual firmness she might use with the top of a beet." Givens is taken aback when he witnesses her calm efficiency, saying, "Good God, woman, you do have nerve." Perhaps he remembers her seeming cold-bloodedness in killing the chickens when he tells Juan to be "careful." He warns Juan that "some day María Concepción will just take your head off with that carving knife of hers." With these clues, Porter indirectly foreshadows the murder of María Rosa later in the story.

Translated Dialogue

In "María Concepción," Porter uses two distinct styles of dialogue. The first is a naturalistic style, sounding like day-to-day conversation. Givens, the boss of the archaeological dig, speaks with this style of dialogue. For example, after he watches María Concepción kill a chicken for his lunch, he declares, "It gives me the creeps." Then, when María Concepción asks his permission to leave, he says, "Yes, yes, run along; bring me another of these tomorrow." There is nothing grand or dramatic in Givens's few speeches. In contrast, many of the speeches of other characters seem old-fashioned or overly formal. A surprising example of this is Juan's reaction when María Concepción comes home after killing María Rosa. The reader would expect him to speak very naturally—perhaps stuttering, given his shock and fear, but his words seem strangely stilted: "Oh, thou poor creature! Oh, madwoman! Oh, my María Concepción, unfortunate! . . . I will hide thee away, I thy own man will protect thee!"

One possible explanation for this difference in the style of the story's dialogue is that Givens is the only American character. His words are not translated for the reader from Spanish but appear on the page as he would have uttered them. The dialogue that has been translated into English from Spanish-speaking characters has a more formal feel. Perhaps Porter intends to capture the feeling of the Spanish language in her translated dialogue. This might also account for her use of the second-person pronouns *thee*, *thou*, and *thy*, although these forms were not used at the time of the story, with *you* and *your* being used instead. The clearly different feel of the Mexican characters' dialogue gives many scenes a more dramatic, almost operatic feel.

Variations in Point of View

Porter uses an unusual narrative structure in "María Concepción." The narration is all written in the third person, but the point of view varies from scene to scene. Sometimes the text is from the point of view of an omniscient third-person narrator. For example, in the opening scene, the story describes María Concepción as she walks out to the archaeological dig to bring Juan and Givens their lunch. The reader sees her as if from some distance, watching her walk down the road, noting the serenity of her expression and the ease with which she carries her pregnancy. Then, however, the point of view seems to narrow in focus. Rather than observing María Concepción from afar, the reader is inside her head. One can almost hear through her ears the bees buzzing, and one is privy to her thoughts as she craves a bit of honey. All throughout the scene where she first sees Juan with María Rosa, the narration remains from María Concepción's point of view; but when she walks away and meets Givens, the perspective shifts. Once again, Porter shows María Concepción from an outside point of view, this time through Givens's eyes rather than an impersonal narrator. While telling the story from Givens's point of view, Porter gives insight into his character: María Concepción's bearing "sometimes reminded him of royalty in exile," but he also feels a colonialist superiority over the people of the village, "a fatherly indulgence for their primitive childish ways." By alternating between various points of view, Porter is able to give insight into the thoughts and emotions of all the central characters.

HISTORICAL CONTEXT

The Mexican Revolution

The early twentieth century, when Porter was frequently traveling to Mexico, was a politically turbulent time for that country. The Mexican Revolution began as a protest by the middle classes against the dictatorship of Porfirio Díaz (1830–1915), an army officer who came to power through a coup. Díaz's policies favored wealthy industrialists and landowners and ignored the needs of the middle and lower classes. Mexico's political system during Díaz's presidency (1876–1911) was stable but corrupt, with elections controlled at the local level by the political allies of Díaz and his wealthy, influential friends.

As the 1910 election approached, Díaz seemed uncertain about running for his seventh term. Francisco Madero (1873–1913), the emerging leader of the political faction opposing Díaz's reelection, announced his candidacy, but Díaz had him arrested and staged a mock election in June 1910. Díaz declared himself the winner, but Madero, who had since been released from prison, called for a revolt among the citizens on November 20. Though the November revolt did not accomplish anything directly, it sparked revolutionary spirit nationwide. Government garrisons were attacked, and skirmishes broke out all over the country. The rebels forced Díaz to resign in the spring of 1911, and Madero took over as president.

The government under Madero was never strong. Various factions pushed their own agendas, resulting in very little being done. A new revolutionary movement started in the north, protesting the lack of reform, and the United States, concerned about the possibility of civil war in Mexico and its effects on American investments, did not offer Madero support. The unrest and violence continued for almost two years. Then the conflict turned particularly bloody in Mexico City in February 1913. Revolutionary forces under Félix Díaz (1868–1945), nephew of the former president, fought with federal soldiers led by Victoriano Huerta (1850–1916) in a battle known as La Decena Trágica, or the Ten Tragic Days. The two leaders met at the US embassy to negotiate and agreed to work together to depose Madero and put Huerta in office. Madero was arrested and, a few days later, assassinated, while Huerta took over as Mexico's president.

Huerta's presidency lasted only until the summer of 1914, when revolutionary groups once again gathered in Mexico City. Huerta fled, and Venustiano Carranza (1859–1920) took over as president. However, other rebel

COMPARE & CONTRAST

- **1920s:** Mexico is still in a period of political and civil turmoil after the Mexican Revolution. Elections are corrupt, and power struggles on both local and national levels often turn violent and bloody.

  Today: Mexico's government is more stable and fair. Although the Institutional Revolutionary Party held power for most of the twentieth century, with the sitting president essentially choosing his successor, now multiple political parties compete for votes, much as in the United States. The Constitution of Mexico, first enacted in 1917, is now amended to guarantee civil liberties and personal freedoms and to outline the country's basic political principles.

- **1920s:** The infant mortality rate, defined as the number of deaths in the first year of life per 1,000 live births, in the United States is 80. The disorganization of Mexico's government and health-care system is such that statistics on infant mortality are not available.

  Today: By the middle of the twentieth century, infant mortality rates declined worldwide; around 1960 the rates were 26 in the United States but 152 in Mexico. As of 2015, Mexico's infant mortality rate is 11. The United States, despite being one of the few wealthiest countries in the world, has a higher infant mortality rate than twenty-seven other countries, at 6 deaths per 1,000 live births.

- **1920s:** Archaeology is a relatively new field in Mexico. In the late nineteenth and very early twentieth centuries, scholars looked to historic documents for information about Mexican cultures before the arrival of the Spanish, but new archaeological methods in the 1920s turn the focus to firsthand research at sites of importance. The American Museum of Natural History conducts many large-scale digs in Mexico and Central America.

  Today: Archaeological digs are conducted all over Mexico, including dozens of sites in what is now Mexico City. Evidence shows that the Spaniards built their city right over the ruins of the Aztec city of Tenochtitlán, with major roads following the same paths. Archaeologists have found clues in murals and human remains supporting common notions of the brutal and bloodthirsty culture of the Aztecs, who dominated other local peoples.

---

leaders did not support Carranza. Chaos and bloody infighting spread. One of the strongest voices against Carranza was Pancho Villa (1878–1923), a bandit turned revolutionary who had helped Madero on the path to the presidency. Villa had many loyal followers, so his objections to Carranza meant the presidency would never be stable. Other leaders yielded to Villa and declared Eulalio Gutiérrez (1881–1939) interim president. Carranza and his allies, however, fought back, and he had American support. Losing ground, Villa blamed the United States. His soldiers executed dozens of US citizens living in Mexico and just over the border. President Woodrow Wilson sent American troops after Villa.

Carranza, clinging to the presidency, attempted to restore order with a new constitution, which was enacted in 1917. The constitution gave the president the power of a dictator but did provide some basic rights to the common people and limited the power of the Roman Catholic Church. In spite of powerful opposition, Carranza stayed in office until 1920, when he tried to crush a railroad strike. All of his supporters left him, and when he attempted to flee the country, he was killed.

María Concepción takes María Rosa's baby as her own (©OLJ Studio / Shutterstock.com)

Some historians see this as the end of the Mexican Revolution, but the government remained unstable for many years thereafter. Adolfo de la Huerta (1881–1955) became interim president, but he served only from June to November of 1920. Álvaro Obregón (1880–1928) was then elected and served a full term. Skirmishes between revolutionary groups and federal forces continued until 1934, when Lázaro Cárdenas (1985–1970), a staunch reformer, took office and instituted the reforms listed in the constitution of 1917, finally bringing an end to the long, bloody struggle.

CRITICAL OVERVIEW

Although Porter wrote poetry and a novel, it is her short stories that garner the most critical attention. She is considered a masterful writer in the genre, having won a National Book Award and a Pulitzer Prize for her *Collected Stories*. Denis Donoghue, in a review of the collection for the *New York Review of Books*, describes Porter as "at least a minor writer of unusual distinction, a stylist, a craftsman."

The *Weekly Standard*'s Brooke Allen agrees, naming Porter "one of the most original artists of her epoch, and one of the most surprising, too." Allen regrets that Porter's "stories, once widely anthologized and held up as models of the genre by countless critics and educators, were almost forgotten." When experiencing the *Collected Stories*, Allen writes, a reader will be "forcibly impressed with the author's imaginative power and descriptive gifts." However, Allen does mention one of Parker's few weaknesses as an author: although Allen believes Parker to be "a consummate short story writer," she was not able to translate her talents to longer works with complete success. Allen asserts that

> the strengths she brought to this craft—the ability to convey instant visual and sensual impressions, the verbal adroitness that allowed her to sketch the essence of a character with precision—proved something of a liability when she turned to the novel form.

Writing for *Studies in Short Fiction*, Alice Hall Petry reviewed a 1995 reprinting of *Flowering Judas*, which includes "María Concepción," praising Porter's skill in adding "layer upon layer of subtext and symbol" to her stories. Petry believes the collection is "a singularly appropriate introduction to Porter's work and to the twentieth-century American short story in general." Berezhanska Yu, in the 2014 essay "Cultivation and Destruction of Gender Stereotypes in 'María Concepción' by Katherine Anne Porter," calls that particular story a "meticulous exploration of the ambivalent nature of female power," one that examines "the unknown and hidden resources of the female identity."

CRITICISM

Kristen Sarlin Greenberg

Greenberg is a freelance writer and editor with a background in literature and philosophy. In the following essay, she examines the influence of community in Katherine Anne Porter's "María Concepción."

"ALTHOUGH MARíA CONCEPCIÓN COMMITS A TERRIBLE CRIME, WHEN SHE IS UNDER SUSPICION, THE COMMUNITY GATHERS AROUND HER BECAUSE HER ACT MAINTAINED THE SOCIAL ORDER."

Author Katherine Anne Porter threw herself into life. She had many tumultuous love affairs and traveled the world. Her trips to Mexico in the 1910s and 1920s to study art exposed her to the dangerous but exciting atmosphere of a country in revolution. She explained to Barbara Thompson Davis of the *Paris Review* that while in Mexico, witnessing the uprising that eventually installed Álvaro Obregón as president, she had "the most marvelous, natural, spontaneous experience of my life. It was a terribly exciting time. It was alive, but death was in it. But nobody seemed to think of that: life was in it, too." Her stories set in Mexico capture some of these passionate extremes—not only life and death, but also loyalty and betrayal, love and hate. Porter's short story "María Concepción" is an ideal example of her style, examining themes of adultery, jealousy, and murder—some of the darkest elements of human interaction. Yet the story also celebrates some of the positive aspects of society, such as responsibility and, perhaps most importantly, community.

In the opening scene of "María Concepción," the title character walks along a dusty road on an everyday errand. Porter establishes María Concepción as strong and reliable; she has "a good reputation with the neighbors as an energetic religious woman." She is also proud. Rather than marry behind the church, as most of the villagers do, she paid for an official license, so she and her husband, Juan, were married by a priest within the church. María Concepción is reliable, and Porter shows her fulfilling her regular chores: bringing her husband and his boss their lunches and taking chickens to market. María Concepción's life seems to be typical of the small town in which she lives, and her neighbors consider her an exemplary member of the community.

The conflict of the story begins when María Concepción strays from her usual path. She passes the house of Lupe the medicine woman and her goddaughter, María Rosa. María Rosa keeps bees, and María Concepción thinks how tasty a bit of honey would be. However, when she makes her way toward the house, she spies María Rosa with Juan, flirting shamelessly. María Concepción is shocked, saddened, and angered by Juan's infidelity.

Though María Concepción is surprised by Juan's adultery, she may be one of the few. Porter shows that Juan does not make much of an effort to hide it. His boss, Givens, teases him about it, saying "She'll catch you yet, and God help you!" Juan does not deny that he has cheated on his wife, nor does he make excuses. He only "laugh[s] with immense pleasure." He seems almost proud that Givens knows about his philandering—as if it is a mark of his manliness. This is a sharp contrast with the seriousness with which María Concepción thinks about her marriage, given her determination to marry inside the church, with a license. Even Givens, who clearly recognizes that María Concepción has a right to be angry at Juan's behavior, does not to seem to condemn Juan—he only wonders what will happen if Juan gets caught.

Juan's attitude is stereotypically sexist. He thinks his own cheating is understandable and, at least to some degree, acceptable, while it is highly unlikely he would tolerate the same behavior in his wife. Givens seems to share Juan's sexist attitudes enough to joke about his infidelities. However, as a story, "María Concepción" is intended not merely to point out social inequality between men and women but rather to highlight a fundamental difference in their roles in society.

Porter clearly sets up the women of the town as the guardians of the community as a whole, and the story's conclusion makes sense when considering María Concepción's actions against this backdrop, as compared with the behavior of Juan and María Rosa. Although María Concepción commits a terrible crime, when she is under suspicion, the community gathers around her because her act maintained the social order. Porter also makes it clear that although men may be in positions of nominal

- The 1992 novel *Jazz*, by Nobel Prize winner Toni Morrison, has themes similar to those in "María Concepción." In 1920s Harlem, middle-aged door-to-door salesman Joe Trace fatally shoots his teenaged mistress, unraveling a story of passion, obsession, and jealousy.
- Darlene Harbour Unrue's *Katherine Anne Porter: The Life of an Artist* (2005) is a well-researched biography that reveals the truth behind Porter's sometimes contradictory accounts of her own life.
- In the award-winning young-adult novel *Girl Unmoored* (2012), author Jennifer Gooch Hummer offers a coming-of-age tale set in the 1980s in which protagonist Apron Bramhall struggles to cope with issues of infidelity, grief, and death.
- Porter's *Ship of Fools* (1962) tells the tale of a group of widely different passengers traveling from Mexico to Europe on a German ship. The novel is an allegory for the rise of Nazism in Germany in the years leading up to World War II.
- F. Scott Fitzgerald's "Winter Dreams," often described as one of his best short stories, was first published in 1922. Protagonist Dexter Green's almost obsessive interest in the beautiful and wealthy Judy Jones provides a skewed view of love that will be familiar to readers of *The Great Gatsby* (1925).
- In addition to her carefully worded prose, Porter also wrote poetry. Though she only published thirty-two poems during her lifetime, she composed hundreds—and destroyed many of them. Darlene Harbour Unrue gathered Porter's complete known poetic works in the 1996 volume *Katherine Anne Porter's Poetry*.

authority, it is the women of the village who are truly in control because they are the keepers of the community.

Upon close examination, we see that, unlike the female townspeople, the male characters are not valued, contributing members of the community. Juan is the worst: he is unfaithful to his wife and abandons her while she is pregnant. He takes a fifteen-year-old girl away from her guardian into a war zone and then barely takes notice of her when she bears him a child; he is affected by the sight of María Rosa and their son, but perhaps it only feeds his pride. His response to it is to head immediately back to the village and call "every man in the . . . pulque shop to drink with him." Juan's actions are selfish, prompted by his own whims and his own pleasures. Even his protection of María Concepción after he learns of her crime is selfish, for he realizes she will be taken to prison if convicted, and he will be alone.

Some of the lesser male characters, though not behaving with Juan's obvious selfishness, also are not important members of the community. The American archaeologist Givens is an outsider. María Concepción thinks of him as the "diverting white man who had no woman of his own to cook for him." A man of his age, without a wife and family, who is likely to return to his home country once his work is finished, is not a vital part of the town's social structure.

A more puzzling example is the military captain at the barracks where Juan is held when arrested. The captain has a clear role in the society of the country as a whole. However, his involvement in the military—a machine of war in this time of revolution rather than a purely protective force—can be seen as tearing down society, endangering it rather than contributing. The captain arrests Juan for desertion of his military duties, but the community of women condemn Juan for the greater crime of having deserted his wife and unborn child. The captain's authority does not seem to relate to the way the women of the town keep everything running smoothly.

Porter does not portray the gender roles in the story simplistically: not all of the characters whose lives work against the community's interests are men. Like Juan, María Rosa does not fulfill her prescribed role in society. Because she is not there to help Lupe, who has "no talent for bees," there is no honey. Lupe then "began to blame María Rosa for running away." The women of the town have little use for María

In her jealousy, María Concepción kills María Rosa (©Hurst Photo / Shutterstock.com)

Rosa, though Lupe does help her when she suddenly goes into labor, and the town does come together around her coffin, though perhaps that is out of respect for Lupe rather than any regard for María Rosa. Even María Rosa's neglect of the beehives—in themselves models of cooperative society—stresses her lack of participation in the usual female role of maintaining the bonds of community.

Similarly, not all of the male characters work outside of or against society. There is one "toothless old man" who declares, when María Concepción is accused of murder, "She is a woman of good reputation among us, and María Rosa was not." Also, the gendarmes who investigate María Rosa's murder can be considered to play an important role in the community. Their job is to maintain order in society. However, in this story, the policemen are governed by the will of the women in the community. These women decide that María Concepción is to be protected because her act restored the way things should be, and the gendarmes do not argue. They recognize the greater power of the community over their own authority, which comes from a distant government.

The women of the town, as the moral authorities and caretakers of the community, decide early on that María Concepción must be protected. Although they see María Concepción as "altogether too proud," they are sympathetic and "pitied her" after Juan left. Even when María Concepción takes offense at Lupe's visits, curses her, and avoids the other women of the village, they are patient and understanding. Old Soledad, who is described as "a thinker and a peace-maker," expresses the consensus of the women: "She is wrong to take us for enemies. . . . All women have these troubles. Well, we should suffer together."

Part of the reason why María Concepción is supported by the town is that, though she has been abandoned by her husband and loses her child very soon after its birth, she continues to fulfill her given role in the community. She takes her wares to the market and attends church. In spite of her personal pain, she does not behave selfishly. In contrast, Juan and María Rosa act without any consideration of the consequences of their actions in terms of others' feelings or the good of the community.

As a result, the women in the village seem to feel little responsibility for María Rosa and Juan. When the two lovers run away, "there was no particular scandal in the village. People shrugged, grinned. It was far better that they were gone."

The events at the end of the story do not bring justice in the traditional sense. For there to be justice, Juan would be somehow punished for his infidelity and abandonment of his wife and child, and María Concepción would be punished for her murder. Other than losing his paramour, which he does not seem very torn up about, Juan suffers few consequences, and María Concepción gets away with her crime. But the story's conclusion restores order in the community. Spurred on by jealousy and anger, María Concepción commits murder. However, once María Rosa is gone, Juan has returned home for good. María Concepción loses her own baby but adopts María Rosa's—not that adopting a second child erases the pain of losing the first; but the story is structured to suggest that the time when Juan was away is erased in terms of the community at large, and all because María Concepción rids society of a disruptive element.

This is why María Concepción is "guarded, surrounded, upborne by her faithful friends." The women of the community gather "around her, speaking for her, defending her," because by doing so they protect the stability of family life and their community's values. Porter portrays the power of the community with an almost mystical air; the community offers María Concepción "reassurance, understanding, a secret and mighty sympathy." The women of the town represent "the forces of life . . . ranged invincibly with her against the beaten dead." It is both the duty and the power of the women in this small town to maintain the social order. The community keeps them strong, and in turn, their strength supports the community, creating a cycle that prevents breakdown from selfish acts.

Source: Kristen Sarlin Greenberg, Critical Essay on "María Concepción," in *Short Stories for Students*, Gale, Cengage Learning, 2017.

SOURCES

"About Katherine Anne Porter," PBS website, September 28, 2002, http://www.pbs.org/wnet/americanmasters/katherine-anne-porter-about-katherine-anne-porter/686/ (accessed September 5, 2016).

"Achievements in Public Health, 1900–1999: Healthier Mothers and Babies," *Morbidity and Mortality Weekly Report*, Centers for Disease Control and Prevention website, October 1, 1999, https://www.cdc.gov/mmwr/preview/mmwrhtml/mm4838a2.htm (accessed September 11, 2016).

Allen, Brooke, "Pale Horse, Pale Writer: Is the Author of 'Noon Wine' a Classic?," in *Weekly Standard*, Vol. 14, No. 7, October 27, 2008, http://www.weeklystandard.com/pale-horse-pale-writer/article/16795 (accessed September 16, 2016).

Atwood, Roger, "Temple of Quetzalcoatl," in *Archaeology*, June 9, 2014, http://www.archaeology.org/issues/143-features/mexico-city/2211-mexico-city-aztec-temple-of-ehecatl-quetzalcoatl (accessed September 11, 2016).

Davis, Barbara Thompson, "Katherine Anne Porter: The Art of Fiction No. 29," in *Paris Review*, No. 29, Winter–Spring 1963, http://www.theparisreview.org/interviews/4569/the-art-of-fiction-no-29-katherine-anne-porter (accessed September 12, 2016).

Donoghue, Denis, "Reconsidering Katherine Anne Porter," in *New York Review of Books*, November 11, 1965, http://www.nybooks.com/articles/1965/11/11/reconsidering-katherine-anne-porter/ (accessed September 6, 2016).

Elson, Christina M., and Kathryn Venzor, "Meso-American Archaeological Collection," American Museum of Natural History website, http://www.amnh.org/our-research/anthropology/collections/collections-history/meso-american-archaeology/ (accessed September 11, 2016).

"Katherine Anne Porter Biography," in *Encyclopedia of World Biography*, http://www.notablebiographies.com/Pe-Pu/Porter-Katherine-Anne.html (accessed September 5, 2016).

"Katherine Anne Porter Papers," ArchivesUM, University of Maryland website, http://digital.lib.umd.edu/archivesum/actions.DisplayEADDoc.do?source=/MdU.ead.litms.0041.xml&style=ead (accessed September 5, 2016).

Knight, Alan, "The Mexican Revolution," in *History Today*, Vol. 30, No. 5, May 1980, http://www.historytoday.com/alan-knight/mexican-revolution (accessed September 5, 2016).

"Mexican Revolution," in *Encyclopædia Britannica*, https://www.britannica.com/event/Mexican-Revolution (accessed September 5, 2016).

"Mexico: Government and Society," in *Encyclopædia Britannica*, https://www.britannica.com/place/Mexico/Government-and-society (accessed September 11, 2016).

"Mortality Rate, Infant (per 1,000 Live Births)," World Bank website, http://data.worldbank.org/indicator/SP.DYN.IMRT.IN?name_desc=true (accessed September 11, 2016).

"Pancho Villa," Biography.com, http://www.biography.com/people/pancho-villa-9518733 (accessed September 6, 2016).

Petry, Alice Hall, Review of *Flowering Judas*, in *Studies in Short Fiction*, Vol. 32, No. 1, Winter 1995, p. 122.

Porter, Katherine Anne, "María Concepción," in *Flowering Judas and Other Stories*, Modern Library, 1935, pp. 3–35.

Roser, Max, "Child Mortality," Our World in Data, https://ourworldindata.org/child-mortality/ (accessed September 6, 2016).

Subramanian, Alexandra, "Katherine Anne Porter: A Brief Biography," Katherine Anne Porter Society website, http://www.kaportersociety.org/ (accessed September 5, 2016).

Yu, Berezhanska, "Cultivation and Destruction of Gender Stereotypes in 'María Concepción' by Katherine Anne Porter," in *Scientific Bulletin*, Vol. 4, No. 13, 2014, pp. 319–22, http://litzbirnyk.com.ua/wp-content/uploads/2014/07/69.13.14.pdf (accessed September 6, 2016).

FURTHER READING

Cather, Willa, *Stories, Poems, and Other Writings*, Library of America, 1992.

Cather is one of the great writers of the early twentieth century. Like Porter's descriptions of Mexico, Cather's settings on the American plains are central to her stories. This volume collects Cather's shorter works, providing a broad overview for a first-time reader.

Frost, Susan Toomey, and Stella de Sá Rego, *Timeless Mexico: The Photographs of Hugo Brehme*, University of Texas Press, 2011.

In the 1920s and 1930s, Brehme was an internationally known photographer. In this book, Frost and de Sá Rego present a beautiful array of his work along with explanations of his artistic process and his place in the history of Mexican art.

Porter, Katherine Anne, *Letters of Katherine Anne Porter*, edited by Isabel Bayley, Atlantic Monthly Press, 1990.

Upon Porter's death in 1980, Bayley, a close friend as well as Porter's literary archivist, selected some of her best letters for publication, giving the world a glimpse into the mind of this talented writer.

Uribe, Alvaro, ed., *Best of Contemporary Mexican Fiction*, translated by Olivia Sears, Dalkey Archive Press, 2009.

In this volume, Uribe has gathered sixteen short stories by some of Mexico's finest prize-winning authors. The collection offers a wide variety of subjects and settings, from small towns to busy cities.

SUGGESTED SEARCH TERMS

Katherine Anne Porter AND Flowering Judas

Katherine Anne Porter AND María Concepción

Katherine Anne Porter AND short stories

Katherine Anne Porter AND interview

Katherine Anne Porter AND women's issues

Katherine Anne Porter AND Pulitzer Prize

Katherine Anne Porter AND poetry

Katherine Anne Porter AND stereotypes

Novel of the Black Seal

ARTHUR MACHEN

1895

Many people may not have heard of Arthur Machen and his "Novel of the Black Seal" (which is a short story, not a novel), but its influence has been seen everywhere in popular culture. The story is the basis of much of modern horror literature, including the idea of the mad scientist. H. P. Lovecraft thought it was one of the best horror stories ever written and molded much of his own work on the story. Lovecraft's entire Cthulhu Mythos is an expansion of Machen's idea in the "Novel of the Black Seal" that an unknown and unimaginably horrible world lurks just below the surface of the seemingly safe and mundane modern world. On the eve of the twentieth century, Machen could no longer, like gothic writers, simply indulge in ancient magic without seeming outmoded to his audience. He had to find a way for his horror to appear validated by science. Machen established the modern literary paradigm in which the mad scientist uses science, or what appears to be science, to discover a new monstrous reality. The story appeared as an inset story in the episodic novel *The Three Impostors*, published as part of Bodley Head's Keynote Series in 1895.

AUTHOR BIOGRAPHY

Arthur Llewelyn Jones-Machen was born in the village of Caerleon in Wales on March 3, 1863. His father, an Anglican vicar, had been obliged to

Arthur Machen *(©Classic Image / Alamy Stock Photo)*

hyphenate the family name with his wife's in order to secure her inheritance. Machen attended a public school with the standard aristocratic classical curriculum, but his family could not afford to send him to university. Machen's childhood in rural Wales shaped his later literary vision. For him, that countryside would always be the entrance to another world. In his *Autobiography*, he recalls,

> When my eyes were first opened in earliest childhood they had before them the vision of an enchanted land. As soon as I saw anything I saw Twyn Barlwm, that mystic tumulus, the memorial of peoples that dwelt in that region before the Celts left the Land of Summer.

In the early 1880s, Machen moved to London, intending to work as a freelance writer. He published some minor works but was eventually forced to take employment as a manuscript editor for the publisher George Redway to secure a stable income. His first significant works were his translations of the *Heptameron* of Marguerite of Navarre (1886) and Casanova's *Memoirs* (1894).

In 1887, Machen married Amelia Hogg, who introduced him into the bohemian counterculture of London. He became close friends with the occultist Arthur Edward Waite, who induced him to join the occult secret society of the Hermetic Order of the Golden Dawn (of which the Nobel Prize–winning author W. B. Yeats was also a member), although Machen did not stay affiliated with the group for long. He was interested instead in the Celtic church tradition, and his spiritual life moved him in the direction of high-church Anglicanism.

In 1894, Machen published his first novel, *The Great God Pan*, which was a notable popular success. A briefer version had been published in the magazine *Whirlwind* in 1891. This was followed in 1895 by *The Three Impostors*, which includes the "Novel of the Black Seal." These works established his main literary themes, which are human degeneration, the rejection of contemporary science as a thin overlay on top of a mysterious and horrible reality, and the existence of a lost, primitive race—really a lost, primitive universe—alongside the everyday world. With *The Three Impostors*, Machen hoped to exploit the enormous popularity of Robert Louis Stevenson's *New Arabian Nights* (1877–1880), but the fad for that style faded quickly, and Machen's text was at the time a popular failure. In a letter of May 9, 1934, to his friend Montgomery Evans, Machen noted that recently an old friend

> had asked me what I really meant, what was the inner sense, of "The Three Impostors." I told him it was a pattern of words—borrowing, I think, from Henry James, who once wrote a good short story, called "The Pattern in the Carpet."
>
> And, by the way, here is an interesting question; why don't we put a beautiful Oriental carpet on the same artistic level as a composition in prose, or "absolute" music, such as a fugue or a symphony? Each has the common advantage of not "meaning" anything.

The book's low sales and his association with the decadent movement after the 1895 trial of the writer Oscar Wilde (on a charge of gross indecency) effectively halted Machen's publishing career. Machen's early novels were celebrated, however, in the critical works of H. P. Lovecraft and would become the foundation of modern horror literature. After *The Three Impostors*' failure, Machen wrote several books that would be published only decades later, including what may be his best work, *The Hill of Dreams* (1907), whose main character is drawn inexorably into a mystical vision of life in Roman Wales. In a series of articles in the decadent journal *Academy* and in his novel *The Secret Glory* (written in the late 1890s but not published until 1922), Machen worked out the idea that the Holy Grail of Arthurian legend still exists today and is guarded by a secret society, an idea embedded in modern popular culture through such derivative works as the Indiana Jones films and Dan Brown's 2003 novel *The Da Vinci Code*.

Machen's first wife died in 1899. In 1901, Machen started a second career as an actor in order to secure a steady income. In 1903, Machen married his second wife, Dorothie Purefoy Hudleston, with whom he had two children. He continued to publish, but his sales could not supply a living for him and his family. In 1910, Machen took a full-time journalistic job as a writer for the *Evening News*. In this capacity, he published a short story in the paper, "The Bowmen," in September 1914. It described British soldiers on the battlefield at Mons in France, at the beginning of World War I in August, praying and being saved from the attacking Germans by the ghosts of the soldiers of Henry V who had died in the medieval Battle of Agincourt. The story immediately became a sensation and was widely republished in newspapers and magazines as well as in pamphlet form. The general public believed that the text had been a news account, and the story became a widespread urban legend to the effect that angels had appeared to save the British army at Mons. (The historical reference of Agincourt was ignored as being too obscure.) In 1915, Machen published a book, *The Angels of Mons: The Bowmen and Other Legends of the War*, explaining in no uncertain terms that the story was fiction, but he was publicly denounced for withholding the sources where he had read of the original story. To this day, the story is accepted as true in some New Age circles.

The early 1920s saw a Machen renaissance during which all of his writings were republished and, together with his newly written autobiography, published in America for the first time. Machen himself was lauded as one of the great writers of his generation. This fad, too, quickly passed, and the late 1920s again saw Machen working as a copy editor. In his last years, Machen had to be supported by a charity subscription organized by his admirers, including T. S. Eliot and George Bernard Shaw. Machen, who seemed by at least 1944 to be suffering from Alzheimer's disease, retired to Beaconsfield in Buckinghamshire, England, and died on December 15, 1947.

PLOT SUMMARY

The "Novel of the Black Seal" is embedded in the text of Machen's novel *The Three Impostors*. The larger work concerns a neo-pagan secret society's attempts to manipulate the book's Sherlockian hero into helping them find a coin of Emperor Tiberius, struck to commemorate a Roman orgy, while at the same time misdirecting him from investigating their own activities. To do this, a series of members of the society go to him and his Watson, Charles Phillipps, and tell them stories that will give him information he needs but which are generally fictitious within the narrative framework of the novel. "Novel of the Black Seal" is one of these stories, which has since often been published as an independent short story. The term *novel* in the title is rather awkwardly used to mean "story."

In the frame story, Phillipps is approached by a young woman known as Miss Lally. She refers to a Professor Gregg, whose *Textbook of Ethnology* Phillipps has read and who was recently reported in the newspaper as having taken a house in the west of England for the summer and drowned in a local river. She tells Phillipps that the truth is very different, and he asks her to explain. She begins the "Novel of the Black Seal" with her own life story. Her father had been an engineer, but he died very young, leaving his widow and two children, Miss Lally and her brother, in poverty. They still had her father's books, however, and the children received an excellent education from reading them. Her brother eventually worked as a Latin tutor. When her mother died, Miss Lally came to London to look for work. She had no success, and with the last of her small amount of money gone, she was about to be thrown out of her rooming house. Having no idea whether she will have to kill herself before she starves, she runs into Professor Gregg, who needs a governess for his children.

Naturally, Miss Lally takes his offer of employment. As the months wear on, she finds herself working more as his secretary than as his children's governess. He dictates to her the text of his scholarly masterpiece, *Textbook of Ethnology*. During this process, she can tell that there is

MEDIA ADAPTATIONS

- An audiobook of *The Three Impostors*, including the "Novel of the Black Seal," read by Jim Killavey, was released in 2011. The run time is six hours and two minutes.

something else he would rather be working on. When they are done, he confesses to her that he has a new project that will make him as famous as Columbus. Gregg shows her an odd collection of objects, letters, and news clippings that mean nothing to her but which he suspects will unlock a new world. He refuses to say more about them, however, since the one time he tried to discuss the matter with his colleagues, they suggested his mind was imbalanced by overwork.

Soon Gregg tells Miss Lally that the household will be moving for the summer to a cottage on the Welsh border, near the town of Caermaen, a town built on an old Roman fort. Once they arrive in this idyllic spot, Gregg confesses that they are not merely on a holiday but that the place is connected to his mysterious collection.

Miss Lally usually takes the children on hikes through the countryside, but on a rainy day she looks at one of the few books in the house, an old Latin geography book that contains the *De situ orbis* of Pomponius Mela and the *De mirabilibus mundi* of Gaius Julius Solinus. (Machen refers to the latter book simply by the author's name since he has only one surviving work.) Miss Lally quotes the Latin text of a chapter of Solinus and gives a translation. It describes a secret race of people who live apart from other men and have nothing in common with them. They hate the sun and speak a language that sounds like hissing. They possess a black stone they call the Sixtystone (Hexecontalithos), since it is inscribed with sixty characters, including the secret and unspeakable name Ixaxar. Gregg happens to come into the room, and she shows him the passage, at which he is clearly taken aback. Though he says he hates to take her only reading material, he tells her he must take charge of the book. The next day, Gregg calls Miss Lally into his study and shows her the black seal she had seen before and asks her to count the characters on it. Aside from two scratches, she confirms it has sixty characters. She realizes that it is the Sixtystone of which Solinus spoke.

Gregg tells Miss Lally that he is going to hire a boy from the village to help with the household chores, though she says the maids actually do not have enough work to do. Later that day, he returns from the village with Jervase Cradock. The boy seems to be mentally handicapped and an epileptic. His father had died before he was born, and his mother had been found wandering hysterical in the woods a few days later. Jervase was born eight months after this episode. Miss Lally learns that the local hills are called the Grey Hills, which she recalls was mentioned in one of the letters in Gregg's mysterious collection as the location of some recent markings that reproduced the same characters as on the black seal.

One day, Miss Lally sees Jervase suffer what she takes to be an epileptic fit. He is carried into the house and, still writhing and hissing, starts to speak in what sounds to her like an alien and utterly horrible language. Gregg comes and carries the boy to the couch in his study, and Miss Lally is "appalled by the glow of exultation that shone on every lineament and feature" of Gregg's face.

The local rector, Mr. Meyrick, comes to dinner in the Gregg household. Gregg steers the conversation to Welsh, and Meyrick says he speaks Welsh fluently and is very familiar even with its regional dialects. Gregg asks him about a Welsh word he heard Jervase Cradock say, but Meyrick insists that neither the Cradock family nor hardly anyone else in the village knows Welsh anymore. The word in question is *Ixaxar*, but Meyrick is certain that it is not a Welsh word.

A few days later, Miss Lally asks directly for an explanation about what is going on, but Gregg is as reluctant as ever to speak for fear of being called a quack. However, he tells her that Jervase had another fit in the middle of the night and that soon he will have completely proved his theory and they will return to London. He expects the last step to be somewhat dangerous for himself. He is amazed that with as much as she knows (that is, as much as the reader knows), she has not figured out the mystery for herself. During this conversation, Miss Lally realizes that a bust of William Pitt (a British prime minister) is sitting on a shelf above Gregg's desk, whereas before it had been on the top of a tall cabinet. She is quite sure of it, since earlier she had noted it when she could find no way for the maids to reach it for dusting. Gregg assures her he had used no stepladder or anything of the kind to move it, but he tells her:

> There is a little puzzle for you; a problem in the manner of the inimitable Holmes; there are the facts, plain and patent; summon your acuteness to the solution of the puzzle.

Miss Lally discovers that a part of the statue has had its heavy coating of dust removed and that the same area is covered with something slimy, such as a snail leaves behind it.

The next day at breakfast, Gregg announces that he is going for a long walk and that, in fact, he might stay overnight in some roadside inn. Miss Lally, filled with dread over what he might be doing and realizing that this will be the search for his final evidences, urges him not to go, but to no avail. He does not return; and by dinnertime the next day one of the servants gives Miss Lally a letter Gregg had left to be given to her if he did not return by then.

The letter begins by telling Miss Lally that if she is reading it, then Gregg must be dead. The letter then directs her to the key of a locked drawer in his desk that contains a summary of his research, which she reads. During his ethnological researches, he had come to the conclusion that reports of demons at witches' Sabbaths, encounters with fairies, and similar occurrences ought to be taken seriously as evidence. He rejected the magical explanations embedded in the reports in medieval and ancient texts but believed there must be some rational explanation. This led him to suggest that, while probably all reports of supernatural events in spiritualist sciences are false, this did not mean that very rare human beings might not possess extraordinary powers. He explains this by what he calls the theory of reversion, whereby a human being might suddenly be able to do something that a lower form of life like a snail might do. He describes how he started amassing evidence. The explanation for fairies, he thought, must be that they are part of some evolutionarily primitive tribe, hidden from the rest of humankind in the wilderness and able to perform seeming miracles by reverting to the forms of more primitive animals. When he read of a young woman and a child who disappeared from country villages, he convinced himself that the best explanation was that they had been kidnapped by this tribe.

He added to this evidence a report of a man who had been beaten to death with a stone ax that had been left beside his body. He had had the black seal in his possession for some time, having bought it from a professional looter of archaeological sites in Iraq (which was all too common a way for museums and scholars to acquire artifacts at that time). The characters on it looked like cuneiform writing, which Gregg could read, but they did not fit any known system of cuneiform text. Once he received a letter from a colleague asking him if he could make sense of a strange graffiti that had been found painted with red dirt on a stone in the Grey Hills (near the sites of the disappearances and murder). None other than Jervase Cradock's mother, in a state of shock, had been found in the middle of the night near the painted stone. She had gone to visit her cousin after her husband died but never arrived and was found a few days later. It was then that Gregg broached his theory to colleagues, only to find himself scorned as a madman. He turned to the script on the black seal, which it took him fourteen years to decipher. He succeeded only when he found a second engraved stone with a copy of part of the black seal inscription, together with a translation into a known cuneiform language. The text was evidently a spell meant to enable a man to be turned into a snake, but as soon as he had translated it, Gregg reacted with horror and burned his work and never replicated it.

Gregg deduced that Mrs. Cradock had been raped by his hypothetical tribe, and therefore her son, Jervase, would have inherited their ability to revert. He confirmed this during Jervase's first fit, when Gregg recognized what he was saying as the text on the black stone, and during his second fit, when he saw a tentacle several dozen feet long extend from the boy's body and move the bust of Pitt, which Gregg likened to a snail extending and retracting its eye stalks. After this, Gregg intended to go into the hills to try to find the lost tribe, leaving the letter in case he did not return. Later, searchers found

Gregg's watch and wedding ring but no other trace of him.

Returning to the frame story, Miss Lally adds that Gregg's lawyer refused to believe the same story she had told Phillipps and gave out the report to the newspapers that Gregg had drowned. Phillipps, however, does believe her, because, he says, Gregg's hypothesis is confirmed by the latest scientific discoveries of spiritualism.

CHARACTERS

Jervase Cradock

Jervase is a youth from the local village near Gregg's summerhouse whom Gregg hires as a houseboy. Miss Lally describes him:

> He was a youth of about fourteen, with black hair and black eyes and an olive skin, and I saw at once from the curious vacancy of his expression that he was mentally weak. . . . I heard him answering the gardener in a queer, harsh voice that caught my attention; it gave me the impression of some one speaking deep below under the earth, and there was a strange sibilance, like the hissing of the phonograph as the pointer travels over the cylinder.

This is meant as foreshadowing to reveal that he is a member of the secret race, if, unlike Miss Lally, the reader can join up the description from Solinus with the particular features the boy possesses.

Mrs. Cradock

Never appearing directly in the story, after the death of her husband, Mrs. Cradock went to visit her cousin and was kidnapped and raped by the inhuman tribe Gregg is investigating, giving birth to her son, Jervase, eight months later. Left insensible by the horror of her experience, she slowly recovered but never discussed what had happened to her.

Professor Gregg

Gregg is described as "a middle-aged gentleman of specious appearance, neatly and correctly dressed." Innocuous in itself, this passage shows some of the way culture has changed in the last century. "Correctly dressed" means that he was wearing a suit, which by 1895 would not have looked that different from a modern suit: a matching jacket and pants, almost certainly of wool, and a tie. The hat that was part of this costume has almost dropped out of use today. Suits have not gone away, but they are no longer universal and may be worn by people of any class or profession. However, in 1895, they were closely tied to social status, and no one employed in a professional capacity—from a politician to a university professor to a bank clerk—would have left the house without wearing one. "Correctly dressed" in the text means he was dressed in a manner befitting and indicating his social station.

Workmen like carpenters would also have worn a suit, but they would probably have had only one, and the difference in material and cut would have been instantly recognizable to anyone familiar with the intricacies of Victorian dress. Like Sherlock Holmes, one could tell a man's profession merely by looking at him. Other tradesmen would have worn other cuts of jackets, but if a man went out on the streets in his shirt sleeves, the police would probably stop him to ask what the trouble was. The use of the word *specious* is also interesting. The root meaning of the word is simply "to make an appearance," and in 1895 it could be used to mean making any kind of appearance. The context here clearly provides the sense of making a good or appropriate appearance. Today, it would be hard to imagine using the word for anything except to denote making a false and deceptive appearance.

Gregg at first seems to be a stereotypical Victorian professor who fits into the urban elite world that Machen himself was always trying to penetrate. The location of the summerhouse Gregg rents, though it is fictitious, is clearly meant to be in Wales. When Gregg says that it is in the west of England, Machen is making fun of supposedly sophisticated Londoners who could not tell the difference. Gregg gradually takes on a more precise character. As mild-mannered as he seems, Gregg is, far more than Mary Shelley's Dr. Frankenstein, the prototype of the mad scientist. The first hint about his pet scientific project comes when Gregg tells Miss Lally, "I covet the renown of Columbus." This is already a bad sign, because he is not talking about the importance of his work but about grasping for fame. At the same time, Gregg is secretive about his work, because he once tried to discuss it with colleagues, and they reacted with condescension and pity. One suggested he was overworked and needed a rest, to which Gregg, as he told Miss Lally, replied, "'In plain terms . . . you think I am going mad. I think not'; and I showed him out with some little appearance of heat."

Once Gregg's theory is revealed later in the story, it is easy to see that his colleagues must have thought him mad, because he had reversed the scientific process and become a pseudoscientist. However, precisely because Gregg had really done that, he is no longer capable of perceiving the problem. His emotional reaction is aroused not by rudeness from the other party, as Gregg would probably say, but by his own defensiveness, since at some unconscious level he must be aware of precisely what he is doing. Similarly, in contrast to his regular scholarly work, which is carefully sourced and reasoned, Miss Lally is impressed by the "vehemence of his tone" when he speaks about his new project. As a skeptic, she is "offended at a hint of the marvellous" and wonders if Gregg is "cherishing a monomania, and barring out from this one subject all the scientific method of his other life." She, too, in plain terms, thinks he has gone mad. The stock scene in countless Hollywood films in which mad scientists denounce the fools who laughed at them and on whom they swear vengeance once their experiments have vindicated them begins with Gregg's statement "My friends ridiculed me to my face, and I was regarded as a madman; and beneath a natural anger I chuckled to myself." It only remained to add: *I'll show them, I'll show them all!* to complete the formula.

Miss Lally

Miss Lally is the narrator of the "Novel of the Black Seal." She presents herself in the text as a governess, a gentle and unassuming woman possessed of the conventional Victorian morality and virtues of her day. Although her daily routine in Gregg's household would naturally have mostly been concerned with his children, whom she would have overseen and, if they were young enough, educated, it is remarkable that other than noting their mere existence, no mention is made of them except in the most incidental manner. The reader never learns their names or even how many children there might be. They are more invisible in the narrative than the servants.

Left orphaned and in poverty at an early age, Miss Lally educated herself from the remnants of her father's library. She taught herself Latin and read moralizing literature such as the medieval *Gesta Romanorum.* In fact, the plot of the "Novel of the Black Seal" hinges on her Latin familiarity. The text that Machen fabricated for Solinus is quoted in Latin and then translated into English by the character of Miss Lally. Part of the reason that Machen sets up this vital part of the plot in this way is to help provide characterization for Miss Lally through the reader's comparing her translation to the original. Naturally, many of Machen's original readers would have been fluent in Latin because of the prevailing system of education in Victorian England. In general, the translation is like indifferent but competent student work. It conveys the sense of the Latin but echoes the word order and other features of the original too closely, using a style that is often called *translationese* in the schoolroom, rather than fluent English. That is why the passage seems so archaic in style. There is a serious mistake, however, in her translation of the first clause of the last sentence: "Cujus lapidis nomen secretum ineffabile colunt." Miss Lally translates this as "And this stone has a secret unspeakable name." She has, however, left out the verb *colunt.* The passage should be translated as "They worship the secret ineffable name of this stone." Since Machen composed the Latin, he hardly made a mistake himself in translating it. Nor does the mistake have the slightest consequence in the later plot of the story. As it is presented, the mistake goes entirely to character: it shows only that Miss Lally is not quite as competent and serious as she presents herself.

It must be remembered that not only is the character of Miss Lally a fictional creation of Machen's, but also, within the larger framework of *The Three Impostors*, the woman who represents herself as Miss Lally is a member of a secret neo-pagan society bent on murder: she is devious, cunning, and depraved and only playing the part of an innocent governess in order to deceive. Bearing this in mind, some of Miss Lally's professed reading habits also go to character. Sir Richard Francis Burton's translation of *The Book of the Thousand Nights and a Night* is hardly the kind of literature that the purportedly chaste and prim Miss Lally would read. The book, although it contains nothing that would be considered obscene today, deals forthrightly with matters of sex, and Burton adds to this his own ethnological discussions of the subject. He knew full well that if he had tried to publish it openly in Victorian Britain, he would have been arrested and tried for obscenity. Therefore, the book was published as a private subscription, originally limited to just a thousand copies. Such a book would no doubt have horrified a truly innocent governess. (Miss Lally's actual reference is to the "supplementary Nights," leaving no doubt that she means Burton's translation.) However, it seems certain to have been high on the reading list of the neo-pagan secret society to which the woman playing Miss Lally belongs. Her referring to it is a slip out of character.

Mr. Meyrick

Mr. Meyrick is the local Anglican pastor in the town where Gregg and Miss Lally spend the summer. He is a member of a local gentry family.

Charles Phillipps

Phillipps is not technically a character in the "Novel of the Black Seal," but in *The Three Impostors*. He does, however, hear the story and speaks briefly with Miss Lally before and after she tells it. He seems remarkably sure of his intellectualism and his scientific credentials, but he is also remarkably gullible.

THEMES

Gothicism

The gothic was a new type of horror literature developed in England at the end of the eighteenth century. The gothic was a reaction to the Enlightenment. During the Enlightenment, the ethos of science finally became dominant in European intellectualism. Belief in the supernatural and demons was dismissed as superstition, since they corresponded to nothing observed in nature. Even Christianity was profoundly changed by the Enlightenment. In intellectual circles, deism replaced medieval faith. The idea that God was a person who went around suspending the laws of physics in favor of miracles like the parting of the Red Sea or the multiplication of the loaves and fishes seemed out of place in the clockwork universe described by Isaac Newton and other early scientists. The role of God was reserved for putting the whole mechanism in motion, leaving little room for a personal, anthropomorphic deity.

The nature of the church changed, too. It was during the Enlightenment that church-sponsored violence stopped. Witches and heretics were no longer tortured and executed, and crusades were no longer called for. The new rational man of the Enlightenment would no longer kill or see people killed for superstitious belief, but the irrational side of culture that the Enlightenment tried to sweep aside was not based on nothing. The human mind is profoundly irrational. The mind evolved to function within the small social network of a family, extended family, and tribe. Those kinds of relationships are modeled in the mind, and so the mind tries to use the model to explain the larger universe, resulting in the magical view of a universe bound by mutual ties of antipathy and affinity and where all actions have anthropomorphic causes. What the Enlightenment called superstition was the imposition of the inner organization of the unconscious mind onto the world, and this naturally persists, despite science's having shown what a poor model of reality that structure is.

The gothic expresses the tension between the traditional world that still lingers inside the reader and the new scientific world that is emerging all around. There were two strains of gothic literature. In a novel like Ann Radcliffe's *The Mysteries of Udolpho* (1794), apparently supernatural events are revealed at the end to have taken place in the orderly scientific universe, and everything that appears to happen by magic is the result of misperception and misunderstanding. In the other kind of gothic novel, such as Matthew Lewis's *The Monk* (1796), the old magical view of the universe is simply taken for granted in stories where magic is used to exorcize ghosts and summon demons. There are certainly many gothic elements in Machen's work, for instance, in the narrator's wild walk through a mist-enshrouded world after she has given up all hope:

> All that I remember of my walk on that Sunday afternoon seems but the broken fragments of an evil dream. In a confused vision I stumbled on, . . . the cloudy world of mist on one side of me, and on the other comfortable villas with a glow of firelight flickering on the walls, but all unreal. . . . In the white silence I stumbled on, as desolate as if I trod the streets of a buried city; and as I grew more weak and exhausted, something of the horror of death was folding thickly round my heart.

Note that she is nearly in an altered state of consciousness (a hallucination or dream), on the border between the real world represented by the lighted houses and the unreal world of the mist. Yet it is the real world that seems unreal to her. The image of the buried city evokes a real place like Pompeii but also the fairy halls buried inside

TOPICS FOR FURTHER STUDY

- *Japanese Gothic Tales* (1996), by Izumi Kyoka and translated by Charles Shiro Inouye, is a collection of horror stories by an author roughly contemporary with Machen and heavily influenced by Western literature. Write a paper based on one of the stories, comparing the styles of the two authors and their approaches to the vocation of horror.
- *Native American Tales and Legends* (2001) is a retelling of North American myths for a young-adult audience by Allan A. MacFarlan. Among the subjects of the myths are tales of dwarfs, giants, and nonhuman races that exist alongside humankind (a common theme in Native American mythology). Write a paper comparing this actual mythological material with the pseudoscientific interpretation of myth presented by Machen.
- Machen was interested in the contrast between the rural life in which he grew up and the urban life he embraced as an adult. This dichotomy was related, for him, to the conflict between traditional and modern ways of life in industrial Britain. He deals with this both explicitly and in a more allegorical fashion in the "Novel of the Black Seal" and extensively in his *Autobiography*. Explore this theme in Machen's work in a report to your class.
- Google's Ngram Viewer (https://books.google.com/ngrams) allows one to track the frequency of word use in English-language publications over the period 1800–2000. Google Books allows one to locate specific uses of words, ranked by popularity or a choice of other criteria and so track their change in meaning over time. Machen, in the "Novel of the Black Seal" uses words like *specious* in a sense that would not, or even could not, be given to them today. Use these analytical tools to track the history of the word *specious* and any other words in Machen's text whose usage looks unusual to you, and make a presentation to your class describing their changing use over time.

ancient tombs in Celtic myth. Machen also moves beyond the gothic. The modern horror story, which Machen created and H. P. Lovecraft would perpetuate, takes a different approach. The story is filled with apparently supernatural elements, which are explained away rationally at the end, but by a rationality that has itself been transformed by taking into account the reality of the supernatural.

Language and Languages

Part of Gregg's researches in the "Novel of the Black Seal" result in the deciphering of the sixty characters inscribed on the seal itself. These were written in a script similar to the cuneiform writing of the ancient Near East but also so different that they could not be easily read. This is the case with the actual writing of the ancient Canaanite city of Ugarit, whose language was written in a small group of cuneiform signs that had been adopted for use as letters in a quasi-alphabet (in that ordinarily cuneiform signs stand for syllables), although these would not be discovered until the 1920s. Gregg works on the problem of the black seal for fourteen years without making any progress, which is not surprising in the case of an unknown language recorded in an unknown writing system. He is eventually able to decipher the black seal when he finds another copy of the inscription together with a translation into a known cuneiform language (though Machen does not relate which one).

Earlier in the nineteenth century, this technique had been used to decipher both Egyptian hieroglyphics, beginning with the famous Rosetta stone, and cuneiform, from the Behistun inscription in

The story is set in rural Wales (©JONATHON barnett / Shutterstock.com)

Iran. If these are the models of deciphering that Machen had in mind, the direct inspiration to hinge the story on an ancient inscribed seal perhaps came from another historical event. From the antiquities market in Greece, the archaeologist Arthur Evans had been collecting Minoan-Mycenaean seal stones written in the scripts today called Linear A and Linear B. In 1894, he began publishing them, just a year before Machen's story was published. Machen may well have been inspired by reading about the then-indecipherable inscriptions on these seal stones. The Linear B script, which was the earliest system for writing Greek, going back to the 1200s BCE, would not be deciphered until the 1950s, whereas Linear A, a similar writing system for recording a non-Indo-European language native to Crete, has never been deciphered.

STYLE

New Arabian Nights

Miss Lally dismisses as quaint what she reads in the Roman geographer Solinus and "thought it fit for Sinbad the Sailor, or other of the supplementary Nights." Machen is here rather obliquely referring to *The Book of the Thousand Nights and a Night*, a work more commonly known as the *Arabian Nights*. This was originally an Indo-Persian collection of folktales that was translated into Arabic in the Middle Ages. The book was immensely popular in the Arab world, and as it was copied and recopied by hand, each manuscript introduced new stories until all together they made a corpus of well over one thousand stories. The famous stories of Sinbad the Sailor were originally an independent story cycle that was incorporated into the *Nights*. Several partial translations of the stories had been made in Europe beginning in the eighteenth century, but the first substantial translation (given the chaotic state of the manuscripts, no edition or translation could ever be considered complete), containing 1,001 stories, was published in 1885 by the British soldier, explorer, and diplomat Sir Richard Francis Burton. Between 1886 and 1888, he published six hundred more stories in volumes he called *The Supplemental Nights*. This is the text to which Miss Lally is referring, but the reference has a deeper significance for the "Novel of the Black Seal."

In 1878, Robert Louis Stevenson published a volume he called *Latter-Day Arabian Nights* (later retitled *New Arabian Nights*). This consisted of two cycles of short stories set in modern-day England. Their connection to the *Nights* was through the use of a frame story rather than in subject matter. The *Thousand Nights and a Night* is set up beginning with the life of an Islamic caliph. He has had several wives, but they have all betrayed him with other lovers and have been executed. He determines that the only way to ensure the fidelity of his future wives is to marry a new wife each day and execute her at the end of the wedding night, but his next wife, Sherazade, begins to tell him a story that is so fascinating that he agrees to spare her until the next night so she can finish it. This recitation goes on for a thousand nights, until he is satisfied she will not betray him. While each story or chapter is a separate self-contained story, they all also go together to make up a larger unified narrative. Several of the stories, or story cycles, are composed in the same way, with a storyteller telling a story in which another storyteller tells a story, and so on, so that the main narrative descends and reascends through many levels of narrative framework. Stevenson used the same kind of structure in his *New Arabian Nights*. This work proved immensely popular, and Machen thought he would capitalize on the idea, writing *The Three Impostors* in the same way, consisting of a frame story in which half of the chapters (including "Novel of the Black Seal") can function as stand-alone stories but also go together to make up a single, unified novel. Miss Lally's comparison, then, is a reference to the nature of the story she inhabits, a joke passed between the author and the reader through the medium of the character.

Pseudepigraphy

Usually, the term *pseudepigraphy* is used to describe a work that claims to be written by someone other than the actual author, as when a medieval alchemical book asserts it was written by the ancient (and mythical) author Hermes Trismegistus. What Machen does in the "Novel of the Black Seal" is somewhat similar. A key point in the plot of the story turns on a passage from the Roman geographical writer Solinus. Solinus was a real historical figure who indeed wrote a geography book entitled *The Wonders of the World.* Machen proceeds to quote a section of it, but the text he gives, in both Latin and a flawed English translation, is entirely Machen's own fabrication. No such passage appears in the text of Solinus. This technique is so rare that it does not have a critical name, but it can certainly be classed with a range of techniques that includes pseudepigraphy. The fabrication of entirely fictitious works of literature, usually to help flesh out a fictional world, is very common in fantasy literature, most notably in the work of J. R. R. Tolkien, who created not only fictional books but also whole new languages. Umberto Eco, in contrast, in *The Name of the Rose* (1980), built his story around the second book of Aristotle's *Poetics*, which was a real book but which was lost by the end of antiquity. In Eco's novel, however, at least one copy survived, and Eco briefly quotes from it, fabricating his own text to represent it. In this case, Eco is re-creating a real but lost work.

HISTORICAL CONTEXT

Latin Literature

"Novel of the Black Seal" is filled with references not only to Latin books but even to obscure Latin books, the knowledge of which on the reader's part plays a greater or lesser part in the understanding of the work. The *Gesta Romanorum* is a book that Miss Lally says she read over and over as a child, helping to teach herself Latin. It is a book that would have been widely read in the nineteenth century when the educated class was fully fluent in Latin. Today, it is a text known only by narrow specialists. The book was compiled in the Middle Ages (perhaps around the year 1300) by giving new versions of more or less well-known stories. The title denotes the rather serious sounding "Acts of the Romans," but its connotation is more like "Ancient stories." It contains a miscellany of stories that all have a distinct and simple moral message. For this reason, it is usually thought that it was compiled for the purpose of providing source material for sermons. Although it provides nothing original, it conveniently collected a variety of stories, some of which were later used as the foundation of works by Chaucer and Shakespeare. Machen mentions the *Gesta* perhaps to suggest the limited depth of Miss Lally's education, and perhaps as well to suggest one way of reading the "Novel of the Black Seal"—as a simple moral tale, in that

COMPARE & CONTRAST

- **1890s:** The Linear, A, B, and C scripts, which represent the earliest phase of writing in Greece, have just been discovered but are not deciphered.

  Today: In the 1950s, Michael Ventris deciphered Linear B, revealing that the scripts recorded forms of the Greek language. There have not been any developments since. Although Linear A still has not been deciphered, it is now clear that it records an unknown language in a different family from any other known language, closer to what Machen imagined in the "Novel of the Black Seal."

- **1890s:** There is little or no international policing of archaeological sites, and those who wish to dig can generally sell whatever they find on the antiquities market, effacing the provenance and context of the objects in question.

  Today: Archaeological excavation is carefully controlled by the host country where the dig is carried out as well as by international bodies and treaties governing artifacts. Nevertheless, a large black market exists, ready to benefit from areas of political anarchy. ISIS, for example, is believed to have sold far more Iraqi and Syrian artifacts than have been destroyed.

- **1890s:** Gorillas were not known to Western science until the 1840s, and it is still barely possible to imagine that an unknown hominid species might exist, which would be a scientific framing of what Machen proposes in the "Novel of the Black Seal."

  Today: With the increasing field study of nature, particularly the widespread use of trail-cams, it is no longer possible that an unknown hominid (e.g., Sasquatch) or similar animal could still exist.

Gregg is seen to have been destroyed by his own pride and his covetousness for knowledge.

Pomponius Mela's book *De situ orbis* has been translated under the title *Description of the World.* Something of Mela's Victorian reputation can be discerned from his entry in the eleventh edition of the *Encyclopædia Britannica*, where his book is described as "dry in style and deficient in method, but of pure Latinity, and occasionally relieved by pleasing word-pictures." Scholarly opinion of Mela today is somewhat better. His work, a geographical survey of the known world, is seen as the first beginning of the establishment of a Spanish national identity. There is something suggestive about Mela for the plot of the novel. Ancient geographers believed that the earth was divided into climatic zones. They conceived of the far north as uninhabitable because of the cold. Below this was the inhabited zone of the Mediterranean, but around the equator they hypothesized that there was a zone uninhabited because of its excessive heat. Logically, there would be corresponding habitable and cold zones in the Southern Hemisphere, though they would be impossible to reach through the torrid equatorial zone. Mela was the only ancient author who even suggested that the southern temperate zone might, in this scheme, actually be inhabited. He refused to speculate about what these *antichthones* living there might be like, but at a minimum they would be an entirely different kind of human from those known in the north, if not something far stranger. This goes to Machen's theme of the hidden race in the "Novel of the Black Seal."

Solinus's *De mirabilibus mundi*, or "On the wonders of the world," is an even less read book than Mela's, largely because it consists of excerpts of other extant works, mainly the *Natural History* of Pliny the Elder and Mela himself. The book was often included in general compendiums of Latin geography in the sixteenth and seventeenth

The protagonist of the story is a professor who finds mysterious writing on a stone (©Roman Samborskyi / Shutterstock.com)

centuries of the kind Miss Lally finds. It lacks a modern English translation, and the text has not even been edited since Theodor Mommsen produced an edition in 1895. This is, of course, the same date as that of the publication of *The Three Impostors*, so one wonders if that publication inspired Machen to use Solinus in his story. However, the quotation attributed to Solinus in the story is entirely Machen's invention.

CRITICAL OVERVIEW

Fantasy or horror literature has traditionally been dismissed by literary critics. Fantasy literature in the twentieth century was largely published in pulp magazines, not serious literary venues. The distinction is more one of class than literary merit. Even the supremely academic J. R. R. Tolkien's work has suffered from this stereotyping. The same problem has for a long time colored Machen's literary reception. He is rarely discussed in the context of the decadent movement, of which he is indisputably a part, and literary critics are often blind to his importance in the foundation of the modern horror story. Consequently, the most important critical discussion of Machen is by the horror writer H. P. Lovecraft. His own writings were deeply inspired by Machen, and in his *Supernatural Horror in Literature* (1927), Lovecraft identifies in Machen's work the great theme of modern horror: the irrational, ancient, gothic world threatening to break out into what seems an ordered, modern reality, proving false everything the modern world thinks it knows about itself.

Machen's juxtaposed treatment of the traditional magical world and the modern scientific world also informs Latin American magical realism, especially through the work of Jorge Luis Borges. Wesley D. Sweetser, in his Twayne survey of Machen, points out that Machen is considered part of the "art for art's sake" movement championed by figures like Walter Pater and Oscar Wilde (through, for example, the fantastic elements in *The Picture of Dorian Gray*), as opposed to the realism represented by the prominent contemporary Russian authors—Leo

Tolstoy and others. Sweetser also finds *The Three Impostors* excessive in its modeling on Stevenson's *New Arabian Nights*, echoing his style and even reusing some of his plots, though not in the "Novel of the Black Seal," which he considers the best part of the book.

Sweetser also notes that the fairy mythology that Gregg attempts to explain in the "Novel of the Black Seal" is based on Welsh folklore. Mark Valentine, in his *Arthur Machen*, relates the fairy theme in several of Machen's stories to the popularity of fairy folklore in the literature of the 1890s, for example in W. B. Yeats's *Celtic Twilight* (1893). The "Novel of the Black Seal," Valentine explains, originally concerned a werewolf, but Machen felt it would not be convincing enough. Valentine explains the use to which Machen put his neo-fairy mythology, appealing to the unconscious fears of his audience:

> Without ever bringing us directly into the presence of the sub-human species that his character has encountered, Machen creates an aura of menace and hideousness about them, in a masterpiece of macabre allusiveness. In doing so, we can have little doubt that he was tapping deep sources of unconscious dread for Victorians—the threat to their civilization from an underclass of sordid, violent, secret and subterranean terrorists, or from frighteningly alien races.

Sondeep Kandola suggests, in "Celtic Occultism and the Symbolist Mode in the Fin-de-Siècle Writings of Arthur Machen and W. B. Yeats" (2013), that the "Novel of the Black Seal" is a satire of W. B. Yeats's attempt to break away from the Order of the Golden Dawn and found his own Celtic Order of Mysteries.

Adrian Eckersley, in his 1992 article "A Theme in the Early Work of Arthur Machen: 'Degeneration,'" notes that Machen was the leading horror writer of the 1890s. He is curious as to why the horror story became so popular just at that time in a Victorian England where religious feeling and belief in the supernatural were quickly ebbing away in the face of rational modernity. He sees Machen as demonstrating that

> from the Enlightenment onwards, the imagery of evil was being translated gradually from a spiritual to a scientific register, just as the function of the priest as society's moral guardian was steadily and imperceptibly being taken over by the medical man; and the priest's sanctions of spiritual damnation were being replaced by the medical man's ideas of biological *degeneration*.

Machen is expressing the views of the popular pseudosciences of eugenics and physiognomy rather than real science.

Kimberly Jackson, however, writing in *Victorian Literature and Culture* in 2013, reads the same material quite differently: Gregg is interested in the possibility of transcending evolution. Stefania Forlini, in her postmodernist reading "Modern Narratives and Decadent Things in Arthur Machen's *The Three Impostors*" (2012), finds that this "tale of the dealings of a secret society of Decadent fetish-worshippers . . . is ultimately a kind of parody of his contemporaries' 'scientific' attempts to read and narrate object culture." She finds the vast scientific collections that were compiled in Victorian museums for scientific analysis to be an expression of the same impulse to control and classify as Dorian Gray's collection of precious *objets d'art* in Oscar Wilde's novel. She rejects earlier readings of the "Novel of the Black Seal" as an expression of eugenicist fears of physical degeneration and sees it instead as a horrible satire of science itself. Contemporary ethnography was well aware of the rapid extinction of traditional cultures in the burgeoning colonial empires. It tended to look away from the biological devastation and warfare that led to the extinction of the people bearing the culture. This was considered progress, with modernity replacing Stone Age cultures. In this regard, Forlini thinks, the primitive secret race in the "Novel of the Black Seal" becomes a nightmare vision of the genocides being carried out against third-world peoples, as the Stone Age throwbacks show up in the British countryside to murder and rape.

CRITICISM

Bradley A. Skeen

Skeen is a classicist. In the following essay, he explores the role of pseudoscience as a protest against the emerging modern world in Machen's "Novel of the Black Seal."

In the nineteenth century, people had to cope with the transformation of intellectual life by science and with the disruption of social and cultural life by industrialization. Though this process had really begun in the eighteenth century with the Enlightenment, in the nineteenth century what had before affected an intellectual elite class now impacted all of society. People often do not like change,

WHAT DO I READ NEXT?

- Robert Louis Stevenson's *New Arabian Nights* (first published in book form as a two-volume set in 1882, thereafter often reprinted, and widely available on the Internet) copied the structure of the original as a series of nested, unrelated, but nevertheless interdependent stories whose success became a model for Machen's *The Three Impostors*. *New Arabian Nights* is often considered to contain some of Stevenson's best writing, especially "The Pavilion on the Links."
- *Ugetsu Monogatari* is a collection of horror stories written by Ueda Akinari in 1776. Although he treats his tales as would a literary author, they are largely drawn from traditional stories of Japanese folklore. The collection has been translated into English several times, either under the transliteration of the title or using the translation *Tales of Moonlight and Rain*, for example, by Leon Zolbrod in 1974.
- H. P. Lovecraft's short story "The Call of Cthulhu" (1928) is closely based on Machen's "Novel of the Black Seal." The story has been frequently reprinted and is posted widely on the Internet.
- *The Great God Pan* (published in full in 1894) was Machen's first novel. Closely related in theme to the "Novel of the Black Seal," it concerns a physical operation (on the brain) to achieve spiritual awakening as well as the reversion of human beings to animal forms.
- *The King in Yellow*, by Robert W. Chambers, is a classic collection of horror stories published in 1895, the same year as Machen's *The Three Impostors*, by a fellow member of the decadent movement. Chambers's stories revolve around a play (after which the collection is titled) that is never quoted from in the stories but which drives insane anyone who reads it. It also follows the *New Arabian Nights* formula but not as strictly as Machen did.
- Rick Yancey's *The Monstrumologist* (2009) is a young-adult novel heavily derived from the "Novel of the Black Seal." It concerns a mad scientist charged with protecting the world from a group of monsters whose reality is incompatible with the framework of modern science.
- John Rhys's *Lectures on the Origin and Growth of Religion as Illustrated by Celtic Heathondom* (1888) was based on the Hibbert Lectures that Rhys delivered in 1886. Rhys was an Oxford don (and would become J. R. R. Tolkien's most important teacher). Rhys hypothesized that Celtic fairy mythology was based on cultural memories of the Celts' contact with the indigenous population of the British Isles. (Celts arrived there only in the Iron Age, displacing the civilization that had built Stonehenge and other megalithic monuments.) In the "Novel of the Black Seal," Gregg enthusiastically (rather too enthusiastically) takes up this idea to postulate his lost race as a remnant of that or an even earlier population. (One wonders if Machen did not have Neanderthals in mind.)

---

particularly change that is forced on them against their will. They can adapt to it and make the best of it and even find a new way of life better than they had before, but that does not always make change more palatable. In the early nineteenth century, romanticism was the first reaction to modernity, an attempt to reconcile the virtues of the past, the sense of meaning available in a cohesive social tradition, with modernity, but it failed by its own standards and did nothing to deflect the advance of modernity.

"THE POWER OF THE NAME OF SCIENCE IS PARADOXICALLY CO-OPTED TO DISPROVE SCIENCE."

The gothic was a popular version of the romantic and simply showed the old world breaking into and replacing the new world, as if the clock could be turned backward. The characters who believe in science and rationality find out that the real world has not changed at all and is filled with ghosts and demons. Machen could not fall back on that position, even in fantasy. Science had become so ubiquitous that it was no longer possible to simply deny it and say the supernatural world is real and science is wrong. Rather, Machen used science, or at least something that looks like science, to validate the supernatural. The power of the name of science is paradoxically co-opted to disprove science. In his story, Machen shows a world that looks scientific and can be accepted as the real world by the reader but, at the same time, reveals that science is fundamentally limited, essentially wrong. Machen's fantasy is able to deny science, but the basically nonscientific world is not an Edenic paradise; rather, it is a place of unimaginable horror. The attack on a world ordered by science and reason takes on the darkest character, expressed in the hidden desires of the human unconscious.

Professor Gregg thinks of himself as a new Columbus—one might more pointedly say a new Darwin—who is going to revolutionize all of science with his fresh discoveries. He believes that he is going to effect what the historian of science Thomas Kuhn called a paradigm shift and establish an entirely new way of looking at the world. In Kuhn's view, science progresses by a series of revolutions. In each cycle, new data are discovered, which increasingly diverge from the explanation offered by existing theories and eventually require a revolution and a new theory to explain the discrepancies between new evidence and existing theory. Since science is a human institution, there is also a generational factor. Young scientists will be more anxious to formulate and accept new theories, since they are not as entrenched and invested in the old theories as their seniors are.

A real world example of such a paradigmatic shift was under way even as Machen was writing. Scientists had observed irregularities in the orbit of the planet Mercury compared with its predicted behavior under Newton's theory of gravity. This suggested not that Newton's theory was wrong (which would be highly unlikely, since it explained almost all observed data) but that it was missing something. Several attempts to find what was missing had been made, but the problem became clear only with a series of articles that Albert Einstein would publish beginning in 1905 establishing the theory of relativity. Far from falsifying Newtonian gravity, it explained it more thoroughly as part of a larger theory with greater explanatory power.

Another example of a paradigm shift relates to the theory of evolution. Charles Darwin was keenly aware that his understanding of inheritance was insufficient. This was changed in the 1890s as the largely ignored work on genetics by Gregor Mendel was combined with Darwinian evolution to produce the modern synthesis. This, in turn, was revolutionized in the 1940s by the discovery of molecular genetics. Again, each new step did not falsify its predecessor but placed it in a better-explained context.

Gregg's work seems superficially similar to these real-life scientific revolutions. Even before she understands just what Gregg has hypothesized, Miss Lally

> began to dread, vainly proposing to myself the iterated dogmas of science that all life is material, and that in the system of things there is no undiscovered land, even beyond the remotest stars, where the supernatural can find a footing. Yet there struck in on this the thought that matter is as really awful and unknown as spirit, that science itself but dallies on the threshold, scarcely gaining more than a glimpse of the wonders of the inner place.

She is envisioning that Gregg's discovery will change existing conceptions of reality, but that is not quite the case. Gregg hints to Miss Lally what he is really up to:

> Life . . . is no simple thing, no mass of grey matter . . . to be laid naked by the surgeon's knife; man is the secret which I am about to explore, and before I can discover him I must cross over weltering seas indeed, and oceans and the mists of many thousand years. You know the myth of the lost Atlantis; what if it be true, and I am destined to be called the discoverer of that wonderful land?

People who hunt for Atlantis are not scientists but pseudoscientists. They use a methodology that superficially resembles science, which perhaps they themselves believe to be science but is not science. They presuppose that Atlantis is real and start hunting for anomalies, bits of evidence that do not look quite right, and then interpret them in whatever contorted fashion is necessary to turn them into evidence of their pet hypothesis. This is exactly the opposite of the way real scientists proceed. Einstein took into account the anomalous orbit of Mercury and looked for a new way to explain it. He did not think of the theory of special relativity and then try to find things like the orbit of Mercury to support it. Science works from data and tries to find patterns in it that can be reduced to laws. These are explained by a hypothesis that makes testable predictions; after every attempt has been made to show that the hypothesis is false, it is recognized as a provisionally valid theory that is the best explanation of all the facts. It is symptomatic of Gregg's misunderstanding of science that he is hopelessly confused about the use of the terms *theory* and *hypothesis*. He constantly describes his vague ideas as a theory when it is no more than a hypothesis.

Gregg nevertheless begins his chain of reasoning with what he already considers a theory, namely, that the description in medieval texts of devils and of fairies are to be explained by a misunderstood reality rather than, for example, by the science of comparative mythology:

> I thought that the purely supernatural element in these traditions was to be accounted for on the hypothesis that a race which had fallen out of the grand march of evolution might have retained, as a survival, certain powers which would be to us wholly miraculous.

Gregg's statement suggests that he believes evolution is teleological, leading as if by design from primitive forms to the high point of humankind. Rather, evolution is contingent, shaping each creature to its immediate environment, but teleology paves the way for explaining the supernatural attributes of his secret race, allowing the creatures to manifest traits of more primitive creatures. (In fact, the traits they manifest are those of snails and snakes, neither of which are ancestral to human beings.) Gregg regularly refers to his hypothesis as a *theory* and fearlessly uses it to explain new facts, despite its never having been tested through experiment.

Only after formulating this theory does Gregg begin to cherry-pick evidence that he can interpret to support it. He assembles "a collection of the strangest significance." This in part consists of what might be termed *industrial accidents*: dislocations from traditional village life caused by industrialization. These include a girl who ran off to the city to look for work and a child who fell down a deep abandoned mine shaft. Since he already has his theory in place, the easiest explanation for these common occurrences comes from asking, "What if the obscure and horrible race of the hills still survived, still remained haunting wild places and barren hills and now and then repeating the evil of the Gothic legend?" It is at this stage that he broaches his ideas to other scientists. If he explained his theory as clearly to them as he did to Miss Lally, then they were certainly right to dismiss him as a crank. They would have recognized that he was doing science backward and hunting for anomalies instead of interpreting evidence. Note that Gregg's explanation for the disappearances, especially that of Jervase Cradock's mother, is a mediator between the folkloric idea of being kidnapped by fairies and the modern trope of alien abduction.

Gregg argues for his theory by analogy, saying that he is like a biologist who,

> roaming in a quiet English wood, had been suddenly stricken aghast by the presence of the slimy and loathsome terror of the ichthyosaurus, the original of the stories of the awful worms killed by valorous knights, or had seen the sun darkened by the pterodactyl, the dragon of tradition.

Gregg's analogy would work only if he were likening his hypothetical case to proven fact. Actually, no one has ever suggested that these kind of prehistoric creatures survived into medieval times to become the basis of mythological narratives about dragons (although there are cases in premodern times where fossils were explained by reference to mythological creatures), except for in two major instances. Neither is quite as fantastic as Gregg's vision of an ichthyosaur, a creature whose appearance and habitat were quite similar to a modern killer whale's, roaming in the forest. One is the case of the Loch Ness monster, a well-known hoax that employed the most desperate reasoning to justify itself. The other is fundamentalist creationism. According to creationists' interpretation of the Bible, nonavian dinosaurs and pterosaurs must have ridden out the flood in Noah's ark and become extinct only later, in historic times. They often point to any mention of dragons or other monsters, like Grendel in *Beowulf*, as evidence that dinosaurs survived until the time such texts were written and may do so even today in the unexplored tropics. They, like Gregg, are looking for any evidence that can be used to support their grievance against modernity rather than objectively considering the whole body of evidence.

At one time, Gregg recommends to Miss Lally that she re-create his research using the Sherlock Holmes method of reasoning. This is best exemplified by Holmes's famous statement in *The Sign of Four* that "when you have eliminated the impossible, whatever remains, *however improbable*, must be the truth." This is a version of scientific falsifiability, working to prove hypotheses false and accepting only those that cannot be proved false (ironically propagated by Arthur Conan Doyle, himself a believer in spiritualism and in fairies), but Gregg does not do this himself. He says, "I remember being struck by the phrase 'articulate-speaking men' in Homer, as if the writer knew or had heard of men whose speech was so rude that it could hardly be termed articulate." He interprets this as evidence that Homer knew a race of inhuman beings in whom the power of speech was rudimentary or nonexistent, making it evidence for his pet theory. However, there are other possibilities, namely, that Homer is simply alluding to men whose rhetorical gifts would not allow them to persuade an army to fight or entertain a group of banqueters, such as the heroes in his poems can do. Gregg did not eliminate these explanations or even consider them, failing in the simplest application of science.

Very often, the motive of pseudoscience is to try to discredit science and the scientific explanation of the world. In its most malignant forms, it claims that scientists really do know the *truth*, that is, the truth offered by the pseudoscience, but are engaged in a sinister worldwide conspiracy to suppress it, and this kind of thinking can be used for all-too-real political purposes. The ultimate reason behind the attack on science itself, the reason that Machen can use pseudoscience to create a simultaneously attractive and repulsive fantasy, is precisely because pseudoscience claims that the world is different from the way science construes it to be. The emotions of the unconscious have a vision of the world that is based on projection. The human mind has evolved to recognize and interact with other people. It makes the world over into a place where human feeling matters and makes sense, absolutely, not merely to other people. Science revealed the world is not that way, but the mind does not want to abandon its fantasy.

"MACHEN WAS, CONSEQUENTLY, IN A POSITION TO REALIZE THAT THE SECRETS BEING IMPARTED WITHIN THE WALLS OF ISIS-URANIA TEMPLE WERE AVAILABLE TO ANYONE WHO HAD THE WHEREWITHAL TO READ AND RESEARCH."

Source: Bradley A. Skeen, Critical Essay on "Novel of the Black Seal," in *Short Stories for Students*, Gale, Cengage Learning, 2017.

Susan Johnson Graf

In the following excerpt, Graf examines Machen's interest in the occult.

Arthur Llewelyn Jones-Machen (1863–1947), who wrote under the shortened form of his name, Arthur Machen, was initiated into the Isis-Urania Temple of the Hermetic Order of the Golden Dawn on November 21, 1899. He and Algernon Blackwood were among the last to be initiated into the original Golden Dawn before internecine feuding and scandal would irrevocable damage the order and lead to schism. The year 1899 was a pivotal one in Machen's life, marking the end of the most creative and productive decade of his life and of almost thirteen years of marriage to his first wife, Amelia (Amy) Hogg, who died of cancer on July 31, 1899.

It is difficult to find direct documentation of Machen's marriage or his spiritual belief before 1900 because he does not write about them. He does, however, write about his Golden Dawn involvement in Part Two of his autobiography, *Things Near and Far*, but he is contradictory throughout the narrative. He makes more negative than positive statements, and they come near the end of *Things Near and Far*, the second installment of his memoirs. There is the often-quoted statement that the "Order of the Twilight Star," a veiled reference to the Order of the Golden Dawn, did nothing for him:

Finding the tentacled monster seems in some ways more real to the narrator than the everyday world
(©Yulia Mladich / Shutterstock.com)

> I supposed that the Order, dimly heard of, might give me some light and guidance and leading on these matters [the strange occurrences surrounding Machen at the time of Amy's death and his "process"]. But, as I have noted, I was mistaken; the Twilight Star shed no ray of any kind on my path.

In the same section of *Things Near and Far*, Machen makes another derogatory statement about the order:

But as for anything vital in the secret order, for anything that mattered two straws to any reasonable being, there was nothing of it, and less than nothing. Among the members there were, indeed, persons of very high attainments, who, in my opinion, ought to have known better after a year's membership or less; but the society as a society was pure foolishness concerned with impotent and imbecile Abracadabras.

Machen also did not believe the story of how the order was founded, as it was claimed to be descended from a Rosicrucian order of antiquity. Machen, with the help of A. E. Waite, determined that the story was apocryphal and that the order was formulated by master masons in the 1880s. Machen was disgusted that some members were gullible enough to believe the story: "Any critical mind, with a tinge of occult reading, should easily have concluded that here was no ancient order from the whole nature and substance of its ritual and doctrine." For Machen, then, the order was, in a very real sense, fraudulent.

On the other hand, Machen praises an order with equal fervor in *Far Off Things*, but this may be Waite's Independent and Rectified Rite of the Golden Dawn rather than the original version of the organization that Machen initially joined:

> I am reminded of one of the secret societies with which I have had the pleasure of being connected. This particular society issued a little MS. Volume of instructions to those who were to be initiated, and amongst these instructions was the note: "remember that nothing exists that is not God." "How can I possibly realise that?" I said to one of the members of the society.

In *Things Near and Far*, just paragraphs before he lambastes the order, he has this to say in introducing the whole topic: "There is one episode of this period of which I may say a little more, that is the affair of the Secret Society. . . . And I must confess that it did me a great deal of good—for the time."

It is hard to come to a definitive conclusion about Machen's attitude toward the Golden Dawn, and it may not be just because he is obfuscating. He truly may have harbored conflicting feelings about his involvement in the Order of the Golden Dawn and its offshoot, the Independent and Rectified Rite. He may have been embarrassed when he thought about it retrospectively, but he also may have had conflicting feelings not long after he was initiated.

One sticking point that caused Machen to rethink his opinion of occult societies was his objection to the idea of initiation as it was practiced in the Order of the Golden Dawn and other occult groups. Here again, however, we find Machen contradicting himself because he found the initiation ceremony compelling at the time he was initiated:

> To stand waiting at a closed door in a breathless expectation, to see it open suddenly and disclose two figures clothed in a habit that I never thought to see worn by the living, to catch for a moment the vision of a cloud of incense smoke and certain dim lights glimmering in it before the bandage was put over the eyes and the arm felt a firm grasp upon it that led the hesitating footsteps unto the unknown darkness: all this was strange and admirable indeed; . . . All this was very fine; an addition and a valuable one, as I say, to the phantasmagoria that was being presented to me.

Five years later, in December 1905, Machen penned a letter to Waite in which he questions the concept of initiation as it was practiced in the Golden Dawn:

> And another point: the average secret society presupposes, as you yourself have said, that the initiator is, in a certain sense, superior to the initiated, superior that is, because he possesses certain information which he imparts to the neophyte; who is by this process, admitted into a circle of knowledge, outside which, (by the hypothesis) he stood, before initiation.

Occult groups are organized around the concept of initiation and the idea that there is secret knowledge that only can be imparted to an elite group: the privileged, spiritually advanced vanguard made up of members. Thus, to question the idea of initiation is to undermine the basis on which occult societies are founded. But question Machen did. Not only did he question, but he also conceived of a different kind of initiation. He proposed a secret society that

> makes no pretense of knowing anything which the outsider, the neophyte, does not know; which has no temple or circle to which admittance is given; which bids its members to look within, & uncover, & remove, & Behold, & Make the Great Interior Entrance—from Within to Within, instead of Without to Somebody Else's notion of Within.

Machen seems to be suggesting a group composed of autonomous mystics who would meet together but maintain a very Protestant sort of personal relationship with whatever they considered to be a supreme state of consciousness.

Machen's objection comes, at least partly, out of the disillusionment he experienced when he got to know the members of the Golden Dawn who were supposed to be initiated into the inmost secrets. He came to know that those people had feet of clay. He complains about Florence Farr Emery and Marcus Worsley Blackden specifically. Both were members of the inner order, and Machen must have expected enlightened behavior from such initiates. Instead, he found that they were "about as complete a pair of 'rotters' as I have ever seen."

Machen's disappointment also may have been the result of his advanced understanding of things occult before he entered the order. Machen did not come to the Golden Dawn as an occult studies greenhorn. He had been deeply immersed in occult studies at least since the time before he was married when he compiled a catalogue of occult texts entitled "The Literature of Occultism and Archeology" for George Redway in 1885. He details some of the works he catalogued:

> There were the principal and the more obscure treatises on Alchemy, on Astrology, on Magic; old Latin volumes most of them. Here were books about Witchcraft, Diabolical Possession, "Fascination," or the Evil Eye; here comments on the Kabbala. Ghosts and apparitions were a large family, Secret Societies of all sorts hung on the skirts of the Rosicrucians and Freemasons, and so found a place in the collection. Then the semi-religious, semioccult, semi-philosophical sects and schools were represented: we dealt in Gnostics and Mithraists, we harboured the

> Neoplatonists, we conversed with the Quietists and the Swedenborgians. These were the ancients; and beside them were the modern throng of Diviners and Stargazers and Psychometrists and Animal Magnetists and Mesmerists and Spiritualists and Psychic Researchers.

Redway also published works by MacGregor Mathers, among them *The Kabbalah Unveiled*, in the 1880s, so Machen may have had access to Golden Dawn materials as early as the 1880s. Machen was, consequently, in a position to realize that the secrets being imparted within the walls of Isis-Urania Temple were available to anyone who had the wherewithal to read and research.

. . . Even if the Order of the Golden Dawn, per se, did not influence Machen's writing, occultism did. He was a voracious reader, an autodidact, and had access, through George Redway and the British Museum, to most available occult sources. He and his first wife shared an interest in occultism and may have engaged in practices together as part of their married intimacy. Finally, Machen continued to think about and study the Kabbalah, the basis for most of the Golden Dawn system, for the rest of his life. In a letter to Waite penned on April 11, 1936, he asks the former head of his order:

> And since we are discoursing of interior things: tell me if I am right in declaring that the Serpent did not ascend beyond Daath (the logical understanding) in the Tree of Life? And furthermore; that being so, we may speak of the world of Kether, & the works of it as uncorrupted? [sic] Or, in terms of literature, may it justly be said that Pope's Character of Addison is of Daath, while Coleridge's *Kubla Khan* is of Kether?

Machen was thinking about whether the energy of nature, "the Serpent," ascended to the border of the highest realms, according Kabbalistic lore. Daath is a path on the Tree of life that acts as the threshold to the realm of Godhead.

Although Machen was thinking about the Kabbalah late in life, it is fair to say that occultism did not remain a central topic for him. An interest in The Holy Graal and the Celtic Church replaced the occultism of the 1890s. His tenure within the Hermetic Order of the Golden Dawn was not lifelong; it probably lasted for eight or so years. He repudiated his involvement after the fact, and he did not advance beyond the grades of the outer order. He learned about the occult independently between 1880 and 1900 by reading on his own and working for Redway. For most of his life, Machen was a High Church Anglican, and his Golden Dawn experience, according to his own assessment, was classed with the excesses of young adult life during the 1890s in London.

"THEREFORE SOME SORT OF WAKING DREAM IS IMPLIED, SO THAT THE PHANTASMAGORIA IS AN EXPERIENCE OF SOMETHING THAT IS LIKE A DREAM WITHOUT BEING LITERALLY DREAMY IN ITS NATURE."

Source: Susan Johnston Graf, "Arthur Machen," in *Talking to the Gods: Occultism in the Work of W.B. Yeats, Arthur Machen, Algernon Blackwood, and Dion Fortune*, SUNY Press, 2015, pp. 57–61,77–78.

Arthur Tearle

In the following excerpt, Tearle explains how Machen's stories blend the supernatural with the scientific.

. . . Machen was one of number of writers who, around the turn of the century, produced supernatural stories and novels which, like many of the experiments and investigations carried out by the Society for Physical Research around the same time, fused science with spiritualism, the psychological with the mystical. Indeed, for a short time Machen was a member of not only the Society for Psychical Research but also the Hermetic Order of the Golden Dawn, an occult group whose experiments Machen described as being "halfway between psychology and magic." Indeed, in a piece published in September 1898 titled "Science and the Ghost Story," Machen wrote with some cynicism that "there are few steps between the laboratory and the séance."

Andrew Lang was another author and psychical research enthusiast who noted the scientific flavour that many of the new ghost stories carried. In "Ghosts up to Date" (1894), he remarked that "ghost stories, the delight of Christmas Eve, have been ravaged and annexed by psychology," and makes the important point:

> Now there are many educated persons, who, if asked, "Do you believe in ghosts?" would answer, "We believe in apparitions; but we

> do not believe that the apparition is the separable or surviving soul of a living or a dead man. We believe that it is a hallucination, projected by the brain of the percipient, which, again, in some instances, is influenced so as to project that hallucination, by some agency not at present understood." To this experience of the percipient, who is sensible, by emotion, by sight, hearing, or touch, or by all of these at once, of the presence of the absent, or of the dead, the name *telepathy* (feeling produced at a distance) is given. Any one may believe, and many do believe, in telepathy, yet not believe in the old-fashioned ghost.

Indeed, his interest in psychical phenomena led to numerous essays on the subject of ghosts and hallucinations. He heard and read a great number of account of ghostly happenings, many of which he found "palpably ridiculous." It is indicative of just how popular such studies were that in 1894, the same year as Lang's essays were published, the Society for Psychical Research published its 400-page "Census of Hallucinations," containing some 830 first-hand accounts of "apparitions." Lang concluded that "the identity of the alleged phenomena, in all lands and all ages, does raise a presumption in favour of some kind of abnormal occurrences, or of a common species of hallucinations." As Roger Luckhurst comments, "The order of this hedged bet—abnormal phenomena before hallucination—indicated that Lang had absorbed psychical research, and was using its categories to order anthropological data." Not only that, but the obvious yet crucial point that Lang, a staunch supporter of the romance genre of fiction, considers the "abnormal" as a more preferable, if not more likely, cause for these apparitions.

For many, including Lang himself, the scientific approach of psychical research and the ultimately imaginative nature of fiction were, however, largely incompatible. As Luckhurst frames it, many viewed "the dogged empiricism of psychical research as ruinous to the hesitation, the suspense between natural and supernatural explanations, theorized by Tzvetan Todorov in *The Fantastic*." And yet the supernatural tales of such writers as Algernon Blackwood and William Hope Hodgson, which began to appear in the early years of the twentieth century, showed that the two disciplines could coexist with some (albeit limited) success. But perhaps it is in Arthur Machen's fiction that hallucination, specifically, is most vividly drawn as a multifaceted and complex phenomenon, akin (yet not identical) to Jonathan Harrison's talk of "quasi-hallucinations," which "differ from ordinary hallucinations in that they are paranormally induced and that they give some objective information about the world, such as that a near relative, whom the quasi-hallucination resembles, has recently died."

Machen, as a keen enthusiast of many things occult and mystical, was well acquainted with the ambiguity surrounding such terms as "ghost," "apparition," and "phantom," and the investigations that were being undertaken at the time to determine the source of ghostly occurrences. His relationship with the ghostly is perhaps mostly famously symbolized through his part in the creation and subsequent popularity of the "Angel of Mons" legend in the First World War. But Machen knew well that the term "ghostly" need not always imply the straightforwardly supernatural. And it is knowledge he puts to good use in his novel *The Hill of Dreams*, while describing the fantasies of the novel's protagonist, Lucian Taylor: "Even as he struggled to beat back the phantasmagoria of the mist, and resolved that he would no longer make all the streets a stage of apparitions he hardly realised what he had done, or that the ghosts he had called might depart and return again." At this point in the novel, we are still unclear as to whether Lucian really has "called" these apparitions, at least consciously, or whether he has been hallucinating, these "ghosts" being the product of his unconscious. Machen well knew the suggestiveness of such phantasmal words; he even toyed with the possibility of calling the novel *Phantasmagoria* while he was engaged in writing it during the 1890s. Such a book would have been very different, or at least our expectations of it, since the "phantasmagoria" itself is so rich in meaning, almost dizzyingly alive with possible senses and implications. It also points up Machen's own attitude to the novel he was writing, namely that it would position itself somewhere between "psychology and magic," inhabiting a borderland between hard scientific fact and mystical, supernatural fantasy.

The word "phantasmagoria" is an intriguing choice. The *Oxford English Reference Dictionary* defines "phantasmagoria" as "a shifting series of real or imaginary figures as seen in a dream" and "an optical device for rapidly varying the size of images on a screen." Several things about this definition are of interest here. First, the word "phantasmagoria" suggests a vision that can be either real or imaginary. This it can be hallucinated, dreamt, or thought; conversely, it can be "real," in the sense that it is not hallucinated, but is actually perceptible, and therefore, to an extent, an objective vision. Second, the word "phantasmagoria" can describe either an abstract experience of moving images or a concrete, tangible "device" for "rapidly varying the size of images on a screen." From Machen's title alone, it is impossible to say with any certainty which of these two senses is intended. The novel could be about a phantasmagoria (that is, sense two) or the novel itself could *be* a phantasmagoria (in sense one). The title refuses to say, left hovering between the real and the possibly unreal or imaginary.

Mark Valentine has remarked, "Machen may have intended in the original title a deliberate ambiguity both about what happens on the hill, and as to the actuality of all Lucian's later visions." That is to say, the either/or of the *Oxford English Reference Dictionary*'s "real or imaginary" points up that a phantasmagoria can imply either something imagined in the mind or something that is actually there, whether by natural or supernatural means. Phantasmagoria is, after all, etymologically linked to the word "phantasm." "Phantasm" itself has an almost spectrally evasive entry in the dictionary: "an illusion, a phantom [. . .] an illusory likeness [. . .] a supposed vision of an absent (living or dead) person." What does the dictionary mean by "a supposed vision." In doubting the veracity of a phantasmal vision, the dictionary attempt to capture the ambiguity or spurious authenticity of the "phantasm." But "vision" itself invites ambiguous readings, suggesting both supernatural (even religious) and psychological (that is, imagined) experiences: how can a "vision" be "supposed" to be anything, when "vision" itself covers a multitude of different experiences? But the real evasion comes when the dictionary tries to explain the origins of the second half of that word, "phantasmagoria." The whole etymological entry reads thus:

> prob. f. F *fantasmagorie* (as PHANTOM + fanciful ending)

The almost comical fancifulness of the entry, descending into language that only vaguely sounds like technical linguistic terminology, is itself interesting. That "fanciful ending," which cannot be traced back to any precedent (or concedent), sounds like a lexicographical cop-out, the dictionary's unwillingness or inability to explain in satisfactory terms the real meaning of the *-agorie* that rounds off the phantasmagoria in the original French. Even the "prob." admits that it cannot say for certain that this is the correct origin.

The phantasmagoria thus suggests an evasion or ambiguity of language, one that cannot be completely done away with. It is perhaps mere coincidence that "phantasm" stems from the Greek meaning "show," while the word "fanciful"—used to such bathetic effect in the second half of the etymology—is also derived from the same Greek root, *phain*, "show." The entry for "phantasmagoria" is not only evasive and uncertain about the facts it puts forward, but there is also a measure of circularity to the language it uses to articulate this uncertainty. The *Oxford English Dictionary*, itself scarcely manages to impart the spurious origins of the word any better: alter claiming that the second part of the word is probably from "-agora," the Greek for "place of assembly," the dictionary goes on to admit, in parentheses: "But the inventor of t e word prob. only wanted a mouth-filling and startling term, and may have fixed on *-agoria* without any reference to the Greek lexicon." So much for that: it is enough to note the trouble the word appears to have caused the most prominent lexicographers. Phantasmagorias are anything but linguistically (or indeed semantically) straightforward.

The *Oxford English Dictionary* itself offers this definition for "phantasmagoria": A shifting series or succession of phantasms or imaginary figures, as seen in a dream or fevered condition, as called up by the imagination, or as created by literary description. The first recorded use of the word in this sense, the *OED* tells us, was 1803. This definition is even more ambiguous and circular: "A shifting series or succession of phantasms or imaginary figures' posits the fact that a phantasmagoria can involve either supernatural images —that is, "phantasms"—or "imaginary figures." So far so good: the supernatural/psychological ambiguity remains. And yet if we turn to the *OED* definition of the word "phantasm," we find the following: "Illusion, deceptive appearance"; "An illusion, an appearance that has no reality; a deception, a figment; an unreal or imaginary being, an unreality; a phantom"; and "An apparition, a spirit or supposed incorporeal being appearing to the eyes, a ghost."

Again, that seems fair enough. A "phantasm" is, broadly speaking, either an "illusion" or a "ghost." And yet the dictionary goes on to admit that this last, ghostly sense is "Now only *poet*, or *rhet*." Thus the outward appearance of the word "phantasm"—that is, that it signifies both supernatural and psychological illusions—is deceptive and illusory, since the essential meaning of 'phantasm' boils down to psychological roots, not supernatural ones. The word retains a ghostly association without signifying anything so ghostly in actual fact. As Terry Castle has put it, "since its invention, the term *phantasmagoria*, like one of Freud's ambiguous primary words, has shifted meaning in an interesting way. From an initial connection with something external and public . . . the word has now come to refer to something wholly internal or subjective: the phantasmic imagery of the mind." But words have a habit of carrying around the ghosts of their former meanings with them, and "phantasmagoria" cannot quite "wholly" shrug off its initial sense.

Before we leave the dictionary definition for 'phantasmagoria' behind us, let us consider one final feature of the main definition: "a shifting series of real or imaginary figures as seen in a dream." "As seen in a dream": that is, as either experienced literally in a dream, or experienced only as though in a dream or dreamlike state. The "as" invites either reading. When we experience a phantasmagoria, therefore, the shifting series of figures we see can either be real (whether that means they are seen through a phantasmagoria, that is, "an optical device for rapidly varying the size of images on a screen" or via some other, perhaps supernatural, means) or imaginary, which implies something dreamed or dreamlike. Therefore, presumably, the imaginary figures can be either deliberately imagined (as in a daydream or other conscious process of thought) or imagined beyond one's control (as in a dream or hallucination). But the idea that a phantasmagoria can involve wilfully imagining a series of shifting figures is almost altogether ruled out by that qualifier, "as seen in a dream": dreams, in the purely psychological sense of the word, are anything but deliberate on the part of the dreamer. Therefore some sort of waking dream is implied, so that the phantasmagoria is an experience of something that is like a dream without being literally dreamy in its nature. It retains a sense of reality, experienced while the spectator is awake and in the real world, which dreams cannot possess. What this definition implies but refuses to spell out is that the phantasmagoria is, essentially, a hallucinatory experience. . . .

Source: Oliver Tearle, "Insectial: Arthur Machen's Phantasmagoria," in *Bewilderments of Vision: Hallucination and Literature, 1880–1914*, Sussex Academic Press, 2013, pp. 109–13.

SOURCES

Batty, Roger, "Mela's Phoenician Geography," in *Journal of Roman Studies*, Vol. 90, 2001, pp. 70–94.

Bunbury, Edward Herbert, and Charles Ramond Beazley, "Mela, Pomponius," in *Encyclopædia Britannica*, 11th ed., Vol. 18, *Medal to Mumps*, Encyclopædia Britannica, 1911, p. 87.

Doyle, Arthur Conan, *The Sign of Four*, Spencer and Blackett, 1890, p. 93.

Eckersley, Adrian, "A Theme in the Early Work of Arthur Machen: 'Degeneration,'" in *English Literature in Transition, 1880–1920*, Vol. 35, No. 3, 1992, pp. 277–87.

Evans, Arthur J., "Primitive Pictographs and a Prae-Phoenician Script, from Crete and the Peloponnese," in *Journal of Hellenic Studies*, Vol. 14, 1894, pp. 270–372, 394, pl. XII.

Forlini, Stefania, "Modern Narratives and Decadent Things in Arthur Machen's *The Three Impostors*," in *English Literature in Transition, 1880–1920*, Vol. 55, No. 4, 2012, pp. 479–98.

Hassler, Sue Strong, and Donald M. Hassler, eds., *Arthur Machen & Montgomery Evans: Letters of a Literary Friendship, 1923–1947*, Kent State University Press, 1994, p. 76.

Jackson, Kimberly, "Non-evolutionary Degeneration in Arthur Machen's Supernatural Tales," in *Victorian Literature and Culture*, Vol. 41, No. 1, March 2013, pp. 125–35.

Kandola, Sondeep, "Celtic Occultism and the Symbolist Mode in the Fin-de-Siècle Writings of Arthur Machen and W. B. Yeats," in *English Literature in Transition, 1880–1920*, Vol. 56, No. 4, 2013, pp. 497–518.

Kuhn, Thomas S., *The Structure of Scientific Revolutions*, University of Chicago Press, 1962, pp. 92–134.

Lovecraft, H. P., *Supernatural Horror in Literature*, 1927, http://www.hplovecraft.com/writings/texts/essays/shil.aspx (accessed August 2, 2016).

Machen, Arthur, *Autobiography*, Richards Press, 1951, pp. 16–19.

———, "Novel of the Black Seal," in *The Three Impostors; or, The Transmutations*, John Lane, 1895, pp. 82–160.

Mela, Pomponius, *Pomponius Mela's Description of the World*, translated by F. E. Romer, University of Michigan Press, 1998, p. 7.

Solinus, Gaius Julius, *Gesta Romanorum; or, Entertaining Moral Stories*, translated by Charles Swan, George Bell & Sons, 1894, pp. v–xv.

Sweetser, Wesley D., *Arthur Machen*, Twayne Publishers, 1964, pp. 115–18.

Valentine, Mark, *Arthur Machen*, Seren, 1995, pp. 36–43.

FURTHER READING

Burton, Richard Francis, trans., *The Book of the Thousand Nights and a Night*, 10 vols., Kama Shastra Society, 1885.

This monumental book is still an authoritative and the most complete translation of the Arabic original. Its structure provided the inspiration for Machen's *The Three Impostors*, especially as mediated through Stevenson's *New Arabian Nights*. Its tales of miracles and adventure hint at the story Machen fabricated to insert into the Latin geographer Solinus. Perhaps more to the point, its stories represent the kind of straightforward tale of the supernatural that simply cannot be made to fit into the post-Enlightenment world, forcing Machen to develop his modern type of horror story.

Eco, Umberto, *The Name of the Rose*, translated by William Weaver, Harcourt, 1983.

The Name of the Rose is a semiotic mystery that turns on the existence and discovery of a lost manuscript of the second book of Aristotle's *Poetics*, of which Eco fabricated a sample in his own text, similar to Machen's fabrication of a passage in Solinus.

Machen, Arthur, *The Hill of Dreams*, Grant Richards, 1907.

Often considered Machen's greatest work, this novel concerns a young man living in a small Welsh town that was once an important city during the Roman occupation of Britain. Increasingly in the novel, he slips back to living a different life in that time.

Reynolds, Aidan, and William Charlton, *Arthur Machen: A Short Account of His Life and Work*, Richards, 1963.

This early biographical work is essentially built on Machen's autobiography, providing more historical context outside of his own perspective.

SUGGESTED SEARCH TERMS

Arthur Machen

Novel of the Black Seal AND Machen

Machen AND The Three Impostors

decadence AND literature

pseudoscience

cuneiform

Solinus

Pomponius Mela

H. P. Lovecraft

Orbiting

BHARATI MUKHERJEE

1988

Bharati Mukherjee identifies herself as an American writer of Bengali Indian descent. She positions herself in mainstream American writing, assimilating in her stories the customs, speech patterns, and pluralistic cultural voices and histories of Americans and American immigrants. Every American came from immigrants, she points out, a fact especially evident in the short story "Orbiting," from her collection *The Middleman and Other Stories* (1988). "Orbiting" re-creates a Thanksgiving celebration, that most quintessentially American ritual of inclusion, where third-generation Italian immigrant Renata deMarco introduces her family to her Afghan refugee boyfriend, Roashan. In this brilliantly compressed mosaic of cultural differences told in the contemporary voice of a young woman who is determined to live her own life, and to help Ro discover his, Mukherjee shows the reader how the United States is rapidly changing in the modern day through its immigrants. Far from being alarmed by this change, she celebrates it, because for her, immigrants represent creative renewal in American life and art. "Orbiting" has also been collected in *Braided Lives: An Anthology of Multicultural American Writing* (1991).

AUTHOR BIOGRAPHY

Bharati Mukherjee was born on July 27, 1940, in Calcutta (now Kolkata), India, to Sudhir Lal Mukherjee, a chemist, and his wife, Bina

Bharati Mukherjee (*©Steve Russell / Toronto Star / Getty Images*)

Mukherjee. The family were Bengali Brahmins living in an extended family arrangement of about forty members in a compound in a middle-class neighborhood. Bharati and her two sisters grew up protected and pampered. Her father had a PhD from the University of London and set up a pharmaceutical company in Calcutta. Sudhir Mukherjee took his family to London in 1947 while he did research there. They returned to India in 1951, where the girls attended the Loreto Convent School, a private school run by Irish nuns. In 1959 Bharati got a BA with honors in English from the University of Calcutta, and in 1961 she earned an MA in English and ancient Indian culture from the University of Baroda. Soon after, she arrived in the United States to attend the Iowa Writers' Workshop on a scholarship. There, she received an MFA from the University of Iowa in 1963 and married fellow writing student and author Clark Blaise, a Canadian American.

Mukherjee began her long teaching career at Marquette University, in Milwaukee, and at the University of Wisconsin–Madison from 1964 to 1965. In 1966 she moved with her family to Canada and taught at McGill University, in Montreal, Quebec. After getting a PhD in English and comparative literature from the University of Iowa in 1969, she worked her way to a full professorship at McGill in 1978. Her first novel, *The Tiger's Daughter*, came out in 1972, and her second, *Wife*, in 1975. In 1973 she went to Calcutta on a sabbatical with Clark, and they began work on a joint nonfiction project, *Days and Nights in Calcutta*, published in 1977. Mukherjee won a Guggenheim Foundation Award in 1978 and in 1980 moved to New York to be a permanent American resident, taking freelance teaching jobs to help support her husband and two sons.

In 1984 as writer in residence at Emory University, she wrote the stories in the collection *Darkness*, published in 1985. She received a National Endowment for the Arts grant and in 1987, again working with her husband, published *The Sorrow and the Terror*, about the 1985 Air India crash. *The Middleman and Other Stories*, including the story "Orbiting," came out in 1988, winning Mukherjee a National Book Critics Circle Award, and the novel *Jasmine* followed in 1989, at which time she moved to California to become distinguished professor at Berkeley. A string of novels followed. *The Holder of the World* was published in 1993 and *Leave It to Me* in 1997. A trilogy about the present, past, and future of Indian women came out centered on the character of Tara Lata with *Desirable Daughters* in 2002, *The Tree Bride* in 2004, and *Miss New India* in 2011. Mukherjee has also written two historical studies of India: *Political Culture and Leadership in India: A Study of West Bengal* (1991) and *Regionalism in Indian Perspective* (1992).

PLOT SUMMARY

The narrative of "Orbiting" is a first-person account of a family Thanksgiving by Renata deMarco, in a running stream of consciousness about this particular Thanksgiving Day in the present, though she brings in bits of memory from other Thanksgivings and other times. It begins as she is in her nightgown on Thanksgiving morning in her own apartment when her father knocks on the door to drop off the turkey. She remembers last Thanksgiving, when Vic, her boyfriend at the time, cooked a cranberry sauce with Grand Marnier. Her father took it as a sign that she was going to marry him, but Vic was a transient boyfriend. The turkey seems too big for their needs this year because brother Danny is in the Marines, and Uncle Carmine just had a bypass. Vic is gone, presumably tripping on dope with other friends. He used to cook and talk at length about their relationship, but now she knows he was only talking about himself. Vic's dad, Vinny Riccio, was on her dad's bowling team. Vic's older brother once tried to date her. He owns a funeral home now. They were all part of the Italian neighborhood.

When her father informs Renata (nicknamed Rindi) that the bird has already been thawed by her mother in view of her small refrigerator, she translates this to her father as her mother's way of saying that she lives in a dump. Her mother is an immigrant who believes that the children should be richer than the parents. Rindi is twenty-seven and only sells jewelry made out of seashells and semiprecious stones, so this studio in New Jersey is all she can afford. She still has not made the bed on the futon sofa. Her father's knees, ruined from being a minor league baseball

MEDIA ADAPTATIONS

- In an interview with Bill Moyers called "A World of Ideas: Conquering America," Mukherjee describes being an Indian immigrant and her wish not to assimilate into American culture, but to change it. The video is thirty minutes in length, produced in 1994 by the Films for the Humanities and Sciences as part of the Moyers Collection Series, in color on VHS.
- In an interview with Paula Marantz Cohen, Episode 31 (Parts 1 and 2) of the Drexel InterView series, recorded at Drexel University in 2006 and uploaded to YouTube at https://www.youtube.com/watch?v=4y56BERx2E0 and https://www.youtube.com/watch?v=q02OsKJqzEo, Mukherjee discusses the evolution of her writing and the experience of being an American immigrant.

catcher, do not allow the sixty-five-year-old formally dressed man to sit on her deck chairs. The deMarcos come from a North Italian family, and scolding is how Italians express love. She and Danny and Cindi grew up with a Calabrian Italian peasant mother and an American-born Italian father.

Renata's father wants to know if her mother has been talking about him to the children. She told him to bring the turkey to get him out of the house. Rindi lies and says no, but her mother is worried about him since he retired and has nothing to do. In her mind, Rindi quickly translates all the family politics. Her father wants to talk about her mother. She knows but does not say that her mother wants to call Doc Brunetti, her father's best friend, and have a talk about what to do with him. Her mother, meanwhile, is just finding herself and signing up for a class. Rindi remembers her immigrant mother constantly telling them about the hardships of her life in Italy, about carrying water from a well, gaslight, and wolves. For a long time, she did not drive a car in America or even leave the house. Now with the children grown, she is finally trying to do something for herself.

Rindi's father complains that she has no dining table. This year is a potluck, and Rindi reflects that she does not have real furniture. She uses folding tables to eat from. But she tells her father that a friend made her a table, and it is in the basement. Jorge, she says, will bring up the table and chairs. Her father asks if Jorge is a new boyfriend. Rindi does have a new boyfriend, but she does not know how to tell her family about him yet. Jorge is the landlady's roomer from El Salvador, who works on an oil rig and is saving to bring his family to America.

When her father leaves, Renata calls her sister, Carla. They changed their names to Rindi and Cindi as teens. Cindi married Brent on a cruise ship. Rindi did not like Brent at first. His father is an Amish farmer from Iowa. He was originally Schwartzendruber but now calls himself Schwartz and owns a discount store in Manhattan.

In her mind Rindi compares her former boyfriend, Vic, who impressed her by speaking of feminism and macrobiotics on their first date, to her current boyfriend, whom the family has not met, Ro from Afghanistan. Ro picked her up in a singles bar, though he does not drink alcohol. She went right to bed with him. In contrast, she remembers how the promising relationship with Vic ended when he told her one morning he was leaving to see the world, and he was not taking her. He asked for the keys to her van and took it.

Rindi tells Cindi they need a roaster for the turkey. Cindi says she will be right over because Brent's twelve-year-old daughter, Franny, is driving her crazy. Rindi wants her sister to like Ro and her mother and father to do more than tolerate him. He has only been in the United States for three months. She tries to call him because she does not know how to use the whole nutmegs he bought her from his Pakistani friend. Ro is a refugee from Kabul. He wants to be an electrical engineer. His father smuggled him out. He is living with an Afghan restaurant owner in Brooklyn, Mr. Mumtaz, who takes in both legal and illegal immigrants. Mr. Mumtaz, or somebody, answers the phone and says he does not know a Ro.

Cindi shows up in the parking lot in her BMW with food. Rindi advises her to get the bored stepdaughter, Franny, involved with the food preparation. When Rindi gets back inside the apartment, the phone is ringing: Ro has called. He is from a macho culture and likes it when men come on to Rindi because then he can show that she belongs to him. He is worried about his cousin Abdul, who has no papers and is locked up in detention. If he gets deported, he will be tortured in Afghanistan.

Rindi's mother and father come early. They are dressed up. Her father married her mother out of a seamstress sweatshop. Her father appoints himself bartender. He asks where the table is, and she says Ro will bring it up. The parents do not understand the name. Just then Ro comes in the door, and her mother screams, seeing a strange man of color entering (with a key). Ro uses his prep-school manners to introduce himself. He is relatively light-skinned but obviously not European looking. He says his name is Roashan. Her father does not shake hands. Rindi kisses Ro in a sexy way so that her parents will know she has slept with him. She suddenly realizes that if Ro asks her to marry him, she will. Ro gives a small bouquet of flowers to her mother and says it is his first Thanksgiving. Rindi explains that he comes from Afghanistan, but her father thinks it means Africa. She explains that the Russians bulldozed his father's estate near Kabul. Mr. deMarco calls him Roy and tries to give him a drink. She says he is a Muslim and does not drink. Ro gets a Tab from the refrigerator.

Brent and Cindi show up with his daughter Franny wearing headphones, listening to music. Brent is a lot older than Cindi and loud and boisterous. Ro is effectively hiding, blending into the plants by the wall. He looks effeminate, Rindi figures, to the Americans. She sees Franny's sarcastic smirk and realizes that Ro is not dressed right. The men are talking sports and try to get Ro involved in the conversation. Rindi knows that he looks stupid to her family but wishes she could tell them how cosmopolitan he is: he has skied in St. Moritz, Switzerland, and knows the casinos in Beirut. The men carry the table from the basement. Ro has scars on his arms. He tells the family about being arrested in Kabul for handing out pro-American pamphlets. The men are embarrassed to hear his passion about a foreign conflict they know nothing of. Ro tells them how he was tortured in jail, and even Franny pays attention. His father had been rich and bribed a guard to release him. He hid in a tunnel for four months until he could get a forged visa. For six days he orbited in an airplane from one international airport to another, until he could get asylum. Now he guts chickens to pay for room and board. He shows his dagger to everyone.

At dinner, Rindi bypasses her father, who usually carves the turkey, and places the bird in front of Ro. He takes out his dagger and carves beautifully. Rindi is proud of her lover, with his scars, and vows to help heal him, to make an American of him, her own offering for world peace.

CHARACTERS

Abdul

Abdul is a cousin of Roashan's, an illegal immigrant from Afghanistan who is locked up by American authorities in a detention center for having no papers and will probably be sent back to Afghanistan, where he will face torture by the Russians.

Doc Brunetti

Doc Brunetti is Mr. deMarco's best friend, of retirement age, as his friend is. They grew up together in an Italian neighborhood and are still in the same church and bowling league. Mrs. deMarco wants to talk to Doc about what to do with her husband, who has retired and is always around the house.

Uncle Carmine

Uncle Carmine is Mr. deMarco's brother, who cannot attend Thanksgiving because he has had heart bypass surgery.

Arturo deMarco

Arturo deMarco was Mr. deMarco's father, Rindi's grandfather, who came as an immigrant from Italy in his mother's womb.

Danny deMarco

Danny deMarco, or "Junior," is not at the Thanksgiving dinner because he is overseas. He is Rindi's brother, one of the three deMarco children, probably the youngest, who dropped out of college to join the Marines.

Grandma deMarco

Grandma deMarco is Mr. deMarco's immigrant mother, who always fixed two Thanksgiving dinners, one American and one Italian, with pasta.

Mr. deMarco

Mr. deMarco, Rindi's father, is a conservative, retired insurance adjuster who has been living in a Catholic Italian neighborhood in New Jersey his whole life. He is solidly middle class and voted for Reagan. He once played catcher for a minor league baseball team and has pain in his knees. He finds Rindi's campy apartment with no real furniture uncomfortable. Rindi likes to shock him with her unconventional lifestyle. Mr. deMarco represents the sort of average American ignorant of other cultures, especially of minority cultures. Once from Italian immigrants, he is now part of the American mainstream and does not have much sympathy for an exotic newcomer like Roashan, who is Muslim, looks and dresses funny, and does not drink alcohol or know about American sports. Mr. deMarco thinks Afghanistan is in Africa. Yet he went beyond his normal class boundaries when he married his wife, a peasant girl fresh from Calabria, in southern Italy, working in a sweatshop. He has explained to the children that his folks came from northern Italy, where they show their family love by scolding one another. He is obviously a good family man but is pushed by this new encounter with Rindi's boyfriend. He already had to adjust to Cindi's non-Catholic husband. Rindi understands and is tolerantly amused by her parents.

Mrs. deMarco

Mrs. deMarco is an earthy peasant girl from a mountain village in Calabria, southern Italy. She worked in a sweatshop when she arrived in America, until Mr. deMarco rescued her with marriage. Rindi probably gets her sexy nature from her mother, who was always open with her daughters about sex. The mother has lived with insecurities from her upbringing, when she did not have electric lights or indoor plumbing. She never lets her family forget her hard background, has seldom left the house, and never learned to drive a car. Now, in middle age, she is beginning to come out of her shell and is taking a class at the local college. She does not know how to handle her husband's retirement because he is under foot all day. She dresses up in a beaded dress for the family dinner and wants Rindi to dress up. The parents dress and act formally, but Rindi tries to get them to loosen up. Her father has always treated her mother as though she is slightly deficient because of her backwoods upbringing and immigrant status.

Renata "Rindi" deMarco

Renata deMarco is the first-person narrator of the story. She is the oldest of the three deMarco children and the observer of those around her, understanding the background and story of each person. She is compassionate and non-judgmental, even toward her former boyfriend Vic, who seems to have been somewhat self-centered and left her without warning. Rindi is twenty-seven with a sense of humor and irony and does not live a conventional life like her parents. With Vic she sampled an alternative lifestyle that entailed macrobiotic cooking and cohabitation without marriage. It is not specified whether she went to college, but she is not working in one of the professions. She and Vic, however, spoke of intellectual matters and were into cinema and Amnesty International, so her point of view is liberal or even radical compared to her family's. She hated her former job taking orders for MCI and now sells jewelry at a boutique and likes her job, not minding her makeshift furniture and quick-made meals of pita bread and sprouts.

Renata is friendly, getting to know those around her, though they might be of a different class or nationality, like Jorge, the handyman from El Salvador. She seems in this way to be more worldly and experienced than her sister Cindi, who went for a conventional marriage to an older man that gave her material security. Rindi seems to have a healthy sexuality and is sure of herself as a woman. She likes Ro's open admiration of her sexuality. His way of making love is not Western, and she responds. Instead of being repulsed by Ro's immigrant status, different race and religion, and lack of money and prestige, she admires his scars and what he has been through, seeing him as a hero and survivor, a Clint Eastwood. He is a man of the world who once was rich and skied at St. Moritz. He has a sophistication that other men, even Vic with his big ideas and talk, lack. She vows to marry Ro and make him an American citizen so he can realize his dreams. This is effectively her own project for world peace, as if for Amnesty International. She is the example of a later-generation immigrant to America who is used to inventing her own life, and she wants to show the ropes to Ro, who is already in the throes of transformation.

Jorge

Jorge is the roomer of Rindi's landlady, Marge. He works on an oil rig and does yard work and odd jobs for her, including teaching her Spanish, while he saves money to bring his family from El Salvador.

Mr. Mumtaz

Mr. Mumtaz is a friend of Roashan's Afghan father who has a fried chicken restaurant in Brooklyn. He employs legal immigrants as waiters and illegal immigrants in the back gutting chickens. Roashan is living with him, gutting chickens, though he has temporary papers.

Tony Riccio

Tony Riccio is Vic's older brother who once tried to date Rindi. Now he owns a funeral home.

Vic Riccio

Vic Riccio is Rindi's former boyfriend from her Italian neighborhood. She and Vic moved in together in a studio apartment in New Jersey in a liberal contemporary arrangement, where he spoke to her of feminism, cooked macrobiotic food for them, and made pottery. She was shocked when he suddenly called it off, wanting to travel and find greener pastures. He took some of her best furniture and her van. She liked Vic for his flair and style and unconventional ways.

Vinny Riccio

Vinny Riccio is Vic's father, who is in Renata's father's bowling league. It is obvious that the Riccios are part of the Italian neighborhood Rindi grew up in. Her father expected her to marry Vic and now is in shock to be meeting a potential son-in-law like Roashan.

Roashan "Ro"

Roashan, or Ro, is Rindi's new immigrant boyfriend, whom she met in a singles bar. He comes from a wealthy Afghan family but was imprisoned by the Soviets and tortured because he was pro-American and handing out pamphlets in Kabul. His father had a garden estate outside the city, but it was bulldozed by the Soviets. His father bribed guards to let Ro out of prison, and he was hidden in a tunnel for four months, until his father could buy him an airline ticket.

Ro had to transfer between a series of international airports until the United States gave him asylum and temporary immigration papers. He now works at Mr. Mumtaz's Afghan restaurant in Brooklyn gutting chickens. He wants to go to university and become an electrical engineer. He looks effeminate to American men, but Rindi finds him very sexy and macho. He likes other men to admire her so that he feels like he has a prize. Rindi finds that his scars and traumas make him more of a man than Brent or her father, who seem like little boys to her.

Brent Schwartz

Brent Schwartz grew up as Brent Schwartzendruber with an Amish family in Kalona, Iowa. He reinvented himself as a Manhattan discount store owner and changed his name to Schwartz. He is called Bernie by the locals. He is divorced, and his ex-wife lives in Florida. His daughter Frannie is staying with him and his new wife, Cindi (deMarco). Brent is torn between loyalty to his daughter and his new wife. There is a lot of tension in their family. Though Brent came from Protestants, he is more like Mr. deMarco than Roashan is, for he drinks and can talk about sports and business. Brent is rich and acceptable. He does not know how to handle his daughter around his new wife. He tries to play up to Franny by insulting or slighting Cindi and making jokes at her expense. In addition, it is hinted that Brent likes to try to fool around with women. Rindi mentions that he has made a pass at her. She did not like him or Cindi's marriage at first but has grown used to it.

Carla "Cindi" (deMarco) Schwartz

Cindi is the younger sister of Rindi by eleven months. The two are close. Cindi was once Carla but changed her name to Cindi when Renata changed hers to Rindi. She met Brent on a cruise and married him on the ship. She has a husband with money who can buy her a BMW, but she is not happy. Her stepdaughter is giving her trouble, apparently trying to alienate her husband from her.

Franny Schwartz

Franny is twelve and obviously traumatized by, or at least indignant over, her father's remarriage. She lives in Florida with her mother and is visiting her father for Thanksgiving. He has spent a lot of money on lawyers to get visitation rights. Franny wears sloppy clothes and carries a Walkman that she listens to constantly. She makes sneers at Cindi and at Roashan. She finally drops her spoiled belligerence when Roashan tells of his torture experience.

THEMES

Immigration

"Orbiting" is the title and also serves as a central metaphor in this story about immigrants in the United States as they leave one culture and seek to join another. Some immigrants come voluntarily, like Renata's Italian family, seeking a better opportunity. Others, like Roashan from Afghanistan, are refugees from the world's violence. Like many other refugees seeking asylum, Ro for several days remained in orbit in international airports, waiting until a country would let him in. He describes a whole culture of refugees who live in airports, orbiting until they can stay somewhere and find a life again. Ro is still in orbit in the story, a transient without roots, living in Brooklyn.

The other characters are in various orbiting positions as well. Renata is circling around in her adult life in some alternative and independent lifestyle, selling jewelry and living in a dumpy apartment, sampling boyfriends, and observing the multiple ironies of life. Her mother and father are adjusting to middle age, with her father retired and her mother interested for the first time in life outside her home. Her sister Cindi, married to a wealthy but boring older man with a teenage daughter, does not exactly fit as either a wife or a stepmom. Franny is the teen who is orbiting her new family with a stepmother she does not like. She checks out of the conflict with music and headphones. The characters are Americans, inventing their lives and adjusting as they go. The story demonstrates that America is a nation of immigrants, some of whom have been here longer and help those who are newcomers. They are in various stages of holding on to the past from one culture or lifestyle and inventing the future in another.

Americanization

Another major metaphor for American life and the process of Americanization is Thanksgiving. It is a holiday that celebrates the moment when one group (American Indians) helped another group (Europeans) to survive and find

TOPICS FOR FURTHER STUDY

- Using such resources as the Gilder Lehrman Institute of American History, at http://www.gilderlehrman.org/history-by-era/hamilton, or the biography *Alexander Hamilton* (2004), by Ron Chernow, give an oral report on the life of Alexander Hamilton (1755–1804), the immigrant from the Caribbean island of St. Croix who became a founding father of the United States. Use the popular musical *Hamilton* (2015), by Lin-Manuel Miranda, with its hip-hop lyrics, winner of eleven Tony Awards and the 2016 Pulitzer Prize for Drama, to elucidate Hamilton's contributions to American government.
- *West Side Story*, the 1957 musical made into a film in 1961, is about the clash of a white teen gang on Manhattan's West Side with a Puerto Rican immigrant gang. The plot, based on Shakespeare's tragic love story *Romeo and Juliet*, features a romance between Tony, a Pole, and Maria, a Puerto Rican, whose friends and family belong to the rival gangs. Both the gang fights and the love story can be seen as metaphors for the process of assimilation into American culture. Make a website on cross-cultural love stories between Americans and immigrants, such as the one in "Orbiting" with Rindi and Ro and the one in *West Side Story*. In an introductory essay on your website, make conclusions about what unexpected contributions immigrants bring to America as illustrated in these love stories.
- Immigration is a controversial topic in many countries today, as war, economic hardship, and natural disasters drive large numbers of people from their homelands each year to neighboring and distant foreign countries alike. Within your class, have individual people or groups take different countries such as the United States, United Kingdom, Germany, Denmark, Canada, France, Pakistan, India, Mexico, and Brazil, to name a few, and report on the immigration situation there: how many flee there, and under what circumstances, and how does the country deal with these issues? What are the reasons for quotas and regulations? What kinds of laws and procedures are in place, especially for families and refugees and guest workers? Which countries have dealt most successfully with immigration in your opinion, and why? Make a group wiki on immigration policies, with the individual research on each country added along with stories and/or visuals to illustrate.
- An immigrant has many challenges to face, such as Ro learning how to take the bus across town or how to interact politely with people of another culture. Even if one knows the language, there are many slang or popular expressions to understand, many gestures that might be missed. Write a short story about someone going through culture shock in a strange country.
- Read the young-adult novel *Illegal*, by Bettina Restrepo, published in 2011, about fifteen-year-old Nora, whose father left her and her mother in Mexico to find work in the United States. When the paychecks he sends home stop with no explanation, Nora and her mother decide they must look for the missing father. They make a dangerous crossing to the United States, where they have to survive as illegal immigrants and a separated family. Discuss as a group the challenges Nora and her family face. Should the United States help such families? If you were to run into someone like Nora, how would you try to help her? Does the United States assist with family reunification? Write up your summary from the discussion to hand in, along with your insights.

a place in the New World. It is the American ideal of all peoples sitting together at one table to share. Ro mentions to the family that it is his first Thanksgiving, and it becomes a sort of ritual or ceremony of acceptance. At first the family is shocked or bewildered by his presence because he is so foreign. Even his posture and head shake are strange. Rindi watches every detail in excruciating suspense, wondering if her family will accept him. Now, in order to gain freedom, like many other immigrants, Ro, once rich, is experiencing downward social mobility, butchering chickens to survive. In her musings on her family and surroundings, Rindi points out the process of Americanization the characters are constantly undergoing, including herself. Each person has an individual drama—her sister, for instance, is married to Brent, a Manhattan store owner who comes from an Iowa Amish family named Schwartzendruber. He changed his name to Schwartz. Renata and Carla deMarco have changed their names to the more American sounding Rindi and Cindi. The name changes indicate how people try to assimilate and create a new identity in America. They are free to scrap the past and make their own place. Rindi's tiny apartment becomes a melting pot on Thanksgiving. Ro's carving of the turkey is his badge of acceptance. He is now an American, with Rindi at his side to help him.

Family Life

The many alternate versions of family life in the United States are symbolized in these characters. The deMarcos are a traditional immigrant family with two cultures. Rindi remembers how her grandmother deMarco served two Thanksgiving dinners, an American one with turkey and an Italian one with pasta. Rindi grew up in an Italian neighborhood that served as a sort of extended family. She went out with Vic Riccio, whose father was on her father's bowling team from church. She almost dated Vic's older brother as well. As in American families, however, the children have made their own choices. Cindi, though brought up Catholic, is married to a divorced German Protestant, Brent Schwartz. She is having a difficult family life with a teen stepdaughter. Brent, trying to keep his daughter, plays up to Franny and excludes his wife from their special relationship. Jorge, the boarder, has a family back in El Salvador and is saving to bring them to the United States. Ro is separated from his family in Afghanistan and has to live in terror, even in the United States, of his illegal immigrant cousins being deported back to Afghanistan, where they will be tortured. Rindi is determined to take Ro in, to marry him, to make him her family. She is the most radical of the deMarcos, living as she chooses. Rindi is not looking at her financial possibilities. She is interested in issues, the arts, macrobiotics, and feminism, and with Vic had belonged to Amnesty International. Vic seemed politically correct but lacked depth. At twenty-seven, Rindi seems interested in settling down, but not with just anyone. Her potential family life with Ro, a former political prisoner and a Muslim, would be anything but conventional.

Female Identity

The female characters in the story are highlighted through Rindi's first-person observations. Her grandmother lived a dual cultural life in an Italian neighborhood. Her father could have married up but married down, finding her immigrant mother in a sweatshop. Her mother hardly left the house from ingrained fear. Rindi, however, sees her middle-aged mother finally coming out, ready to sample American opportunity by taking a class to expand her knowledge. Cindi takes a conventional route by marrying an older established man with money. She has a different set of challenges—the kind that come with divorce, second families, and hostile stepchildren. Franny, the child of divorce, is rebellious. She is rude and listens to her music.

Rindi, the main character, is the one who does the most overt experimentation with her female identity. She compares two men in her life, Vic and Ro, to see how far she has come. Rindi represents the option of women since women's liberation in the 1960s to try various relationships. She had lived openly with Vic without marriage. He could speak about feminism, and this caught Rindi's attention. On the other hand, Ro is from a macho culture and treats Rindi as a sexy woman, something she responds to. She does not see Ro as others do. He is at once more sophisticated and more primitive than other people she knows. He comes from a life-and-death culture, and it makes Rindi feel alive. She wants to give and protect. Her instincts are activated. She actually glows with fulfillment after being with him. She is also impressed with Ro as a human being in a

The story is set at Thanksgiving (©Alexander Raths / Shutterstock.com)

struggle for freedom and wants to be on his side. While she and Vic talked about ideas, Ro is a living example, someone she can admire and learn from.

STYLE

Modern Short Story and Stream of Consciousness

The modern short story is a short narrative with a unified plot generally striving for a single effect or revelation for the main character. Though the modern short story typically concerns the everyday world of realistic events and settings, it can also be exotic, using complex symbols to suggest deeper meanings. James Joyce, Katherine Mansfield, and Joseph Conrad helped to make the twentieth-century short story a highly polished form, with surprise turns and philosophical depth. Mukherjee became proficient with this form at the Iowa Writers' Workshop. She has expressed admiration for such writers as Bernard Malamud, Alice Munro, Flannery O'Connor, Raymond Carver, and John Cheever.

Mukherjee's "Orbiting" concerns a single Thanksgiving Day with the Italian deMarco family, who meet daughter Renata's new boyfriend, an Afghan refugee named Ro. The first-person narrator, Renata, tells the story through stream of consciousness, meaning that she does not tell the story in a straight plot line but digressively, going back and forth in memory while reporting current dialogue as well. In stream of consciousness, the character's traits are revealed as well as the events, for the reader is directly in the narrator's mind. The story of Rindi's former boyfriend Vic, for instance, is pieced together from details she relates in flashes throughout the story. Her family background, sister's marriage, and boyfriend Ro's flight from Afghanistan all come out in accumulated bits and pieces through her associations and thoughts. Mukherjee calls this a zigzag style of narrative. The author says she finds her stories through voice, that special consciousness and point of view of a certain character, whether told in first or third person. When she can hear the character's thoughts in her mind, the story unfolds itself to her. Rindi is a distinct voice who hears the other distinct voices around her.

Maximalism, Overlapping Stories, and Compression

In her essay "Immigrant Writing: Give Us Your Maximalists" (1988), Mukherjee claims that American fiction writers have become minimalists, writing simple sentences and unimaginative stories with social criticism left out, promoted to become mainstream best sellers. She wants to invigorate American writing with "maximalism" that illustrates the lives of a new America of immigrants. Immigrants have overlapping cultures. They can represent many generations of compressed history within a single person. Immigrants are bursting with stories to be told, and they will not tell them the same way as predictable best sellers. Mukherjee's own ideal is the maximalist technique suggested to her by Indian Mughal painting.

Though Mukherjee likes to be identified not as "postcolonial," but rather as "American," she uses techniques from the culture she came from, from Indian art. She describes her storytelling in an essay called "A Four-Hundred-Year-Old Woman," in *American Studies Newsletter*, as like the old South Asian Mughal miniature paintings. This miniature style derived from Persian art and was used in the Mughal Empire in sixteenth- to nineteenth-century India by Hindu, Muslim, and Sikh artists in secular court paintings. Depictions of plants, animals, portraits, and clothing were realistic but stylized and put into elaborate decorated frames. These miniatures are jammed with detail, little universes within a larger one, and multiple stories told within one scene, for there are many points of focus and everything happening at once. It may look chaotic, but the frame provides the coherence. In "Orbiting," this technique is seen in the amazing compression that in a few paragraphs can illuminate Rindi's story as well as produce little cameos of her family members, friends, and Ro in his flight from Afghanistan. These other little stories are framed in and by Rindi's consciousness and are of equal importance to the story. Rindi is not exclusively privileged over the others. They are all inventing their lives as they go, she shows. Their many stories add up to the freedom to choose alternatives.

Immigrant Literature

Mukherjee places her writing within American immigrant literature rather than within postcolonial or Indian diasporic literature. It is an important distinction for her, because she wants to show immigrants reinventing their lives in a new place rather than pining for what is lost. Other examples of immigrant literature include *Call It Sleep* (1934), by Henry Roth, about Jewish immigrants in New York; *Pnin* (1957), by Vladimir Nabokov, about a Russian refugee professor in America; *The Namesake* (2003), by Jhumpa Lahiri, about immigrants from Kolkata in New York; and *The Brief Wondrous Life of Oscar Wao* (2007), by Junot Díaz, about Dominican immigrants in New Jersey. More than just colorful storytelling, immigrant literature can reinspire American literature, for in Mukherjee's view, immigrant writing is part of mainstream American literature. The United States is a land of immigrants, and the theme of immigration is therefore prominent and meaningful to the nation's melting-pot identity.

HISTORICAL CONTEXT

Afghanistan

Roashan's home country, Afghanistan, is a mountainous region bordered by Pakistan and Iran. The country has been swept by many conquerors, including Persian Zoroastrians, Alexander the Great, the Maurya Empire of India, Islamic conquest by Arabs, the Mongol invasion of Tamerlane, and the Mughal rule of India. After World War I, Afghanistan, under its monarchy, began to modernize with a secular culture. Mohammed Zahir Shah ruled from 1933 to 1973, during the time when Kabul was a thriving modern city of business, but this lifestyle was mainly enjoyed by the upper classes, like Roashan's father, who had an estate outside the city.

During hard economic times in 1978, in a bloody coup—dubbed the Saur Revolution—the Afghan Communist Party, with close ties to the Soviet Union, took over. When the Soviet Union invaded with its forces in 1979, Afghanistan became part of global Cold War politics. The United States's Carter administration secretly funded the mujahideen guerrilla fighters to defeat the Soviets. In "Orbiting," Ro is persecuted for being an American supporter and escapes a Soviet prison in Kabul to make his way toward New York. After the fall of the Communists in 1992, the right-wing Taliban seized Kabul in 1996, imposing their

COMPARE & CONTRAST

- **c. 1988:** Refugees like Roashan in Mukherjee's story are fleeing an Afghanistan controlled by the Soviet Union.

  Today: Afghanistan is terrorized by Islamic militant groups like ISIS (Islamic State in Iraq and Syria) and the Taliban, and thousands of Afghans continue to leave the country to seek security and employment.

- **c. 1988:** Immigration laws of 1980 and 1986 address the growing number of refugees and illegal immigrants in the United States. A legalization program for illegal aliens who came before 1982 is established, as is a streamlined temporary-worker program.

  Today: President Obama's executive order giving amnesty to illegal aliens, issued because a gridlocked Congress cannot move forward on the growing immigration crisis, is defeated by the Supreme Court in June 2016. Immigration becomes a major issue in the 2016 presidential campaign.

- **c. 1988:** Multicultural courses are popular in schools and colleges for study of unfamiliar cultures among minority and ethnic groups such as African American, Native American, Latino, and others.

  Today: Films, novels, TV shows, and other popular media increasingly depict a mainstream American culture composed of multiple races and ethnic groups together in the workplace, the neighborhood, and intercultural romances and marriages.

extreme repression and ethnic cleansing on the country. Ahmad Shah Massoud created the Northern Alliance against the Taliban, supported by the United States, while the Taliban was supported by Pakistan, al Qaida, and Osama bin Laden. Massoud was assassinated two days before the attack on the Twin Towers on September 11, 2001.

The recent Afghan-American war began in 2001 after the 9/11 attack on the United States by al Qaida, a Sunni extremist group founded by bin Laden that called for global jihad. The United States along with the Afghan Northern Alliance, which united ethnic groups against the Taliban, ousted the Taliban in 2001. The war then shifted to a Taliban insurgency, which slowly gained ground. In 2009, President Barack Obama announced an escalation of American military involvement that entailed sending an additional thirty thousand soldiers. Osama bin Laden was killed by a Navy SEALs special operation in Pakistan on May 2, 2011. Although American troops soon began withdrawing from Afghanistan, a military presence remained to combat terrorism, under the 2012 Enduring Strategic Partnership Agreement with President Hamid Karzai. Afghanistan is now a non-NATO American ally. Afghans have constituted one of the largest recent refugee populations, fleeing to Pakistan, Iran, Europe, and the United States.

History of American Immigration

With the founding of the United States in 1789 by constitution, it was established as a country composed of immigrants and has expanded and progressed through immigration over the years. European settlers came to find economic opportunity or to escape religious persecution. There have been three larger waves of modern immigration that have modified the history of the country. One was in the 1840s and 1850s, largely from Ireland and Germany; the second from 1890 to World War I, from eastern Europe and Russia; and the third after 1965, when immigration laws opened the borders to people of any origin. The first two waves are associated with the change of the United States from an agrarian economy to an industrial one. Immigrants, such as Polish steelworkers, Irish policemen, Jewish garment workers, Slovak coal miners, Italian construction workers, Chinese railroad workers, and Japanese and Mexican agricultural workers, supplied the labor to support this urban shift. These European and Asian groups were gradually assimilated into what was perceived as an Anglo-American core identity, based on the United States' emerging from its colonial struggle with Great Britain. Yet people of all nationalities and ethnic groups were called "American," for they had voluntarily jumped into the melting pot of the new country and accepted the values of democracy, hard work, and equality as primary. On the other hand, the liberation of slaves after the Civil War brought another group into the picture, African Americans, forced immigrants, who had to fight for their American identity over the next century. They were joined by various American Indian groups in the 1960s, not immigrants, but treated as outsiders by white immigrants and their descendants.

The Naturalization Law of 1795 spelled out the terms of citizenship, including forswearing allegiances to any other country; however, dual citizenship for Americans has been recognized as acceptable since 1952. The Fourteenth Amendment confers citizenship as a birthright to those born on American soil. Other restrictions have been enacted by law. Chinese were stopped from entering in 1882; Mexicans and Filipinos were deported during the Great Depression to save jobs for white Americans; Japanese were incarcerated during World War II as possible traitors. Legislation between 1864 and 1917 barred convicts, beggars, prostitutes, the sick and disabled, and the illiterate. The 1891 Immigration Act made immigration a national issue controlled by Congress and federal courts.

Assimilation to some degree has been the expected ideal in the United States. It was feared that the less European-looking immigrants were less likely to assimilate, and the quota system was enacted in legislation of 1921, 1924, and 1927 to control the numbers entering from each national or ethnic group. After World War II, the quota system was felt to be an insult. There were major displacements of populations after the war, and more refugees were allowed in. The wave of immigration that opened up after the liberal 1965 Immigration and Nationality Act, abolishing quotas and mention of race, for the first time brought massive numbers of immigrants from outside Europe, along with new challenges. First, many came illegally; second, they were largely nonwhite; third, there were fewer industrial jobs waiting for them. Many immigrants since that act have been refugees from war-torn areas, like Ro in Mukherjee's story, or those escaping poverty in Mexico and South America. Factory jobs once helped immigrants transition from the lower to the middle class. Now, the jobs open are in information technology, health care, and other service sectors. There is greater job competition because the US economy is not the center of the world economy the way it once was, what with other emerging giants such as China, India, Brazil, and the European Union. A city like New York, once predominantly European American, has become a global city composed of half nonwhite citizens. The scenario has rapidly changed from the 1960s because of various civil rights movements, when racial and postcolonial issues began to be addressed and recognized, embraced under a broad title of "multiculturalism." This milestone ideally meant that groups who had been marginal or invisible would be included in the new dialogue of the "melting pot." Mukherjee's "Orbiting" is a snapshot of such a post-sixties American society. Immigration is a fact of life in the world today, with millions of people living outside the land of their birth.

Indian Diaspora Writers

The Indian diaspora writers include those born in India emigrating to the West and writing in English. These authors have become world-renowned, telling the stories of Indians and their encounters with other cultures. Mukherjee first considered herself an expatriate writer like Nobel laureate V. S. Naipaul, an Indian born in Trinidad, who writes of the loss of Indian culture in such books as *A House for Mr. Biswas* (1961) and *India: A Wounded Civilization* (1977). Expatriate writers are voluntary exiles who often look back with nostalgia or criticism to a way of life they can no longer accept, like Rohinton Mistry, the Canadian Parsi writer who describes the period of Indira Gandhi's state of emergency in *A Fine Balance* (1995). Anita Desai, who has lived in the United States and taught at MIT, has written in psychological terms of modern Indian lives, as in *Clear Light of Day* (1980). Her daughter, Indian novelist

Although the family still values their Indian heritage, Mukherjee uses their lives to explore what it means to be American (©Monkey Business Images / Shutterstock.com)

Kiran Desai, won the Booker Prize for *The Inheritance of Loss* (2006), about the postcolonial loss of identity for Indians in both the United States and India. Mukherjee moved in sympathy from V. S. Naipaul's position as expatriate to Salman Rushdie's position as immigrant, who, born in Bombay, is now a British citizen and has won the Booker Prize for *Midnight's Children* (1981). Rushdie is interested in the past but, like Mukherjee, more interested in the ability to reinvent one's identity.

Mukherjee's Stand on Multiculturalism vs. Interculturalism

"Multiculturalism" was originally a broad term meaning the acceptance of cultural diversity. Mukherjee moved to Canada with her Canadian husband, Clark Blaise, in 1966, living in Toronto and Montreal. She took a teaching position at McGill University and became a Canadian citizen. Canada had already passed the Bicultural and Bilingual Act in 1969 to address differences between its French- and English-speaking populations. In 1971 Prime Minister Pierre Trudeau announced that Canada would be the first country in the world to adopt a multicultural policy, respecting diverse cultures. In the 1970s other groups began to immigrate to Canada from Asia, Africa, and the Caribbean, and the problems of racism increased. The Multiculturalism Act in 1988 was passed to affirm equal protection under the law for all groups. Mukherjee was a citizen and full professor with tenure at McGill and yet was harassed in public places as a person of color. Canada's "multiculturalism," as she has remarked, turned out to emphasize ethnic or racial difference. Ethnic minorities may have rights, but they are still racially distinct and not easily assimilated into the mainstream. Mukherjee wrote her essay "An Invisible Woman," for which she won an award, for the popular Canadian magazine *Saturday Night*, explaining why she could no longer make her home in Canada, with its multicultural policy representing a form of separatism and not a hybridity of cultures.

She uprooted her husband and two sons and left Canada in 1980. Excited about becoming an American citizen, in 1988 she wrote the essay "Immigrant Writing: Give Us Your Maximalists" for the *New York Times Book Review*, calling for a new immigrant writing to reinvigorate American mainstream literature. She was not a marginal multicultural or postcolonial author. She wanted to speak for immigrants who were moving into the mainstream just as she was. In "Orbiting" and the rest of her 1988 collection, *The Middleman and Other Stories*, her characters are caught in clashes of cultures but are flexible and creative. "Interculturalism" is the way to speak of a pluralism where immigrants do not assimilate into a fixed core culture, but change the mainstream as much as they are changed by it in a dynamic and mutual interchange. Mukherjee celebrates what she sees as an America changing for the better because of third-world immigration. "Orbiting" represents this shift in perspective on what it means to be American today.

CRITICAL OVERVIEW

Mukherjee's *The Middleman and Other Stories* (1988), which won the National Book Critics Circle Award, was proof of the goal announced in her essay "Immigrant Writing: Give Us Your Maximalists," to write about America in the making through its immigrants. Her characters learn how to forge a new identity in a new country. The book was published a few months after she herself excitedly became a US citizen. The stories represent an expansion of character types beyond Indian expatriates that she allows to speak for themselves in their own voices, including Americanisms and slang, rather than using an omniscient point of view as she had before.

Elizabeth Ward's review of *The Middleman* for the *Washington Post Book World* comments on the fact that all the author's characters in these stories inhabit a borderland caught between two worlds, like Maya in "The Tenant," trying to find a place. They are restless, moving around, leaving the past behind and looking for a future. Jonathan Raban, in his review of *The Middleman* in the *New York Times Book Review*, notes that Mukherjee writes her own version of the global diaspora, with immigrants, legal and illegal, on the move, inventing their lives from one minute to the next. In a review of *The Middleman* in the *Voice Literary Supplement*, Polly Shulman feels that the story "Jasmine" in this volume offers a depressing view of new immigrants, for she sees Jasmine as sexually exploited in an encounter with her employer.

This brings up the point that Mukherjee's stories, though acclaimed by both critics and the reading public, often provoke controversy or multiple interpretations. For instance, S. Alliya Parveen, in *Immigrants and Immigrant Literature by Bharati Mukherjee: A Study*, published in 2013, sees an example of how European Americans are being challenged by Asian immigrants in the story "Orbiting." The deMarco family is disturbed by Ro's non-American appearance and behavior. Parveen interprets Renata as moved by Ro, but "with the attitude of a colonizer, she feels that she can redeem him from his poor condition," vowing to make him into an American.

On the other hand, Carole Stone, speaking of the stories in general and "Orbiting" in particular in "The Short Fictions of Bernard Malamud and Bharati Mukherjee," takes the view that "the voices of Mukherjee's narrators add divergent values to America, proposing to share the center in a new way." In this interpretation, Renata is not colonizing Ro but telling her family to move over to make room for him.

In his introduction to *Conversations with Bharati Mukherjee*, Bradley C. Edwards comments that in *The Middleman and Other Stories*, "Immigration as reincarnation becomes a major theme in Mukherjee's fiction." She is interested in how immigrants can transform themselves into new persons. Edwards notes that *The Middleman* "elevated Mukherjee among the elite of American writers."

CRITICISM

Susan K. Andersen

Andersen is a teacher and writer with a PhD in English literature. In the following essay, she focuses on the character of Rindi deMarco and the qualities that make her the perfect narrator for Mukherjee's theme of American diversity in "Orbiting."

WHAT DO I READ NEXT?

- Diana Abu-Jaber's novel *Crescent* (2003) concerns Sirine, an Iraqi American cook in Los Angeles, and her love for an Iraqi refugee whom she misunderstands because she grew up in America and he grew up in Iraq.
- *The Meagre Tarmac*, a 2011 collection of short stories by Clark Blaise, Mukherjee's husband, tells linked stories about successful Indian immigrants to North America. The book was well received with favorable reviews.
- Khalid Hosseini's *The Kite Runner*, published in 2003, tells the story of Amir, a wealthy young Afghan boy in Kabul, and his growing up through the fall of the monarchy and escaping to America during the Soviet occupation, as Roashan does. As an adult, Amir goes back to Afghanistan to rescue a boy from the Taliban.
- Sara Howell's series of books published in 2014 for young readers called "The American Mosaic: Immigration Today" includes separate volumes called *Refugees*, *Undocumented Immigrants*, and *Famous Immigrants and Their Stories*. Issues, laws, and rights are described simply and clearly, as are the path to citizenship and inspiring stories of those who made it.
- Jamaica Kincaid's 1985 novel *Annie John* is the coming-of-age story of a young girl in Antigua, in the Caribbean, who feels she must leave home for nursing school in England to make a new life for herself.
- Rohinton Mistry's 1987 title *Swimming Lessons, and Other Stories from Firozsha Baag* is a collection of eleven short stories, including the much anthologized "Swimming Lessons," illustrating the double lives of Indian Parsi immigrants in Toronto.
- Bharati Mukherjee's novel *Jasmine* (1989) tells of a Punjabi teen whose husband is killed by a terrorist bomb. She moves to America and keeps reinventing her life, changing her names, in an effort to survive, though violence seems to follow her.
- *Other Immigrants: The Global Origins of the American People*, by David M. Reimers, came out in 2005, showing the effects of US immigration since 1965. The large numbers of immigrants coming from Latin America, the Caribbean, and Asia, shifting the ethnic balance in the United States, is a plus, not a minus, he points out. Reimers is a professor emeritus from New York University.
- The novel *The Joy Luck Club*, by Amy Tan, published in 1989, tells the immigrant Chinese stories of three mothers and four daughters in San Francisco.
- Anzia Yezierska's *Bread Givers* (1925) tells of the hard lives of Jewish American immigrants on the Lower East Side of New York. Sara Smolinsky does not seek marriage like her older sisters but wants an education.

On a first reading of Bharati Mukherjee's "Orbiting," from her 1988 collection *The Middleman and Other Stories*, it seems a simple realistic account of a multicultural Thanksgiving dinner centered around an Italian immigrant family, the deMarcos. Even though there are surprises, like an Afghan refugee's suddenly erupting into the scene using his own key to enter Rindi deMarco's apartment and giving her a sexy kiss in front of her shocked parents, the story could seem similar to many other stories and films about bringing a boyfriend home to the family on Thanksgiving. From the first sentence, however, when we are

"RINDI IS THE PERFECT NARRATOR FOR MUKHERJEE'S PROJECT OF SHOWING HOW IMMIGRANTS BECOME PART OF THE MAINSTREAM OF AMERICAN SOCIETY AND WHAT AMERICAN FREEDOM IS ALL ABOUT."

immersed in the first-person stream of consciousness of Rindi's mind, we enter a unique world, her world, her life on her terms, which she firmly lets the reader in on through her casual, easy, and confident manner, her way of noting the chaos around her without being disturbed. She remains in the center, as though orchestrating all this diversity into something harmonious. Rindi is the perfect narrator for Mukherjee's project of showing how immigrants become part of the mainstream of American society and what American freedom is all about. She is twenty-seven, positioned as the recipient of decades of immigrant life in America, and further back, traditions from Italy, but young enough to still be "orbiting" in her own life, seeing where it will lead, without rigid ideas of the future. She identifies herself as a liberated woman, able to move ahead to her own drum without bending to the pressure of criticism. She is the most flexible character in the story, provocative, but a peacemaker, accepting the stories of others, willing to take everyone in.

Rindi is a third-generation Italian immigrant, thoroughly Americanized in her manners and thinking, yet not assimilated into middle-class values. Her sister has married a rich businessman. Cindi has material wealth, status, and a BMW, but she is unhappy. Rindi has carved her own niche. She is on the social fringes with a lack of an educated profession, selling jewelry in a boutique and living in a funky third-floor apartment with no real furniture. Instead of bemoaning this situation, Rindi makes it clear that she has chosen her own life. She likes her job and lived an alternative unmarried radical lifestyle with her former boyfriend, Vic, including macrobiotic cooking and membership in Amnesty International. Amazingly, Rindi is not embarrassed about her lack of social status or wealth or her sexual freedom with men in front of her family. She maintains a live-and-let-live attitude, characteristic of a later generation of independent immigrant women.

Within Rindi's consciousness is the memory of her Italian great-grandmother who was pregnant with her grandfather as she passed through Ellis Island. Similarly, she is saturated with her mother's memory of growing up in the wild Calabrian landscape of Italy, her life as a sweatshop seamstress in America, and the rigid insecurities that she does not let go of until middle age. Her father's life as a veteran and baseball player and a bowler in the church league, his friendships in their Italian neighborhood—all these are conveyed economically in Rindi's memory, accounting for the family traits and relationships. Mukherjee has commented that immigrants to this country have fascinating stories; they have lived heroic lives and have had to compress hundreds of years of their homeland history and American history in their own consciousness. She gives a hint of this breadth in Rindi's character, for her mother and grandmother are still alive in her, though she is her own person.

"Orbiting" is an illustration of what Mukherjee calls maximalism, the cultural richness possessed by immigrants. "Mine is not minimalism, which strips away, but compression, which reflects many layers of meaning," she said in a 1989 interview with Sybil Steinberg. The layers of meaning in "Orbiting" include the several strands and histories of ethnic identity in American life that Rindi takes for granted because they are now part of her; the long process of assimilation of earlier immigrants like her father and mother; and the current friction with the entry of Asian refugees, who have just as much right to be accepted, Rindi asserts. To unpack Rindi's reflections in this story is to uncover American history itself, for Rindi is aware of herself as an immigrant, as Mukherjee has said of herself in a 1987 interview with Geoff Hancock: "I am an immigrant, living in a continent of immigrants."

By this statement Mukherjee, a South Asian, makes a place for nonwhite immigrants in the American mainstream. And this is what "Orbiting" does by introducing Roashan, the Afghan refugee, into the Italian American Thanksgiving celebration. Mukherjee does not call herself a minority, an expatriate, or an Indian American. She refers to herself as an

American. In this story, she is illustrating how immigration to America no longer means the Italians, Germans, and Irish. These groups that once stuck out have been assimilated. Now, the melting pot is enlarging to include people of color—Asians, Africans, and Latin Americans. This story registers the shock of this fact on Rindi's Euro-American family as they take in Ro's darker skin, different posture, manners, and violent history. As Italians, they had to make their way in their day, as Rindi explains. She understands her mother's worry about her apartment, because her mother "has the simple, immigrant faith that children should do better than their parents." She also comments on the journey of her brother-in-law Brent from German Amish roots in Iowa as a Schwartzendruber to his current incarnation as Bernie Schwartz, a successful electronics store owner in Manhattan. Without criticizing or fighting with her family, she tries to fairly represent them, as she does also with Jorge, who does cleaning and yard work for her landlady, also teaching her Spanish, to get money to bring his family from El Salvador. When she tells her father about Jorge, he responds as if El Salvador is "messy and exotic, at the very rim of human comprehension." She reflects on her father's ignorance of the world with humor and tolerance. Rindi also tries to do justice to Roashan's story, though they are still getting to know each other. He buys her real whole nutmegs from a Pakistani, and she tells him how to get across town on the bus. She has learned things from him that have suddenly opened her up to a new reality.

Ro is fearful, with only a temporary work permit, living among illegal immigrants, worried about being sent back. If he or any of his cousins get deported they face torture in a Soviet prison. Rindi mentions,

> When I'm with Ro I feel I am looking at America through the wrong end of a telescope. He makes it sound like a police state, with sudden raids, papers, detention centers, deportations, and torture and death waiting in the wings.

This too is part of the American reality for immigrants, Mukherjee shows. Critics have wondered why Mukherjee's stories have so much violence in them. There are murders, rapes, suicides, robberies, betrayals, terrorism, and life in the criminal underground. This is a world that immigrants often have to traverse, as she points out in her novel *Jasmine* and in the story "The Middleman." Mukherjee mentioned in the interview with Geoff Hancock that her characters "may be immoral or amoral, but they operate in a deeply moral world." She also suggested in a 1996 interview with Tina Chen and S. X. Goudie that the best literature is more than just realism: "No fine fiction, no good literature, is anchored in verisimilitude. Fiction must be metaphor. It is not transcription of real life but it's a distillation and pitching at higher intensification of life." Violence in Mukherjee is thus often a metaphor for the extreme psychic transformation immigrants must undergo, as Ro is in the middle of experiencing here.

The reader is shown the trauma of Ro's life from another point of view, from Rindi's. She is changed by Ro's drama, and she allows her family to be changed by it as well. Franny, Cindi's stepdaughter, is a spoiled child who thinks she has troubles until she hears how Ro was tortured in a Soviet prison. Brent and Mr. deMarco seem to think Ro is effeminate in appearance; he cannot share their male talk about sports, and he does not drink alcohol. Rindi believes, however, that his manhood is far more potent than theirs. He has a direct sexuality that she has never encountered before, and his courageous flight from Afghanistan and his scars to prove it make him more of a man in her eyes than they can understand. They are children compared to him. They begin to see her point of view when she bestows on him the symbolic job of carving the turkey, ordinarily reserved for the patriarch of the family. She gives the honor to Ro, a sort of initiation into her family and American life, an acceptance. He uses his own dagger as a swashbuckling symbol of his exotic masculinity, carving the bird to perfection and demonstrating his manhood to everyone's satisfaction.

Rindi's acceptance of others makes her an exponent of the American dream. She wants to help Ro realize his goal of becoming an electrical engineer. She wants to help him forget the past and reinvent himself. This optimistic view of America as embodying what the author calls "the will to transform" was explored by Mukherjee in an interview with Francisco Collado Rodríguez in 1994. She does admit that there is some selfishness and greed in pioneers who go forward in acts of self-making. There is perhaps a thin line between pioneering and

Renata is worried about bringing her boyfriend home to meet her family *(©India Picture / Shutterstock.com)*

using one's will in a coercive manner. That coercion is the dark side of this will to transform, if used at the expense of others. In this story, however, Mukherjee seems to be celebrating the Whitmanesque view of America as inclusive of the rights of others to find a space on these shores for renewal. Mukherjee often uses the terms "unhousement" and "rehousement" to describe the process of changing cultures. In the interview with Geoff Hancock, she explained: "Unhousement is the breaking away from the culture into which one was born. . . . Rehousement is the rerooting of oneself in a new culture. This requires transformations of the self." This is the process of "orbiting"—unhousement, rehousement, and transformation. At the end of the turkey carving, Rindi has a vision of Ro, naked, with his scars. She comments, "I am seeing character made manifest." The scars are his badge of courage, the proof of the start of his transformation from Afghan to American. None of the immigrant stories Rindi mentions were easy. Immigration seems to be about character building, with scars as part of the process. Rindi frames all of this within her consciousness, making her the perfect narrator for illustrating the mutual interchange between Americans and immigrants. She is changed as she watches and facilitates Ro's change.

Source: Susan K. Andersen, Critical Essay on "Orbiting," in *Short Stories for Students*, Gale, Cengage Learning, 2017.

Alison B. Carb

In the following interview, Mukherjee talks about writing the stories in The Middleman.

Bharati Mukherjee: The stories were done in two intense flurries, although I had been thinking about the book for a long time. As soon as *Darkness* was published in 1985, I started working on stories for *The Middleman*. One cycle of stories was written over an eight-month period during a semester off from teaching and on an NEA grant. Then my work was interrupted while I was teaching and writing the book on the Air India crash, *The Sorrow and the Terror*, with my husband. Once that book was over, I wrote another cycle of stories for *The Middleman* over the summer of 1987. So it

"MY AIM IS TO EXPOSE AMERICANS TO THE ENERGETIC VOICES OF NEW SETTLERS IN THIS COUNTRY, NOT ONLY THROUGH MY OWN WRITING BUT BY EDITING AND REVIEWING THE FICTION OF WRITERS FROM NONTRADITIONAL NATIONS, INCLUDING INDIA, SRI LANKA, EGYPT, AND SOUTH AFRICA."

took me about a year and a half to write this book if one includes the break in between.

Carb: Where did you get the idea for the book?

Mukherjee: It grew out of an incomplete novel about a man who served in the Army in Vietnam, and who, after the war, becomes a professional soldier and hires himself out in Afghanistan and Central America. While I was working on that novel, a character with a minor role, a Jew who has relocated from Baghdad to Bombay to Brooklyn, took control and wrote his own story. He attracted me because he was a cynical person and a hustler, as many immigrant survivors have to be.

So Alfie Judah, the protagonist in "The Middleman," travels around the world, providing people with what they need—guns, narcotics, automobiles. The story takes place in an unnamed country in Central America where he becomes involved in a guerilla war.

Incidentally, the Vietnam veteran, Jeb Marshall who comes from Miami, is featured in his own story in this collection, called "Loose Ends." A large number of these stories are told by native-born Americans, but even when I write about them I tell how their lives are affected by newly arrived or first-generation Americans.

For example, one of my stories, "Fighting for the Rebound," is narrated by an Atlanta stockbroker who falls in love with a former millionaire's daughter from the Philippines, who supports Marcos. As a writer, my voice is supple and I can enter diverse characters' lives and let each of them speak for themselves.

The new, changing America is the theme of the stories in *The Middleman*. For me, immigration from the Third World to this country is a metaphor for the process of uprooting and rerooting, or what my husband Clark Blaise in his book *Resident Alien* calls "unhousement" and "rehousement." The immigrants in my stories go through extreme transformations in America and at the same time they alter the country's appearance and psychological make-up. In some ways, they are like European immigrants of earlier eras. But they have different gods. And they come for different reasons.

Carb: What is special about this collection?

Mukherjee: I write about well-known American establishments, such as the family, in unique ways. In my stories, the families are not the American families which we are accustomed to reading about in fiction. The American family has become very different, not just because of social influences and new sexual standards, but because of the interaction between mainstream Americans and new immigrants.

For example, there's a story in *The Middleman* entitled "Fathering," in which the secure life of a yuppie living with his girlfriend in a small town in upstate New York is disrupted when the half-Vietnamese child he had fathered in Saigon comes to visit.

In another story, "Orbiting," a New Jersey woman of Italian origin invites her parents and her Afghan boyfriend for Thanksgiving dinner at her home and a crisis occurs over who should carve the turkey, her father or the boyfriend. My stories are discomfiting because they challenge accepted codes of behavior in this country and show the changes taking place here.

Carb: Do you see changes in your writing style in The Middleman*?*

Mukherjee: My style has changed because I am becoming more Americanized with each passing year. American fiction has a kind of energy that fiction from other cultures seems to lack right now. The stories in *The Middleman*, I like to think, have this energy and passion as well. Each character and story suggests a different style.

When I sit down in my study to write, I don't immediately say, "I have to write an experimental story." The story idea itself dictates the appropriate voice for it and how lean or fleshy a paragraph might be. I write some stories from a very authoritative third person point of view. With others I use an intimate, textured style and a first person point of view.

My first novel, *The Tiger's Daughter*, has a rather British feel to it. I used the omniscient point of view and plenty of irony. This was because my concept of language and notions of how a novel was constructed were based on British models. I had gone to school in London as a young child and later to a British convent school for elite young women in postcolonial India, where we read English writers like Jane Austen and E. M. Forster.

By the time I wrote *Darkness* I had adopted American English as my language. I moved away from using irony and was no longer comfortable using an authoritative point of view. In addition, I started to write short stories instead of novels. The short story form requires us to express our thoughts concisely and not waste a single sentence or detail.

Carb: How does your writing contrast with that of other India-born writers?

Mukherjee: There is a large difference between myself and these authors. Unlike writers such as Anita Desai and R. K. Narayan, I do not write in Indian English about Indians living in India. My role models, view of the world, and experiences are unlike theirs. These writers live in a world in which there are still certainties and rules. They are part of their society's mainstream. Wonderful writers as they are, I am unable to identify with them because they describe characters who fit into their community in different ways than my naturalized Americans fit into communities in Queens or Atlanta.

On the other hand, I don't write from the vantage point of an Indian expatriate like V. S. Naipaul. Naipaul, who was born in Trinidad because his relatives left India involuntarily to settle there, has different attitudes about himself. He writes about living in perpetual exile and about the impossibility of ever having a home. Like Naipaul, I am a writer from the Third World but unlike him I left India by choice to settle in the U.S. I have adopted this country as my home. I view myself as an American author in the tradition of other American authors whose ancestors arrived at Ellis Island.

Cab: Which authors do you think your writing most closely resembles?

Mukherjee: (Emphatically) I see a strong likeness between my writing and Bernard Malamud's, in spite of the fact that he describes the lives of East European Jewish immigrants and I talk about the lives of newcomers from the Third World. Like Malamud, I write about a minority community which escapes the ghetto and adapts itself to the patterns of the dominant American culture. Like Malamud's, my work seems to find quite naturally a moral center. Isaac Babel is another author who is a literary ancestor for me. I also feel a kinship with Joseph Conrad and Anton Chekhov. But Malamud most of all speaks to me as a writer and I admire his work a great deal. Immersing myself in his work gave me the self-confidence to write about my own community.

Carb: How does your writing differ from Malamud's?

Mukherjee: When you are from the Third World, when you have dark skin and religious beliefs that do not conform to those of Judaism or Christianity, mainstream America responds to you in ways you can't foresee. My fiction has to consider race, politics, religion, as well as certain nastinesses that other generations of white immigrant American writers may not have had to take into account.

I was born into a Hindu Bengali Brahmin family which means that I have a different sense of self, of existence, and of mortality than do writers like Malamud. I believe that our souls can be reborn in another body, so the perspective I have about a single character's life is different from that of an American writer who believes that he only has one life.

As a Hindu, I was brought up on oral tradition and epic literature in which animals can talk, birds can debate ethical questions, and monsters can change shapes. I believe in the existence of alternate realities, and this belief makes itself evident in my fiction.

Carb: Do you think American readers and editors have been receptive to your work?

Mukherjee: Yes. Americans have a healthy curiosity about new writers and new ideas. American publishing houses have been far more ready to receive my writing than have houses in Canada, where the attitude in the sixties and seventies was that if one hadn't played in snow and grown up eating oatmeal one didn't have anything relevant to say to Canadian readers.

I was touched when one of my "immigrant" stories, "The Tenant," which was printed in a small literary quarterly, the *Literary Review*, was read by people and eventually made it into *The Best American Short Stories 1987*.

Writing short stories helped too. As soon as I started writing them, my work became more available to American readers than my novels had been. The novels were not easily obtainable because initially there were no paperback editions. This past year they were reissued by Penguin Books.

Unfortunately, one of the difficulties that writers like myself face are editors of large-circulation magazines who are unwilling to risk publishing writers whose fictional worlds are not intensely familiar or overtly sellable. They say my work is "too strong" for their readers.

Carb: What other difficulties have you experienced as a writer?

Mukherjee: (In a low, strained voice) I had a very bad time during the 1970s when my husband and I lived and taught in Canada. I had gone there with him because his family lived there. The seventies were horrendous years for Indians in Canada. There was a lot of bigotry against Canadian citizens of Indian origin, especially in Toronto, and it upset me terribly when I encountered this or saw other people experiencing it.

There was a pattern of discrimination. I was refused service in stores. I would have to board a bus last when I had been the first person on line. I was followed by detectives in department stores who assumed I was a shoplifter or treated like a prostitute in hotels. I was even physically roughed up in a Toronto subway station.

I found myself constantly fighting battles against racial prejudice. Toronto made me into a civil rights activist. I wrote essays about the devastating personal effects of racism. For many years I didn't find the strength to turn my back on Canada and do what I really wanted to do: write fiction.

But in 1980 I did leave. We were living in Montreal at the time. I resigned my full professorship at McGill University and came to the United States with my family. I felt guilty about pulling my husband and sons away from what was home, but it was a question of my own self-preservation. It was the only way I could think of removing myself from the persistent hurt.

Being in the U.S. was a tremendous relief after Canada. I suddenly felt freed to write the thousands of stories inside my head. In the U.S. I wasn't continuously forced to deal with my physical appearance. I could wear Western clothes and blend in with people on a New York City street. America, with its melting pot theory of immigration, has a healthier attitude toward Indian immigrants than Canada. Although this country has its share of racial problems there are human rights laws and ways to obtain legal redress in the courts.

Carb: Do you find it easy or difficult to write?

Mukherjee: I *like* to write but finding the time isn't easy. It would be ideal if I could write from nine to three or four every day. But I have so many jobs to do, teaching, lecturing, writing articles and reviews, taking care of my family, that I can't write as much as I would like. When I do sit down at the word processor in my study, I'm ready to go and the writing just flows. Especially where short stories are concerned. I hear a voice inside my head and start typing. Not everything I write appears in a book though, I'm a great reviser.

My husband, Clark, also helps me with my fiction. He is an American-Canadian author. Like me, he teaches in the English Department at Columbia University. We work well on joint writing projects such as the nonfiction books we did, *Days and Nights in Calcutta*, about our year-long stay with my family in India in 1977, and *The Sorrow and the Terror*.

We have an intensely literary marriage. We talk about writing and Clark is a very good audience for my work. He reads it and comments on it just as he did when we were students in the Writers' Workshop at the University of Iowa, where we first met.

Carb: Were you interested in writing before graduate school?

Mukherjee: Yes. I always knew I was going to be a writer. I had wanted to write since I was a child. The world of fiction seemed more real to me than the world around me. I started my first novel when I was about nine or ten. It came to seventy or eighty pages. It was about English children and was set in England.

But it wasn't until I was in high school in Calcutta that I started writing short stories for school magazines. I don't remember what these stories were about and I want to forget them (laughs), but I recall writing one from Napoleon's point of view. My imagination was stimulated by reading about European history and Western civilization. By the time I was at college I decided that I wasn't going to be a chemist like my father. I enjoyed writing far too much.

Carb: You have come from a complex background and world. Is it hard for you as a South Asian immigrant writer to convey the immigrant experience to native-born American audiences?

Mukherjee: No, no, no. My task as an author is to make my intricate and unknown world comprehensible to mainstream American readers. This is what good novels and stories do. If my fiction is effective, unexplained and cultural aspects about the Indian community in Queens or the Korean community in New York will become accessible.

We immigrants have fascinating tales to relate. Many of us have lived in newly independent or emerging countries which are plagued by civil and religious conflicts. We have experienced rapid changes in the history of the nations in which we lived. When we uproot ourselves from those countries and come here, either by choice or out of necessity, we suddenly must absorb two hundred years of American history and learn to adapt to American society. Our lives are remarkable, often heroic.

I attempt to illustrate this in my novels and short stories. My characters want to make it in the new world; they are filled with a hustlerish kind of energy, like Alfie Judah in *The Middleman*. Although they are often hurt or depressed by setbacks in their new lives and occupations, they do not give up. They take risks they wouldn't have taken in their old, comfortable worlds to solve their problems. As they change citizenship, they are reborn.

My aim is to expose Americans to the energetic voices of new settlers in this country, not only through my own writing but by editing and reviewing the fiction of writers from non-traditional nations, including India, Sri Lanka, Egypt, and South Africa. By doing this I hope to make editors aware of how these writers are changing the scope and structure of American fiction.

Source: Alison B. Carb, "An Interview with Bharati Mukherjee," in *Conversations with Bharati Mukherjee*, edited by Bradley C. Edwards, University Press of Mississippi, 2009, pp. 25–31.

"IT IS A STORY MUKHERJEE APPEARS TO HAVE DELIBERATELY WRITTEN AS HER THANKSGIVING OFFERING FOR THE MELTING-POT PROCESS OF AMERICAN CULTURE THAT WAS ALLOWING IMMIGRANTS FROM ASIA TO SUCCESSFULLY ROOT THEMSELVES IN THE NEW WORLD AND TO TRANSFORM IT AS WELL AS THEMSELVES."

Falcru Alam

In the following excerpt, Alam describes "Orbiting" as "the most optimistic story" in the collection.

. . . Renata de Marcos, the narrator of "Orbiting," has no problems with having an affair and giving herself up wholly to her Asian-American boyfriend, Roshan. An upper-class refugee from the civil war in Afghanistan, Roshan works in a restaurant in New York and plans to eventually earn a degree in electrical engineering. Despite being cosmopolitan and well-bred, he has a foreignness of manners and a sensibility that Renata finds irresistible. "Orbiting" is therefore not a story where the narrator-protagonist has to come to terms with her feelings for an alien. Instead, the problem Mukherjee poses is whether the rest of Renata's family will accept Roshan as one of their own. Older Americans themselves, will they take to her Afghan boyfriend? Renata's father, we gather, is a second-generation American of Italian origin, her mother a Spanish woman her father met on a European holiday. Her sister Cindy is married to an Amish American named Brent. All of them, however, have been more or less transformed by America and have come to accept its values and its culture. Will they approve of someone as unassimilated as Roshan is?

Renata is afraid, then, that in having become completely Americanized, her family will not remember their own immigrant past and will find Roshan too exotic for their tastes. Consequently, she is quite tense about the outcome of the Thanksgiving dinner where her family will get the opportunity to meet Roshan for the first time. "All over the country," she reassures herself before the dinner, "women are towing new lovers home to meet their families" (*Middleman*). But while the fact that he is totally unlike any man she has ever known is the reason she feels so attracted to him, she cannot help reflecting as she introduces him to her family that "my parents are so parochial" (*Middleman*).

As the Thanksgiving Day dinner encounter begins, all her worst fears about the dinner turning into a disaster seem to be coming true. Her father, for example, thinks Afghanistan is somewhere in Africa and starts calling Roshan Roy. Roshan, for his part, says something about the odorlessness of American flowers, which she knows her mother will find offensive. He then makes her father's face go livid by declining to drink whiskey with him because drinking is a taboo in his religion. Franny, Brent's petulant teenage daughter from a previous marriage, starts smirking at Roshan's obvious foreignness. Brent tries to help by getting Roshan involved in a conversation about professional basketball, but Roshan admits he knows nothing about the game. Renata knows that Roshan "is so sophisticated, he could make monkeys" out of them all, and yet she is afraid her family was beginning to see him as "a retard" (*Middleman*).

At the end, though, the Thanksgiving Day dinner turns out to be a success, and Roshan proves to be quite a hit with Renata's family. What finally endears him to them is his passionate exposition of the situation in Afghanistan and the circumstances that led him to flee his country. It is something of a "revelation" for Brent, for instance, that "a reasonably educated and rational man like Ro would die for things that he . . . has never heard of and would rather laugh about" (*Middleman*). Renata's father is stunned by the intricacies of the route Roshan took to come to America and begins to appreciate the meaning of Thanksgiving more clearly than he has ever done before. Roshan impresses also with his carving skills; he does such a good job on the turkey that he has even Franny "practically licking his fingers" (*Middleman*). As for Renata, her feeling for Roshan has now been transformed into hero worship. In fact, as the story ends, she comes to see Roshan as the archetypal American hero, "Clint Eastwood, scarred hero and survivor," a man beside whom her father and brother-in-law are children (*Middleman*). She realizes, of course, that there are things American that Roshan has still to learn, but she knows that these are relatively simpler than what he has already experienced. Ro is her chance, she is convinced, "to heal the world" (*Middleman*).

"Orbiting" is without a doubt the most optimistic of the stories of *The Middleman*. Liew-Geok Leong's comment on the story is very apt: "In the movement from immigrant subcultures to mainstream culture that *The Middleman* represents, 'Orbiting' is striking for the very Americanizing process it celebrates" (Leong, 498). It is a story Mukherjee appears to have deliberately written as her Thanksgiving offering for the melting-pot process of American culture that was allowing immigrants from Asia to successfully root themselves in the New World and to transform it as well as themselves. Certainly it substantiates Mukherjee's claim that what she wants to do through her fiction is more than tell a story or create a memorable character and that her ultimate intention is "to redefine the nature of *American* and what makes an American" ("Woman").

The Middleman and Other Stories thus approaches from a variety of angles the striking changes occurring in American society and culture as well as in the American psyche by new and nontraditional immigrants to the country. Throughout the volume Mukherjee keeps directing the reader's gaze at the interpenetration of America by Asians. Seen as a whole, the stories point to an American landscape that is starting to be dotted with Asian ghettos and businesses. The Indian settlement of Flushing, Queens; the Brooklyn neighborhood that Roshan has dubbed "Little Kabul"; names such as Patel or Abdul; and "the aisles of bok choy and twenty kinds of Jamaican spices" at the Atlanta Farmers' Market are some of the instances inserted by Mukherjee to remind her readers that "the US of A is still a pioneer country" ("Fighting for the Rebound," *Middleman*). The pages of *The Middleman* are full of people such as Mr. Venkatesan of "Buried Lives" who wish "to flee abroad and seize the good life as had his San Jose cousin," of new Americans dreaming the American dream and realizing or half-realizing that dream in startling ways. Mukherjee also fictionalizes the way people shed parts of themselves and acquire new identities in America, the way in which the American melting pot makes in no time a Ro or a Roy out of a Roshan. Jonathan Raban is therefore right to say in his review of *The Middleman* that, taken together, the volume represents "a romance with America itself, its infinitely possible geography, its license, sexiness and violence" (Raban, 22).

One other point Raban makes about *The Middleman* is that it is a distinctive collection at least partly because of the dexterity with which Mukherjee uses the monologue form in most of the stories and the "rapturous affection and acuteness of ear" Mukherjee displays in capturing "the idiom of America in the 1980s." This aspect of Mukherjee's accomplishment reminds Raban of the success of Nabokov, another immigrant writer whose 1950 novel *Lolita* exhibited his ability to capture the idiom of contemporary America. Seeing it from the perspective of its use of American speech, Raban calls *The Middleman*, too, "a consummated romance with the American language" (Raban, 22).

Mukherjee has claimed that from *Darkness* onward she had "begun appropriating the American language" ("Woman"). But only in Shawn Patel's narrative of his quest to find wholeness in a fragmented world in "Saints" has Mukherjee handled the monologue form with anything like the adroitness she displays in representing American speech in almost all the stories of *The Middleman*. In "A Wife's Story" Panna Bhatt comments on the way her diction has changed in the time she has spent in America. Bhatt's comments on this change reveal something of the attention that Mukherjee pays to the nuances of the spoken language in situating a character: "That part of my life is over, the way *trucks* have replaced *lorries* in my vocabulary" (*Middleman*). But Panna can also sound poetic as she depicts the sun breaking through over New York City: "The summer sun pushes through fluffy clouds and dapples the glass of office towers" (*Middleman*).

Both Jeb Marshall's Vietnam experience and the atmosphere of menace that surrounds him come out clearly in his one-sentence account of his success in killing his boss's rival: "I did what I was paid for; I eliminated the primary target and left no traces" (*Middleman*). Griffs fondness for stock-market jargon, for sports metaphors, and for the appurtenances of yuppie life are everywhere in evidence in his narrative in "Fighting for the Rebound." Sometimes Mukherjee experiments with mixing registers and in showing her characters moving between languages. Gita Rajan thus points out the way Mukherjee shows Eng shuttling "between perfectly normal, American use of the English language and curses/war slang in Vietnamese" in "Fathering" to reveal "her position between two cultures and her splintered psyche" (Rajan, 239). While Mukherjee's ability to reproduce the American vernacular and to introduce the idioms of new immigrants is impressive in *The Middleman*, her ear for Indian English seems to have deteriorated considerably in the volume; when someone such as Dr. Chaterji speaks in "The Tenant" he almost becomes a parody of Indians speaking English.

On the whole, though, *The Middleman and Other Stories* shows a confident Mukherjee working dexterously on her theme of the making of new Americans and ringing all kinds of fascinating variations on that theme. Reviewers were almost unanimous in their praise of Mukherjee's handling of her subject matter and her skillful use of the American language. It is no wonder that the volume garnered for Mukherjee her only major laurel to date, the National Book Critics Circle Award for Fiction, and that it was a commercial as well as a critical success. Indeed, it is not too much to say that with the publication of *The Middleman* Mukherjee had registered her claim to be considered one of the leading authors of contemporary America. The widespread acclaim for the book would be eventually followed by one or two tough-minded critiques of it (see Knippling, 143—61), but from now on Mukherjee's presence in American letters could no longer be ignored. . . .

Source: Falcru Alam, "The Exuberance of Immigration," in *Bharati Mukherjee*, Twayne, 1996, pp. 96–99.

SOURCES

Chen, Tina, and S. X. Goudie, "Holders of the Word: An Interview with Bharati Mukherjee," in *Conversations with Bharati Mukherjee*, edited by Bradley C. Edwards, University Press of Mississippi, 2009, p. 83; originally published in *Jouvert: A Journal of Postcolonial Studies*, Vol. 1, No. 1, 1997.

Edwards, Bradley C., ed., Introduction to *Conversations with Bharati Mukherjee*, University Press of Mississippi, 2009, p. xv.

Gerber, David A., *American Immigration: A Very Short Introduction*, Oxford University Press, 2011, pp. 2–51, 73, 80, 86, 101–108.

Hancock, Geoff, "An Interview with Bharati Mukherjee," in *Conversations with Bharati Mukherjee*, edited by Bradley C. Edwards, University Press of Mississippi, 2009, pp. 11, 14, 19; originally published in *Canadian Fiction*, No. 59, May 1987, pp. 30–44.

Mukherjee, Bharati, "A Four-Hundred-Year-Old Woman," in *The Writer on Her Work*, edited by Janet Sternburg, Vol. 2, Norton, 1991, pp. 33–38.

———, "Immigrant Writing," in *New York Times Book Review*, August 28, 1988, p. 29.

———, "An Invisible Woman," in *Saturday Night*, No. 96, March 1981, pp. 36–40.

———, "Orbiting," in *Braided Lives: An Anthology of Multicultural American Writing*, Minnesota Humanities Commission, 1991, pp. 238–52.

Parveen, S. Alliya, *Immigration and Immigrant Literature by Bharati Mukherjee: A Study*, Centre for South and Southeast Asian Studies, University of Madras, 2013, p. 99.

Raban, Jonathan, Review of *The Middleman and Other Stories*, in *New York Times Book Review*, June 19, 1988, pp. 1, 23.

Rattansi, Ali, *Multiculturalism: A Very Short Introduction*, Oxford University Press, 2011, pp. 8–16, 27–43, 151–53.

Rodríguez, Francisco Collado, "Naming Female Multiplicity: An Interview with Bharati Mukherjee," in *Conversations with Bharati Mukherjee*, edited by Bradley C. Edwards, University Press of Mississippi, 2009, p. 66; originally published in *Atlantis*, Vol. 17, Nos. 1–2, May–November 1995, pp. 293–306.

Shulman, Polly, "Home Truths," in *Voice Literary Supplement*, June 1988, p. 19.

Sollors, Werner, *Beyond Ethnicity: Consent and Descent in American Culture*, Oxford University Press, 1986, pp. 6, 11, 13, 25, 55, 66, 151.

Steinberg, Sybil, "Bharati Mukherjee," in *Conversations with Bharati Mukherjee*, edited by Bradley C. Edwards, University Press of Mississippi, 2009, p. 34; originally published in *Publishers Weekly*, August 25, 1989, pp. 46–47.

Stone, Carole, "The Short Fictions of Bernard Malamud and Bharati Mukherjee," in *Bharati Mukherjee: Critical Perspectives*, edited by Emmanuel S. Nelson, Garland, 1993, p. 224.

Ward, Elizabeth, "Notes from a New America," in *Washington Post Book World*, July 3, 1988, p. 9.

FURTHER READING

Knippling, Alpana Sharma, "Toward an Investigation of the Subaltern in Bharati Mukherjee's *The Middleman and Other Stories* and *Jasmine*," in *Bharati Mukherjee: Critical Perspectives*, edited by Emmanuel S. Nelson, Garland, 1993, pp. 143–60.

> Knippling questions Mukherjee's stance of situating herself as a spokesperson for other minorities in her fiction.

Magill, David, "Performing Community: Teaching Ethnic American Literature through the Short Story Sequence," in *Multiethnic American Literatures: Essays for Teaching Context and Culture*, edited by Helane Adams Androne, McFarland, 2015, pp. 170–71.

> A short-story sequence by an ethnic author—such as Mukherjee's *The Middleman and Other Stories*—is deemed a valuable teaching tool for re-creating the experiences of a whole community outside the mainstream culture, showing alternate ways of living.

Marconi, Giovanna, and Elena Ostanel, *The Intercultural City: Migration, Minorities and the Management of Diversity*, I. B. Tauris, 2016.

> These professors from IUAV University of Venice are researchers for a project by UNESCO to include international migrants in city planning. They cite scholars from a range of disciplines on how to plan for the mass migrations now taking place in the world. They give examples of solutions from around the globe where minority contributions have strengthened cities.

Markandaya, Kamala, *Nectar in a Sieve*, G. P. Putnam's Sons, 1954.

> This best seller describes the urbanization of India and the endurance of the poor. Markandaya, novelist and journalist, left India for Britain and always maintained her status as an expatriate looking back, as opposed to Mukherjee's philosophy of assimilation.

Mukherjee, Bharati, and Clark Blaise, *The Sorrow and the Terror: The Haunting Legacy of the Air India Tragedy*, Viking, 1987.

> Mukherjee and her husband undertook a nonfiction account of the Sikh terrorist act of blowing up Air India Flight 182 in 1985, killing all aboard, including many whole families. Although the flight originated in Canada and had Canadian citizens on board, most Canadians did not see it as related to them because the passengers were Indian Canadians. Mukherjee's experience of interviewing the families of victims resulted in her short story "The Management of Grief," in *The Middleman and Other Stories*.

Nelson, Emmanuel S., ed., *Ethnic American Literature: An Encyclopedia for Students*, Greenwood, 2015.

> Entries include biographies and works by ethnic authors, as well as topics such as African

American poetry, bilingualism, and border narratives. Mukherjee's novel *Jasmine*, for instance, is featured, as it is frequently taught in classes.

SUGGESTED SEARCH TERMS

Bharati Mukherjee

Orbiting AND Mukherjee

The Middleman and Other Stories

American immigration

multiculturalism in Canada

Air India Flight 182 crash

Indian diaspora writers

history of Afghanistan

Calabria, Italy

Iowa Writers Workshop

Calcutta OR Kolkata AND India

Clark Blaise

The Signalman

CHARLES DICKENS

1866

"The Signalman," a short story by Charles Dickens, was first published in a special 1866 Christmas issue of *All the Year Round*, a literary magazine launched and edited by Dickens beginning in 1859. Its full title as it appeared in the magazine is "No. 1 Branch Line: The Signalman." The story is one of a set of short stories collected under the special-issue title *Mugby Junction*, including work by Charles Collins, Amelia B. Edwards, Andrew Halliday, and Hesba Stretton. Although "The Signalman" can stand alone, the stories are linked by a framing device, the "gentleman for nowhere," who enjoys the freedom of retirement to explore the railroad lines in and around fictional Mugby Junction. "The Signalman" is also available in *Charles Dickens' Christmas Ghost Stories* (1992), his *Complete Ghost Stories* (1997), and other collections.

Dickens is generally thought of primarily as a novelist, but he published dozens of short stories, including a number of ghost stories. Modern readers are likely to be familiar with his most famous ghost story, *A Christmas Carol*, featuring Ebenezer Scrooge, but he wrote several others, some of which appeared as interpolated tales in novels such as *The Pickwick Papers*. "The Signalman," also a ghost story, rode a wave of public fascination with stories of the supernatural, the eerie, and the uncanny—and with railroad accidents. The story, in which a mysterious apparition foretells

Charles Dickens *(©Everett Historical / Shutterstock.com)*

disasters on the railroad, is based in part on a historical railroad accident that Dickens's readers would almost certainly have recalled: the Clayton Tunnel rail crash of August 25, 1861, which claimed the lives of twenty-three and injured 176 people, making it the most catastrophic rail accident up to that time. Dickens was also likely motivated by his own experience with a railroad accident: On June 9, 1865, he was traveling with his mistress, Ellen Ternan, and her mother when his train derailed near Staplehurst, in Kent, England. For the rest of his life, he was apprehensive about traveling by train, especially higher-speed express trains. "The Signalman" relies on details of the management of train traffic through tunnels, when signals have to be transmitted quickly and accurately to ensure that the tunnel is clear of one train before another can enter.

AUTHOR BIOGRAPHY

Dickens was born in Landport, near Portsmouth, Hampshire, England, on February 7, 1812, the second of eight children of John Dickens and Elizabeth Barrow. His improvident father, a clerk in the Navy Pay Office, ran into financial troubles and was imprisoned for debt in Marshalsea debtors' prison, an experience Dickens drew on heavily for his novel *Little Dorrit*. To help with the family finances, the twelve-year-old Dickens was sent to work for several months during this period and beyond. He earned six shillings a week pasting labels on bottles of shoe blacking at Warren's Blacking Warehouse, an experience he drew on for his autobiographical novel *David Copperfield*. The experience had a lifelong haunting, humiliating effect on him, because his education was interrupted and he was forced into association with coarse, vulgar boys with whom he had nothing in common.

Dickens began his professional career as an office boy for a lawyer. He later worked as a freelance court reporter and then as a reporter for two London newspapers. His first short story, "A Dinner at Poplar Walk," was published in 1833. In 1836, tapping his experience as a journalist, he published *Sketches by Boz*, a series of descriptions of London life (Boz was his pen name). That year, he assumed the helm as editor of a new magazine, *Bentley's Miscellany*, and married Catherine (Kate) Hogarth, whose father was the editor of the *Evening Chronicle*. In time, the couple had ten children, but they separated in 1858. The separation was likely triggered by Dickens's relationship with Ellen Ternan. Ternan was an actress he met while appearing in an amateur theatrical production of *The Frozen Deep* (1856), a play he cowrote with his friend, colleague, and frequent collaborator, Wilkie Collins.

Dickens's first novel was *The Pickwick Papers* (1836–37), which, like most of his novels, was published serially. The novel became a publishing phenomenon, encouraging Dickens to continue writing. In the following years, he wrote *Oliver Twist* (1837–39), *Nicholas Nickleby* (1838–39), *The Old Curiosity Shop* (1840–41), and *Barnaby Rudge* (1841). His work was popular not only in England but also in North America. New Yorkers congregated at the wharf waiting for the last installment of *The Old Curiosity Shop* to determine the fate of its heroine, Little Nell. In 1842, Dickens made his first reading tour in Canada and the United States. The impressions, many of them disparaging, he formed during this tour found their way into *American Notes* (1842) and *Martin Chuzzlewit* (1843–44). During a second American tour in 1867–68, Dickens tried to mend fences with the Americans he had offended.

During the 1840s and 1850s, Dickens continued to write with almost obsessive fervor, publishing "A Christmas Carol" (1843), *Dombey and Son* (1846–48), *David Copperfield* (1849–50), *Bleak House* (1852–53), *Hard Times* (1854), *Little Dorrit* (1855–57), and *A Tale of Two Cities* (1859). He was also the editor of *Household Words*, a magazine he founded in 1850. When that magazine ceased publication in 1859, he launched a new one, *All the Year Round*, which included "The Signalman" in 1866. He continued to enjoy great popularity, and in the 1850s and 1860s, he traveled throughout England, Scotland, and Ireland giving highly successful public readings from his novels. While enjoying his status as England's most popular, even revered, novelist, he was active in amateur theatricals and in various benevolent causes.

During the 1860s Dickens's health deteriorated, but he continued to write, producing two of his most highly regarded novels, *Great Expectations* (1860–61) and *Our Mutual Friend* (1864–65). A profound event in his life was the Staplehurst railway crash of 1865, which caused ten deaths and forty injuries. Dickens, who narrowly escaped death or serious injury, was commended for his efforts to help those who were injured, but he was permanently shaken by the accident, which was caused in part by a mistake on the part of the signalman. In 1870 he was working on *The Mystery of Edwin Drood*, which remained unfinished after he had a stroke. He died at age fifty-eight, at Gadshill, near Rochester, Kent, England, on June 9, 1870.

MEDIA ADAPTATIONS

- "The Signalman" was adapted by the BBC as *A Ghost Story for Christmas* in 1976. The production was directed by Lawrence Gordon Clark and starred Denholm Elliott as the signalman. The running time is thirty-eight minutes.
- In 2007 Naxos Audiobooks released an audio version of "The Signalman" read by Stephen Critchlow. The running time is thirty-two minutes.
- John Sessions reads "The Signalman" for the Dickens compilation *The Signalman & Other Ghostly Tales*, released by Textbook-Stuff.com in 2010. The running time is thirty-two minutes.
- In 2011 Sonolibros released a Spanish-language audio recording of "The Signalman" under the title "El Guardavias." The running time is twenty-seven minutes.
- Matthew Harper has adapted "The Signalman" as a stage script, which is available at the http://www.lazybeescripts.co.uk/Scripts/script.aspx?iSS=2230 webpage of Lazy Bee Scripts.

PLOT SUMMARY

"The Signalman" is set at a railway tunnel. The narrator, standing atop a steep cutting, shouts "Halloa! Below there!" to a railway signalman below. After he catches the attention of the signalman, the narrator asks whether there is a path he can take to come down to speak to him. Before he receives an answer, a train speeds by. After the train passes, the narrator repeats his query, and the signalman points with his red flag to a path two or three hundred yards down the line. The narrator zigzags down the path to the level of the railroad tracks, observing along the way the damp ooze and earthy smell of the jagged stone walls of the cut. The line stretches off into the distance in one direction, but in the other it enters an imposing tunnel marked by a red light. The two men approach each other, but each seems wary of the other. The signalman seems to think that he has seen the narrator before.

The signalman points out the details of his job, which is not onerous but requires watchfulness. He attends to the train signal, the light, an iron handle (presumably to shunt a train onto another track), and an electric bell. He tells the narrator that during his idle hours, he has taught himself a language and studied fractions, decimals, and algebra. Occasionally, when the train schedule is light, he is able to climb briefly out of the cut to the sunshine above. He takes the narrator into his signal box (a small building where the signaling mechanisms can be kept in a controlled environment and where the signalman can take shelter) and shows him his entry book, a telegraphic instrument with a dial and needles, and a bell. When the narrator observes that he seems highly educated for such a job, the signalman confesses that he had been a student of natural philosophy earlier in life but had wasted his opportunities.

As the signalman goes about his work, he seems troubled and apprehensive, and he twice looks at the alarm bell as though it is ringing, although the narrator hears nothing. In response to the narrator's questions, he confesses that he is troubled and tells the narrator that he will explain why the next night. As the narrator leaves, the signalman cautions him not to call out when he reaches the top of the cutting or when he arrives the next evening. He hints at some supernatural agency behind the narrator's initial calls to him, and he questions the narrator about the words he used when he called out to him.

The narrator arrives at the path at eleven the following evening. The signalman takes him into his box and relates a story involving someone else he has seen (later referred to as a specter) who also shouted, "Halloa! Below there!" The specter was standing by the red light of the tunnel and seemed to be vehemently signaling a warning, but when the signalman ran toward him, he disappeared. The signalman sent an inquiry by telegraph in both directions along the line, but the responses assured him that all was well. The narrator is initially convinced that what the signalman saw was the result of a physical malady, and that what he heard was caused by the wind playing on the telegraph wires. Then, however, the signalman reports that within six hours, an accident occurred on the line, resulting in deaths and injuries of passengers, who were carried out of the tunnel over the spot where the specter had stood. Several months later, a similar incident occurred. The specter appeared near the red light and appeared to be mourning. That day, a train emerged from the tunnel. The signalman saw commotion inside and stopped it, and in one of the compartments, a beautiful girl had died.

The signalman reveals that the specter returned the previous week. Again it was waving its arms in the gesture that said, "For God's sake, clear the way!" The narrator continues to believe that the signalman is hallucinating and questions him about whether he has heard the bell in the signal box. The signalman is convinced that the appearance of the specter presages a dreadful calamity, and he wishes he had enough information to avert it. The narrator resolves to accompany the signalman to a medical practitioner.

The following evening, the narrator returns to the signalman's box. Before he arrives, however, he sees at the mouth of the tunnel a man waving his arm at a small group of other men, presumably railroad officials. When he descends and asks the men what has happened, one answers that the signalman was killed that morning, run down by an engine driven by a man named Tom. As Tom was driving the train through the tunnel, he saw the signalman standing on the tracks, lamp in hand, but he did not have enough time to stop the train. He did, however, shout the spectral words: "Below there! Look out! Look out! For God's sake, clear the way!" In a brief coda, the narrator notes that the engine driver used the very words both that the signalman had heard and repeated and that the narrator himself had conceived for the gesture but had never spoken aloud.

CHARACTERS

Narrator

The unnamed narrator is the gentleman for nowhere who forms the framing device for the set of stories in *Mugby Junction*. Earlier stories in the set provide background information about him. He tells the story of his encounters with a railroad signalman. He describes himself as "a man who had been shut up within narrow limits all his life, and who, being at last set free, had a newly-awakened interest in these great works." He appears to be a highly rational, practical man, for he resists belief in coincidence and attributes the signalman's visions to a medical malady.

Signalman

The signalman is a railroad employee who works near the entrance to a rail tunnel. He is responsible for the safety of the trains passing through, controlling their movements and warning (by telegraph) other signalmen up and down the line of the potential for danger. The narrator calls the unnamed signalman "intelligent, vigilant, painstaking and exact." The signalman on three occasions sees a specter that foretells impending calamities: a train crash, the death of a young woman, and his own death.

Tom

Tom is the name of the railroad engineer who drives the engine that kills the signalman.

THEMES

Technology

During the nineteenth century, the British reading public was adapting itself to new technologies and scientific developments. The steam engine was a relatively recent technological innovation that was being harnessed in a number of industries, including the textile industry. By the middle of the nineteenth century, looms were being powered almost entirely by steam, and the textile industry was one of the main drivers of the Industrial Revolution in Britain. Steam power was used to drive the nation's trains. The British rail system was effectively launched in 1825, and by the time Dickens wrote "The Signalman," rail lines extended the length and breadth of the British Isles. The rise of the rail system made the movement of people and goods more efficient, but in the resulting cultural shift, personal bonds and the rural values promoted by cottage industries were lost to impersonal technology. Many of Dickens's readers approached technologies such as rail travel with trepidation, because—despite the means taken to ensure the safety of the traveling public, including telegraph signals, lights, flags, and bells—accidents happened. The signalman's need to keep these devices at hand suggests that workers were being converted into cogs in industrial machines. Even though signalmen such as the one in Dickens's story were watchful and conscientious, disasters were a fact of life in the new technological age. "The Signalman" taps into that anxiety about technological progress and the potential for both dehumanization and disaster.

Spirits

"The Signalman" depends for its effects on spirits and spiritualism, the belief that spirits, such as those of the dead, can communicate with people. The story's sense of eeriness is developed from the beginning with the signalman's wary reaction to the narrator. The setting of the story, with its darkness and dampness, adds an element of ghostliness. As the signalman begins to unfold his story to the narrator, the reader learns that the signalman has seen a ghostly figure at the entrance to the train tunnel. This figure seems to be warning the signalman of an impending disaster—a disaster that subsequently occurs. Later, the same specter reappears and rather than issuing a warning seems to be mournful. His grief is borne out by the later discovery of the death of a beautiful woman in a train compartment. The story reaches its climax with the third appearance of the specter, which again seems to be warning the signalman of something and uses words that, it turns out, are used by the driver of the engine that kills the signalman.

In Dickens's world, ghosts and apparitions tend not to be threatening or to pose a danger to humans. Rather, ghosts, such as the specter in "The Signalman," often appear desperate and helpless. The specter waves its arms frantically but is unable to avert the impending disaster. It appears to be saddened by the death of the woman in the train compartment but cannot prevent it. This treatment of the specter reinforces the story's technology theme. The futility of its efforts and of the efforts of the signalman suggests the helplessness that can result from reliance on impersonal and dangerous technologies.

Loneliness

A third theme that is closely tied to the other two is loneliness and isolation. The signalman of Dickens's story is completely isolated, connected to others only by means of the telegraph. Furthermore, neither the signalman nor the narrator has a name. Each is an anonymous character caught up in a changing world that can only partially be understood. Each initially wonders whether the other is a ghost. As the story opens, the reader has no idea who the narrator and the signalman are. The narrator's greeting provides no real

TOPICS FOR FURTHER STUDY

- Turn "The Signalman" into a radio play. Try to incorporate sound effects. With a classmate, record your play, then play it for your other classmates, inviting them to comment.
- Conduct research on the history of railroads in Britain. In particular, focus on the cultural impact of the railroads, trying to answer the question: How and to what extent did the development of the rail system alter British society? Present the results of your findings in an oral report.
- Read Amelia B. Edwards's 1881 short story "Was It an Illusion? A Parson's Story," available in *The Collected Supernatural and Weird Fiction of Amelia B. Edwards* (2009). The tale involves a school inspector who spots ghostly figures while traveling on a road in northern England. Write an essay explaining how this story and "The Signalman" both create tension between rationalism and the uncanny. (Edwards was one of the contributors to *Mugby Junction.*)
- Prepare a series of drawings or sketches for an illustrated edition of "The Signalman." Post them on your website and invite your classmates to comment. As an alternative, consider adapting the story as a short graphic novel.
- Investigate the history of spiritualism in the nineteenth century. What did spiritualists believe? Who were the major figures in the movement? What frauds were perpetrated? How did interest in spiritualism make the reading public more interested in ghost stories? Present the results of your findings in an oral report for your classmates.
- Roald Dahl compiled fourteen ghost stories for young adults in *Roald Dahl's Book of Ghost Stories* (1984). Included are well-known classics by Robert Aickman, Edith Wharton, Sheridan Le Fanu, and F. Marion Crawford and tales by less familiar writers such as L. P. Hartley, Rosemary Timperley, Jonas Lie, Mary Treadgold, and A. M. Burrage. Select one of the stories from the collection and explain in a written report themes and other aspects it has in common with "The Signalman."
- Imagine that you are the signalman in Dickens's story. Compose a series of tweets that you believe the signalman might have sent had such technology been available to him. Invite classmates to respond to your tweets.
- Conduct research into the female folk figure called Nuestra Señora de la Santa Muerte, generally referred to more simply as Santa Muerte, Spanish for "Holy Death" or "Sacred Death." This figure is venerated by Hispanic Catholics, primarily in Mexico and the American Southwest. As a personification of death, she is connected with healing, protection, and safe delivery to the afterlife. Compile images and descriptive text, and present the results of your findings to your classmates in a multimedia presentation.

---

information, and the signalman's response is vague and provides no clue to his identity. The systems that are set up for communication are impersonal and metallic: bells, telegraphs and telegraph wires, gauges with dials. The signalman deals with the daily anxiety that a disaster may happen, but he works in complete isolation, having no coworkers to share his anxieties with. The train that rushes by, however, has a forceful presence, a vital energy, in contrast to the powerlessness of the narrator and the signalman. The human actor occupies a barren landscape where he is alone, isolated, hardly real, and unable to tame the monstrous trains that pass through and potentially wreak havoc.

The story's narrator speaks to a railway signal-man, who believes he is being haunted
(©R-Bac Photography / Shutterstock.com)

STYLE

Point of View

"The Signalman" is narrated from a first-person point of view. That is, the story is told by one of the participants rather than by a third-person authorial voice. The narrator in the story is never named, but he plays an important role, serving as a witness to the revelations of the signalman. The reader first encounters the narrator as he appears at the top of the cut where the rail lines are located. He appears to be simply exploring the rail lines in and outside of Mugby Junction. When he spots the signalman below, he is eager to strike up a conversation and, it appears, learn what he can about the operation of the railroads. He also learns that the signalman has had encounters with a specter that foretells disaster. The narrator, however, appears to be a practical, rational man who does not believe in coincidences but does believe in the call of duty, such as the duties imposed on the signalman. He dismisses the notion that the signalman has seen a ghost. Rather, he ascribes the signalman's visions to a physical malady, and he believes that the bells the signalman hears are the result of the wind whistling through the overhead wires. He expresses his intention of accompanying the signalman to a medical practitioner.

In a brief coda to the story after the signalman's death, the narrator comments on the coincidence that the engine driver's warning to the signalman consisted of the same words that the signalman indicated had been haunting him and that the narrator used. The narrator still seems to be resistant to the notion of an otherworldly explanation for the events on the rail line. Earlier in the story, he confesses: "I have speculated since, whether there may have been infection in his mind." The first-person point of view reinforces the story's conflict between the rational and everyday on the one hand and the otherworldly and uncanny on the other.

Suspense

"The Signalman" relies on suspense for much of its effect. Dickens produces this effect in a

COMPARE & CONTRAST

- **1860s:** The rail system in Britain is transforming how the people of England travel and goods are transported, supplanting inefficient horse-drawn vehicles on uncertain roads.

  Today: The British rail system consists of 9,790 miles of tracks; travelers can board trains at any one of more than 2,500 stations.

- **1860s:** British railroads generally use a semaphore system for train signaling, along with various colored lights to signal clear (green), caution (yellow), and danger (red).

  Today: British railroads use cellular telephones, signal post telephones, and radio devices along with a complex system of semaphore signs to communicate information to train crews.

- **1860s:** The Railway Regulation Act of 1840 governs railroad safety and establishes procedures for investigating accidents.

  Today: Various rule books for signaling and other matters are promulgated by Britain's Rail Safety and Standards Board.

- **1860s:** The British rail system is powered by steam engines.

  Today: Plans are under way to increase electrification of the British rail system to 51 percent of the system by 2021.

number of ways. At the beginning of the story, he does not identify the characters by name or by role. The narrator shouts a greeting to a man below, inviting the reader to speculate on the roles of the two men in the story. As the two meet, an eerie, supernatural atmosphere pervades the scene as the signalman appears to wonder whether he is seeing a ghost. Similarly, the narrator begins to think that the signalman, with his "fixed eyes and . . . saturnine face . . . was a spirit, not a man." The suspense builds as the signalman seems reticent about telling his story. In the signal box, he seems to be hearing the railroad warning bell ring, although the narrator hears nothing. The signalman hints at troubles, but he will not say what they are, although he questions the narrator closely about his initial greeting. The reader is almost halfway through the story before learning that what troubles the signalman is his vision of a specter that has foretold a train accident and then the death of a woman. The signalman's sense of foreboding and doom is underlined by his frantic demonstration of the specter's arm gestures and repetition of its words. All of this is prologue to the third appearance of the specter, which has occurred not in the past but in the dramatic present, leaving the reader in suspense about what will happen. When the narrator appears on the scene for the last time, he sees a man gesticulating, momentarily raising for the reader the possibility that the narrator is now seeing the specter. The suspense of the story is brought full circle with Tom, the driver of the engine that kills the signalman, who reports the words he used in trying to warn off the signalman: "Below there! Look out! For God's sake, clear the way!"

HISTORICAL CONTEXT

Industrial Technology in Great Britain

"The Signalman" was written when Great Britain was riding the crest of a wave of industrialization. Beginning in the eighteenth century and continuing well into the nineteenth, the British economy, fueled by advances in science and technology, underwent radical transformations. Perhaps the chief technological development was the steam engine, which allowed machinery to function more rapidly, without having to rely on human (or animal) muscle power. To feed the steam engines, great quantities of coal were needed, leading to expansion of the mining industry—which itself was fueled by steam power. Additionally, industries such as textiles and metalworking were made more efficient by technological progress. These increases in productivity enabled Britain to export its surpluses—everything from glass, guns, and grain to cotton and woolen goods and pins—contributing to the growth of the transportation and maritime industries. By the mid-nineteenth century, Britain was forging its reputation as the workshop of the world.

Industrialization led to changes in the landscape. New towns formed at the centers of industrialization and along transportation routes. As the nation became increasingly urbanized, large numbers of people left the countryside, altering the social fabric of rural society. Rural inns where travelers in horse-drawn carriages stopped for the night were replaced by urban hotels along the rail lines. As the rail system spread, the movement of goods and people became quicker, more efficient, and more reliable. Coastal towns became connected to the rest of the country. New and improved roads, along with new iron bridges, erased physical barriers and eased communication with and transport to smaller towns in the rural shires. The architecture of growing urban centers began to change as new public buildings such as town halls, libraries, and museums were constructed.

Progress came at a price. The extensive use of coal in cities contributed to air and water pollution. Urban centers became overcrowded as people who in earlier generations would have earned their livings as rural laborers relocated in search of factory jobs. People were often apprehensive about the new technologies, considering them mysterious, forbidding, and replete with the potential for accidents. Such was the case with the railroad industry, which was launched in Britain in 1825 with the opening of the first rail line. In 1830 the country suffered its first rail accident. On September 15 of that year, the Duke of Wellington opened the Liverpool and Manchester railroad line. One of the dignitaries in attendance was William Huskisson, a member of Parliament, president of the board of trade, and cabinet minister who strongly backed the construction of the rail line. During the ceremonies, he descended to one of the tracks, where an open door on one of the carriages knocked him under (perhaps against) a moving car, killing him. Despite continuing efforts to make train travel as safe as possible, including the passage of regulatory acts and the implementation of other technologies to improve communication along rail lines, rail disasters such as the Clayton Tunnel crash of 1861 took place. It is in the context of anxiety about new and frightening technologies that Dickens, himself a survivor of an 1865 rail crash, wrote "The Signalman."

The signal-man hears a warning bell ringing, but no one else can hear it (©nik sriwattanakul / Shutterstock.com)

CRITICAL OVERVIEW

Some critics analyze "The Signalman" as a reflection of its historical milieu. Karen M. Odden, for example, in *Victorian Review*, examines the story in light of the effects of public anxiety about railways and rail disasters on literature:

> As historians have shown, the early railway crash was widely understood to be a different kind of accident from those that came before—shocking and overwhelming in its size, speed, and effects. Unlike a farming or carriage accident, it made no distinctions based upon class, gender, occupation, or age; and it could injure hundreds of people at once. Unlike a factory accident, the railway crash brought together the machine with not only the workers who produced the means of transportation but also the consumers. Unlike natural disasters, the blame could often be attributed.

Odden also notes that stories such as "The Signalman" "provided critics fertile ground for Victorian notions of 'shock' (and, later, hysteria and trauma)." She further points out how stories such as "The Signalman" anticipated developments in the understanding of the psychology of trauma:

> In fiction, the railway crash becomes a device that creates gaps in the narratives as well as gaps in the protagonists' memories, and the accidents often cause characters to repeat events unwittingly or unwillingly. In other words, these novels enact at the level of structure some of the very elements that Freud and Breuer later medicalize as attributes of hysteria and trauma.

Ewald Mengel, in an article in *Studies in Short Fiction*, focuses on the way in which the story reflects views regarding the impact of technology on society:

> In "The Signalman," Dickens's fears and apprehensions as to the dehumanizing effects of technological progress on man and the dangers of the Industrial Revolution take the form of images that have the quality and suggestiveness of a nightmare. The story reveals the insufficiency of mathematical logic and a purely scientific outlook on life and asserts the existence of dark forces in the life of man that turn him into a blind tool of fate and resist all attempts at rational explanation.

Regarding the railway, Mengel notes: "Dickens showed himself deeply aware of the changes it caused, and became uneasy when he considered the speed with which the transformation of society was effected and the old rural tranquility of England destroyed." He further remarks that the story embodies attitudes toward forces that control man's destiny:

> The allusions to the fate of the signalman from the beginning create an atmosphere of doom. More particularly, they create the feeling that the life of this man is predetermined by forces beyond his own control.

Other critics have focused their attention on issues surrounding the nature and structure of ghost stories and Dickens's treatment of the supernatural, otherworldly element of the story. In an article in the journal *Criticism*, David Seed first comments on the roles of the signalman and the narrator as they attempt to analyze the nature of the events that have happened. He argues that both, not just the narrator, make the attempt:

> It is facile to attribute the role of analyst purely to the narrator. If anything the signalman shows just as much eagerness to ransack his experience for their significance, and in a way he *does* understand it better than the narrator. The latter stays doggedly with his pathological explanation, whereas the signalman accepts the predictive function of the apparition and asks himself what death is coming next.

Seed also comments on the ambiguity of the story's resolution:

> Rather than giving us a complete resolution, the ending brings into question the interpretation to which the narrator was the most strongly attached, namely the pathological one. He (and the reader with him) has actually experienced the prediction and seen the result.

Seed does, on a different note, praise the story for "the use of everyday materials, . . . its method of understatement, its teasing movement backwards and forwards between particular facts and tentative explanations, the scruple of narrator and apparent rationality of the signalman." He concludes by calling the story a "successful, if tantalizing, appeal to the reader's intelligence."

Deborah A. Thomas, in *Dickens and the Short Story*, notes:

> Historians of the short story have sometimes called attention to "The Signalman" for special, if somewhat biased, praise as the only one of Dickens' stories that, in the words of Henry Canby, "employed the technique of Poe with ease and effectiveness."

Refuting the notion of a debt to Edgar Allan Poe, Thomas, like Seed, discusses the story's resolution: "The question of whether or not a specter from some world beyond the visible one actually appeared to the signalman is left unresolved." She concludes:

> Dickens has skillfully depicted in the central character of "The Signalman" the unsettling, uncanny sensation that the incredible may, after all, be credible and then reproduced this sensation for the narrator and, ultimately, the reader.

Taking a unique perspective, John Daniel Stahl, in the *Dickens Studies Newsletter*, characterizes the story as "a fairy tale set in the context of an industrial wasteland, told with Dickens's exact eye for social reality." Stahl goes on to assert that "several clues . . . add up to the surprising implication that the narrator is actually a revenant." (A revenant is a figure who has returned, usually from the dead, after an absence; the word is the present participle of the French *revenir*, meaning "to return.") Stahl explains:

> Not only does the narrator appear to be the signalman's double, we may suspect that he is the signalman's ghostly alter ego, his own spirit returning across the bounds of time and death, to visit himself before the inevitable fatal accident.

Stahl, praising the story for its economy and sophistication, notes:

> A series of puzzling, obscure signals is presented—the action of the gesticulating figure, the spectre in an attitude of mourning, the ghostly ringing of the bell—creating an interrelated pattern of urgent yet cryptic messages in a subtler and more many-layered story than a fairy tale.

Stahl concludes:

> The story as a whole is symbolic. Its power lies in its ability to present us with a mysterious world much like our ordinary one, yet strangely heightened. . . . The story . . . communicates a sense of the incommunicable; it presents a world in which there are signals that have some awful significance, but the signals are confusing.

In this light, the story is highly ironic, for the signalman is unable, in Stahl's view, to interpret the signals he receives.

CRITICISM

Michael J. O'Neal

O'Neal holds a PhD in English. In the following essay, he examines the use of setting in "The Signalman."

"THE NARRATOR IS BEING INITIATED INTO A DEMONIC REALM INHABITED BY SPIRITS OF THE DEPARTED. IT IS A DANK, UNNATURAL, UNHEALTHY, SUBTERRANEAN WORLD THAT IMPRISONS THE SIGNALMAN AND THAT IS DISCONNECTED FROM THE SUNLIT, RATIONAL, UPPER WORLD OF THE NARRATOR, WHO CAN COME AND GO AS HE PLEASES."

The term *setting* as applied to a narrative primarily refers to its physical backdrop: urban, rural, or wilderness; indoors or outdoors; desert or forest; mountains or flatlands; grand mansion or hovel; major thoroughfares or backroads; leafy suburban neighborhood or inner city; earth or outer space. *Setting* can also refer to less specific and concrete characteristics of the narrative's backdrop. Thus, it may refer to the daily life and occupations of the characters. An example would be the distinction between farm, factory, and office or between military and civilian life. *Setting* can refer to the historical period in which the narrative takes place: Is it set in wartime or peace? In a particular historical era, such as the Renaissance or the Victorian era? In the present or in an imagined future? Additionally, *setting* can refer to the season of the year or, at times, a single day (James Joyce's *Ulysses* and Virginia Woolf's *Mrs. Dalloway* are novels that take place over the course of a single day)—or even a single hour of the day (Kate Chopin's "The Story of an Hour," for example). Finally, *setting* can refer to the social, cultural, religious, psychological, economic, or emotional environment that surrounds the characters and guides, directs, or reflects their actions. Examples include the Protestant Reformation, the Crusades, the Industrial Revolution, the Dark Ages, the Cold War, and the atomic age.

"The Signalman" relies heavily for its effects on setting in its various forms. After the narrator's initial greeting, the first paragraphs of the story call attention to the physical setting, relying on visual, olfactory, and tactile images, including temperature, to create a sinister, foreboding atmosphere. The narrator indicates that he is standing at the top of a deep cutting, looking down at the signalman below in a deep trench. While the signalman is mired in gloom and darkness, the narrator has to

WHAT DO I READ NEXT?

- Dickens made a tradition of publishing special Christmas issues of his periodicals. In the 1859 Christmas issue of *All the Year Round* he published "The Haunted House," a portmanteau that includes stories by five other authors, among them Elizabeth Gaskell and Wilkie Collins. Dickens wrote three of the tales. "The Mortals in the House" and "The Ghost in the Corner Room" frame the set. The first of these, along with "The Ghost in Master B's Room," can be found in Dickens's *Complete Ghost Stories* (1997). The webpage https://ebooks.adelaide.edu.au/d/dickens/charles/d54hh/index.html contains the entire set.
- Dickens's most famous ghost story is "A Christmas Carol," first published in 1843, which features Ebenezer Scrooge, Bob Cratchit, Tiny Tim, and the ghosts of Christmases Past, Present, and Future. The story, widely adapted for film and television, is also available in the *Complete Ghost Stories* (1997).
- One of the contributors to *Mugby Junction* was Amelia B. Edwards, who wrote numerous ghost stories, including "The Four-Fifteen Express." The story can be found in *The Phantom Coach: Collected Ghost Stories* (1999).
- Wilkie Collins, a close friend and colleague of Dickens, was the author of several ghost stories, including "Mrs. Zant and the Ghost" (1885; first published as "The Ghost's Touch"), available in Collins's *Little Novels* (1981).
- For younger readers, *The Dark-Thirty: Southern Tales of the Supernatural* (2001), by Patricia McKissack, is a series of tales inspired by African American history from the slave era to the civil rights era. The "dark-thirty" of the title refers to the half hour before twilight, when the telling of such eerie stories is said to have the most impact.
- *The Oxford Companion to British Railway History: From 1603 to the 1990s* (1999), edited by Jack Simmons and Gordon Biddle, is a six-hundred-entry encyclopedia that provides a comprehensive overview of the British railway system.

---

shade his eyes because of the glare of the sunset. After the narrator asks how to make his way down to the railroad tracks, the signalman points to a path some two or three hundred yards down the line—but not before a train rushes past, announcing its presence first with a vague vibration and then with a violent pulsation. By this time the reader understands that the narrative is taking place at a railroad junction, but the details of the setting's description are ominous and foreboding.

To descend to the tracks, the narrator has to follow a rough zigzag. The sense the reader has is one of isolation: The rail line passes through empty countryside, and the signalman spends his solitary working life down in the deep cutting through which the tracks pass. The narrator observes that "the cutting was extremely deep, and unusually precipitate," suggesting a feeling of vertigo and disorientation. Readers may be reminded of the pits, cellars, and tombs of a story by Edgar Allan Poe ("The Pit and the Pendulum," "The Cask of Amontillado") or the eerie castles of the gothic novelist Ann Radcliffe. The walls of the cutting consist of clammy stone that becomes oozier and wetter as the narrator makes his way down the path. When the narrator reaches the bottom, he finds on either side of the signalman's post "a dripping-wet wall of jagged stone, excluding all view but a strip of sky." Later the narrator refers to the unhealthy damp of the atmosphere surrounding the signal box, and the signalman refers to "the wet stains stealing down the walls and trickling through the arch." The narrator goes on to compare the place to a great dungeon. It has an "earthy, deadly smell; and so much cold wind rushed through it, that it struck chill to me, as if I had left the natural world." The cutting ends at a dark tunnel, which has a "barbarous, depressing and forbidding air." Its red light strikes one as a satanic eye peering out of the darkness, or perhaps like the eye of a dragon that could burst forth at any moment, breathing fire and smoke much in the way that trains do.

The effect of these images is to suggest that the railroad cutting is more than just a physical setting. They imbue the setting with mythic, sinister possibilities. They suggest a lower world, a descent into the Hades of classical mythology. The rail line becomes a modern-day, industrial version of the river Styx, the dividing line between the upper world inhabited by the narrator and the lower underworld inhabited by the ominous-looking signalman, a "dark sallow man, with a dark beard and rather heavy eyebrows." Just as the Styx is one of several rivers that converge at the center of the underworld, so Mugby Junction serves as the convergence of a number of rail lines in a modern technological underworld. Later, the eerie, otherworldly quality of the setting is suggested by images of the aeolian harp, a stringed musical instrument played by the wind and named for the Greek god Aeolus, the god of the wind (although in Homer's *Odyssey* Aeolus is a mortal characterized as the keeper of the winds). Responding to what he calls an imaginary cry heard by the signalman, the narrator says: "Do but listen for a moment to the wind in this unnatural valley while we speak so low, and to the wild harp it makes of the telegraph wires." It seems that the narrator is being initiated into a demonic realm inhabited by spirits of the departed. It is a dank, unnatural, unhealthy, subterranean world that imprisons the signalman and that is disconnected from the sunlit, rational, upper world of the narrator, who can come and go as he pleases.

The setting of "The Signalman" is not solely symbolic, however. The setting also has a literal, historical reality and significance. Here is a description of the signalman's job:

> Had he much to do there? Yes; that was to say, he had enough responsibility to bear; but exactness and watchfulness were what was required of him, and of actual work—manual labour—he had next to none. To change that signal, to trim those lights, and to turn this iron handle now and then, was all he had to do under that head. Regarding those many long and lonely hours of which I seemed to make so much, he could only say that the routine of his life had shaped itself into that form, and he had grown used to it.

The narrator further observes,

> In bright weather, he did choose occasions for getting a little above these lower shadows; but, being at all times liable to be called by his electric bell, and at such times listening for it with redoubled anxiety, the relief was less than I would suppose.

The stark routine of the signalman's job, one that keeps him tethered to bells and dials and the telegraph, seems particularly dismal in light of the fact that in former years he had been a student of natural philosophy (science) and attended lectures. A life that held promise of more stimulating things has been reduced to one of numbing routine.

It would be difficult to overestimate the symbolic significance of the railroads in Britain during the nineteenth century. When Dickens was born in 1812, Britain was largely a rural, agricultural nation, even though transformations had been under way since the previous century, and London had long been a metropolis. Much of the population still lived in bucolic towns and villages in tranquil, rural shires, the kind of places preserved in the Barsetshire novels of Anthony Trollope, most of which appeared in the 1860s. Cottage industries such as weaving and other domestic handicraft trades formed an important part of the British economy. The chief feature of this type of social and economic system was its stability. Workers were vested in their daily activities. They had a place in a social order and performed tasks that they understood, often with families and their community close at hand. Their jobs put them in touch with the natural order and rhythms of things. Life moved at a less hectic pace than it would in future years. The rising and falling of the sun, the phases of the moon, and the passing of the seasons sang the cadences of their lives.

Dickens, however—and he was not alone—saw the technological developments taking place in Britain as an image of alienation. They threatened to create a culture of brute laborers,

After one warning from the bell, there is a terrible accident on the railway (©Lloyd Smith / Shutterstock.com)

superseded by machines, performing numbing, repetitive tasks and disassociated from their work, their families, and their familiar social and natural environments. Moreover, he saw technology as embodied in the railroad as a physical threat. The railroad is a nightmarish emblem of raw, uncontrollable, malevolent power, the kind of power exhibited when a train first passes before the narrator of "The Signalman." In Dickens's 1840s novel *Dombey and Son*, a railroad engine does not simply kill the novel's villain, James Carker, but brutally annihilates him:

> He heard a shout—another—saw the face change from its vindictive passion to a faint sickness and terror—felt the earth tremble—knew in a moment that the rush was come—uttered a shriek—looked round—saw the red eyes, bleared and dim, in the daylight, close upon him—was beaten down, caught up, and whirled away upon a jagged mill, that spun him round and round, and struck him limb from limb, and licked his stream of life up with its fiery heat, and cast his mutilated fragments in the air.

Words such as these could almost be used to describe the signalman and his violent death, a rending of his body that follows on the enervation of his soul.

The brilliance of "The Signalman" is due at least in part to Dickens's masterly linking of the symbolic and the literal, his ability to create a powerful, mythic image of a historical reality that was transforming the society in which he and his readers lived.

Source: Michael J. O'Neal, Critical Essay on "The Signalman," in *Short Stories for Students*, Gale, Cengage Learning, 2017.

Jill L. Matus

In the following excerpt, Matus speculates that "The Signalman" resulted from trauma Dickens experienced.

. . . I turn now to Dickens, who is represented in Carpenter's work, as we saw earlier, as the writer intimately engaged with the imaginative reconstruction of the self through memory, and who also was fascinated by mesmerism over a long period and in a variety of ways. Not only was Dickens a close friend for many years of Dr. John Elliotson, the great pioneer of mesmerism in England, and witness to a large number of displays of animal magnetism, he was himself a practicing mesmerist. Fittingly, he took the role of the Doctor in Elizabeth Inchbald's eighteenth-century farce, *Animal Magnetism* (1788), a play that formed a double bill with *The Frozen Deep* (1857) and was performed in private theatricals (Winter 148). According to Fred Kaplan, Dickens, by the time he went on his Italian trip in 1844, was able to magnetize a range of subjects and was primed to develop an intense relationship with Augusta de la Rue, helping to relieve her "convulsions, distortions of the limbs, aching headaches, insomnia, and a plague of neurasthenic symptoms" through frequent mesmeric therapeutics (Kaplan 77). He was in fact practicing a form of psychotherapy, and working on the assumption that her altered state revealed aspects of personality and psyche that were hidden from her ordinary consciousness. Dickens relied on techniques such as "sleep-waking" and mesmeric trance (77). Through questions to his mesmerized patient, he formulated theories of what was causing her ailments and attempted to battle the dominating phantoms that surfaced when she was in a state of altered consciousness. Though Dickens never abandoned his belief in an independent fluid as the physical basis of magnetism, it was clearly the relation between conscious and unconscious selves that fascinated him about the magnetized state. Dickens seemed to understand that the mesmerized state offered the prospect of finding out what it is we know, but do not know that we know. What later trauma theory would propose was that the traumatized subject, though not somnambulist or mesmerized, was in a state akin to these "altered states." Shock or fright could produce the effect of making memory inaccessible; trance, nightmare, or flashback could return the victim to the unprocessed and terrible knowledge of the traumatic event. Although such propositions were not part of the discourse of nervous shock at the time Dickens suffered his accident, they are nevertheless the stuff of "The Signalman." I want to suggest, then, that because Dickens was sympathetic to the possibility of unconscious knowledge, and because he was adept at manipulating the literary possibilities within the genre of the ghost story, in this story he is able to articulate more about the relation of trauma and memory than was available to him in the current discourse on nervous shock. In so doing, he powerfully anticipates the formulations of Freud and later trauma theory.

> "IN 'THE SIGNALMAN,' DICKENS EXPRESSES THE INTERNAL DISLOCATIONS ASSOCIATED WITH THE EXTERNAL ACCIDENT."

The genre of the ghost story and trauma narrative have much in common, since to be traumatized is arguably to be haunted, to be living a ghost story: it is "to be possessed by an image or event" (Caruth, *Trauma* 5). It may then seem tautological to say that Dickens's story of uncanny possession is a story of trauma. But even though Dickens's ghost stories frequently objectify states of mind, not all ghost stories are expressive primarily of trauma—*A Christmas Carol* (1843), for example, is a notable exception. In ghost stories, as in trauma, the sanctity of ordered time is violated as the past intrudes on the present. In its depiction of both the signalman's distress and the narrator's responses, this story dwells on powerlessness, heightened vigilance and a sense of impending doom, uncanny reenactment, and terror at the relived intrusion. These are all legitimate aspects of a tale of horror; they are also all characteristics of trauma. Just as Augusta de la Rue's "phantoms" emerged in the mesmerized state, so in the ghost story Dickens could give play to the phantoms or specters that intruded as hallucinations to demand that the possessed subject revisit areas of experience not fully assimilated. The ghost story was a way of probing unusual psychological states. As Dickens wrote to Elizabeth Gaskell in 1851, ghost stories were illustrative of "particular states of mind and processes of the imagination" (qtd. in Schlicke 249). The possibilities in the ghost story allow Dickens in "The Signalman" to confront the disjunction in subjectivity that trauma occasions as he dramatizes the emphatic gap between knowledge and cognition, signing and meaning, the shocking external occurrence and its internal assimilation and representation. The story is Dickens's way of pondering that fateful and fatal gap in the tracks at Staplehurst, a creative way of articulating his personal experience of railway shock that seems, from the vantage point of the present, uncannily prescient of the direction and emphasis that trauma studies would take in the next century.

Perhaps the most compelling aspect of trauma to which the story gives voice is the feeling of powerlessness in the survivor, who may not recall the traumatic event but has an overwhelming sense of impending and unavoidable doom. In the story, the narrator one evening passes a signalman's remote box, hails the signalman, and shows that he wishes to descend to the box and talk to him. The signalman tells the narrator of a "spectre" who has been haunting him. Indeed, he takes the narrator initially to be an apparition or ghost, the very same as the one that has appeared to him on the line near his signal box a number of times. On one occasion, the "spectre" appeared before a terrible collision; then again before the death of a young lady on the train. The signalman imagines that the apparition's reappearance precedes a further tragic event. That turns out to be the signalman's own death. Dickens's story focuses obsessively on the signalman's anguish at receiving a warning in time, but finding it impossible to heed because he does not know about what exactly he is being warned.

With some justification the story could be read as a fantasy of revenge against signalmen, though in the Staplehurst disaster, strictly speaking, it was not the signalman who blundered. The foreman on the job miscalculated the time of the train's arrival; the flagman was too close to give adequate warning of the train's approach. In the story, the signalman is too close to the train and does not or cannot heed the warning as the engine bears down on him. Ironically, the signalman lives in a state of heightened vigilance, yet dies because he is unable to read the precise import of the warning; he is powerless to prevent his own death on the tracks. But there is also the sense that the signalman does not want to prevent his death. In this way, he may be seen as exemplifying the death drive that Freud associates with traumatic reenactment: he does not heed the whistle and literally allows death to overtake him as the train comes upon him from behind and cuts him down. On the one hand, Freud saw traumatic reenactment as the life-affirming attempt to master the stimulus retrospectively through repetition; on the other, he later came to see the daemonic content of reenactment as evidence of the death instinct. If the signalman in some sense exemplifies the death instinct, the story as a whole may be seen as a traumatic reenactment: Dickens returns imaginatively to the site of the railway accident in order to master a stimulus that resists mastery.

Dickens's story also apprehends the repetitive cycle of trauma. Based structurally on the principle of repetition, "The Signalman" reveals the hallmark of trauma as unbidden repetition and return. In Dickens's story the trauma repeats and accumulates. Not only is the signalman compelled to witness a terrible train disaster, he is tantalized through the "spectre's" visitations by an impossible clairvoyance. The trauma compounds as the signalman is twice forewarned but is both times unable to avert death and disaster. After the first terrible accident on the line, the signalman thinks he has recovered from witnessing the carnage: "Six or seven months passed, and I had recovered from the surprise and shock." At that point, the specter appears to him again and the next calamity occurs: "I heard terrible screams and cries. A beautiful young lady had died instantaneously in one of the compartments and was brought in here, and laid down on this floor between us." Now the specter has appeared again, signaling to him some further calamity about to occur on the line, and prompting, the signalman laments, "this cruel haunting of him." Haunted not only by the past, but by a past that seems to project itself into the future, the signalman is subjected to relentless repetition and can avail himself of neither hindsight nor foresight.

As it is understood today, trauma is the inability to know the past as past—it is therefore a "disease of time" in which the events of the past continually obtrude on the present in the form of flashbacks and hallucinations (Young 7). Traumatic memory is the return that does not recognize itself as a return. Like the train disaster that is literally a disruption of linearity, the narrative of "The Signalman" disrupts linear sequence. In part, this sense arises from the clairvoyant specter, whose gestures enact and predict each of three train disasters before they occur. The sense of disturbed linearity or chronology arises also from the fact that the narrator seems to be taking part in something that has already happened. That is, the narrative is itself part of some uncanny repetition. The fact that the narrator uses the words, "For God's sake, clear the way," themselves repeated many times in the course of the story, could suggest that the narrator has just repeated his part in the replay of a past he "knows" but does not know he knows.

In support of this line of thinking, the narrator from the outset seems inexplicably drawn to approach the signalman, all the odder because initially he says he is not someone given to starting up conversations. Understandably the signalman imagines that the narrator is himself a further spectral illusion, especially since the narrator hails him with the exact words that the specter has already used. After a time the signalman seems reassured that the rational, skeptical narrator is not a ghost, and confides his story to him. By persistently dismissing as "imagination" what the signalman says he has seen, by construing recurrence as coincidence, by remaining stubbornly unbelieving, the narrator refuses to witness the signalman's hallucination or spectral illusion. He refuses, in effect, to witness the trauma. But it is arguably inscribed upon him nonetheless, and he is now (as narrator) participating in the repetition by telling the story of it. When the narrator arrives at the tracks for the third time, he is struck with a "nameless horror" because he sees the "appearance of a man" in the tunnel and clearly thinks he is seeing a ghost. The horror that oppresses him passes when he sees that the figure is a real man. Horror gives way to fear that something is wrong. He then learns of the signalman's death. All would appear to be resolved for the rational narrator, except for the fact that the words the engine driver called out were the very ones in the narrator's thoughts. Despite the matter-of-factness of the coda, it is clear that the narrator too will be haunted by the words, "For God's sake, clear the way."

It is this widening implication and involvement that warns the reader against focusing only on the signalman and seeing him as a pathological case. Graeme Tytler, for example, has diagnosed the signalman as suffering from monomania—a clinical condition in which the patient is obsessed by one dominating idea. A man with a one-track mind, the signalman is undeniably fixated. But he could equally well be diagnosed as suffering from Abercrombie's spectral illusion or Wigan's split self. John Stahl, meanwhile, has seen in the story a critique of industrialization in Dickens's representation of the alienated labor of the signalman and the stress his job entails. But rather than pathologizing the signalman as a "case of partial insanity" or substituting an alternate diagnosis stemming from stress in the workplace, I want to emphasize how the narrator and reader are drawn into the ongoing trauma, and the way the entire narrative is shaped by and expressive of the logic of trauma.

If the specter can be seen as an articulation of the signalman's traumatized consciousness, the narrator shares characteristics of the signalman that suggest he is not just a detached interlocutor, auditor, or reporter. The signalman thinks initially that the narrator is a specter; the narrator has a "monstrous thought" that the signalman is a spirit. Each finds himself in a position that makes him feel compelled to act and assume responsibility for the general safety of those on the line. When the signalman sees the apparition for a third time, he is (literally) beside himself to interpret the warning and forestall the disaster. But he cannot. Similarly, the narrator feels himself compelled to act: "But what ran most in my thoughts was the consideration how ought I to act, having become the recipient of this disclosure." The narrator is less worried about the uninterpretable spectral warnings than he is about the mental stability of the signalman and his job performance under present stress. He resolves to try to calm the signalman as much as possible and to return the next morning to visit with him the "wisest medical practitioner [. . .] and to take his opinion." He is also too late. The specter appears to the signalman on three occasions; the narrator descends to the signalman's box three times; the words the narrator uses are the words that the ghost has used and the train driver will use; the gesture that the signalman describes is given words by the narrator but, significantly, he does not speak these words—"For God's sake, clear the way"—before the engine driver tells the narrator that those are in fact the words he used. The narrator, the signalman, the specter, and the engine driver are all bound together in a series of overlapping occurrences and repeated occurrences and expressions, in a history that seems to have begun before the narration begins and will continue after it ends.

Trauma vexes the boundaries between outside and inside; recent theorists have remarked that trauma is a situation in which the outside goes inside without mediation (see Caruth, *Unclaimed Experience* 59). In "The Signalman," Dickens expresses the internal dislocations associated with the external accident. Measuring the distance between Dickens's article "Need Railway Travellers Be Smashed?" and his story "The Signalman" we see—genre and overt intention notwithstanding—a shift in emphasis in Dickens's growing apprehension of railway disaster. This shift in Dickens is very much in line with what railway historian Ralph Harrington has suggested about perceptions of railway disaster in the period. Whereas the railway was associated initially with the external destruction of landscape in its construction and of people in the wake of its accidents, it came later to provoke anxieties about internal disruption. Harrington also notes that the later part of the nineteenth century saw a change in the way people viewed accidents. Rather than private (individualized) happenings they became public ones, affecting or concerning the whole of society (1–2). The paradox of railway shock, then, for the Victorians, was that what seemed insignificant and hidden—delayed nervous shock without physical injury—was nevertheless public in its significance. This paradox is articulated in "The Signalman," where, although the emphasis is on the internal disruption and fragmentation of trauma, there is undeniably a public dimension to the experience, both the signalman's sense of being at once responsible yet powerless, and in the communication or transmission of the trauma to the narrator.

As the editor of widely read journals, and in his novels and stories, Dickens espoused many public causes, championing the individual plight and exposing the public responsibility for what may have appeared to be merely personal or private hardship. Dickens, it is fair to say, is preeminently the Victorian writer who claims the public dimension of private trauma. No stranger to traumatic experience before the railway accident, as his continual, fictive reenactments of abandonment and childhood abuse attest, Dickens was perhaps brought through the Staplehurst accident to a sharper intimation of the nature of trauma than ever before. He lost his voice in that accident to find it later, as I have argued, in articulating in this story of ghostly clairvoyance and hindsight the characteristics of trauma barely broached in the discourse of nervous shock during the 1860s.

Source: Jill L. Matus, "Trauma, Memory, and Railway Disaster: The Dickensian Connection," in *Victorian Studies*, Vol. 43, No. 3, Spring 2001, p. 413.

SOURCES

Canby, Henry Seidel, *The Short Story in English*, Henry Holt, 1909, p. 270.

"Charles Dickens and the Staplehurst Crash," in *Rail Album*, March 2004, http://www.railalbum.co.uk/articles/charles-dickens.htm (accessed June 27, 2016).

Cody, David, "Dickens: A Brief Biography," Victorian Web, http://www.victorianweb.org/authors/dickens/dickensbio1.html (accessed October 25, 2016).

Dickens, Charles, *Dombey and Son*, Oxford University Press, 1950, p. 779.

———, "The Signalman," in *Complete Ghost Stories*, Wordsworth, 1997, pp. 260–71.

"Dickens, Charles," in *Merriam-Webster's Encyclopedia of Literature*, Merriam-Webster, 1995, pp. 324–25.

"Display Report," UK Office of Rail and Road website, http://dataportal.orr.gov.uk/displayreport/report/html/c35e0c28-324f-4168-81b9-be197963f251 (accessed July 8, 2016).

"11% of the UK Rail Network to Be Electrified under Network Rail's £4bn National Electrification Programme," Rail.co.uk, March 10, 2014, http://www.rail.co.uk/rail-news/2014/uk-rail-network-to-be-electified-under-network-rail-programme (accessed July 8, 2016).

"First Railway Accident: A Personal Narrative of the Tragic Event," in *Liverpool Mercury*, 1913, http://www.old-merseytimes.co.uk/huskisson.html (accessed July 13, 2016).

Garber, Megan, "Serial Thriller," in *Atlantic*, March 2013, http://www.theatlantic.com/magazine/archive/2013/03/serial-thriller/309235 (accessed July 13, 2016).

Hudson, Pat, "The Workshop of the World," BBC website, March 29, 2011, http://www.bbc.co.uk/history/british/victorians/workshop_of_the_world_01.shtml (accessed July 12, 2016).

Manolopoulou, Artemis, "The Industrial Revolution and the Changing Face of Britain," British Museum website, https://www.britishmuseum.org/research/publications/online_research_catalogues/paper_money/paper_money_of_england__wales/the_industrial_revolution.aspx (accessed July 8, 2016).

Mengel, Ewald, "The Structure and Meaning of Dickens's 'The Signalman,'" in *Studies in Short Fiction*, Vol. 20, No. 4, Fall 1983, pp. 271–80.

Odden, Karen M., "25 August 1861: The Clayton Tunnel Rail Crash, the Medical Profession, and the Sensation Novel," in *Victorian Review*, Vol. 40, No. 2, Fall 2014, pp. 30–34.

Regulation of Railways Act, August 10, 1840, Railways Archive, http://www.railwaysarchive.co.uk/docsummary.php?docID=57 (accessed July 7, 2016).

Rolinson, Dave, "Signalman, The (1976)," BFI Screenonline, http://www.screenonline.org.uk/tv/id/141623/index.html (accessed June 27, 2016).

Seed, David, "Mystery in Everyday Things: Charles Dickens' 'Signalman,'" in *Criticism*, Vol. 23, No. 1, Winter 1981, pp. 42–57.

Stahl, John Daniel, "The Source and Significance of the Revenant in Dickens's 'The Signal-man,'" in *Dickens Studies Newsletter*, 1980, pp. 98–101.

"Standards and the Rail Industry," UK Rail Safety and Standards Board website, http://www.rssb.co.uk/standards-and-the-rail-industry (accessed July 7, 2016).

Thomas, Deborah A., *Dickens and the Short Story*, University of Pennsylvania Press, 1982, pp. 136–38.

FURTHER READING

Cox, Michael, and R. A. Gilbert, eds., *The Oxford Book of Victorian Ghost Stories*, Oxford University Press, 2003.

> The volume collects thirty-five ghost stories published in Victorian England from 1850 to 1910. Among the authors represented are Dickens, Wilkie Collins, Sheridan Le Fanu, Henry James, Robert Louis Stevenson, and Arthur Conan Doyle. The volume highlights the contribution of women to the genre with selections from Elizabeth Gaskell, Rhoda Broughton, and Charlotte Riddell. A helpful feature for researchers is the volume's "Select Chronological Conspectus of Ghost Stories, 1840–1910," a listing of all the collections of ghost stories or fiction collections that included ghost stories during those years.

Dickens, Charles, *Charles Dickens: The Complete Short Stories*, Rutilus Classics, 2016.

> This volume includes all sixty-two of the short stories Dickens published. It is the first in the publisher's series titled Complete British Short Stories and is available only for Amazon Kindle.

Griffin, Emma, *A Short History of the British Industrial Revolution*, Palgrave Macmillan, 2010.

> This volume provides a succinct account of the Industrial Revolution in Great Britain, during which the railway system depicted in "The Signalman" was developed. The book emphasizes steam power as the engine of economic growth.

Kaplan, Fred, *Dickens: A Biography*, Johns Hopkins University Press, 1998.

> Named as a notable book of the year by the *New York Times*, Kaplan's biography of Dickens was first published in 1988. It explores some of the contradictions and conflicts in Dickens's personality and describes his successful career, expansive circle of friends, and crumbling marriage.

Paterson, Michael, *Voices from Dickens' London*, 2nd ed., David & Charles, 2007.

> This work paints a portrait of nineteenth-century London. It reproduces first-person accounts by residents and visitors as well as newspaper articles and passages from Dickens's writing. The book provides insights into the difficulties faced by people living in this immense city at a time when it was growing and changing dramatically.

SUGGESTED SEARCH TERMS

British railroad history

Charles Dickens

Clayton Tunnel AND railroad accident

Dickens AND Christmas Carol

Dickens AND All the Year Round

Dickens AND Mugby Junction

Dickens AND The Signalman

Industrial Revolution AND England

Staplehurst AND railroad accident

Victorian ghost stories

The Streak

WALTER DEAN MYERS

2000

Included in *145th Street: Short Stories*, a collection by renowned young-adult author Walter Dean Myers, is the story "The Streak," about luck in the life of a high-school basketball player. By the end of his life and career—he died in 2014—Myers had established himself as the reigning patriarch of young-adult literature written about, and in some ways specifically for, African Americans. Having been raised in Harlem, where he ended up in fights in elementary school when other children mocked his manner of speech, Myers was familiar with the urban conditions experienced by disproportionate numbers of African Americans and other minorities, and moreover the lives they lived under those conditions. As a writing career came into view, Myers realized that both the African American and the broader American communities would benefit from more literature featuring the true-to-life inner-city protagonists that he was capable of representing.

For all Myers's laurels for bringing race to the forefront of young-adult literary conversations, "The Streak" is essentially a universal tale of life and chance. It begins with the aftermath of a basketball game in which the narrator, Jamie Farrell, plays a lamentable role. As the story proceeds, his friend Froggy starts to question his luck, and soon Jamie does as well—and with the upcoming junior dance in mind, he can only hope that good fortune is on the horizon.

Walter Dean Myers (©New York Daily News Archive / Getty Images)

AUTHOR BIOGRAPHY

Myers was born Walter Milton Myers on August 12, 1937, in Martinsburg, West Virginia, to George and Mary Green Myers. The family was large and poor, and tragically, when Walter was three, his mother died giving birth to her eighth child. Unable to raise the family on his own, George allowed Herbert and Florence Dean to become foster parents to Myers and two of his sisters; the children were taken to live with the Deans in Harlem. Herbert Dean proved so mesmerizing a storyteller that Myers would often fear meeting the fictional monsters and creatures in their apartment. Florence read aloud to him from *True Romance* magazine, and by age five, he could read the newspaper to her. But in school, Myers was ostracized because of his imperfect speech; he often ended up in fights and for escape turned to reading, especially comic books. After a fight in fifth grade, his teacher, Mrs. Conway, caught him reading a comic book and tore it up. Later, to make it up to him, she brought him a pile of her own books to start reading. In turn, to make the regular classroom task of reading aloud easier, she permitted him to write his own stories and poems (and exclude unpronounceable words) and read those aloud.

Myers attended Stuyvesant High School in downtown Manhattan, one of New York City's best public schools. However, he was disheartened by racism there, and though teachers tried to encourage his writing—he even won prizes in contests—he knew his parents would be unable to afford college. He dropped out at sixteen. Inspired by the British poet Rupert Brooke, Myers joined the US Army; three years later, he withdrew. In 1957, he rejoined his parents at their new home in Morristown, New Jersey, and worked various odd jobs before moving back to New York City. There he met and married his first wife and had two children, though the marriage soon ended.

Myers's dedication to becoming a writer had grown strong, and through the 1960s, he published stories and poems in various magazines, including *Black World* and *Negro Digest*. In 1968, a contest inspired him to try his hand at a children's book. His effort, *Where Does the Day Go?*, won the contest and was published in 1969. The following year, he was hired by the Bobbs-Merrill Publishing Company, which felt a need for an African American editor, allowing him an ideal position from which to further his career. He officially changed his name to Walter Dean Myers—a tribute to his foster parents, the Deans—in publishing *Fly, Jimmy, Fly!* (1974). Meanwhile, he married his second wife, Constance, in 1973, and she soon gave birth to his son and later literary collaborator, Christopher.

When another editor was impressed by what was then a short story, Myers spontaneously charted out what would become his first young-adult novel, *Fast Sam, Cool Clyde, and Stuff* (1975). In the ensuing decades, Myers penned one highly praised title after another, primarily for young adults, touching upon virtually every literary genre there is. Returning to school, he finally gained a bachelor of arts from Empire State College in 1984. He received the Coretta Scott King Award for *The Young Landlords* (1980), *Motown and Didi* (1985), *Fallen Angels* (1989), *Now Is Your Time! The African-American Struggle for Freedom* (1992), and *Slam* (1996). His novel *Monster* (1999), with graphic art by his son Christopher, won the American Library Association's inaugural Michael L. Printz Award for young-adult literature. *145th Street: Short Stories* was published in 2000. In all, Myers wrote over fifty titles. He died of natural causes on July 1, 2014, in New York City.

PLOT SUMMARY

"The Streak" opens with narrator Jamie Farrell expressing that the reader should remember his name in case he is famous someday. His friend Froggy Williams unfortunately knows nothing about basketball. In conversation, Jamie relates how earlier that evening he missed the easy layup that should have won the game for his high-school team. To make matters worse, he dropped his sports drink in the locker room, and the glass bottle shattered, an inconvenience for everyone. Froggy expresses a modicum of sympathy. Jamie heads home and that night has a bad dream about a shattering basketball.

Before biology, Jamie notices a poster for the junior dance, and—after a passing student chides him for blowing that layup—he muses aloud about asking a girl named Celia Evora, though Froggy says Jamie has no chance with her. At the end of biology class, Jamie is about to submit his major slide project when he drops it on the floor and wrecks it. Mr. Willis gives him a zero. In the cafeteria, Froggy tells Jamie he might be a "streaker"—someone who goes on streaks with good and bad luck. Jamie scoffs at the idea of luck. As they leave, Jamie takes Froggy's milk carton and tosses it in the garbage, but it bounces off of the trash can into the lap of Maurice DuPre. Jamie runs. He later hears that Maurice was chasing Froggy around the gym.

On the way home from school, Jamie stops at a burger joint and starts eating the potato wedges he ordered—until he realizes he has no money. He pretends they taste strange, but the manager sees through his deception, and Jamie gets a smack on the head as he dashes out. Shutting himself in his room at home, he hesitates to answer when the phone rings. When he finally decides to answer after all, he bangs his ankle on a dumbbell. He sees stars. On the phone is Mr. Bradley, who reports that Jamie badly failed his English test. His leg is bleeding; he ices it and calls Froggy, who reassures him that the streak will eventually end, probably with some stroke of good luck.

Jamie's sister, Ellen, gets home and starts giving him a hard time. After she mocks him with a fresh egg, he disgustedly tosses it back in her direction—and realizes moments later that it landed back in the carton on the counter perfectly, unbroken. He marvels over the miracle to Ellen, who is skeptical of his sanity. Jamie calls Froggy again, and they determine that because the unlucky streak consisted of seven bad things, now his lucky streak will feature seven good things—with six left, after the egg landing. Jamie expresses his intention to immediately ask Celia to the dance. He envisions the scene playing out in the hall at school.

The next day in math class, Mr. Galicki reports that Jamie excelled on his parallelogram quiz. Froggy points out that he has five lucky things left. Jamie starts getting nervous. As he feeds one quarter into the cafeteria soda machine, he is told by his teammate Tommy Smalls that the machine is out of order—but Jamie immediately receives a soda anyway. He mentally elaborates his plan for asking Celia to the dance: to buy her some roses and go to her house. He calls first, only to be told by Mrs. Evora that Celia is in the hospital for a flower allergy treatment; Jamie guesses, correctly, that roses are the problem. Mrs. Evora affirms that she will tell Celia about Jamie's phone call.

Taking Mrs. Evora's revelation of the rose allergy as another stroke of luck, Jamie counts three remaining. Meanwhile, he is running low on money. That evening, his father enters his room to give him a lecture about avoiding drugs; he concludes by giving Jamie one hundred dollars to treat himself as he pleases, so as not to feel like he is deprived of good things in life. More worried than ever that the streak is running out, Jamie calls Froggy, who warns him that his luck is out of control. Trying to avoid any activity, Jamie starts making up a list of the lucky things so far. However, worrying that this will bring about more luck, he crumples the paper and makes an improbable cross-room shot toward the wastebasket. He fears it will go in, so he dives over and tries to block it. Just then Ellen opens the door, and the paper ricochets several times and goes into the wastebasket. Jamie is beside himself. He has one stroke of luck left.

At the game the following day, Jamie tells his coach he cannot play on his injured ankle, to avoid being lucky in a game in which his school, Ralph Bunche, is not even expected to be competitive. However, the team does well and is down by just one point late in the game, when another guy on their team fouls out; Jamie has to play or they will be short a man. As the clock ticks down, he gets the ball and tries to make a floating pass toward Tommy at the hoop, but the buzzer sounds, and the ball goes in; Ralph Bunche wins. Jamie basks in the glory but laments that his streak has been used up.

The next day, Jamie sees Celia in the hall but presumes that his luck has run out. He is certain she will surely decline an invitation to the dance, but she starts chatting and soon asks him to the dance. His affirmative response leaves her delighted but unsurprised, because this has been her lucky week. Celia reports that her mom was so impressed by Jamie's concern for her allergy that she is letting her go to the dance, but only with him. She asks him to pick her up early. After she leaves, Froggy finds Jamie stunned in the hallway, and Jamie declares that "the whole world is on a streak." Froggy doubts his comprehension of the term, but Jamie cares not.

CHARACTERS

Mr. Bradley

The English teacher, Mr. Bradley, calls Jamie at home to report that his recent failure has put his course grade in jeopardy.

Coach

Jamie's basketball coach does not pressure him to play on his injured ankle until the team absolutely needs him.

Maurice DuPre

Maurice is the school thug who plays his part in the unlucky streak by getting milk poured on his lap and trying to get revenge on Jamie—or at least on somebody, perhaps Froggy.

Celia Evora

The girl of Jamie's dreams is a shapely Dominicana with a beautiful smile. After getting wrapped up in his own lucky streak—which ends before he can take full advantage of it—Jamie is pleasantly surprised to learn that Celia has been nursing a lucky streak herself, culminating in her asking him, in a reversal of prescribed gender roles, to the dance. Celia clearly respects her mother's wishes about whom she spends her time with.

Mrs. Evora

Celia's mother mistakenly believes that Jamie called specifically to ask about her allergy, which proves a boon to Jamie's mission of taking Celia to the dance. In light of how considerate and gentlemanly he proved himself, Mrs. Evora will allow only Jamie to take Celia.

Ellen Farrell

Ellen, Jamie's twelve-year-old sister, seems to relish getting her older brother riled up. She finds his superstitiously motivated behavior rather bizarre.

Jamie Farrell

Jamie is both the narrator and the central protagonist of his story about an unlucky streak that leads into a lucky one. Jamie is a high-school junior and plays on the school basketball team. He seems to favor his best friend, Froggy, in part for the wisdom Froggy shares and in part for the sense of superiority he gets by virtue of Froggy's confusion about sports and other things. Jamie may be a little self-centered—he does not seem to mind that Froggy was getting chased around the school by a large and angry student because of his own milk-spilling mistake—but of course, he is telling a naturally self-centered story, so one cannot draw too many conclusions based on where his narrative interests lie. Jamie is intent on, and succeeds in, making clear every step along the way in his long streak of bad and then good luck, with an almost scientific interest in all that took place.

Mr. Farrell

Rather comically, Mr. Farrell steps in to give Jamie a drug lecture straight out of a public-service television commercial, then provides Jamie with one hundred dollars just when he has started worrying about funds for the dance.

Mr. Galicki

Mr. Galicki, Jamie's math teacher, tells the class that Jamie excelled on his pop quiz.

Jerry

In the story's second game, Jerry's in-bounds pass is deflected to Jamie.

Ramona Rodriguez

Ramona is the friend who gave Celia's phone number to Jamie.

Tommy Smalls

Tommy is the one who passes the ball to Jamie under the hoop in the first game. He is also the one Jamie tries to pass the ball to under the hoop in the second game.

Froggy Williams

Froggy, a member of the school band, is more intellectual, less athletic, and perhaps less socially attuned than his best friend, Jamie, but the two have an excellent rapport. Jamie typically plays it cool, and Froggy follows his lead, but when Jamie gets overheated about things, Froggy uses rational explanations to help his friend wrap his mind around his situation. Froggy does not hesitate to speak the truth to Jamie, or at least what he perceives to be the truth, such as regarding his chances of bringing Celia to the dance.

Mr. Willis

Mr. Willis is Jamie's biology teacher. Whether in view of past disappointments (which seems likely) or for some other reason, Mr. Willis refuses to believe that Jamie accidentally destroyed his crucial slide project. Still, a zero grade seems harsh, encouraging Jamie to believe Froggy's theory about bad luck.

THEMES

Failure

Although it proves to be concerned primarily with the idea of luck, the narrative in "The Streak" is set up through Jamie's concern over a series of debilitating failures. The first of these is his missing the layup that should have won the basketball game for his team. Some readers may see Jamie's failure much the way Froggy seems to see it: so, he missed a shot; people miss shots in basketball all the time. However, the rigor of a sports team leads to the expectation that, with practice, there are certain basic aspects of a game that one should be able to do without failing or with an extremely low rate of failure. A football receiver should catch a pass that hits him in the numbers; a baseball player should catch a fly ball hit right at him; and a basketball player should make an open layup.

As they say, practice makes perfect, but as anyone who plays sports knows, sometimes one fails to make a routine play and can offer no explanation. Perhaps there is an obvious cause: maybe a defender bumped the receiver's elbow; maybe the fly ball was lost in the sun; maybe the basketball player failed to jump as high as expected because his legs were tired. Or sometimes there really is no explanation for why a player could make one hundred layups without missing in practice but fail when it matters the most—and yet of course, that is where the explanation must lie: the pressure of performance, when things matter most, with people watching, can introduce a layer of self-consciousness that disrupts one's ability to focus, meaning the littlest variables or even just a slip of the mind can throw a person off. All this is to say that oftentimes, failure simply happens, whether owing to chance, fate, karma, or a butterfly flapping its wings in China. Jamie also has academic failures, on tests; apparent moral failures, like helping himself to food before being sure he can pay for it; and what appear to be mere accidents, though perhaps he was insufficiently careful with the science project.

TOPICS FOR FURTHER STUDY

- Read the Major Jackson poem "Urban Renewal XVIII," which is oriented toward young adults and was published in Jackson's verse collection *Hoops* (2006); the poem can also be found on the Poetry Foundation website. Imagine and record a dialogue between Jackson's narrator and Jamie Farrell, taking place in whatever medium you choose—such as online forum, e-mail, actual letters, conversation at a coffee shop, video chat, or something more surreal (like one's spirit visiting the other at a key point in time). Present the dialogue to your class.
- In terms of narration, Jamie's cool, masculine, elliptical style is in certain ways reminiscent of that of Nobel Prize winner Ernest Hemingway. Choose a suitable story by Hemingway—those featuring protagonist Nick Adams, such as "The Three-Day Blow," would be good choices—and write a paper in which you compare Hemingway's and Myers's stories with regard to concision, masculinity, emotionality, and compassion.
- Read the biblical book of Job, in whatever version appeals to you most (such as with regard to archaic versus modern language), and consider Job's situation alongside Jamie Farrell's. Then write an essay in which you consider such points of comparison and contrast as the degree of seriousness, the role of friendship, the importance of belief, and the lesson implicitly learned by the reader (whether the author intended the lesson or not).
- Choose any one country or culture and research cultural conceptions with regard to luck, chance, fate, and so forth. In many instances, such conceptions will be founded in religion and may involve rituals not unlike those in which superstitious athletes engage. Give examples of such rituals where possible. Especially interesting choices might be India, China, Persia, and Egypt. Relate your findings in the form of a multimedia presentation, and share your project with your class.

But the failures that seem most important to Jamie are the ones that affect his community.

Community

From an all-encompassing perspective, the biggest problem with the missed layup is not that Jamie's practice has not yet made him perfect, nor that his team lost the game (though that part surely stings), but that the failure disappoints his teammates and the general school populace. One of the prime motivators, as one hones one's basic skills in team-sport practices, is that the rest of one's team depends on one's individual ability to succeed on the field or court. Baseball players have to work together, through moments of individual effort, to get three outs each inning. Soccer players must all be able to deftly handle and pass the ball, while relying on the forwards to lead the scoring. Basketball players have to execute plays with the proper movements and passes, and wide-open shots must be made for the team to prevail.

What is interesting is that players themselves all understand what it must be like to be the one who fails at an important moment. Everyone has moments of insufficiency in some form or another, but few end up costing their teams games through such moments. Thus, players tend to be highly sympathetic toward each other after such on-the-field or on-court failures. (On the other hand, the shattered glass in the locker room seems to represent plain old carelessness and comes across as quite irritating.) Less forgiving, ironically, can be fans, who invest themselves emotionally in teams perhaps because otherwise their lives lack vigor and perceived importance. It is as if sports players are representing their communities whether they mean to or not, and thus get both the rewards of communal glory in victory and the blame for letting the community down in defeat. In the story, the harshest response from Jamie's missed layup seems to come from a girl who bumps him in the hall. When the broader community seems to have turned its collective back on Jamie, he naturally turns to the most important part of his personal community: his best friend, Froggy.

Friendship

Froggy and Jamie make for an interesting pair of companions. They seem rather different in many ways—one is in the band, while the other plays basketball; one is an intellectual, the other simply lives in the here and now; one is rational, the other is emotional. It is perhaps precisely in their opposing natures that some friends come to be "best"—they complement each other, each providing the other a perspective that may otherwise be lacking with regard to important issues. Froggy indeed proves the best of friends to Jamie in that he helps him pull himself together and think about things rationally when the worst of his streak is starting to overwhelm him. Jamie is apparently being deliberately dramatic or comical in saying, "Froggy, I give up, man. . . . I'm on a death streak and I know I'm probably headed right on out the world"; that is, he does not seem to be genuinely suicidal. However, when a friend expresses such thoughts, one does not dismiss them as mere playing around but recognizes that this is a call for help of some kind—perhaps a melodramatic one, but perhaps a serious one disguised as melodrama—and what one should do is help the friend out of the situation, however one can.

Froggy encourages Jamie to take a step back from his situation and consider that this is all, really, a matter of chance. One cannot expect so many unfortunate things to happen to one on a regular basis, Froggy argues (although if Jamie's study habits are as poor as the story suggests, he perhaps should expect to regularly fail with schoolwork), and so such an unfortunate streak may lead to a counter-streak of fortunate things. It does not matter whether Froggy's reasoning makes perfect sense; if one considers coin flips, for example, a series of seven heads does not make it any more likely that one will now flip tails seven times in a row. What matters is that the reasoning appeals to Jamie in a way that allows him to put a positive spin on the situation. The psychic upshot is as simple as Jamie being able to tell himself, "Things will get better." Sometimes it takes more than just those words to bring the idea home; the words must be given life with a story, or an experience, or perhaps even superstition.

Superstition

At first Jamie refuses to believe that luck affects anything in his life. At Froggy's first positing a streak of some kind, Jamie replies, "I don't believe in luck or streaks or whatever else you're talking about." It is easy for one who has always been fortunate—or fortunate enough—to believe that luck has had nothing to do with it. In fact, believing against luck allows people in fortuitous positions to themselves take more credit for having gotten there; in this sense, not believing in luck is often a matter of pride or egotism. However, Jamie's pride has been thoroughly leveled by the time he gets deep into his unlucky streak, what with the community failures, the poor test performances, and the interpersonal missteps. Therefore he seems to reach a point where he actually needs to believe in the idea of luck in order to persevere, to feel capable of facing the world and whatever it might throw at him next; he needs to believe that his luck will change, perhaps dramatically.

Something almost magical happens with that first lucky event, the tossing of the egg right back into the carton. This minor miracle, of course, reflects not at all on Jamie's qualities or abilities as a person; he was not consciously trying to land the egg directly in the carton. Nonetheless, because he has invested in the superstition of the idea of the streak, and the idea that when his luck changes he will get to ride out a counter-streak, the egg miracle changes his entire outlook on life. He is able to delve back into his activities and feel something like luck practically flowing through his body: "When I got to school I was feeling good." Maybe this feeling is only a sensory mirage or simply his blood circulating better with the release of tension, but it is not too far-fetched to perceive that Jamie's believing in his turned luck is actually what improves his situation.

Superstition, a hallmark of many devoted athletes, is sometimes derided as having no place in a modern, scientific, rational society; but Jamie demonstrates how, believed in fully enough, a superstition can actually be a means of taking advantage of the world in ways that rationality alone cannot allow. Of course, this belief also leaves Jamie obliged to conceive that once the good luck has counterbalanced the bad luck, his luck has run out. It is fortunate then that Celia was infused with belief and faith in a lucky streak as well, or she might never have asked him to the dance.

After Jamie misses a shot in an important basketball game, he worries it was the beginning of a streak of bad luck. *(©Vasilyev Alexandr / Shutterstock.com)*

STYLE

First Person

Myers's stories in *145th Street* are praised for the appeal and power of the narrating voices, with Jamie's being singled out as especially compelling. There seem to be several reasons for this. One is Jamie's self-assurance. The confidence he expresses in the opening paragraph, in suggesting that the reader may want to remember his name in case he is famous one day, may be consciously overblown, but in that sense it remains genuine: with this opening Jamie communicates that he believes in himself, as well as in what he has to say, and these are very appealing qualities not just in storytellers—the listener or reader wants to trust that they are being taken somewhere worth going—but in people in general. Confident people naturally bring the more uncertain and hesitant people along with them in their wake (for better or for worse).

Another facet of the narrator's appeal is his clear sense of humor, which typically operates in the subtle/deadpan range. For example, after his story about smashing the glass bottle in the locker room and inconveniencing everyone, Jamie highlights Froggy's failure to grasp the significance of the event in his life simply by recording Froggy's one-word response to the story and adding his own minimalist take on that response: "'Oh.' That's what Froggy said." This is much like Jamie as narrator turning to the reader, pointing his thumb at his friend, and shaking his head, as if to say, *Sometimes people just don't understand* or *Can you believe this guy?* The gesture of confidence in the reader is likely enough to make most smile, if not laugh aloud. Finally, one might posit that there is something vaguely "cool" about Jamie—perhaps this is a combination of his confidence, his sense of humor, and other qualities that one cannot necessarily at first put a finger on.

Youth Dialect

In this story, as in much of Myers's fiction featuring first-person narrators, the language used includes certain phrasings in the sort of dialect one might attribute either to Jamie's

COMPARE & CONTRAST

- **c. 2000:** With the NBA's existing systems of free agency and salary restriction, the best teams tend to have pairs of stars—Michael Jordan and Scottie Pippen, Karl Malone and John Stockton, Kobe Bryant and Shaquille O'Neal—operating with key supporting casts. In 2000–2001, the salary cap is $35.5 million per team.

  Today: The most successful NBA teams feature trios of big-name stars. In order to trump the Cleveland Cavaliers' trio of LeBron James, Kyrie Irving, and Kevin Love, the Golden State Warriors add Kevin Durant to the trio of Stephen Curry, Klay Thompson, and Draymond Green, fostering more disparity between the best and worst teams than the NBA has ever seen. The salary cap in 2016–2017 is over $94 million.

- **c. 2000:** The percent of NBA players identifying as African American, having risen as high as 82 percent in the 1994–1995 season, is 78 percent as of the year 2000.

  Today: As of 2015, 76 percent of NBA players are African American.

- **c. 2000:** A teenager going through tough times may need to arrange frequent interactions with a close friend for support, whether in person or over the telephone, typically at home on a landline—although cell phones are gaining in popular usage, especially in cities.

  Today: The vast majority of teenagers have their own cell phones, and misfortune is likely to be instantly shared via text message or even broadcast via social media so that entire circles of friends can counter the misfortune with flattering comments and good vibes.

youth, his urban environs, or perhaps his status as African American. Race seems to be less of an influence on the dialect as presented, however, in part because the reader cannot even be sure that Jamie should be seen as a young African American man until, as he starts to use up his lucky streak, he tells himself, "Calm down and think hard, my Nubian selfhood." *Nubian* refers to the dark-skinned African peoples who occupied a kingdom straddling modern-day Egypt and Sudan along the Nile River. Aside from this reference and Jamie's envisioning Celia "looking tan," Myers leaves out any reference to skin color or race. This does not mean that the idea of race is absent from the story; one presumes, for example, that the character Ramona Rodriguez is Latina. However, race is not really on Jamie's mind, and consequently it is not on the reader's mind either. As such, Jamie's stridently youthful verbal formulations—"he doesn't know scratch about ball"; "I can't pop her when she's running her weak girl game"; and "dreaming about laying some serious lip on Celia"—effectively represent the sort of slang-peppered and casual, if practiced, mode of communication that youth, perhaps especially urban youth, of all races might be expected to use.

HISTORICAL CONTEXT

Basketball in American Culture

The focus of "The Streak" is the idea of luck or superstition, not basketball, and yet because the two on-court episodes frame the streak and seem to carry the most weight out of all the un/fortunate events, the sport carries a special significance. This is especially the case because the episodes so fully mirror each other, representing the first of seven strokes of bad luck and the last of seven strokes of good luck, and with the plays themselves effectively inverted: in the

Several things go wrong for Jamie–accidentally breaking things, leaving his wallet behind, and angering a bully. (©udrall / Shutterstock.com)

first Jamie is receiving a pass under the basket and blows it, in the second Jamie is passing to someone else under the basket but unintentionally scores.

One scholar who has considered the cultural relevance of basketball in America is Michael Mandelbaum, in *The Meaning of Sports: Why Americans Watch Baseball, Football, and Basketball and What They See When They Do*. He considers basketball largely as a postindustrial game, representing the churning out of points through repetitive cycles almost as if in a factory. Another is Craig A. Forney, who in *The Holy Trinity of American Sports: Civil Religion in Football, Baseball, and Basketball* similarly examines the game as one signifying ever-accelerated societal progress in the improvement of people's lives and material circumstances, as the scores climb steadily by two or three points at a time. As such, the ease with which scoring is sometimes achieved evokes in the viewer's mind the facility with which work brings success—just like practice makes perfect. Forney writes, "The smooth and sweet moves in a game resemble the convenient flow of efforts . . . of progressive movement to an easier life. Players almost effortlessly lay the ball in over the field goal rim or gently kiss the basketball off the backboard for a lay up." This formulation may help explain why students at Jamie's school can be so upset with him over something that ultimately has nothing to do with them, unless they are on the basketball team; the success of the players on the team with which one is affiliated—whether by school or city or just devoted fandom—signifies success in life for the people in one's extended community. This also explains why fans can be so possessive about their favorites, saying things like, "Alas, my team lost last night."

Among his other sweeping observations, Forney attributes special significance to the game of basketball for African American communities, especially in light of the slavery, racism, and discrimination that have marred US history. The idea of racial uplift has been at the forefront of many African Americans' minds since Emancipation and, in cultural terms, especially through the Harlem Renaissance of the 1920s, the civil rights movement of the 1950s and 1960s, and Black Power through the 1970s. Forney declares,

> More than any other area of professional life, basketball depicts remarkable progress for people of African descent, expressing the improvement from harsh discrimination of the past. . . . Black individuals dominate the game, disclosing a significant advancement from strict exclusion not so long ago.

Forney observes that the pace and appeal of the game of basketball dramatically improved with integration: "Largely by way of innovations from blacks, games follow fast-paced, explosive, and high-flying style." Myers, of course, does not intend in this story to create a thrilling sports scene and so bypasses intense descriptions of the action. As with the rest of the story (excluding Jamie's one comment to his Nubian self), there is nothing racialized about the basketball scenes.

Forney also considers sports as not just realms that reflect society but as a kind of civil religion, especially for those who loyally watch and root for their favorite teams at games (whereby they do, after all, contribute effort and energy to the team's success). In this social environment, "Notorious losers . . . generate belief in a 'curse' at work to cause their chronic losing, convinced of a determining influence by some diabolical and greater force." Humankind, of course, has been using superstition to externalize poor performance as bad luck and at times personify the sources of misfortune for thousands of years.

CRITICAL OVERVIEW

Not merely a prolific author, Myers has earned wide critical acclaim for his works, including a multitude of Coretta Scott King Awards and other honors. Regarding *145th Street*, a *Publishers Weekly* reviewer was greatly impressed. Myers's vivid prose is said to create a "pulsing, vibrant community"; the narratives are rendered especially compelling by "voices of witty, intelligent teens" who establish "an inviting, conversational tone"; and the collective portrait is one of people "sitting on the front stoop swapping stories." Jamie Farrell, as both narrator of his own story and a secondary character in other stories, is "a standout." The reviewer concludes that "most readers will find that they could settle in for hours" with the collection.

Like the *Publishers Weekly* writer, a *Horn Book* magazine reviewer was impressed with the range of the stories in *145th Street*, as Myers—who is seen to have "a sure skill" for the demands of the genre—proves deft at everything from "brash comedy" to "moody romances" to the darker tones of tragedy. The reviewer concludes, "Myers has a great, natural style . . . and is completely at home in a Harlem depicted without adulation but with great affection."

In the *Dictionary of Literary Biography*, Carmen Subryan lauds Myers's ethical intentions and his ability to connect with young readers of all stripes. She declares that Myers

> is concerned with the development of youths, and his message is [that] young people must face the reality of growing up and must persevere, knowing that they can succeed despite any odds they face. Furthermore, this positive message enables youths to discover what is important in life and to reject influences which could destroy them.

In the essay "'Keepin' It Real': Walter Dean Myers and the Promise of African-American Children's Literature," R. D. Lane likewise affirms that Myers addresses important contemporary youth issues with "meritorious resolve." Lane observes, "Clearly, Myers's fiction is regarded as seminal in the discourse of children's and young-adult literature." Writing in 1998, Lane saw that a common problem with pop-cultural treatments of African American experience was that they tended to present either idealized overachievers, like TV's Cosby family, or the grittiest of street denizens, as in the film *Menace II Society*. Lane sees Myers as achieving a crucial balance in his various literary portrayals:

> Myers has not only discovered a solution to the moral quandary regarding what aspects of realism should be presented to young readers, but he has excelled—particularly in the area of illustrating, interrogating, and problematizing how black masculinity comes to be shaped and (under)developed by socio-environmental nuances of class and experience.

Subryan acknowledges that Myers "is recognized as one of the premier writers for books for young black people," yet she affirms that his "books demonstrate that writers can not only challenge the minds of black youths but also emphasize the black experience in a non-racist way that benefits all young readers."

CRITICISM

Michael Allen Holmes

Holmes is a writer with existential interests. In the following essay, he suggests that "The Streak" posits coolness as approaching a transcendental oneness with the universe—like, sort of.

One thing that is crystal clear by the time the reader finishes the first paragraph of Walter Dean Myers's short story "The Streak" is that Jamie Farrell is *cool*—or at least he thinks he is cool. It is hard to come up with a single definition of what it means to be cool that will fit any community or situation. Certainly chess players use the term in different ways than gymnasts, who use it in different ways than football players. One cannot quite refer to a person as "cool" and have the full sense be immediately understood. However, one universal implication is a degree of social superiority; in any group, the coolest person is the one who somehow holds dominion over the group, whether intentionally or not—the person to whom everybody else looks up and even models oneself after, largely because of some unspoken sense that this person has life best figured out, especially with regard to one's attitude toward it.

It is hard to determine, sometimes, how valuable it is to be cool. In some respects, the cool person really has mastered not only the current circumstances but him- or herself, that is, has the highest degree of self-understanding—or so it seems. On the negative side, coolness can represent little more than a superficial sense that a person is the best at what are actually relatively, or even absolutely, insignificant things, like driving a car at unsafe speeds, smoking a cigarette with the proper blasé disposition, or making fun of other people's foibles. Jamie offers readers an interesting case study in coolness, in that he is in a position in which cool people do not often put themselves: telling a story that potentially reveals much about his innermost fears, hopes, and dreams. In the spaces between Jamie's narrative responsibilities and his status as a cool person, one can get a sense for what might really be at the bottom of the idea of coolness.

In considering what coolness means, it is helpful to first turn to a dictionary. *Merriam-Webster's Collegiate Dictionary*, 11th ed., needs several discrete, if related, definitions to

ONE CAN CONCEIVE THAT WHEN JAMIE MISSED THE LAYUP, HE LOST THE TAO."

encompass the different connotations the word *cool* can carry in the sense under discussion: "marked by steady dispassionate calmness and self-control"; "lacking ardor or friendliness"; "marked by restrained emotion"; "free from tensions or violence"; "fashionable, hip"; and "very good: excellent." Before turning to Jamie with such qualities in mind, it might be fruitful to consider a character who is presented as rather *un*cool: Froggy Williams.

It is Jamie, of course, who first suggests that, even if he is "definitely for real," Froggy is essentially uncool—a notion that should be taken with a grain of salt, coming as it does from a narrator who has the aplomb to instruct the reader to take care to remember his own potentially famous name. The problem, anyway, is that Froggy "doesn't know scratch about ball." The statement is somewhat opaque—*scratch* may be taken to mean "anything," but what kind of *ball* is Jamie referring to? This is one aspect of coolness as socially signified: the assumption of a level of background knowledge that allows one to understand what is being referred to with a minimum of clues. It many city locales, where well-maintained fields are hard to come by, the only kind of "ball" around is basketball. Those in the know will immediately get the reference; those aspiring to coolness will figure things out before long; and the uncool ones are those who need to ask all kinds of questions to make sense of things.

Thus do we find Froggy responding to Jamie's story with question after question—"So what happened?"; "Tommy didn't see you?"; and "Yeah?"—never quite indicating that he really understands the import of the episode. Froggy knows well enough to note that Jamie should not have missed the layup, asking, "Why you do that?" However, Jamie's immediate response is enough for Froggy to fully understand the situation rationally and thus consider it resolved. In fact, at the end of this

WHAT DO I READ NEXT?

- Myers has made basketball an integral part of the Harlem setting and plot of several young-adult novels. These include *Hoops* (1981), about a teenager facing ethical questions; *Slam!* (1996), about a teen who has to balance his street life with his magnet-school education; and *Game* (2008), about a young man's attempts to make it to Division I in college and ultimately the NBA.
- Although it has been published in the form of a juvenile book complete with illustrations, *The Lucky Stone* (1979), by Lucille Clifton, carries the literary weight of an epic short story about the course of African American history. Connecting episodes dispersed over time is a lucky stone that merits its appellation.
- Readers who find Jamie's voice appealing may enjoy Dominican American author Junot Díaz's short-story collection *This Is How You Lose Her* (2012), in which recurring narrator Yunior delivers tales of romance gained and lost in a most masculine style of both living and writing. The collection is advised for mature readers, owing to language and sexual content.
- An intense portrait of the role of basketball in one teenager's depraved inner-city life is presented in the memoir *The Basketball Diaries* (1978), by (white) punk musician Jim Carroll. The book covers a period when the author was a New York City teenager addicted to heroin. It was adapted into an acclaimed 1995 motion picture starring Leonardo DiCaprio and Mark Wahlberg.
- One of the superstitions of basketball is that, especially in cases where the referees seem to have gotten a call wrong, the ball itself will set things straight; for example, if a player is sent to the free-throw line on a defensive foul that should have been called an offensive foul, the player is considered more likely to miss one or both shots. This superstition is featured in the title of Yago Colás's intriguing sociological study *Ball Don't Lie! Myth, Genealogy, and Invention in the Cultures of Basketball* (2016).
- An in-depth exploration of the significance of basketball as intertwined with the realms of music and spirituality—both religious and secular—is provided by Onaje X. O. Woodbine in *Black Gods of the Asphalt: Religion, Hip-Hop, and Street Basketball* (2016).

---

exchange, from the definitions above, one might conceive of Froggy as the "cool" one, remaining relatively unconcerned with the situation, while Jamie seems too emotionally invested in what has taken place. Yet the implication is that Froggy fails to recognize how important sporting events are in social terms; it can be cooler to be invested in athletics, tests of bodily performance, than to believe that the ability to perform under pressure is irrelevant.

Froggy might be further assessed as uncool for other reasons. Regarding the sports drink Jamie had in the locker room, Froggy points out, "WonderAde is cool," but a rule of thumb, when it comes to this sort of thing, is that cool people do not feel a need to label things as cool; that quality ought to be self-apparent, and only those still trying to figure things out invest in the label itself. Further minor clues include Froggy's drinking milk in the cafeteria (worrying about nutrition); his coming from band practice (an activity that also involves performance under pressure, but not in such an athletic sense—and only soloists hold a spotlight all for themselves the way athletes inevitably do); and his making overly intelligent references, such as to the lambada, a dance with which Jamie is unfamiliar. The dance itself, being highly sexualized, might be considered cool (or, more accurately, hot), but holding and wielding knowledge about the dance indicates a degree of intellectualism, of placing value on *knowing* things over actually *doing* them or simply *being* in the world, which is not usually considered cool.

By now, to one versed in Eastern traditions, it becomes apparent that coolness as commonly understood carries some of the hallmarks of genuine spiritual transcendence. Take, for example, *Webster's* mention of "dispassionate calmness and self-control." One of the primary goals of the Buddhist monk is to gain freedom from overly passionate emotions, to recognize that the world is ever-evolving, that change and loss must be accepted, and that the passion that brings attachment also brings suffering. It is through mastering one's passionate responses that suffering can be eased, perhaps brought to an end entirely. The ultimate goal of the Zen Buddhist, *nirvana,* means "extinguishment," that is, the extinguishing of one's passions, among other aspects of the self.

In "The Streak," Jamie may not have perfect control over his passions—he gets rather worked up about a number of things that happen in the course of the story—but in his narration he often either makes deliberate efforts to minimize the presentation of his emotional state or reveals an intention to quell his passions in reality. For example, when the girl bumps him in the hall and suggests he might be a traitor, Jamie does not respond with aggression or a comeback insult, as many would; rather, he lets (or tries to let) the insult roll right off his back. Immediately following the girl's comment, he narrates, "When she left I turned my attention back to the junior dance." Surely this leaves something out: perhaps Jamie felt a tinge of genuine shame, or shook his head at the girl, or (improbably) stuck out his tongue behind her back, but he does not make a point of belittling the girl for the reader, of cutting her down to size in order to make himself seem bigger. Thus, whether in the story's reality or in Jamie's narration—or both—he neutralizes the interaction by refusing to engage with the girl in a negative way. As the scene continues, Froggy suggests, likewise somewhat insultingly, that Jamie has no chance with the beautiful Celia. Jamie might use this comment as fodder for an argument or a counter-insult, but of course Froggy is his friend, not an enemy, and again Jamie seems intent on playing down any passionate response: "That got my jaw a little tight, but I didn't say anything. I just went on in and sat through the longest biology class I have ever had in my life."

Jamie next suggests for himself a degree of coolness in declining to invest any faith in Froggy's idea about lucky streaks. Notably, this idea is acquired from a book, which perhaps gives it less credence from a "cool" person's point of view—that is, it derives not from lived experience but from the deliberate acquisition of knowledge. Once again, this correlates with an Eastern outlook, specifically Taoism. Taoist texts attributed to the likes of Lao-tzu and Chuang-tzu take a skeptical view of the attainment of knowledge, something lauded by the likes of Confucius, whom the Taoist philosophers single out for ridicule. Confucius took a very prescriptive view of nearly everything in life, from academics to work and family relationships to the mourning of loved ones. To follow such prescriptions, of course, one must attain knowledge of them.

The Taoists, to the contrary, are inclined to throw out the behavioral rule books—indeed all the rule books—and advise simply living in accord with the dictates of virtue. They hold up as not just idyllic but ideal the precivilized state when people simply went about their daily village business without making a point of attaining knowledge and then using that knowledge to materially improve their circumstances. Knowledge, in the Taoists' opinion, inevitably leads to hierarchies, which lead to discrimination, which leads to disruptions in the fabric of society. So again, Jamie's refusal to invest himself in book learning is suggestive both of being "cool" and of an aspect of a philosophy aiming at the achievement of an existential balance—of oneness with the Tao, the Way that infuses all of life and the world. Also, in accord with the conception of the Tao underlying the workings of the world, it does not necessarily behoove one to believe in luck as something that can be lost or acquired or wielded. One cannot "take advantage" of the Tao, as one might with luck. Yet the net result of what the Taoist conceives is similar: if one is in sync with the Tao, with the natural flow of the universe, then one will find oneself in a better position to live well in the world. If one has lost touch with the Tao, such as by failing to live virtuously, then the natural flow of the universe will be against one, and trying to live in contentment will be like trying to constantly swim upstream; defeat is inevitable.

In this sense, one can conceive that when Jamie missed the layup, he lost the Tao; perhaps his ego led him to prematurely believe the layup would simply go in—the shot would make itself, so to speak—such that he failed to consciously physically execute the action. That is, he may have gotten lost in a layer of egotistic abstraction instead of being perfectly at one with the present moment as he was living it. An emphasis on full absorption in and engagement with the present moment is a hallmark of Zen (as basketball coaching legend and noted Zen adherent Phil Jackson can attest). Once Jamie believes that a lucky streak is upon him, on the other hand, and he is freed of the physical and mental tensions that seem to have contributed to his "unluckiness"—kinesthetic failures and absent-minded distractions account for six of his seven misfortunes—he finds himself practically flowing with the Tao, and as such everything seems to go his way.

In a word, Jamie becomes cool again (even if his sister, who sees him in his most psychologically exposed moments, would suggest otherwise). He can respond to his math teacher by saying, "Yeah, wazzup?"; he can coax a soda out of the drink machine when no one else can; he can take the cash from his dad without bothering to say thank you—or at least without narrating even a hint of interpersonal thankfulness; and he can do all these things with a level of emotional disengagement that affirms his stature as cool. (Arguably he has a minor hiccup when he feels a need to report, in buying only half a dozen roses for Celia, that "six is cool," which goes against the aforementioned rule of thumb about labeling. However, in this case Jamie must be given some credit for being responsible with his limited finances and not placing too much stock in material purchases; whether or not six roses instead of twelve is actually cool, he deserves credit for what is effectively an antimaterialist stance. Of course, he is probably reassuring himself more than the reader of the coolness of a half dozen.) Regardless of the evidence, one need not conclude for oneself that Jamie proves himself cool; when his "shot" wins the game against Carver, and he takes it all in stride—he knows that *he* does not really deserve the credit, but rather his streak (or the Tao) does—everybody is left talking about, as Jamie reports, "how cool I was with it."

It must be acknowledged that there seems to be one problem with Jamie's apparent coolness and/or oneness with the Tao: he is not an entirely virtuous person. This may be the locus where coolness and transcendental oneness most sharply diverge: the person considered cool is quite often the one who is specifically *not* virtuous. Cool people do not care about things, like the grades they get on tests, or other people's feelings, and so forth. This seems to be an extension of that dispassionate manner that the dictionary speaks of and which Buddhism and Taoism also speak of. Yet these are forms of dispassion that do not accord with virtue. Achievement on tests may seem irrelevant, but compare the high-school dropout who is obligated to work as a convenience-store clerk with the graduate who is enabled to become a social worker, or an environmental lawyer, or a teacher; clearly one is doing more ethical good for humanity than the other, not to mention better providing for family financially. Not caring about tests is tantamount, in the long run, in some cases, to not caring about other people in the world. Buddhism advises dispassion toward oneself, but it also insists upon compassion toward others.

For Jamie, not caring about others' feelings seems to be an issue. What matters after he spills milk in Maurice's lap is that he gets away; Maurice's later chasing Froggy seems to be little more than a comedic epilogue to the episode from Jamie's self-centered perspective. When he starts munching on potato wedges he cannot pay for, what matters is that, again, Jamie gets away, not that the food will end up wasted and the manager will be liable for the loss. When the miscommunication between himself and Mrs. Evora leads to Jamie getting a date with Celia, he reveals no intent to set the record straight, however dishonest it might be to build a relationship on such a deception—a deception that was, after all, unintentional, but which he does not correct even when he has the chance. One can conclude that Jamie is cool, but he may not quite be one with the Tao.

Still, whether Jamie is virtuous or not and whether he is one with the Tao or not, the story treats him kindly in the end—and the reader likely appreciates this. It is as though Jamie

In the end, the girl Jamie likes asks him to the dance, and he recovers his equilibrium. (©bikeriderlondon / Shutterstock.com)

has done his time, so to speak, through the first half of the story, in enduring his seven misfortunes; and after sinking so low, the reader naturally wants him to be raised back up in the end. It is in the story's conclusion that the story makes Jamie's existential merit and even the idea of the Tao most evident. As Jamie narrates after the interaction with Celia, during which he decidedly plays it cool (note the lie about not having thought about the dance), he is left "standing in the hallway leaning against the wall." Once again, it seems that Jamie's narration leaves something out, namely, the full degree of his emotional response to the situation. He might have reported that his heart was beating out of his chest, or he was short of breath, or he was more thankful than he had ever been in his life; something along these lines must have been the case, for why else would Froggy ask, "What happened? . . . You okay?"

Jamie is clearly in some kind of a daze—perhaps a transcendental one, as it seems, because his somewhat irrational response is, "I just figured out that the whole world is on a streak." Froggy is stumped; as far as he understands the notion of a streak, Jamie's words simply do not make sense. Again this represents something of a Taoist or Zen precept: a belief that irrationality sometimes trumps rationality. That is, sometimes an irrational expression, an irrational verbal formulation, like a paradox, is superior to a rational one, because it bypasses that realm of knowability and knowledge that takes one outside of the living present and into the world of mental abstractions. That is, if something cannot be understood rationally—perhaps like Jamie's last statement—it can only be approached irrationally, with feelings and intuition, through immersion not in knowledge but in lived reality. Froggy may believe that Jamie simply does not understand what the word *streak* means, but as Jamie observes, that rational meaning is, in that (transcendental) moment of his, irrelevant. What Jamie says may not accord with the strict definition of a *streak*, but he might well have communicated precisely the same thing if he had said, "I just figured out that the whole world is *one with the Tao*." The world indeed is, in the end, though people do not always know it; but when they know it, as Jamie would say, "It's all good."

Source: Michael Allen Holmes, Critical Essay on "The Streak," in *Short Stories for Students*, Gale, Cengage Learning, 2017.

Susan Bailey

In the following review, Bailey points out how the reappearance of characters throughout the book highlights the feeling of community in Myers's novel What They Found: Love on 145th Street.

The story begins at a funeral in Harlem. However, this is no ordinary funeral, as most do not include a barbeque, a hair salon, and a fashion show. Teenage Abeni must hold her family together and draw upon support from the community as she fulfills her dying father's last wish for an unconventional funeral to raise money for his family's new salon, the Curl-E-Cue.

After the funeral, the crowd disperses and the author takes us into their individual daily lives. This composite novel's street setting becomes a collection of narratives told from the point of view of the young adults of today's Harlem. Myers does an excellent job of crafting characters with real problems to which many modern youth can relate. Each chapter is told from the point of view of a different character. There are dozens of plotlines, many of which begin in the Curl-E-Cue salon. One advantage of this structure is that even the most reluctant reader can be kept interested because the stories develop and resolve so quickly.

Not all of the characters' stories have a fairytale ending, and many of the plotlines fail to come to a neat resolution. Wrapping up each story without any loose ends, however, would not be true to the real-life experiences these characters face, and would be unsatisfying for the reader. At the end of many chapters, the only thing that has changed is the character's attitude toward his or her situation.

Although all the stories are different, many of the characters appear on the periphery of multiple narratives so the effect is that of a community whose members have individual and unique problems but are all tied together through shared experience and circumstance. The setting is vital to the individual and collective stories. Walter Dean Myers grew up in Harlem and does an excellent job recreating his living, breathing neighborhood on the pages of this novel. This neighborhood community is full of people with problems, passions, beauty, poverty, life, and loneliness. Each character's struggle to overcome circumstances brings the individual pieces of the puzzle together to create an overarching picture of self-affirmation and discovery.

As are all Myers's novels, this book is well written, and the individual stories catch the attention of the reader and leave them wanting more. The variety of characters in many different circumstances gives ample opportunity for most readers to find at least one character with whom they can relate. Whether it is a young woman wondering if there is something wrong with her because love does not seem to work for her the same way it works for the other girls in the neighborhood, or a young man dealing with the consequences of taking the "easy" way out by using gun violence to make some money to buy his baby son a birthday present, every reader will find a character that seems to fit.

While the age and gender of the characters vary throughout the book, most of the characters are young adults, trying to find out where they fit in the world. This book would be an excellent choice for sophomores or juniors in high school, especially those growing up in an urban setting.

Source: Susan Bailey, Review of *What They Found: Love on 145th Street*, in *Journal of Adolescent & Adult Literacy*, Vol. 51, No. 4, December 2007, p. 361.

Publishers Weekly

In the following review, the anonymous reviewer compares the stories in Myers's collection 145th Street *to stories traded between neighbors while relaxing on the front porch.*

In a kind of literary *Rear Window*, Myers (*The Blues of Flats Brown*) uses 10 short stories to create snapshots of a pulsing, vibrant community with diverse ethnic threads, through all of its ups and downs. Beginning with the tale of a wry character who stages his own funeral on a sweltering 4th of July to celebrate the money he has received from canceling his life insurance policy, Myers then follows with a chilling story of a cop shootout gone wrong. Many of the stories are told through the voices of witty, intelligent teens; Jamie Farrell, in particular, is a standout as he relates his changing luck in "The Streak" and makes other cameo appearances. But even the more poignant stories told in the third person—such as that of Billy Giles, a middling fighter hired by the local gym to make contenders look good, and "Angela's Eyes," infused with superstition, in which Angela possesses the ability to foresee death and destruction through her late father's eyes—keep an inviting, conversational tone. Myers creates an overall effect of sitting on the front stoop swapping stories of the neighborhood. Most readers will find that they could settle in for hours and take it all in.

Source: Review of *145th Street: Short Stories*, in *Publishers Weekly* online, September 3, 2007.

Horn Book

In the following review, the writer praises Myers's natural style as displayed in 145th Street.

The first in this collection of ten stories is a brash comedy about a man who wants a fancy funeral while he's still around to enjoy it ("Funerals bring out the best in people. Am I lying or flying?"), but the tone abruptly darkens in the second, where a dog is thought to be the only victim of a police shooting until a boy finds the body of a child ("A feeling came over me, like I was lying on a beach at the edge of a lost world with a wave of hurt washing over my body"). Too many collections have found popular YA novelists ill at ease with the short-story form, but Walter Dean Myers here demonstrates a sure skill for its demands. Tightly focused and selectively detailed, with contemporary Harlem as their common setting, the stories here each feature a small cast grappling with a single situation. Sometimes humorously, as in "The Streak," about Jamie, convinced his lucky streak is going to run out before he gets to ask Celia to the dance; sometimes dramatically, as in a story about a girl whom neighbors are convinced predicts death in her dreams. Two of the best stories are moody romances. In "Kitty and Mack: A Love Story," two unlikely lovers defeat pride, stubbornness, and false ideas of manhood to find their way to each other; "Fighter" seems a few pages lifted straight from the Harlem Renaissance, as it tells of a third-rate boxer whose wife wants him to give up the ring. Myers has a great, natural style ("The girl was fine. Not just kind of fine, not just take another look fine, but, like, take the batteries out of the smoke alarms when she came by fine") and is completely at home in a Harlem depicted without adulation but with great affection.

"CRITICS AGREE THAT HE HAS A FINE EAR FOR DIALOGUE, WHICH BECOMES ONE OF THE MAJOR MEANS HE USES TO DEVELOP CHARACTERIZATION AND AUTHENTICATE SETTINGS. PARTLY BECAUSE THEIR SPEECH SEEMS REAL, HIS CHARACTERS SEEM REAL, TOO."

Source: Review of *145th Street: Short Stories*, in *Horn Book*, Vol. 76, No. 2, March 2000, p. 198.

Rudine Sims Bishop

In the following excerpt, Bishop analyzes Myers's style.

MYERS THE GENERALIST

Myers is proud to be an Afro-American young adult novelist, but he is first of all a writer and can and does write about other people, in other genres, and about other topics. He has written short stories, nonfiction magazine pieces, nonfiction children's books, books for older elementary-age readers, mysteries, adventure stories, easy-to-read science fiction, picture books, and a new novel offering some blank space and invitations for the reader to add his or her own writing to the book.

The adult stories, published in the seventies, reveal some of Myers's versatility. The stories offer a different world view from that in his work for young people. There is some bitterness ("How Long Is Forever?"), tragedy ("The Vision of Felipe"), loneliness ("The Going On"), insanity ("The Dark Side of the Moon"). One or two may be precursors of the work to come. "The Vision of Felipe," set in Peru, features a gentle, sensitive, and compassionate young boy, who when orphaned by his grandmother's death goes off to the city to seek his fortune. Felipe is in many ways similar to Tito, the Puerto Rican boy in *Scorpions*. Like Tito, Felipe has been greatly influenced by his beloved grandmother's teachings, and his relationship with his friend Daniel is in some ways similar to that between Jamal and Tito. Other stories are related to Myers's young adult work only in that they explore similar topics. "Juby" includes a white person studying voodoo, though the story is in a much darker vein than *Mojo and the Russians*. The dialect used in the narrative has a Caribbean flavor similar to the one in *Mr. Monkey and the Gotcha Bird.* Both "Juby" and "Gums," in which a grandfather and his young grandson are overcome by their fear of a personified Death, may have their roots in the scary stories Myers remembers his father telling. "Bubba" features a white soldier who is part of the military escort for the funeral of a Black soldier killed in Vietnam. He spends the night in the home of the deceased soldier's mother and has to confront the issue of racism as it sometimes operates in the military. The issue is one of those touched on in *Fallen Angels*.

Myers has also produced two nonfiction books for young people, *The World of Work* and *Social Welfare*. *The World of Work* draws on the knowledge Myers acquired when he was a vocational placement supervisor for the New York State Employment Service. It is a guide to selecting a career, including descriptions of numerous jobs, their requirements, the method of entry, possibilities for advancement. True to his storytelling self, Myers introduces *The World of Work* with an imaginative speculation about how a hungry cave man might have created for himself the first job.

Social Welfare is a brief history and explanation of the welfare system, how it operates, who it serves, its problems, and some possible solutions. Both are well written—clear and straightforward. Both are over ten years old and somewhat dated, although *Social Welfare* is not nearly as dated as its author might wish it to be, given his expressed desire for change in the system. The books are nonfiction that is accurate, clear, and interestingly written.

Myers is willing to take risks with format, genre, and style, and he does so with varying degrees of success. *Brainstorm* is a science fiction story written with a limited vocabulary and designed for reluctant or remedial readers in fifth through eighth grades. Although Myers says that he would like to "bring some good literature" to the easy reader form, the restrictions on length and vocabulary make that a difficult task. It *is* possible to do what he did with *Brainstorm*—present interesting but undeveloped characters in a fast-moving plot. *Brainstorm* appeals also because it uses black-and-white photographs of a diverse group of teenagers who are the crew of a space ship sent to an alien planet to investigate the cause of a spate of "brainstorms" that have been destroying humans on earth.

Brainstorm received reasonably good notices, but the reviews of *The Black Pearl and the Ghost* range from scathingly negative to a cheerful acceptance of the book as spoof and a recognition of its good points. *Kirkus* called it "clunkingly obvious . . . hollow, creaky." The *Children's Book Services* reviewer found it "static . . . neither well-written nor interesting . . . trivia." On the other hand, *Booklist* saw "funny characters . . . sprightly pace," and *Horn Book* accepted it as "exaggerated in style and designed to meet the tastes of children."

A good reviewer must consider what the author was trying to do. *The Black Pearl and the Ghost; or One Mystery after Another* is a spoof meant for children somewhere between ages seven and ten. The humor starts with the subtitle (the book consists of two mysteries, one after another) and continues through the joke shared with the reader but not the ghost-busting detective. It is a profusely illustrated book, although not quite a picture book, and an important part of the story is told in Robert Quackenbush's amusing pictures.

Myers's books for elementary school readers, including his picture books, show a vivid imagination at work. His realistic stories, *Where Does the Day Go?* and *The Dancers*, are built on premises that were unusual at the time of their publication: a group of Black and Hispanic children speculating about a natural phenomenon and receiving answers from a Black father, and a Black boy from Harlem intrigued by ballet. *Fly, Jimmy, Fly* shows a young boy using his imagination to soar above the city. *The Golden Serpent*, set in India and illustrated by the Provensens, sets up a mystery that it leaves unresolved. *The Dragon Takes a Wife* takes the traditional knight-fights-a-dragon tale and twists it to make the dragon the protagonist, as Kenneth Grahame did in *The Reluctant Dragon*. Then Myers adds a touch of Blackness in the form of Mabel Mae Jones and her hip, rhyming spells. Although *Kirkus* called it "intercultural hocus pocus," other reviewers found it amusing, even delightful. The imaginative humor works. *Mr. Monkey and the Gotcha*

Bird dips into African and Caribbean folk traditions for its narrative voice and its trickster monkey who outsmarts the gotcha bird who would have him for supper.

Myers's novel for readers under twelve, *Me, Mop, and the Moondance Kid*, echoes some of the concerns and qualities of his young adult novels. The story is told by T.J., who, along with his younger brother, Moondance, has been recently adopted. Their task is to help their friend Mop (*M*iss *O*livia *P*arrish), who is still at the orphanage, to be adopted too, preferably by the coach of their Little League team, which they are trying to turn into a winner. The style is typical Myers: T.J.'s narration is easygoing and humorous, characters are credible and likable, the plot moves along briskly, and the human relationships are warm.

Sweet Illusions is a young adult novel, published by the Teachers and Writers Collaborative, that experiments with format. It is an episodic novel focusing on teenage pregnancy. Not only is each chapter narrated by a different character, but at the end of each chapter the reader is invited to help create the story by writing a letter, a song, a list, a daydream. Lined pages are available for writing directly in the book (with a caution about not writing in library books). The characters are Black, white, and Hispanic, and all of them are learning of the difficulties and responsibilities involved in becoming parents. Both the young women and the fathers of their children tell their stories, which raise hard issues involved in teenage pregnancy: decisions about abortion and adoption, parental and community attitudes toward the mothers, irresponsibility on the part of the fathers, continuing their education, providing for the child. The book works. Myers has, in a brief space, managed to create believable characters with individual voices. Their stories are unique and at the same time recognizable to anyone who has thought about or grappled with the problems of teenage pregnancy. The purpose is to provoke thought, which happens as readers get caught up in the characters and their stories.

In spite of its workbook format, *Sweet Illusions* received some serious critical attention. *Booklist*, for example, gave it high praise, calling it "an astute, realistic consideration of some of the problems associated with teenage pregnancy, valuable for personal reading as well as classroom discussion." Further, the reviewer found that "Myers' profiles are quick and clever; his characters, stubborn, confused, and vulnerable, draw substance and individuality from tough, savvy dialogue and credible backdrops." It is an unusual book that succeeds because it draws on Myers's highly developed craftsmanship.

THE MYERS CRAFT

Myers has developed a number of strengths as a writer. Critics agree that he has a fine ear for dialogue, which becomes one of the major means he uses to develop characterization and authenticate settings. Partly because their speech seems real, his characters seem real, too. Myers approaches his characters with warmth and sensitivity; he understands the concerns of young people. His first-person narratives project an intimacy that invites readers immediately into the world of the protagonist. Once there, his flair for drama keeps the pages turning.

When he wants to write humor, he knows how to create it with characterization, with language play, and with situations. Even in his serious books, humor is sometimes interjected, as in the scene in which a Hari Krishna and a Black Muslim fight over saving Tippy's soul in the bus station in *It Ain't All for Nothin'*. When the focus of a Myers book is humor, as in *Mojo and the Russians*, a reader may often laugh out loud.

Critics have not paid much attention to Myers's ability to turn a phrase, to create sharp, clear images outside the context of dialogue, but some of his figurative language is particularly apt. In *Won't Know*, he describes the house the seniors live in as seeming to "squat in the middle of the block, . . . thinking of itself as slightly better than the rest. It gave you the feeling that if it had been human it would have been a fat old man who used to have a lot of money." *Fallen Angels* is replete with vivid figurative language that brings to life the experience of war.

As has been pointed out in the discussion of the novels, critics are not unanimous in their praise of Myers's work. Reviewers who have found flaws in his craft have focused on three areas: credibility (e.g., *Mojo and the Russians*, *The Young Landlords*, *The Nicholas Factor*), unevenness in plot (e.g., *Won't Know Till I Get There*, *Crystal*, *Hoops*, *The Legend of Tarik*), and weak characterization (e.g., *The Nicholas*

Factor, The Legend of Tarik). These assessments are not unanimous, however: for every reviewer who found one of those aspects flawed, another found it strong.

The charges of lack of credibility occur in his humorous novels and in the adventure stories and can be answered by examining Myers's style and the genre in which he is writing. In his humorous novels, some critics respond to the exaggeration that is a part of a Black rhetorical style by testing the escapades of the young people against reality and finding them unbelievable. The adventure stories, too, employ some exaggeration, which may displease some reviewers.

Some of the urban novels, such as *Won't Know Till I Get There* and *Hoops*, have been described as slow moving. This unevenness may also be attributed to an aspect of Black rhetorical style, narrative sequencing, in which there is a tendency to meander off the route to the point one is trying to make, to take the long way when the direct route would be quicker.

The accusation of weak characterization came in response to *The Nicolas Factor* and *The Legend of Tarik*, both of which incorporate enough of the elements of the romantic adventure novel to influence the character development in the direction of types. Ironically, Myers has also been praised for his ability to create credible, well-delineated characters.

Myers's strengths as a novelist far outweigh his occasional shortcomings. In the *Horn Book* review of *Fallen Angels*, Ethel Heins referred to Myers as "a writer of skill, judgment, and maturity." He has honed that skill on a set of books that have earned him a place as one of the most important writers of young adult literature in the country today.

THE FUTURE

Myers loves his work. He seems always to be juggling a number of different projects—a book on Black history, a fictional book about a singer who moves from the church to secular music, another book on the order of *Sweet Illusions*, another picture book, even a book of nursery rhymes. "As a writer there are many issues I would like to tackle. I am interested in loneliness, in our attempts to escape reality through the use of drugs or through our own psychological machinations. I am interested in how we deal with each other, both sexually and in other ways, and the reasons we so often reject each other."

He has achieved some status in the field and is eager to stretch, to explore any and all kinds of ideas, to break away from whatever restrictions seem to be imposed on him because he is a Black writer. At the same time, he will continue writing about the lives of ordinary Black people, "to tell Black children about their humanity and about their history and how to grease their legs so the ash won't show and how to braid their hair so it's easy to comb on frosty winter mornings." May he keep on keepin' on; it ain't all for nothin'.

Source: Rudine Sims Bishop, "The Present and the Future: Myers the Artist," in *Presenting Walter Dean Myers*, Twayne, 1991, pp. 97–103.

SOURCES

Forney, Craig A., *The Holy Trinity of American Sports: Civil Religion in Football, Baseball, and Basketball*, Mercer University Press, 2007, pp. 1–4, 84–99.

Gram, B., "Low Post-Blackness: Race and the Status of the NBA," in *Seven Scribes*, April 9, 2015, http://sevenscribes.com/low-post-blackness-race-and-the-status-of-the-nba/ (accessed September 1, 2016).

Ishola, Olubunmi, "An Interview with Walter Dean Myers," in *World Literature Today*, Vol. 81, No. 3, May–June 2007, pp. 63–65.

Lane, R. D., "'Keepin' It Real': Walter Dean Myers and the Promise of African-American Children's Literature," in *African American Review*, Vol. 32, No. 1, Spring 1998, p. 125.

Mandelbaum, Michael, *The Meaning of Sports: Why Americans Watch Baseball, Football, and Basketball and What They See When They Do*, PublicAffairs, 2004, pp. 199–216.

Martin, Lori Latrice, *White Sports/Black Sports: Racial Disparities in Athletic Programs*, ABC-CLIO, 2015, p. 82.

Myers, Walter Dean, "The Streak," in *145th Street: Short Stories*, Delacorte Press, 2000, pp. 55–72.

"NBA Salary Cap History," RealGM, http://basketball.realgm.com/nba/info/salary_cap (accessed September 1, 2016).

Patrick-Wexler, Diane, *Walter Dean Myers*, Steck-Vaughn, 1996, pp. 5–33.

Review of *145th Street: Short Stories*, in *Horn Book*, Vol. 76, No. 2, March 2000, p. 198.

Review of *145th Street: Short Stories*, in *Publishers Weekly* online, September 3, 2007, http://www.publishersweekly.com/978-0-385-32137-2 (accessed August 30, 2016).

Rochman, Hazel, "The Booklist Interview: Walter Dean Myers," in *Booklist*, Vol. 96, No. 12, February 15, 2000, p. 1101.

Subryan, Carmen, "Walter Dean Myers," in *Dictionary of Literary Biography*, Vol. 33, *Afro-American Fiction Writers after 1955*, edited by Thadious M. Davis, Gale Group, 1984, pp. 199–202.

FURTHER READING

McBride, Georgia, ed., *Very Superstitious: Myths, Legends and Tales of Superstition*, Month9Books, 2013.

This anthology targeting young adults features a variety of stories retelling and playing off of the sorts of superstitious legends that have lingered in popular culture over the years.

Myers, Walter Dean, *What They Found: Love on 145th Street*, Wendy Lamb Books, 2007.

In this novelistic short-story collection, Myers returns to the dynamic setting of *145th Street*, this time focusing on blossoming romance.

Rovira, Alex, and Fernando Trías De Bes, *Good Luck: Creating the Conditions for Success in Life and Business*, Wiley, 2004.

This title in the classic self-help tradition affirms that one can indeed "make one's own luck," advocating mind-sets, perspectives, and patterns that can indirectly bring about positive results in one's endeavors.

Wolff, Alexander, *Audacity of Hoop: Basketball and the Age of Obama*, Temple University Press, 2015.

This volume explains how basketball played a significant role in the life of the man who would become the first African American president, Barack Obama. He played beginning at the age of ten, and he impressed many with his athleticism while fitting regular pick-up games into his presidential schedule, demonstrating his commitment to physical fitness and advocating the positive effects of participating in team sports.

SUGGESTED SEARCH TERMS

Walter Dean Myers AND The Streak

Walter Dean Myers AND 145th Street

young-adult fiction AND luck OR chance OR superstition OR karma OR fate

young-adult fiction AND basketball

basketball AND superstition

basketball AND hot streaks

New York City AND basketball culture

street basketball AND tournaments

Stuart Scott AND African American sports culture

Where the Gods Fly

JEAN KWOK

2012

In an interview with NPR's Tamara Keith, author Jean Kwok discussed the culture clash experienced by many who chase the American dream. While they may be excited to learn all about their new home, immigrants and their children feel the draw of the familiar world they leave behind. Kwok explains that the pull between

> East or West or old or new—that is something that so many of us experience in our lives. And certainly for immigrants . . . it's a constant struggle. And it's that struggle that is so interesting and that can lead to so much richness.

Kwok examines this richness in much of her work, including her short story "Where the Gods Fly," which was short-listed for the 2012 Sunday Times EFG Private Bank Short Story Award and can be found on the author's website. The narrative follows the thoughts of a concerned mother as she decides to put an end to her daughter's study of ballet in favor of more practical pursuits. It is no simple decision, being influenced by issues of family, money, and heritage.

AUTHOR BIOGRAPHY

Kwok was born in Hong Kong. She was the youngest of seven and describes herself as "a dreamy, impractical child" who surprised everyone when she did well in school. The family moved to New York when she was five years

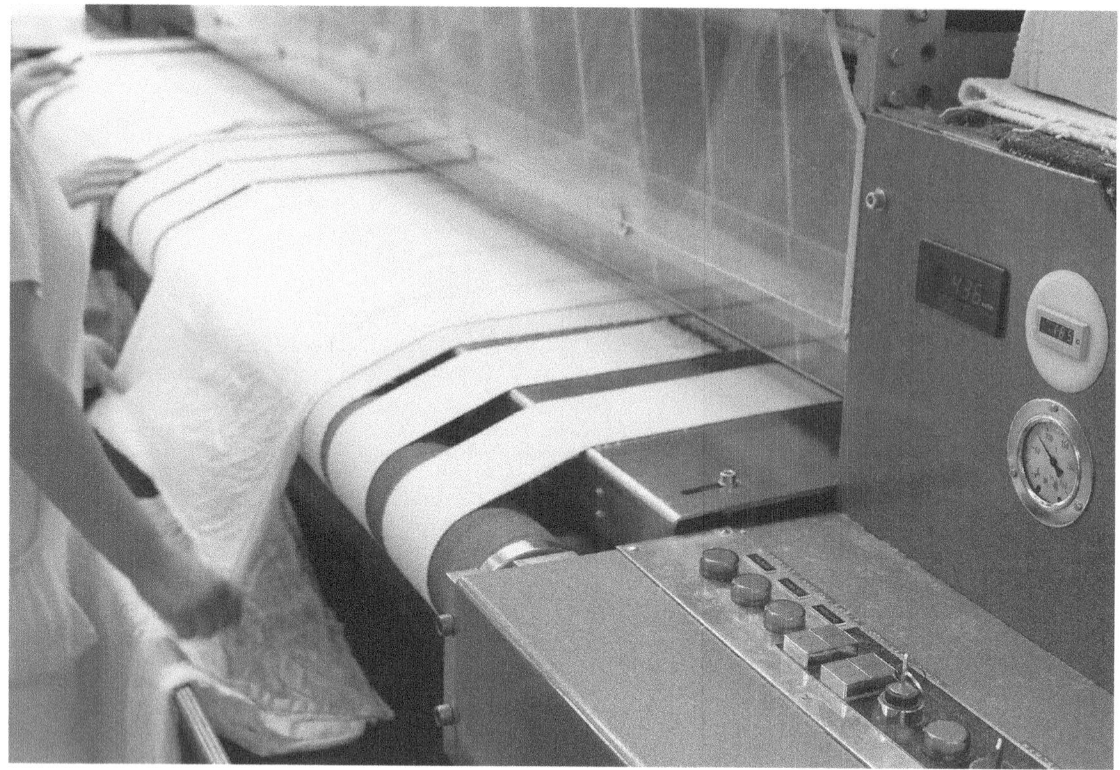

Pearl's parents work long hours in a factory to pay for their expenses, including her dance school tuition (©xtrekx / Shutterstock.com)

old, and their lives changed drastically. Because none of them spoke English, Kwok's parents could only find work in a clothing factory, and Kwok herself struggled in school, which back in Hong Kong had been the one place where she felt she excelled. She quickly learned English and earned top grades once again, but she and her siblings had to work with their parents in the sweatshop to earn enough money to live on. They lived in an apartment with roaches and rats in a condemned building in which the heating system did not work.

By the time Kwok was accepted into Hunter College High School, a school for gifted students, her family's situation had improved, but she knew she would have to earn a scholarship to be able to afford college. During her senior year of high school, she worked in various science labs, hoping the experience would give her an advantage. She began her college career at Harvard University taking courses in physics, believing it to be a practical choice, but she soon changed her major to English. Though she worked several jobs to pay the school expenses not covered by her scholarship, she found more time for extracurricular activities than she ever had before and discovered that she loved to dance. After graduating with honors from Harvard, she continued her studies at Columbia University, earning a master of fine arts degree, but not before working for a few years as a professional ballroom dancer.

Before starting graduate school, Kwok took a trip to Honduras, where she met her future husband, Erwin. Kwok put out her first publication while at Columbia: a short story printed in *Story* magazine. Upon finishing her master's degree, she moved to the Netherlands, her husband's home country. There, she worked as a translator and taught English at Leiden University until she finished her first novel, *Girl in Translation* (2010). The book is somewhat autobiographical, describing the experiences of a girl who lives a double life: going to an exclusive school every day while none of her friends know that she works in a sweatshop at night. Kwok's second novel, *Mambo in Chinatown* (2014), reflects her experiences as a woman who never felt graceful before learning to dance and gaining a sense of her own beauty.

Kwok's writing has been featured in *Time*, the *New York Times*, *USA Today*, *Newsweek*, and *Vogue*. Her short story "Where the Gods Fly" was short-listed for the 2012 Sunday Times EFG Private Bank Short Story Award and was published that same year in an anthology with the work of the other contest honorees. As of 2016, Kwok was living in the Netherlands with her husband and two sons and was working on another book.

PLOT SUMMARY

"Where the Gods Fly" has a first-person narrator, a woman born in China but living in America who is trying to make a big decision: whether to withdraw her daughter from her ballet classes or allow her to continue. As the mother weighs her options, she remembers various scenes starting from when they first came to the United States.

The narrator recalls when her daughter, Pearl, first attended school in America. She is a smart girl who "had already learned to multiply and could read a Chinese newspaper," but because she cannot speak English fluently, she misunderstands the teacher's instructions and later hides her papers, which are covered with red Xs. Pearl also feels out of place because of her looks. She notices that the teacher favors a pale, blond boy, "with hair so white he looks like an egg"—a marked contrast to Pearl with her dark hair.

Because the narrator and her husband have to work long hours at a clothing factory to make ends meet, they cannot be home when Pearl leaves school. They try leaving Pearl in their shabby apartment on her own, but she is anxious while waiting for them to come home, seeing faces in the wallpaper pattern and fearing ghosts. The narrator does not want to bring Pearl to the factory. Many other children of immigrant families work there alongside their parents, but the narrator hopes for a better life for Pearl. Nor does she want Pearl in the factory breathing the "clogged air, thick with fabric dust that clung to our skin like a veil."

At school Pearl begins to feel more comfortable with her peers. However, when she is asked for play dates, her parents refuse, feeling they cannot invite guests to their "stained apartment," which is plagued by rats and roaches. Pearl is too young to be bothered by their poverty, but her mother is ashamed.

The narrator remembers when Pearl began studying ballet. A ballet instructor visits Pearl's third-grade class and singles out Pearl, choosing her to receive a scholarship. The instructor's appraisal of Pearl is puzzling to the narrator—she loves Pearl but believes her to be plain. Although her parents do not care about dance instruction, they use the after-school lessons as free child care. It is still a financial strain to afford ballet shoes and the proper clothes for lessons, but they buy one set of leotard and tights, and Pearl washes them out every night in the bathroom sink.

Years pass, and as Pearl's dancing lessons give her confidence, she begins to act like a typical American teenager. She spends a lot of time on the phone with friends, which worries her mother, especially since she cannot follow English well enough to understand what Pearl is laughing about. Her parents are still strict, not allowing Pearl to attend dances and parties with her classmates, and she runs the water in the bathroom—the only place where she has privacy—to mask the sound of her disappointed crying.

The mother expresses regret that she could not do more for her daughter. She worries that she should have stopped Pearl's dance lessons sooner, because dancing is such a frivolous skill, but Pearl's father started to get sick when she was fourteen. The narrator spent what little time and energy remained after work to tend to her ill husband.

Also when she is fourteen, Pearl is asked by a prestigious ballet school to audition. The mother describes the audition in great detail, explaining how the ballet teacher speaks in Russian with the other judges and dismisses some of the girls because of the flexibility of their bodies, without giving them the chance to dance. When Pearl dances, her mother is taken aback at her skill and beauty but also afraid—the grace and power of her dancing make her seem like an alien creature.

Pearl is accepted to the ballet school and thrives there for a couple of years, but fate intervenes. The narrator explains, "In China, people died of evil spirits, curses, and old age; here, they call it cancer." In spite of her efforts to keep her husband alive, he dies. Now the narrator turns to thinking practically. She watches Pearl dance and worries that her daughter is a stranger to her. She is afraid that dancing is not a skill that can earn a living: "something too ephemeral to grasp."

The narrator decides to withdraw Pearl from the ballet school. Studying "accounting or dentistry" would be more practical. The narrator thinks that someday, if Pearl is strong enough, she, too, will be able to stand in the swirling winds of fate, "searching for the place where the gods fly," seeking the right path.

CHARACTERS

Narrator

The unnamed first-person narrator of "Where the Gods Fly" is a Chinese immigrant, a hard worker, and a protective, devoted mother. She and her husband came to America with their daughter, Pearl, and worked hard in a sewing factory to give their little girl a good life. However, in spite of all of her sacrifices, the narrator feels guilty that she could not do more. Because she and her husband had to work long hours, they had to leave Pearl on her own in their apartment, though she was really too young to be left without supervision.

The narrator never seems to feel at home in the United States, likely because she must spend every waking hour working in the sweatshop to make ends meet. She is not able to experience American life and culture and learn about it. She never learns English, relying on Pearl to translate for her even after they have lived in America for years.

The love the narrator feels for Pearl shines through the story: she aches to see her daughter retreating from the world, is confused by all the changes in her life, and is desperate to keep her out of the factory. She does not want her daughter to be doomed to a dead-end job in a sweatshop. Nor does she dream of ballet stardom for her daughter; she sends her to ballet lessons as free child care so that Pearl will not be alone at their dismal, roach-infested apartment for hours before her parents can make it home from work.

At the ballet-school audition, the narrator is shocked to see how her daughter has changed. Pearl is beautiful, graceful, talented, and confident, and her mother fears the changes in her daughter because she does not understand them. When her husband dies of cancer, the narrator worries for Pearl's future and decides to put an end to Pearl's study of ballet, intending to force her into a more practical ambition.

Pearl

Taken from her home and thrust into an American school, Pearl faces many obstacles. She is sometimes scared, as when she imagines faces in the wallpaper and conceives they are ghosts, though this is understandable in a very young girl left alone for hours after school before her parents come home from work. Pearl notices beauty. Her mother is too ashamed of their shabby apartment to invite guests over, but Pearl sees only "the dances the sun does in the window" and is too accustomed to "the floor strewn with the mattresses" and the leftover fabric her mother "brought home from the factory to cover the worn table" to be embarrassed by these signs of her family's poverty. However, Pearl knows she is different from her classmates, and as she struggles to improve her English, she gets poor grades. Her mother is saddened to see that Pearl is "conspicuous in her foreignness."

Once Pearl begins ballet classes after school, she blossoms. Her grades improve. She begins to "smile more," and her mother notices that "instead of quietly studying or reading, she started to spend her free time on the phone." Like any American teenager, she wants to be with her friends and cries when her parents will not allow it. Pearl changes: "She used to keep everyone at a certain distance; soon, it was only her family she kept away—she embraced the American world now that it embraced her."

The narrator does not understand the evolution of her daughter from "intense, quiet child" to independent young woman. When she watches Pearl at the audition, she sees a side of her daughter she has never seen before. She is shocked that she "no longer recognized my daughter. . . . She flew, she turned and leapt like water in motion, weightless and infinitely powerful." Feeling guilty for all the time she spent working to support Pearl financially, the narrator wonders, "Was this then, what had been happening while I cooked rice, folded the sheets, worked the sewing machine?" Not understanding that her daughter has changed in part because of living in America and in part because of simply growing up, the narrator attributes the changes to the ballet training.

Russian Ballet Teacher

When Pearl is fourteen years old, she auditions for a prestigious ballet school. One of the judges at the audition is a tall, red-haired woman who lifts each girl's leg to see how she moves. Though she and the other judges are pleased by what they see in Pearl, the narrator notes the calculating way they look at their potential students. The narrator believes that the judges "are people with no compassion; it has been carved out and replaced with discipline, muscle, and bone."

Sun

Sun is the narrator's husband and Pearl's father. As Pearl excels in her dance lessons, the narrator struggles to keep her husband alive, "feeding him boiled fish intestines and octopus limbs for nourishment, crushed salted bumblebees for his constant cough." However, when Pearl is fifteen, her father dies of cancer. Without her husband, the narrator fears for Pearl's future. As the narrator struggles to reach her decision about removing Pearl from her dance school, she prays, "Ah Sun, why did you leave us so fast? We still have need of you. . . . Help us turn these winds of fate around." However, Pearl's father cannot offer advice, and the narrator must make her own choice.

THEMES

Immigrant Life

A major aspect of many of Kwok's works is detailed description of immigrant life. A specific focus is the feeling many immigrants have of being outsiders. The narrator in "Where the Gods Fly" seems to feel the family's outsider status for her daughter's sake rather than her own. Although she has "no one in this country, relative or neighbor," this bothers her not because she herself is lonely but rather because there is no one to look after Pearl. As a parent, the narrator does not like to see her daughter "conspicuous in her foreignness" among her classmates, with her "shock of black hair and tawny skin in a classroom of pale freckled children." Even when Pearl starts to fit in and make friends at school, she remains alienated. Her parents, ashamed of their shabby, bug-infested apartment, will not allow her to invite friends over to play. Later, when Pearl is a teenager, she wants to go out with friends, but her parents forbid that as well, fearing what kind of influence her American friends will be.

Part of the reason the narrator is not bothered by her outsider immigrant status is that she moves in a very small circle in the world. She does little other than work and head home for a short evening with her daughter before falling into bed, exhausted. Speaking Chinese only is sufficient for most of her daily activities, because she needs to speak English only when she heads into Pearl's world of school and ballet class. The narrator expresses the desire "to learn English . . . for my daughter more than for anything else." She fears that she will not be able to understand her assimilated daughter if they do not speak the same language—the distance between the immigrant and her new home threatens to divide the family.

Guilt

The mother's guilt that she could not do more for Pearl is a strong thread throughout the story. When they first come to America, the narrator and her husband try to leave Pearl on her own after school, but the mother says she "could not stand coming home to see her little face in the window of the dark apartment." Because she works constantly, even bringing home sewing from the factory to keep earning pay, however meager, in the evening, the mother is not able to give Pearl her time and attention the way she wishes she could.

She also regrets that she cannot afford more indulgences—such as an occasional hot dog from a street vendor. The lack of money causes the mother to feel guilty in subtle ways too, such as when she sees Pearl washing out her single leotard every night so that it will be ready for dance class the following day; the mother does not expressly say she wishes she could afford at least one other outfit for Pearl's classes, but the regretful tone is clear.

As the story builds, the narrator admits that she had been "too busy with work to spare time for most of Pearl's recitals." This is not the lack of interest sometimes seen in workaholic parents. Rather, the narrator and her husband must work virtually every moment to support themselves; on the rare occasions when they were able to attend a recital, the narrator

TOPICS FOR FURTHER STUDY

- Using online and traditional print resources, research the history of sweatshops in the United States as well as the current struggle to ensure fair labor conditions for all. Create a website to share what you have learned, including links to organizations fighting sweatshops and helping underpaid workers.
- Reread "Where the Gods Fly," paying particular attention to the narration. Because Kwok uses a first-person narrator, readers cannot be certain that the information she provides is true and unbiased. Write an opinion paper explaining whether you think the narrator is reliable. Provide examples from the text to support your opinion.
- In the story, the narrator is a practicing Buddhist and describes her view of fate as winds pushing people in the directions willed by the gods. If you are not strong, the narrator believes, the winds "can topple you over and roll you into the earth." In contrast, "if you have the strength to withstand their blows, they can propel you to where the gods fly." Pearl explains to her mother an alternate concept of fate, which she likely learned about in school: the Greek myth of the Fates, the "three sisters who spin and cut the thread of life." Using online and traditional print resources, research various cultures' ideas about fate. Pick three examples that you find interesting and share them with your class in a formal presentation.
- Read Marina Budhos's young-adult novel *Tell Us We're Home* (2010), which focuses on three girls, Maria, Jaya, and Lola, all of whom are daughters of immigrant domestic workers. The main conflict of the story arises when Jaya's mother is accused of theft. Imagine that Kwok's Pearl attends school with Budhos's characters and hears about the accusation. Write a story in which other students are giving Jaya a hard time. Think about how Pearl would react. Would she be more likely to believe that Jaya's mother is innocent because she understands that immigrants are often marginalized and treated unfairly? Pearl's experience in dance has given her confidence, but would she be confident enough to speak up and defend Jaya? Or would she keep quiet for fear of being bullied herself?

explains, "there'd been the constant struggle to keep myself awake through my exhaustion." The mother prays to Buddha to make Pearl understand that "all I have done, I have done because it was the only choice I had." However, even though she feels she has had no choice but to work constantly to keep food on the table, she still feels guilty that she could not do more.

STYLE

Flashback

In "Where the Gods Fly," very little happens in the present tense of the story. The narrator is in a temple. She bows to the Buddha statues and hears monks ringing a gong. Most of the story consists of flashbacks—the things the narrator considers as she contemplates a big decision. The flashbacks are often memories of the family's adjustment to living in a new country. The narrator recalls sending Pearl off to school, "so tiny" in her "red sweater." Pearl quickly becomes frustrated that she does not understand the assignments or why the teacher likes the fair-haired "egg-boy" better than her. The anxious mother also remembers Pearl's fear at being left in the apartment on her own, imagining she sees faces of ghosts in the wallpaper. The mother's wish that she could have done more for her daughter is clear in some of the flashbacks, as when she thinks of the way Pearl

The first-person narrator is a Chinese American mother concerned about her daughter, Pearl
(©Vladimir Volodin / Shutterstock.com)

would pull her mother's "skirt beside every hot dog stand we passed in the street, never daring to ask but yearning with her eyes."

Many of the early flashbacks are small moments like this—almost a snapshot of a moment that the narrator remembers. However, the final flashback is more detailed, describing Pearl's audition at the prestigious ballet school. The narrator describes the twelve hopeful girls all in a line. Some are never allowed to dance, dismissed because of the condition of their bodies. The mother recalls the stern judge with red hair, speaking Russian, and the intense surprise she felt at seeing her daughter dance.

The flashback method works well in the story, because each event is part of the evidence that the narrator uses to make her decision to withdraw Pearl from her ballet classes. By using the flashbacks, Kwok makes the narrative flow naturally, following the course of the mother's thoughts.

Language

When Kwok came to America as a little girl, she and her family spoke little English. She and her siblings learned the language quickly and were soon translating for their parents. This experience made Kwok aware of the barrier language can be for new immigrants, and she often explores the issue in her work. On her website, the author explains her thoughts on the subject when writing *Girl in Translation*:

> I wanted to put the reader into the head and heart of a Chinese person. I wanted to give English-speaking readers a unique experience: to actually become a Chinese immigrant for the course of my novel, to hear Chinese like a native speaker and to hear English as gibberish. And for my readers to experience something thousands of immigrants live with every day: what it's like to be intelligent, thoughtful and articulate in your own language, but to come across as ignorant and uneducated in English.

In *Girl in Translation*, Kwok portrays the frustration and confusion one feels when one cannot speak and understand a language. However, Kwok also explains that she was interested in showing the other side of this equation. Because her own mother "never really learned to speak English," she sometimes came "across as very simple. I wanted people to hear how eloquent, wise and funny she really was in Chinese." Kwok does exactly this in "Where the Gods Fly." Although the reader knows that Pearl must translate what her teachers say to her mother—much like Kwok herself did as a child—the story is not presented in halting, half-learned English. Rather than phrase the prose the way it would sound if the narrator were speaking, Kwok uses traditional, grammatically correct English to show the eloquence of the narrator's thoughts—as if translated from the Chinese—even if she cannot express herself fluently in English.

HISTORICAL CONTEXT

Immigrant Assimilation: Melting Pot or Salad Bowl?

Decades ago, when people spoke of the assimilation of immigrants in the United States, they often used the phrase "great American melting pot." As people chose to make their homes in America, they brought their language, culture,

Pearl enrolls in ballet classes because her parents hope it will help her integrate in her new home (©Shutterstock)

and traditions from their homelands, but for the most part they learned to speak English and tried to conform to mainstream culture. More recently, rather than a melting pot, the metaphor used more often is that of a salad bowl or a mosaic: instead of elements melting and blending into a homogeneous whole, various cultural elements remain separate but come together to create a lively mixture.

This is not a completely new idea. In spite of the traditional expectation that immigrants would assimilate, various communities have settled together upon their arrival in America, in neighborhoods referred to by names such as Chinatown or Little Italy. There are many reasons why people would opt to settle among their own countrymen and resist assimilation. Some do not speak fluent English. Others simply fear the unfamiliar ways of doing things in their new country. Some come to America only to take advantage of plentiful jobs and decent wages before returning home. Indeed, many Chinese migrant workers in the western United States in the nineteenth century, such as those hired to help build the great western railroads, faced criticism and discrimination because they were judged to have settled in America only temporarily rather than seeking to start a new life.

American immigration has been changing since the passage of the 1965 Immigration and Naturalization Act, also known as the Hart-Celler Act. This set of laws put an end to the quota system, which set a limit on the number of people who could immigrate to the United States from each country. The quota system was hugely biased, allowing many more new immigrants from Europe than from other continents. The policies enacted in 1965 concentrated on reuniting families and bringing in skilled workers and resulted in increased immigration from Africa, Asia, and Latin America.

Today, there is some controversy about the assimilation of American immigrants. Because many choose to live in the United States but maintain most aspects of their homeland's culture, including language, some Americans fear that something essential in American identity will be lost if newcomers refuse to adapt. Tom Gjelten, in his *Atlantic* article "Should Immigration Require Assimilation?," quotes historian Arthur Schlesinger Jr., who writes that the salad bowl approach to assimilation "belittles *unum* and glorifies *pluribus*," threatening the traditional common goal of the country, which he sees as an effort "not to preserve old cultures, but to forge a new American culture." Schlesinger sees the interest in and stress on multiculturalism as divisive, driving various groups of Americans apart rather than unifying them.

Other scholars view Schlesinger's assertion as closed-minded—based on an unfairly biased view of what America should be. For example, Gjelten also quotes Molefi Kete Asante, a professor of African American studies at Temple University, who explains in his book *The Painful Demise of Eurocentrism* that

> the American idea is not a static but a dynamic one. . . . We must constantly reinvent ourselves in the light of our diverse experiences. One reason this nation works the way it does is our diversity. Try to make Africans and Asians copies of Europeans . . . and you will force the disunity Schlesinger fears.

Not all critical attention paid to Kwok's work has been positive. Monica Chiu, in her essay "Spheres of Influence in Jean Kwok's *Girl in Translation*: The Classroom, the Blog, and the Ethnic Story," concedes that the book was popular with readers and many critics. "The novel successfully debuted on both sides of the world: in Hong Kong, Kwok's city of origin, as well as in the United States," Chiu writes. However, Chiu takes on a sarcastic tone, calling the novel a "well-rehearsed tale of immigrant hardship brimming with bootstrap mentality and clinched with a feel-good conclusion only slightly dampened by heartbreak." Chiu also dismisses the writing style as unworthy of notice, asserting that the book is "written in middling prose" and "rife with irrational narrative leaps."

However, most critics see the promise in Kwok's stories, especially in her ability to capture the emotions and experiences of immigrants and their families. Rochman explains that as *Girl in Translation*'s Kimberly fumbles her way through mainstream American society, "her misunderstandings are both hilarious and wrenching." Overall, Rochman believes that "immigrants, new and old, will find much to savor" in Kwok's fiction.

CRITICAL OVERVIEW

Although "Where the Gods Fly" has not received much specific critical notice, Kwok's novels have gathered mostly positive reviews. For example, Annie McCormick, reviewing an audiobook of *Girl in Translation* for *Booklist*, describes it as a "charming coming-of-age tale." Also writing in *Booklist*, Hazel Rochman praises the emotion Kwok includes in the book, calling it a "contemporary immigration story of heartbreaking struggle." A review in *Publishers Weekly* draws attention to Kwok's skill in portraying family relationships, because "it is the portrayal of Kimberly's relationship with her mother that makes this more than just another immigrant story." Kwok's *Mambo in Chinatown* received similarly positive notice from reviewers. *Booklist*'s Joanne Wilkinson describes it as a "winning second novel" and points to the way "Kwok infuses her heartwarming story with both the sensuality of dance and the optimism of a young woman coming into her own."

CRITICISM

Kristen Sarlin Greenberg

Greenberg is a freelance writer and editor with a background in literature and philosophy. In the following essay, she examines the various elements influencing the narrator as she makes her decision in Kwok's "Where the Gods Fly."

Jean Kwok's short story "Where the Gods Fly" is undeniably immigrant literature. The story addresses many of the obstacles faced when first arriving in a new country—the disorientation of not knowing the language, as well as the discomfort of feeling like an outsider and looking different from those around you. However, the story also focuses on the relationship between an overworked woman, recently widowed, and her daughter. Kwok provides a fascinating snapshot of a significant moment in the life of this worried, grieving mother as she contemplates a major decision. Her daughter, Pearl, has excelled in dance, but the mother thinks it is time for the girl to turn her attention to studies that will ensure a job and a steady lifestyle.

WHAT DO I READ NEXT?

- In Jeanette Ingold's young-adult novel *Paper Daughter* (2010), protagonist Maggie explores her relationship with her father after his death by immersing herself in an investigation into family secrets. In the process, she struggles with issues of personal and ethnic identity and learns about America's checkered history regarding immigration issues.
- In *The Weight of Water* (2013), young-adult author Sarah Crossan tells the story of Kasienka, who leaves Poland with her mother to find a new home in England. Like the narrator and Pearl in "Where the Gods Fly," Kasienka's mother struggles to earn enough to get by, while Kasienka herself tries to fit in at a school where nothing is what she is used to.
- Madeline Y. Hsu examines the history of immigrants from China in the United States in her 2015 book *The Good Immigrants: How the Yellow Peril Became the Model Minority*. Early American immigration laws were discriminatory, barring many immigrants from Asian countries, and the discrimination continued until the middle of the twentieth century.
- Kwok's first novel, *Girl in Translation* (2010), centers on Kimberly Chang, who as a child moved from Hong Kong to New York with her mother. Kim struggles to balance the different pressures she feels: the poverty of her home life, her mother's expectations, maintaining top grades in school, and the love she feels for a boy who feels nothing like the ambition that drives Kimberly.
- Amy Tan's novel *The Joy Luck Club*, which was published in 1989 and adapted into a film in 1993, was a runaway best seller. The story focuses on two eras: 1949, when four women leave China to come to America, and forty years later, when their daughters take center stage. Tan explores the complicated nature of mother-daughter relationships in this modern classic of American immigrant literature.
- Michaela DePrince's memoir *Taking Flight: From War Orphan to Star Ballerina* (2014) reveals the power of dance to inspire and uplift. Because of a skin condition that makes spots appear on her skin, DePrince was sometimes called a "devil child" in the orphanage where she lived in Sierra Leone before she was adopted by an American family at age four. Her family encouraged her love of dance, and she eventually enrolled in the Jacqueline Kennedy Onassis School at the American Ballet Theatre and became the youngest principal dancer with the Dance Theatre of Harlem.

It is clear throughout the story that the narrator has made many sacrifices for her daughter out of love and devotion to her well-being. At the very beginning of the story, the narrator establishes how hard she works to provide for the family. She and her husband spend all of their "waking hours at the factory in Chinatown." Although she feels guilty for missing Pearl's dance performances, she is not often able to be away from work to attend; when she does, she is so exhausted that she struggles to stay awake. Although the family lives in poverty and could benefit from the extra money Pearl could earn working at her parents' side, the narrator believes that "Pearl was too young, or so I argued, to breathe in that clogged air, thick with fabric dust that clung to our skin like a veil."

The phrase "or so I argued" makes it clear that there is someone—others at the factory

> "CONSCIOUSLY, THE NARRATOR BELIEVES SHE IS DOING WHAT IS BEST FOR HER DAUGHTER IN GUIDING HER TOWARD A MORE PRACTICAL PURSUIT. HOWEVER, KWOK SUBTLY REVEALS THAT THE NARRATOR'S MOTIVATION IS, IN PART, SELFISH."

whose own children work there or perhaps even Pearl's father—who think Pearl should already be hard at work, but the narrator has an "instinct to protect her" from the life that would likely follow from doing physical labor from a young age. When the narrator imagines Pearl working in the factory, she sees

> her entire life pulled taut before her like thread—her thin fingers worn callused and red by years of sewing in the factory, then, if she was lucky, marriage to some office clerk, a pack of children, and finally, Pearl the woman submerged under the struggle to feed and clothe them all.

In short, the narrator imagines a life for Pearl similar to the one she herself leads, the drudgery of grueling work day after day with no hope of anything better in the future.

Kwok hints that the narrator might once have had hopes of something better for herself. She explains that when she "was a girl in China, I was not permitted to go to classes." What little learning she collected she "picked up through lingering at the table, pretending to dust or sweep, as my brothers studied." She describes how her mother, "a progressive woman, knew what I was doing and not only allowed me this but would leave their books where I could find them when no one else was home." With this detail, Kwok provides an interesting perspective on the mother-daughter relationship, showing that the narrator's mother might also have dreamed that her daughter would find a better life than she herself had.

This might explain why the narrator wanted to come to America. If girls were not allowed the same education as their brothers in China, perhaps the narrator hoped for more equitable treatment for Pearl in the United States. The mother understands the value of education. Although she allows Pearl to attend dance lessons, she pulls her daughter aside to stress that

> dancing is not something you can keep, like food, or a house, or a university diploma. A few minutes, an hour, and it is gone. If you had an education, you wouldn't have to be dependent on your husband.

Pearl "did not listen" to this advice. Perhaps she is too young to heed the warning, or perhaps she dreams of being a professional dancer and will not consider other paths—Kwok sticks closely to the narrator's point of view in the story, so while the reader sees Pearl's behavior through her mother's eyes, there is little insight into Pearl's thoughts and emotions. This is not a flaw in the story but rather a reflection of the central thread of the mother's feeling and fearing the distance between them.

When Pearl first starts to fit in at school and begins her studies in dance, the narrator sees positive signs. As the "glory of her dancing passed into her life at school," Pearl is happier, doing "better in her classes" and seeming "to smile more." At first, the narrator is "pleased" about her daughter's improved mood, but conflict arises. Pearl's friends invite her "to movies, get-togethers, holiday dinners," but her parents want her to behave like "a proper Chinese girl" and will not allow her to go out with her friends. Disappointed, Pearl locks herself in the bathroom, "the only place she could be alone," and the narrator can hear "her sobbing through the sound of running water."

In spite of her parents' protectiveness, however, Pearl "embraced the American world now that it embraced her." Like many teenagers, she spends a lot of time "talking and laughing on the telephone with her American friends, jabbering in English much faster than she could speak Chinese by then." Her mother is concerned, in part because she does not understand the conversation: "She could have been giggling over anything—boys, drinking—how could I know? It was just babble to me, her own mother." Because she is worried, the narrator admits that "a part of me wanted to run over and wrench the phone from her hands."

The pivotal moment comes when the narrator watches her daughter at the audition for the prestigious ballet school. When Pearl begins to dance, she seems transformed. The narrator "no longer recognized my daughter. Every glance, every limb, the arch of her hand, curve of leg, was suspended in beauty and a terrible poignancy." Mystified, the mother wonders, "Was this then, what had been happening while I cooked rice, folded the sheets, worked the sewing machine? When had this change, this great gift, come upon my daughter?" Rather than being proud of her daughter's skill and beauty, however, the mother is taken aback.

It seems as if the narrator regrets not putting an end to Pearl's dance career at that time, which she describes as the moment when "evil winds had begun to foment." Instead, the mother is distracted by her husband's illness. He has cancer, and his wife fights to keep him alive. Because of the distance she sees forming between herself and her daughter, likely increased by the stress and worry of her husband's illness and the sadness of his death, the narrator decides to withdraw Pearl from the ballet school. She thinks she is doing what is best for her daughter. While pondering the direction their lives have taken, the narrator thinks,

> Everything has been blown by the winds of fate; here I am in America, my husband has just died, and my daughter is pursuing something too ephemeral to grasp. I have let the winds take us where they will for too long; now, I act upon my choice.

In a relatively small number of words, Kwok masterfully illustrates the complicated nature of making a decision. A multitude of feelings and experiences affect the narrator's thinking as she ponders whether to allow Pearl to continue dancing. Consciously, the narrator believes she is doing what is best for her daughter in guiding her toward a more practical pursuit. However, Kwok subtly reveals that the narrator's motivation is, in part, selfish. She sees Pearl's dancing and "no longer recognized my daughter." She is afraid of losing her daughter and acts to keep her close.

Perhaps rather than Pearl's dancing, the real problem is that the mother is never able to create a true home in America. She never learns to speak English. She never has a job that lets her do more than barely scrape by, and although she does not explicitly state that she dislikes the work, it seems unlikely she could gain a feeling of satisfaction sewing seam after seam in a clothing factory. After approximately a decade in America, the narrator seems to have made no friends. Apart from having no time to socialize, she has never had a home she felt proud of, so she has never invited guests. The narrator explains that she left Pearl alone at home after school because she had "no one in this country, relative or neighbor," who could babysit. This highlights her total lack of community.

Pearl thrives in dance class, and as she improves, her popularity increases *(©Ronnie Chua / Shutterstock.com)*

Clearly the narrator never feels as if she belongs in America. Without any kind of friendship or support, she clings to Pearl, hoping to keep her within the same small sphere of existence so that she is not completely alone. It is easy for the narrator to pin the blame for the potential loss of her daughter on ballet school, but in truth the struggles of immigrant life contributed far more to her isolation, making it impossible for her to find any kind of happiness or fulfillment.

Source: Kristen Sarlin Greenberg, Critical Essay on "Where the Gods Fly," in *Short Stories for Students*, Gale, Cengage Learning, 2017.

Joanne Wilkinson

In the following review, Wilkinson describes Kwok's book Mambo in Chinatown *as "heartwarming."*

Clumsy 22-year-old Charlie Wong had hoped to become a noodle maker, like her famous father, but instead toils away night and day as a dishwasher in New York City's Chinatown. Her mother, once a star dancer for the Beijing Ballet, passed away when Charlie was 14, and she has spent the years since looking after her younger sister, Lisa. And it's Lisa who recognizes that Charlie's job saps all of her happiness and energy. Lisa encourages Charlie to accept a receptionist's position at a ballroom dance studio in Midtown Manhattan, and, for the first time, Charlie begins to realize that she may have inherited her mother's talent. Soon she is entirely transformed, teaching beginning students and competing in a dance competition. Not everyone is happy with the change, especially her father. Drawing on her newfound confidence, Charlie attempts to navigate the great divide between Eastern and Western cultures. In her winning second novel (after *Girl in Translation*, 2010), Kwok infuses her heartwarming story with both the sensuality of dance and the optimism of a young woman coming into her own.

Source: Joanne Wilkinson, Review of *Mambo in Chinatown*, in *Booklist*, Vol. 110, Nos. 19–20, June 1, 2014, p. 38.

Hazel Rochman

In the following review, Rochman predicts readers will find "much to savor" in Kwok's work.

Drawing on Kwok's personal experience, this debut novel tells a contemporary immigration story of heartbreaking struggle and wild success. Ah Kim, 11, leaves Hong Kong in the 1980s and moves with Ma into a freezing Brooklyn slum apartment infested with roaches and rats. The hostile teacher calls "Kimberly" a cheat when she gets good grades. After school, she helps Ma reach her quota in a clothing factory in Chinatown, sometimes until midnight. In simple, searing, richly detailed prose, Kwok captures the anguish of the struggle, including the illegal factory work and child labor, but eventually, as fortunes change, the novel becomes a rags-to-riches story (Kimberly gets into a top high school and then Yale). Success, however, brings the universal immigrant lament of not fitting in. Kim cannot get the rules of fighting and flirting, and her misunderstandings are both hilarious and wrenching. "I wanted to be part of things but I had no idea how." And, always, there are those who don't make it. Immigrants, new and old, will find much to savor here, from the drama of family secrets to the confusing coming-of-age.

Source: Hazel Rochman, Review of *Girl in Translation*, in *Booklist*, Vol. 106, No. 15, April 1, 2010, p. 22.

Publishers Weekly

In the following review, the anonymous reviewer describes the story of Girl in Translation *as "moving."*

This audiobook is the perfect match of narrator and material. Grayce Wey's performance as immigrant Kimberly Chang feels absolutely authentic. As the adult Kimberly looking back at her life, Wey has just a touch of a Chinese accent (appropriate for a character who's lived in America for two decades), and her tone conveys bittersweet regret even while knowing she made the right choice. But when speaking as the younger, newly arrived Kimberly, Wey's Chinese accent is much heavier, and we can hear Kimberly's confusion, anxiety, and struggle to adjust to this new culture. Wey perfectly evokes Kimberly's growing assertiveness and determination, her teenage longing, joy, and pain when falling in love for the first time, and her conflicted feelings when making difficult decisions about her path in life. A moving and memorable listen.

Source: Review of *Girl in Translation* (audiobook), in *Publishers Weekly*, Vol. 257, No. 29, July 26, 2010, p. 68.

Annie McCormick

In the following review, McCormick praises an audiobook adaptation of Kwok's novel Girl in Translation.

This heartfelt debut novel is told from the perspective of Kimberly—an 11-year-old Chinese immigrant who lives with her mother (Ma) in a Brooklyn slum in the 1980s. Smart as a whip, young Kimberly is a good student but has trouble adjusting and fitting in socially with a new culture and her classmates. Ma works long hours in an unsanitary clothing factory in Chinatown. Kimberly excels in school, which helps her gain admission to a top high school and college. Wey reads Kimberly with a slight Chinese accent and Ma in a believably more thick Chinese dialect. Her reading of the many minor characters adds a touch of variety—a schoolteacher speaks in a New York accent, a librarian sounds Middle Eastern, and a housing-complex neighbor uses slow, southern speech patterns. Wey transitions with ease and grace from American dialects to various levels of Chinese accents. This charming coming-of-age tale, marked with skilled narration, will captivate listeners.

Source: Annie McCormick, Review of *Girl in Translation* (audiobook), in *Booklist*, Vol. 107, No. 1, September 1, 2010, p. 57.

Laura Castellano

In the following interview, Kwok talks about the similarities between herself and the character Kimberly in her novel Girl in Translation.

You have a lot in common with the main character Kimberly. You worked in a clothing factory in Chinatown as a girl. You lived without heat in Brooklyn, and you excelled in public school and won scholarships to private schools. Was writing this therapeutic for you?

I think every act of writing is therapeutic in a way. What I think is wonderful about writing and fiction is that you can take something that was difficult, and writing about it transforms it into something positive. Because we were very poor when we came to the U.S. and had to work in a factory, live in an apartment without heat, and we'd been quite a well-to-do family before immigrating, there was a lot of shame associated with our poverty. It was something we never talked about.

You write moments of humiliation with a little bit of humor. Does this lightheartedness come from experience?

Absolutely. It was important to me to not have this be a dark book. I think there are difficult things that Kimberly and her mother experience, but in the end they triumph because they are dignified people with integrity. I think it's important to have humor and to be able to laugh at these things in your life, because they make the burden lighter.

Kimberly's mother never learned to speak English. How did that affect their lives?

My mother never really learned to speak English. She worked from day to night, always in the kitchen with skirts and belts that she brought home from the factory. She was always falling asleep because she was so tired. To Americans she comes across as very simple. And in writing this book, I wanted people to hear how eloquent and wise and funny she really was in Chinese, and also to see how simple a mother, like Kimberly Chang's mother, could be in English. Normally, you see a character only in one language, but now you can see her reflected in both languages.

You live in Holland now. Where do you consider home?

I love Holland and I love the Dutch people, but New York will always be my home. I think it's hard for people in America to realize, but America is a great dream for many, many people. It really is. But we came here, and we expected to see the beautiful skyscrapers of Manhattan, and instead we were put in the slums of Brooklyn. Jr was really different from what we expected.

Source: Laura Castellano, "Q&A: *PW* Talks with Jean Kwok," in *Publishers Weekly*, March 15, 2010, p. 35.

SOURCES

"About Jean," Jean Kwok website, http://www.jeankwok.com/author.shtml (accessed August 30, 2016).

Branigin, William, "Immigrants Shunning Idea of Assimilation," in *Washington Post*, May 25, 1998, http://www.washingtonpost.com/wp-srv/national/longterm/meltingpot/meltingpot.htm (accessed September 1, 2016).

Chiu, Monica, "Spheres of Influence in Jean Kwok's *Girl in Translation*: The Classroom, the Blog, and the Ethnic Story," in *The Transnationalism of American Culture: Literature, Film, and Music*, edited by Rocío G. Davis, Routledge, 2013, p. 186.

"FAQ," Jean Kwok website, http://www.jeankwok.com/faq.shtml (accessed August 30, 2016).

Gjelten, Tom, "Should Immigration Require Assimilation?," in *Atlantic*, October 3, 2015, http://www.theatlantic.com/politics/archive/2015/10/should-immigration-require-assimilation/406759/ (accessed September 1, 2016).

Keith, Tamara, "A Noodle-Maker's Daughter Falls for Ballroom Dancing in *Mambo*," NPR website, http://www.npr.org/2014/07/05/328187558/a-noodle-makers-daughter-falls-for-ballroom-dancing-in-mambo (accessed August 30, 2016).

Kwok, Jean, "Where the Gods Fly," Jean Kwok website, 2011, http://www.jeankwok.com/Where_the_Gods_Fly.shtml (accessed August 30, 2016).

McCormick, Annie, Review of *Girl in Translation* (audiobook), in *Booklist*, Vol. 107, No. 1, September 1, 2010, p. 57.

Review of *Girl in Translation*, in *Publishers Weekly*, March 15, 2010, pp. 34–35, http://www.publishersweekly.com/978-1-59448-756-9 (accessed August 30, 2016).

Rochman, Hazel, Review of *Girl in Translation*, in *Booklist*, Vol. 106, No. 15, April 1, 2010, p. 22.

"Sunday Times EFG Short Story Award 2012," BookTrust website, http://www.booktrust.org.uk/d/prizes/5/2012 (accessed August 30, 2016).

"U.S. Immigration since 1965," History.com, http://www.history.com/topics/us-immigration-since-1965 (accessed September 3, 2016).

Wilkinson, Joanne, Review of *Mambo in Chinatown*, in *Booklist*, Vol. 110, Nos. 19–20, June 1, 2014, p. 38.

FURTHER READING

Gordon, Jennifer, *Suburban Sweatshops: The Fight for Immigrant Rights*, Harvard University Press, 2005.

Sweatshops are often seen as a thing of the past or a product of the inner city, but Gordon's book shows that the sweatshop mentality is still prevalent in all kinds of communities. In addition to documenting the problem through personal stories of immigrant workers, Gordon offers some solutions to help workers get fair treatment and a decent wage.

Howrey, Meg, *The Cranes Dance*, Vintage, 2012.

Howrey's novel takes a look at the love, guilt, and competition that complicate the relationship between sisters Kate and Gwen Crane, dancers in a renowned New York ballet company.

Kwok, Jean, *Mambo in Chinatown*, Riverhead Books, 2014.

Protagonist Charlie Wong is twenty-two years old, living with her widowed father and younger sister in Chinatown. Although she was born in New York, Charlie has rarely strayed out of her familiar neighborhood. A job at a ballroom dance studio broadens her horizons, forcing her to find balance between her own life and the expectations of her family, her heritage and her identity as an American.

Lee, Erika, *The Making of Asian America: A History*, Simon & Schuster, 2015.

Lee offers a detailed account of the role Asian Americans have played in the development of the nation, from sixteenth-century sailors and indentured "coolies" to modern-day immigrants.

SUGGESTED SEARCH TERMS

Jean Kwok AND Where the Gods Fly

Jean Kwok AND immigrant literature

Jean Kwok AND interview

mother-daughter relationships AND immigrant literature

dancing AND immigrant literature

immigrants AND sweatshops

religion AND immigrant literature

Buddhism

The World's Greatest Fishermen

LOUISE ERDRICH

1982

Louise Erdrich, one of the most prominent and highly regarded Native American novelists of the late twentieth and early twenty-first centuries, began her career in fiction with the award-winning story "The World's Greatest Fishermen." Erdrich is of Chippewa heritage—the nation's name is better transcribed as Ojibway or Ojibwe—and grew up in North Dakota, where her parents taught at an Indian boarding school. She is an enrolled member of the Turtle Mountain Band of Chippewa, centered in the reservation town of Belcourt, where she has never lived but has frequently visited family. Her father was of German descent, and Erdrich's characters typically have varying proportions of Indian heritage, ranging from full-blooded and traditionally minded to mostly white in terms of both genes and culture.

Erdrich wrote "The World's Greatest Fishermen" with the assistance of Michael Dorris, also an author of literature about Native Americans, who was then her husband and frequent collaborator. The story takes place in a reservation town but is largely narrated by a young woman named Patsy, who, as Erdrich did, lives off the reservation. Thus, she is not entirely at home among her Indian relatives but can consider their actions with exacting perception. First published in *Chicago* magazine in October 1982, the story was revised and retitled to become "The World's Greatest Fisherman," the first chapter of Erdrich's award-winning

Louise Erdrich *(©Ulf Andersen / Getty Images Entertainment / Getty Images)*

debut novel *Love Medicine* (1984). The original version of the story is included in Erdrich's 2009 collection *The Red Convertible: Selected and New Stories, 1978–2008*. The story addresses, with discretion, sexual activity, the influence of alcohol, and domestic violence.

AUTHOR BIOGRAPHY

Karen Louise Erdrich was born in Little Falls, Minnesota, on June 7, 1954. The town where she grew up, Wahpeton, North Dakota, is in the Red River valley, along the state's eastern border, much of which was originally part of the home territory of the Turtle Mountain Chippewa. The original US designation of the tribe as Chippewa still stands even though it represents a mispronunciation of Ojibway. The present-day Turtle Mountain Reservation is a small parcel of land in north-central North Dakota. Erdrich's parents both taught at the Bureau of Indian Affairs boarding school in Wahpeton. Erdich's mother (who was three-quarters Chippewa and one-quarter French) was the daughter of Patrick Gourneau, the Turtle Mountain Chippewa's tribal chair, who lived on the reservation with his wife. Gourneau was a beader, powwow dancer, and storyteller who impressed on his granddaughter the value of stories. By high school, Erdrich enjoyed reading poetry and recording thoughts and observations in a journal.

Erdrich left her home region for the first time to attend Dartmouth College, in Hanover, New Hampshire, in 1972, as part of the school's first coeducational class. It was also in 1972 that Dartmouth, founded in 1769 with a commitment to Indian education as part of its mission, finally established a Native American studies program. Through the department's classes, Erdrich gained greater appreciation for and interest in her Ojibway background. She majored in English with a focus on creative writing, and she won the school's Cox Prize for fiction and a poetry prize.

After earning her BA degree in 1976, Erdrich worked for a short time for the North Dakota Arts Council as an itinerant poet and teacher. In 1977, she worked on a public television documentary about the Northern Plains

Indians. Erdrich's other early work experience included time as restaurant server, lifeguard, sugar-beet weeder, cucumber picker, and photograph developer. She earned an MA degree from Johns Hopkins University, in Baltimore, in 1979. She then moved to Boston to become editor and communications director of the *Circle*, the newspaper of the Boston Indian Council. Her interaction with urban mixed-blood Indians left her more and more inspired to write about her own experiences and perspectives. In 1981, she married Michael Dorris, a writer and formerly a professor of hers at Dartmouth. Erdrich became mother to Dorris's three adoptive children (one of whom was severely debilitated by fetal alcohol syndrome), and the couple had three more children. Dorris assisted a great deal in Erdrich's development as a writer and also published his own work, but they eventually separated in light of revelations of Dorris's abuse of his children. Dorris's claims of Modoc heritage also came into question, because they could not be verified by any tribal records. Dorris committed suicide in 1997.

Erdrich's rise to literary fame began with her winning the Nelson Algren Award in 1982 for her short story "The World's Greatest Fishermen," which was written over the span of two weeks with the award competition in mind. In 1984, she published both her first poetry collection, *Jacklight*, and her first novel, *Love Medicine*, which received a variety of awards. Though reviews of *Jacklight* were favorable, Erdrich found the medium of poetry both too intimate and too constricting. What she really wanted to do was be a storyteller. She went on to write several more novels presenting different episodes and periods in the lives of her fictional Ojibway, mixed-blood, and white characters in the Turtle Mountain region, including *The Beet Queen* (1986), *The Bingo Palace* (1994), and *Last Report on the Miracles at Little No Horse* (2001), a finalist for the National Book Award. Erdrich's fictionalization of life at Turtle Mountain is often likened to William Faulkner's extended exploration of his fictional Yoknapatawpha County, Mississippi. Erdrich also wrote other works of fiction, a nonfiction book, and juvenile literature, including *The Birchbark House* (1999). Her novel *LaRose* was published in 2016. As of that year, she lived in Minnesota and owned an independent bookstore, Birchbark Books, devoted to supporting Native literature, art, and culture.

MEDIA ADAPTATIONS

In 2009, Symphony Space produced a recording, available via audio streaming online, in which Erdrich discusses her collection *The Red Convertible* with Amy Goodman, and Sonia Manzano reads an excerpt from the book. The running time is one hour, twenty-three minutes.

PLOT SUMMARY

I

"The World's Greatest Fishermen" opens on June Kashpaw wandering the cold streets of Williston, North Dakota, on the day before Easter as she waits to leave on the noon bus. When a man (Andy) summons her with a rap from inside a bar window, she at once enters to drink with him, thinking perhaps she knows him. He offers her the egg he has been peeling, which she eats, then devouring two more. After June asks where the party is and then mentions that she has only a little while before her bus leaves, the man, an engineer, sweeps her in his arms and takes her in his truck to another bar.

Later on, in a bar (perhaps yet another), June is startled to consciousness by a vision of a lethal hose. She tells the engineer he has got to be different.

Going to the ladies' room, June finds herself in the bathroom stall suddenly having a sort of out-of-body (or just out-of-clothing) experience. She drops and picks up the knob to her room's front door, which functions as the key, and returns to the engineer.

They end up in his truck well out of town on a county road. She helps him along on the way toward copulation, shifting her clothing appropriately, but he only manages to grind ineffectually before falling asleep on her. Squeezed up against the door, she manages to open it and tumble out as if being born. She collects herself and walks toward town—then has the idea of walking north instead of bothering with the bus, despite thin boots and a coming snowstorm. The storm proves to be the worst Easter storm in forty years, but June is described as somewhat miraculously making it home.

II

The aunts Zelda and Aurelia are preparing pies in the kitchen and talking about how June (their cousin) has met her end. Zelda offers sensationalized versions of June's recent life, but Aurelia insists that nothing untoward (like spousal abuse) has been proved. A first-person narrator has taken over, the daughter of Patsy, sister of the two aunts. They debate the proper preparation of hard-boiled eggs. They talk about the Indian teacher Little Patsy is going to marry. Delmar and his wife Lynette drive up with their son, Delmar Junior; they also have Grandma and Grandpa Kashpaw in the car.

Grandma emerges from the car and tells Lynette to inform the senile Grandpa that the car has stopped. Lynette is busy changing and pinning the baby's diaper, but Delmar chastises her for not immediately heeding Grandma. Zelda helps pull Grandpa from the car, and he becomes reacquainted with Patsy (the narrator).

Patsy narrates the history of Grandma and Grandpa and his twin, Uncle Eli (Patsy's great-uncle). Grandpa has reached the winter of his life, and Delmar Junior is in a similar sort of winter as his life begins.

The women congregate in the kitchen, a store-bought ham in the oven, and Grandma recalls a time the children gave her trouble: Aurelia and Gordie were preparing to hang June from a tree branch, but Zelda told on them, and Grandma came out to rescue the tearful June and punish the others. June consequently was punished for using foul language. Everyone in the kitchen laughs uncontrollably at the memory.

Delmar drives off with Lynette in his car—purchased with the life-insurance money from June's death, which was ruled accidental—to pick up Gordie and Uncle Eli. Delmar was reportedly June's favorite child.

As the pies cool, the women wait for Delmar and the others to return. Patsy scores a point over Zelda in the banter about wisdom in marriage.

When Delmar and Lynette return, Zelda offhandedly criticizes Lynette—who seems overwhelmed by her baby's demanding nature—for having a child before marrying. Lynette abruptly leaves the room to nurse the baby, then returns. Aurelia suggests that Zelda should leave soon if she wants to see June's grave, but Zelda points out that Delmar (who would drive) will be drunk from the beer seen in his car.

Patsy goes out to see Delmar, who is drinking alone in his car. He suggests that Lynette does not fit in. Patsy says to give her a chance. Uncle Gordie pulls up, and Eli gets right out, but Gordie's ailing feet slow him down. Inside, Eli eats heartily. Zelda, Aurelia, and Grandma head into town—with Aurelia driving Gordie's car—instructing Patsy to not let the men eat the pies.

III

The men talk about hunting deer and skunk. When Lynette suggests that, unlike Zelda, she would be willing to eat skunk meat, Delmar ridicules her. They talk about foxes and local dialects. When Eli instructs them in genuine Indian language—his mention of *Michifs* indicates those of mixed Indian and white ancestry in the region, who speak a mixed rather than pure language—Lynette suggests the descendants need to learn their heritage quickly, before it disappears. Delmar shouts at her. He acknowledges Eli as the greatest hunter but calls himself the greatest fisherman. His hat, which Lynette has made for him, attests as much, but he gives the hat to Eli, who wears it stoically. Delmar, acting drunk, soon runs outside. Gordie begins telling a joke, and Lynette also leaves. Gordie tells the joke as Delmar shouts at Lynette outside. Eventually they hear things breaking and go out: Lynette is locked in the car, which Delmar is smashing in his attempts to get at her. Gordie wrestles Delmar to the ground. Lynette runs inside and starts smoking. She talks about the hat Eli is still wearing, then asks to wear it and takes it. Eli puts his own hat back on.

Delmar Junior cries out from the other room, and Lynette goes to him. Gordie brings in Delmar, who slumps over the kitchen table, and then tells Eli that the two of them are leaving. Patsy goes outside with Lynette, who is drinking steadily and occasionally offers

Patsy the bottle, and they walk down the hill to look at the northern lights and lie down. They talk about dreams.

Patsy wakes up, finds Lynette gone, and heads to the house. Inside, Delmar is trying to drown Lynette in the sink. Patsy pummels him ineffectually and finally bites his ear, interrupting the abuse. As Delmar primes himself to renew an attack against one of the women, Patsy notices the destroyed pies. She curses Delmar, who shamefacedly rushes out, stepping on his hat. Patsy brings the hat to the baby's room and rests there. When she goes out, she realizes that Delmar and Lynette are getting intimate first outside, then in the car.

In the morning, Patsy does what she can to repair the pies, a hopeless task.

CHARACTERS

Andy

The man who summons June from a bar and takes her around town has a large wad of money. He is a mud engineer, which reminds June of one she knew who was killed by a pressurized hose. She seems to think of Andy as someone who will at least give her money in exchange for a fling but perhaps even prove a lasting companion. Later, calling her Mary, he merely passes out drunk on top of her.

Aurelia

Little sister to Zelda, Aurelia seems to be more compassionate and accepting of people's foibles. On the other hand, she and Gordie are the ones who prepare June for hanging while playing as children, indicating Aurelia's mischievous side. Her mention to Patsy that she has a friend to see in town presumably means a man she is having a romantic relationship with.

Johnson the Swede

The Swede was Zelda's first husband, and the marriage is described as disastrous. From the vague but apparently cutting comment that Patsy makes—"*He* stayed with his wife"—it seems that perhaps the Swede was already married when he met Zelda, ultimately voiding his marriage with her.

Delmar Kashpaw

Delmar is the son of June and Gordie. He merits sympathy because his mother has recently died, but the aunts and Eli do not necessarily approve of his purchase of a relatively fancy Firebird with the life-insurance money. In his relationship with his wife, Lynette, with whom he has a son, Delmar acts the villain, constantly shouting at and bullying her and even trying to drown her. He has served in the US Marines and at least seems to have a good-natured relationship with Patsy.

Delmar Kashpaw Jr.

Delmar's baby son wears cloth diapers with pins that give Lynette trouble.

Uncle Eli Kashpaw

Uncle Eli is Grandpa Kashpaw's twin. He has a strong presence compared with that of his senile twin brother. He carries knowledge and memories of Cree traditions of the past, as with hunting, and when Delmar ceremoniously gives Eli his "World's Greatest Fisherman" hat to wear, Eli assumes the bearing of a chief (while knowing that Delmar must be humored in light of his drunkenness). Eli raised June after her mother died, but his relationship to her mother is left unclear.

Gordie Kashpaw

Gordie was apparently treated poorly by his wife, June. The narration suggests (because Delmar is said to take after her) that she was verbally abusive when drunk. Gordie was in a car accident and had his face stitched up but is deemed no less good-looking for the scars. He does what he can to tamp down Delmar's raging anger when Delmar drunkenly smashes his car trying to get at his disobedient wife. The house where the story takes place, once Grandpa's, is now Gordie's.

Grandpa Kashpaw

Grandpa Kashpaw and Uncle Eli are twins. Grandpa has mostly lost touch with the world, hardly knowing what is going on around him or remembering his family members. Grandpa and Grandma have raised a total of ten children. He lives with Grandma in a retirement home. The additional land Grandpa still owns is rented out to a wheat farmer, and Gordie lives in the house situated on the original allotment, land set aside for an Indian reservation.

June Kashpaw

June is the cousin of Zelda, Big Patsy, Aurelia, and Gordie and was raised by Uncle Eli (Little Patsy's great-uncle) after her mother died, although Eli's relationship to June's mother is unclear. The story opens with June's lamentable day in Williston, North Dakota. Needing money, having spent the last of what the previous man in her life had given her on a bus ticket home to the reservation where the rest of the story will take place, June makes insinuating remarks to a mud engineer with an appreciable wad of cash. He takes the bait and brings her outside town in his truck, but he proves too drunk to complete intercourse. June leaves and ends up bravely, almost transcendently, walking north—only to die when her heart stops along the way. Delmar, June's son, is said to take after her.

Grandma Vitaline Kashpaw

Grandpa and Grandma have raised six of their own children along with four adoptive children. Grandma, the mother of the aunts who populate the story, retains the bearing and presence of a matriarch in her old age. Her telling the story about little June almost being hanged by her cousins functions as a way of grieving June's passing through remembrance and laughter.

Lynette

Lynette, the mother of Delmar's child, is of Norwegian descent. Zelda describes her as having the build of a truck driver, presumably large. Lynette bristles at Delmar's abuse but seems to feel obliged to humor him. She may be trying to gain the upper hand over Delmar by supporting Eli when he starts to offer instruction in the Cree language. But her suggestion that the family's heritage will all be gone when Eli dies, coming from a white person, is profoundly insensitive.

Patsy

Little Patsy, the narrator, is the daughter of Big Patsy, who does not appear in the story. Patsy, though old enough to be counted among the aunts in the Kashpaw family, does not have children or a husband yet, so she still feels childlike around everyone else. She is planning on marrying an Indian man who was her teacher, presumably at the college level. (Her mother, Big Patsy, is apparently the second of Grandpa and Grandma's children and married her high-school teacher.) Patsy has traveled a fair distance to visit with the family before her marriage, but she seems not to have bargained for the violence that dominates the funereal reunion.

Zelda

Zelda is apparently the oldest of Grandma and Grandpa's children (at the least, she is older than Aurelia). She often tries to tell others in the family how to do things right. She is rather judgmental, as in her opinion of Delmar's choice of a white woman as a mate.

THEMES

Poverty

Erdrich's characters, nearly all of whom have some Indian blood, if not being full-blooded, cope with various trying circumstances in their lives. Many of these circumstances can be traced to the US historical process of depriving tribes of nearly all their traditional natural resources and restricting them to reservations. But Erdrich provides little to no historical background, leaving the reader with the characters' present-day troubles in isolation.

One of the first apparent issues as June Kashpaw's story unfolds is poverty. June has almost no money, and whether owing to insufficient education, family problems, or other matters, she also seems to have few options for how to make money. It is not clear whether June is a prostitute. She has recently received money from at least one man, and it is implied that she routinely receives money from men. The manner in which she induces the mud engineer to take her along with him suggests a deliberate attempt to remedy her lack of funds. Yet the narration never specifies whether he must pay for her company. It seems more likely that she intends to first allow him to enjoy her company and then tell him she needs money. It is worth recognizing this distinction because in the United States, prostitution is illegal. Although few women choose it above all other professions, some do choose it out of necessity. Erdrich's story suggests that for some women, especially impoverished women, prostitution, even with the moral stigma attached to it, is preferable to severe poverty, which can entail hunger, cold, and eventually death.

TOPICS FOR FURTHER STUDY

- "The World's Greatest Fishermen" presents an array of characters of depth—enough for Erdrich to have expanded the story into the novel *Love Medicine*. Create a website or other representation that uses a family tree or other format to present all of the story's characters, and create links or text boxes in which the individual characters introduce themselves in the first person and comment on their own life situations and on any characters in whom they have especial personal interest. For example, Lynette would have something to say about Delmar. A key part of the task is channeling the characters' distinct voices.
- Write a story that takes place at a family reunion and base it on what you have experienced during your own family's get-togethers. Feel free to take a real episode and use real names in an essentially autobiographical story, or change names and alter personae for the purpose of creating a more intriguing—or less revealing—fictional scenario. For example, writers often combine multiple real-life people into one character or divide one real-life person into more than one character.
- Read Eric Gansworth's young-adult novel *If I Ever Get Out of Here* (2013), about a seventh-grader living on the Tuscarora Reservation, which presents a more positive portrait of Native American life than Erdrich's story does. Write an essay in which you compare the approaches taken by Erdrich and Gansworth, commenting especially on the feelings stirred and impressions created in the reader by the narratives.
- Research Native Americans and the consumption of alcohol, which was known to some tribes before European contact but became a problem with the more widespread production and consumption of alcohol in Euro-American culture. Write a research paper that introduces the historical context and discusses the reality of alcohol use among present-day Indian populations.

Alcoholism

June is probably not clearheadedly choosing prostitution or a similar exchange on this evening, in part because of the role of alcohol consumption by both parties involved. June seems to allow herself to spend time with the engineer, Andy, in the first place only because she imagines (perhaps disingenuously) that she may know him. She even thinks of him in terms that suggest a long-term relationship, but only after a few drinks and a trip to the restroom, as though she needs to loosen her morals before engaging in the relationship as a sort of transaction. That is, the alcohol may allow her to deceive herself into thinking that she is satisfied with the way she is solving her money problem. Moreover, the influence of the alcohol on her brain contributes to her making the unwise decision to head north on foot at night wearing thin boots in a snowstorm. More than unwise, this drunken decision proves fatal.

Alcohol is consumed with abandon through much of the novel that this story grew into, *Love Medicine*. There are characters, like Zelda, who frown upon drinking, but those who drink tend to dominate the scenes, often to the others' chagrin. Among the Kashpaws, Gordie seems to have no qualms about driving drunk (or at least Patsy's narration suggests as much). Most prominently, Delmar drinks heavily throughout the day, and at length Uncle Eli can only take pity on his profoundly intoxicated state. This state directly relates to Delmar's raging against Lynette, including when he is determined to drive off despite his drunkenness but she locks herself inside the car (and he vents his rage against the machine), and later when he even tries to drown her in the kitchen sink.

Domestic Violence

With Delmar's acts of drunken aggression, the story brings into focus the problem of domestic violence. For whatever reasons, Delmar has taken an antithetical attitude toward his partner, the mother of his child, and finds every opportunity to insult and belittle her. He may, at heart, feel resentful toward white people in general. Even when Lynette cannot fulfill a request to communicate something to Grandpa because her mouth is full of pins for the baby's diaper, Delmar holds the purported failure against her, threatening violence if she fails to do as asked. That this is a vicious circle soon becomes apparent: Lynette, rendered unbalanced by the threats and insults, releases her tension or tries to restore her status in the family in ways that offend Delmar further. For example, she claims that she would eat skunk meat and suggests that the family heritage will die out with Eli, and Delmar further berates and abuses her. When she tries to do something decent like prevent him from driving drunk, which could result in the death of innocent people on the road, not to mention his own, he takes this as further insubordination and turns his violent impulses on his own car because he cannot reach her.

Delmar has his own bottled-up tension, from whatever sources—being in the marines has surely primed him for physical activity, of which he may need more in his domestic life. Whether from lack of self-control, indifference, or genuine hate, but regardless with the assistance of alcohol, he acts out this tension in the form of domestic violence. That Delmar and Lynette are still capable of intimacy does not suggest that the violence is not a problem; it suggests that Lynette perceives that she is trapped in the relationship and that simply to survive she needs to make peace with Delmar in any way possible.

Family

In a story that seems to offer little hope for the characters involved, the one thing that they all fall back on is family. Before her untimely death, June realizes that if she needs help she can still rely on support from her ex-husband Gordie, who as the father of her children remains family. The sisters Zelda and Aurelia, though often bickering over minor matters, clearly appreciate the antagonistic rapport they have developed over the years. They have lost their cousin June, but they still have each other and their mother, who can look back and help them laugh—and even cry—over a story from their childhood that reinforces the notion that even when family members find themselves at cross-purposes, they remain family. When Delmar's spirits sink low while he is under the influence, he is reinvigorated in part by thinking of how much he loves his great-uncle Eli. When he turns violent, his father is the one to subdue the rage and try to set him straight. Even Delmar and Lynette, for all their antagonism, ultimately appreciate each other's company, and ideally, one way or another, they can provide Delmar Junior with a stable environment in which to grow up.

June Kashpaw is lost in a blizzard after a failed romantic encounter (©Andriy Solovyov / Shutterstock.com)

Patsy, as narrator, sometimes seems a step outside the family, not entirely a part of it. But she seems to bond with Lynette over a drink or two, and she saves her when Delmar is on the verge of drowning her. Patsy seems to recognize that she can only offer a temporary fix to Delmar and Lynette's problems and grows almost despondent even amidst the intense fight. But the sight of the destroyed pies—the fruits of the women's efforts to bring the joy of good eating to the family reunion—brings out Patsy's rage. Delmar, despite having shown little shame over his treatment of Lynette, seems genuinely ashamed at the affront to his aunts, indeed to the entire Kashpaw family, as if even in his compromised state of mind he can recognize that whether times are smooth or tough, family can be more important than anything.

STYLE

Shifting Narration

Erdrich writes with a postmodern sensibility. One way that emerges in this story is in the instability of the shifting narration. The story opens by following June Kashpaw from an omniscient but limited third-person perspective, which details her actions and offers insight into her state of mind and specific thoughts. The narration is limited in that it does not similarly detail the thoughts of other characters, such as Andy, but only allows the reader to know what June knows.

The reader becomes intimately acquainted with June only for her to disappear from the story. As part II begins, the reader learns that June has died during her late-night snowstorm trek. The narration still seems to be third-person until, after nine brief paragraphs of dialogue, the narrator declares, "I gave Aurelia my pickles." Suddenly the reader realizes that the narrator, Patsy, is present in the scene. The reader becomes familiar with the world of the story through a character who dies, leaving the reader unanchored in the text. Then there appears a first-person narrator who herself has limited familiarity with the community of the story. She professes to feel like somewhat of an outsider among the aunts. Together, the shifts in narration point toward the impossibility of fully knowing the events and people of the story—exactly how June has died, what motivates the other characters, and so forth. This denial of sure knowledge leaves the reader in a state of bare absorption of what takes place, likely in a heightened state of sensitivity to the story's reality.

Fragmentation

The shifting narration is an example of the fragmentation that postmodernism embraces as part of the human condition. Another respect in which the narrative is fragmented is the frequent textual breaks. Divided into three parts by roman numerals, the text is also divided into separate scenes, sometimes with no discernible break in the action. For example, when Grandma and the aunts are reminiscing about June's near hanging as a child, one section ends with Grandma saying of Patsy, "She called June. . . . " After a divide, the next section begins with the narrator asking, "What did she yell?" There is no discernible break in the action here, other than perhaps a pause as Grandma laughs and cries too much to finish her thought. This may be seen to signal a switch in Patsy's understanding of that old story, which she had heard incompletely from her mother. The story contains several similar breaks, where it is unclear why the text has been broken up. Perhaps this is intended merely to cater to modern-day readers' shorter attention spans: a text can feel easier to read if it is broken up into small portions. Or Erdrich may have had something else in mind, and different readers may or may not take note of or have opinions about the breaks.

Some readers may be reminded of how classic films are frequently shot from a single camera angle for the durations of long scenes, which require sustained performances from the actors not unlike on the theatrical stage. Modern films, to the contrary, often feature rapid shifts between camera angles even in scenes where little is happening, simply because the shifts demand more attention from the viewer's brain and thus make the film more exciting to watch—or at least seem more exciting. Often these kinds of perspectival or narrative tricks conceal shortcomings such as substandard acting or plotting. Erdrich's story is very well plotted and written, however, and the frequent textual breaks might be considered unnecessary.

HISTORICAL CONTEXT

Native Acculturation on the Great Plains

The writing of literature with Native American protagonists can be especially complex because the events in the various nations' communal histories—the forcibly altered ways of life, the required shifting of homelands, the genocide—have echoed over the generations to affect nearly everyone at the individual level. Thus, if a respected white author like Edward Abbey, writing on impressions gathered while working at a welfare office in the Southwest, produces a novel like *The Monkey Wrench Gang* in which the Indian characters are invariably drunk or ineffectual, one rightly objects to a collective depiction that is bound to propagate stereotypes without bothering to account for the history that has left Native Americans in their situations. Though Erdrich is of Ojibway descent, "The World's Greatest Fishermen" runs a similar risk in that many, if not all, of the Indian characters seem down and out in one way or another. No less a figure than the Native American Renaissance founding mother Leslie Marmon Silko has gone so far as to question, in the words of the critic Susan Pérez Castillo, "what she perceives as Erdrich's ambivalence about her Indian origins."

COMPARE & CONTRAST

- **1980s:** With prices for oil spiking to an all-time high in 1980, North Dakota, especially in oil-producing localities like Williston, experiences a boom. By 1984 prices slip, and by 1986, they bottom out.

  Today: In April 2016, North Dakota oil sources report the largest monthly drop in crude oil production in state history, in part owing to inclement weather that prevents the drilling and fracking of new wells. With crude prices having dropped by 50 percent since 2014, producers resort to spending cuts and layoffs.

- **1980s:** Prostitutes find clients by performing face-to-face assessments, for example, by lingering on street corners in certain areas.

  Today: Much prostitution is arranged online, and there are occasional reports of prostitutes being murdered by those posing as clients who use false pictures and identification to lure prostitutes as victims.

- **1980s:** Native American authors feel limited by cultural obligations and often reach back in their tribal history or depict unsettling aspects of their more recent historical tribulations.

  Today: Indian authors demonstrate more freedom in writing works in such genres as fantasy, science fiction, and magical realism.

Although the various Indian nations have their distinct histories, many aspects of US oppression and forced acculturation were common to most, if not all, with especial similarities among tribes in specific regions. Indians of the Great Plains, for example, across the central and northern Midwest of the United States, including the Ojibway and Cree, generally lived in portable tipis and depended on the buffalo herds for sustenance. Neither of these practices accorded with Anglo US cultural doctrines of land ownership and permanent agriculture. If white US expansion was to proceed westward in accord with Manifest Destiny, small nations of Indians could not be permitted to roam wide swaths of land, settling here and there as the seasons and migrations dictated, when otherwise entire permanent towns and cities and vast farmlands could occupy the same areas.

Whites also did not intend to make special concessions so that the buffalo herds could follow their natural routes of migration, taking up what could again be productive farmland. Buffalo herds gradually vanished—though recent attempts have been made to revive them—because desperate tribes, hounded by US authorities, had to cull more buffalo from herds than they otherwise would have, thinning numbers; because white fur traders offered so much money that many buffalo were killed merely for their hides; and because one of the US military's tactics in Indian wars was to slaughter entire herds and leave them as carrion so as to cut off tribes' food supplies.

Plains tribes did engage in small-scale agriculture, but the tools and practices used did not resemble the mechanized approaches that whites encouraged in the course of acculturation, which was accomplished primarily through Indian children's forced attendance at boarding schools. Moreover, in many Native American cultures, farming was considered women's work, and because women were considered weak, the men did not want to be perceived as lowering themselves in the eyes of their peers. Where men, women, and their families did devote themselves to farmwork, traditional tribal ethics dictated that an abundance of food would be shared with family and neighbors, indeed with anyone in need. When the primary source of food is buffalo meat, such generosity makes communal and evolutionary

June's family comes together for her funeral, and many conflicts arise (©Robert Hoetink / Shutterstock.com)

sense, because only so much time can pass before a slaughtered buffalo can no longer be eaten. The case is different with agricultural produce, especially grains and vegetables, which can last for longer periods of time. But a sudden change in circumstance does not necessarily produce a sudden change in cultural usages and understandings.

The historian Robert H. Lowie, in *Indians of the Plains*, puts matters in perspective:

> An important personality problem, for the males, was finding a suitable substitute for the ancient goals. With the buffalo gone and warfare a thing of the past, they found it very hard to discover any objectives that made life worth living. Some strongly expressed the sentiment that they preferred the old existence with all its hazards, but with the chance for glory, to the pedestrian career of a farmer or mechanic.

Such thoughts seem especially useful in considering a character like Delmar, who makes himself out to be little more than a villain. In defense of his person (if not his actions), to begin with, he has just lost his mother—and her life was apparently one of prostitution (among white men) in a city off the constraining reservation, another echo of past oppression. The US capitalist culture of acquisition has encouraged him to purchase a car with the life-insurance money he received after June's death. But can one be surprised if he harbors aggressive impulses not only toward that broader culture but also toward the very car that would seem to matter so much to him? A white reader may frown upon his temperamental destruction, or near destruction, of his own new vehicle as the result of the workings of an irrational or unbalanced mind. With history in view, however, it is easier to see Delmar as someone trapped between the traditional masculine Indian life that viral white culture has denied him and the not-so-brave new world that would have him value things, like cars, that he would actually rather not. As such, the alcohol is not so much rendering him irrational as simply allowing him to release the ungovernable tension of life as a subjugated postcolonial subject.

CRITICAL OVERVIEW

Erdrich is, in the words of *Dictionary of Literary Biography* writer Peter G. Beidler, "one of the most important contemporary Native American writers." Ever since she began winning awards for both short and long fiction, her novels have been highly anticipated and widely reviewed, generally with appreciation for the poetic qualities of the narration and the gritty realism—or sometimes surrealism or magic realism—of the narrative.

Beyond its originally being honored with the Nelson Algren Award and its five-thousand-dollar prize, critical consideration of "The World's Greatest Fishermen," as with Erdrich's other short stories, has been limited because her novels—over a dozen altogether—have drawn such extensive attention. Regarding *The Red Convertible*, a *Kirkus Reviews* contributor notes that in the context of Erdrich's "complex fictional universe," the thirty-six stories "resonate like favorite melodies." Assessing her style in some of the stories as "not exactly realism, yet strangely realistic mythmaking," the reviewer concludes with an observation on the challenges of following the webs of relations between the characters and the occasional fragmentation of the narratives: "Erdrich requires a degree of commitment not every reader will make, but fans will find that these stories distill her body of work to its essence."

In the *New York Times Book Review*, Liesl Schillinger opens a review of *The Red Convertible* by noting that although some international writers are uneasy with the Americanness of US literature—"the hybrid nature of our national makeup, the variety and breadth of our landscape, our mania for self-invention and reinvention"—that very Americanness represents "the strength of our letters. And few of our contemporary writers exemplify its adaptive vitality better than Louise Erdrich." Schillinger calls Erdrich "a wondrous short story writer" whose collection is "a keepsake of the American experience." The reviewer also calls her "a master tuner of the taut emotions that keen between parent and child, man and woman, brother and sister, man and beast." Schillinger declares, "With great delicacy, Erdrich handles the emotions of indelicate people, as they're tripped up by the uneven terrain of their lives."

A critic who has considered the text of "The World's Greatest Fishermen" in depth as the first chapter of *Love Medicine* is Susan Farrell. Writing in the *Explicator*, Farrell discusses the Christian symbolism and implications of the final episode of June's life, which takes place on the day before Easter and leading into the night. Farrell notes that the egg is a Christian symbol of rebirth and renewal and that this resonates with June's eating eggs at the bar (and the aunts' later discussion of cooking hard-boiled eggs) and the sense in which her fall out of Andy's truck into the cold gives her "a shock like being born." The motifs of water, fishing, and fishermen all tie into this thematic analysis.

Beidler affirms that Erdrich writes "some of the most sophisticated fiction and nonfiction being produced in the United States." He observes,

> Like life itself, her writing sometimes appears disjointed, but she raises virtually all of the issues important to an understanding of the human condition: accidents of birth and parentage, falling in love, generosity, greed, psychological damage, joy, alienation, vulnerability, differentness, parenting, aging, and dying.

In *The Chippewa Landscape of Louise Erdrich*, Allan Chavkin declares that Erdrich's "brilliant, complex prose style and her unique vision are responsible for her immense critical and popular acclaim." He affirms, "Often viewed as an outstanding practitioner of modern fiction, Louise Erdrich should be regarded as one of the country's most important writers."

CRITICISM

Michael Allen Holmes

Holmes is a writer with existential interests. In the following essay, he argues that the dominant motif in "The World's Greatest Fishermen" is the dead end.

One sometimes reads critical work that takes a story to task for simply not going anywhere. Perhaps the characters do not develop, perhaps no action of any apparent significance takes place, or perhaps the story simply comes across as a static poem, a snapshot of a moment that may resonate over time but in ways that the story does not make apparent or even suggest at all. Many authors intend to write such a story in a style that is more a portrait or a vignette. There is nothing wrong with such a story, and some of the best stories can be described as such. Although the plot of "The World's Greatest Fishermen" goes somewhere—it leads up and

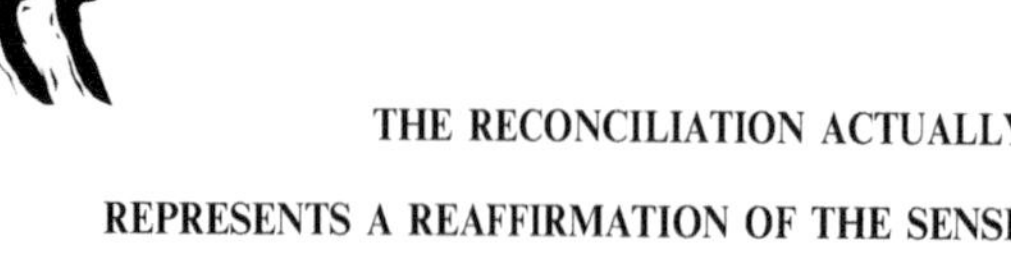

THE RECONCILIATION ACTUALLY REPRESENTS A REAFFIRMATION OF THE SENSE OF THE RELATIONSHIP AS A DEAD END."

into a definitive moment of action, Delmar's attempted drowning of Lynette and Patsy's reaction to it—there is the unpleasant sense that none of the characters are going anywhere. Their lives are stuck in neutral, and Patsy seems to be thrown into reverse by her participation in the family's near tragedy rather than propelled forward into the marriage and life that await her. It is interesting to consider both the ways in which the story is full of dead ends and what one can conclude about the story on the basis of this profusion.

The mood of the story is rendered tragic by the sense of the opening episode: the evening leading up to June's death of exposure. Easter itself is a time marked by death, the death of Christ as leading up to his resurrection. However much Christianity may celebrate that resurrection, there is still an air of profound mourning about Good Friday and the events of the passion of Christ. Given the symbolism of egg and fishermen that the story explores, along with Zelda's indication that being Catholic is a quality that this extended family of Native Americans holds essential to an individual's well-being, the connection to the religion's traditional time of bodily death (if also spiritual rebirth) is strong. In this sense, the reader's being extended June's perspective just before her death—which is presented with underlying implications of rebirth, especially where, despite the depth of the snow, "June walked over it like water and came home"—effectively brings the reader outside the world of the living with June's death. The reader proceeds to look upon the story much as June's spirit might, perhaps in a spirit of lament and regret.

The mood darkens as the day of the Kashpaw reunion progresses. There is a lightness to the aunts' interactions, but the event of their cousin's death casts a pall over the atmosphere. Moreover, both Zelda and Aurelia prove to have foibles of a sort that suggests a sad circularity to their lives. Zelda is constantly nagging Aurelia about doing things properly, and when the topic of Zelda's disastrous marriage is repeatedly raised, the reader gets the impression that somehow Zelda is partly to blame for the disaster. The story makes no mention of either Zelda or Aurelia's having a husband or children, although the characterization of Zelda's having a first marriage implies a second. There is only reference to how "most of the uncles, aunts, children had driven up to Spirit Lake to fish and camp" for the day and night, and so perhaps these two aunts' spouses and offspring are among them. But in the context of the story, Zelda is alone. When Patsy makes a wry narrative observation after Aurelia's rather caustic comment that June "couldn't get much more ruined than dead," it seems to apply especially to Zelda:

> They were like my mother in their rock-bottom opinionation. They were so strong in their beliefs that there came a time when it hardly mattered what exactly those beliefs were; they all fused into a single stubbornness.

Erdrich's precise meaning has to be teased out, or perhaps intuited, because the abstraction of her language—part of her postmodern sensibility—allows for ambiguity. But Patsy seems to be indicating that Zelda and Aurelia constantly hold people to impossible standards, or read the worst out of any situation. The stubbornness of which Patsy speaks seems to be a psychological dead end—a refusal on the aunts' part to adapt their understanding of life to changing circumstances, to the point where what they actually think is irrelevant. They are figured as embodying a pessimism that denies any psychological advancement whatsoever. Aurelia seems buoyant enough through much of the story, but when she winks at Patsy over the prospect of meeting a male friend in town, the reader has to wonder whether she is still, at her advanced age (presumably mid-forties or later), just hitting it off with whichever man of the moment presents himself; perhaps cheating on her husband, suggesting a dead-end marriage; or is prostituting herself much in the way June had, an ominous possibility. The sense of life's being a dead end not only for the aunts but also the entire family—symbolized by Gordie's driving his car in circles upon arriving at the house—is suggested by Zelda herself later in the story when she wonders aloud, "Are we ever getting out of here?"

WHAT DO I READ NEXT?

- Having read "The World's Greatest Fishermen," one would naturally next turn either to other stories in *The Red Convertible* (2009) or to *Love Medicine* (1984), which features an adapted version of the story as its first chapter.
- Another well-known author of Ojibway descent is Gerald Vizenor, who is enrolled in the Minnesota Chippewa tribe. Among his works are the nonfiction volume *The People Named the Chippewa: Narrative Histories* (1978) and the novel *Bearheart: The Heirship Chronicles* (1990), which is set in a postapocalyptic United States where fossil fuels have been used up.
- Leslie Marmon Silko's novel *Gardens in the Dunes* (1999) focuses on a group of Native American women from the Sand Lizard tribe—a fictional clan—who are determined to stay off reservations on the border between Arizona and California and maintain their traditional ways.
- *Easter Ann Peters' Operation Cool* (2012) is a young-adult novel by Jody Lamb that follows twelve-year-old Easter as she copes with her mother's alcoholism and the effects it has on her family, personal, and social lives.
- The acclaimed Nigerian author Chimamanda Ngozi Adichie made her novel debut with *Purple Hibiscus* (2003), which follows fifteen-year-old Kambili Achike as she goes through life while dealing with a father who is verbally and physically abusive toward Kambili, her mother, and her brother.
- The scholar Thomas W. Hill has written an ethnographic study titled *Native American Drinking: Life Styles, Alcohol Use, Drunken Comportment, Problem Drinking, and the Peyote Religion* (2013), which focuses on case studies from the communities of Sioux City, Iowa, and the Winnebago in Nebraska.

There is also the problem of the near hanging of June, which Aurelia was partly responsible for and which turns the women's reunion in the kitchen from one of warmth and good food to one of peals of laughter over the grim recounting of an event that could have easily, with one kick of the box on which June was standing, led to her actual death. It is hard to imagine a grimmer situation to laugh over, a darker sense of comedy.

The mood darkens even further when Delmar graces the scene. The text makes clear the effect he has on the spirits of the company. Patsy reports thoughts like, "I saw him clench his jaw and then felt a kind of wet-blanket sadness coming down over us all." Delmar's comments are consistently delivered in a register that would make most people freeze with discomfort if they heard one family member talking to another in such a way. What is a bystander to say when a young man is unjustly taking his partner to task for not trying to verbally communicate something to a senile old man while bearing several diaper pins in her mouth? Delmar soon exhibits a temper that suggests that few would be inclined to deliberately cross him merely to make a point about etiquette or compassion or fair treatment. Yet his treatment is indicative of a level of disrespect that, sadly but unsurprisingly, crosses the line into violence, even nearly fatal violence. Too often, only after such an event do people look back and recognize that perhaps they ought to have gone out on a limb to help protect someone who was in the position to be a recurring, if not permanent, victim.

The sense of Lynette's position is brought out with the episode in which she tells Patsy about her dream. As the women lie on the ground looking up at the stars, Patsy somewhat whimsically imagines the sky to be the place where "all the world's wandering souls were dancing," with June herself "dancing a two-step for wandering souls." With this repetition, it is as if the sky, the realm of the spirits after death, is positioned as the place where wandering souls belong. For the Indians, it seems, only those who accept life as a dead end remain living. The scene's emotional implications deepen when Lynette reveals her dream, in which she flies up to the moon but upon landing "didn't dare take a breath." This is unpleasant enough to imagine, but Patsy has an especially strong reaction: "I felt crushed when she said that. It seemed so terribly sad." Lynette confirms that she "was scared to breathe," and this seals the figuration of her own life as a dead end, where escape—which is suggested to be something she can only fantasize about, given the dream destination of the moon—is impossible, at least if she wants to survive, because upon escaping she can only be left to asphyxiate in the world outside her relationship. By extension, the Native American characters generally are figured as risking asphyxiation if they leave the world of the reservation, however restrictive and even abusive (in historical terms) that world is.

In this dead-end narrative world, it is perhaps explicable that Patsy, whose life holds the promise of marriage to an educated Indian man, experiences the sudden onset of nihilism at a most surprising moment, in the heat of the violence that Delmar inflicts on Lynette and that Patsy herself is obliged to inflict on Delmar in order to preserve Lynette's life. Somehow, even though Delmar's fists are clenched for fighting as he regards the woman he apparently wants to kill and the woman who has bitten through his ear, Patsy finds herself able to say, "He was deciding who to hit first, I thought, and it seemed not much to matter. I stared at him for a moment, then lost interest." However much adrenaline might be flowing through her body, she seems to come to a sudden recognition of the dead-end sense of everything that surrounds her—the petty aunts, the dead cousin, the abusive father—and to thus withdraw her emotional investment in the scene, indeed in the family. Such is the case, at least, until she sees the destroyed pies—even dessert is a dead end—and is enraged at the way in which Delmar and Lynette are not only imploding their own relationship but also pulling down the people who are doing everything they can to sustain the bodies and morale of the family. Her rage is so powerful that she loads every bit of indignity she can muster into the insult and blame she casts Delmar's way. Almost astonishingly—until one realizes that he may be abusive but is not inhuman—he is so deeply ashamed that he storms out. It is a relief when Delmar and Lynette seem to reconcile, using an intimate physical act to dissipate the tensions of the violent encounter. On the other hand, it is quite upsetting: the couple's pattern of resentment and abuse can only be expected to continue. The reconciliation actually represents a reaffirmation of the sense of the relationship as a dead end.

If the story were to have one saving grace, it would seem to be Patsy herself. Her life seems to hold promise, although the sense of Patsy's self communicated through her narration almost positions her as too timid to make much of her life. The notion that Patsy may be too timid for life is exploded when she manages a life-saving aggressive act in a time of crisis, but the way she has been sucked into Delmar's world of violence suggests that there is a tradition of family misfortune that she will be unable to avoid continuing through her own life. If the fate has not already been sealed, the story's last lines, describing Patsy's hopeless efforts to rescue the pies, make certain the sense of the entire story as a grand dead end: "I worked carefully. But once they smash there is no way to put them right."

What then, if anything, should the reader conclude about a short story that paints such an unpromising picture of life for modern-day Native Americans whose lives seem to be characterized by alienation, dislocation, and the impossibility of progress? One cannot doubt that the story depicts a fairly loyal depiction of life on a North Dakota reservation, given the familiarity that Erdrich had with that milieu. The extent to which Erdrich's position matches Patsy's is certainly relevant, reinforcing the autobiographical and thus presumably realistic nature of the story. This is not to say that Erdrich's family can be presumed to have experienced what takes place in the story, but only that there is no reason to think that she is exploiting or sensationalizing a milieu that must mean so much to her for the sake of a good story.

If there is a problem with the way the story presents its characters and circumstances, it lies with the limits of the story—indeed with the limits of the short-story form. Fuller details about the aunts' familial circumstances would lend their lives more momentum. As sad as a separation between Delmar and Lynette would be, especially for their son, the split would be for the better if their relationship is as abusive as the story portrays. Patsy especially could be seen to be going somewhere important with just a little more narrative extension. Sure enough, Erdrich made a point of addressing all of these issues precisely through narrative extension,

After the funeral, two young cousins gaze up at the Northern Lights (©Frozenmost / Shutterstock.com)

turning this one story into the opening chapter of an award-winning novel. It may be a sad and difficult story to get through, one that paints a darkly complicated picture of life on a reservation, but one can keep in mind that Erdrich saw fit to shed more light on the circumstances of the Kashpaws and on other Indian families, not only in her debut novel but also in numerous others in her body of work. If one wants to hear better things about the Kashpaws and Native Americans in general—which, as with all of life, must be taken in stride along with the worse things—all one has to do is keep reading.

Source: Michael Allen Holmes, Critical Essay on "The World's Greatest Fishermen," in *Short Stories for Students*, Gale, Cengage Learning, 2017.

SOURCES

Beidler, Peter G., "Louise Erdrich," in *Dictionary of Literary Biography*, Vol. 175, *Native American Writers of the United States*, edited by Kenneth M. Roemer, Gale Research, 1997.

Berkley, Miriam, "*PW* Interviews: Louise Erdrich," in *Publishers Weekly*, Vol. 230, August 15, 1986, pp. 58–59.

Bruchac, Joseph, "Whatever Is Really Yours: An Interview with Louise Erdrich," in *Survival This Way: Interviews with American Indian Poets*, Sun Tracks and the University of Arizona Press, 1987, pp. 73–86.

Castillo, Susan Pérez, "Postmodernism, Native American Literature and the Real: The Silko-Erdrich Controversy," in *Nothing but the Truth: An Anthology of Native American Literature*, edited by John L. Purdy and James Ruppert, Prentice Hall, 2001, pp. 15–22; originally published in *Massachusetts Review*, Vol. 32, No. 2, Summer 1991, pp. 285–94.

Chavkin, Allan, ed., Introduction to *The Chippewa Landscape of Louise Erdrich*, University of Alabama Press, 1999, p. 1.

Erdrich, Louise, "The World's Greatest Fishermen," in *The Red Convertible: Selected and New Stories, 1978–2008*, pp. 26–52.

Farrell, Susan, "Erdrich's *Love Medicine*," in *Explicator*, Vol. 56, No. 2, Winter 1998, pp. 109–12.

George, Jan, "Interview with Louise Erdrich," in *North Dakota Quarterly*, Vol. 53, No. 2, Spring 1985, pp. 240–47.

Lowie, Robert H., *Indians of the Plains*, University of Nebraska Press, 1982, pp. 184–97.

"North Dakota's Oil Bust in the 1980s," in *A Brief History of North Dakota Oil Production*, June 2, 2011, https://northdakotaoil.wordpress.com/2011/06/02/north-dakota%E2%80%99s-oil-bust-in-the-1980s (accessed September 5, 2016).

Review of *The Red Convertible*, in *Kirkus Reviews*, December 1, 2008.

Scheyder, Ernest, "North Dakota Oil Output Posts Biggest Drop in History," Reuters website, June 15, 2016, http://www.reuters.com/article/us-north-dakota-oil-production-idUSKCN0Z12GI (accessed September 5, 2016).

Schillinger, Liesl, "All American," in *New York Times Book Review*, January 4, 2009, p. 11.

Shucard, Alan, "Louise Erdrich: Overview," in *Contemporary Poets*, 6th ed., edited by Thomas Riggs, St. James Press, 1996.

FURTHER READING

Bancroft, Lundy, *Why Does He Do That? Inside the Minds of Angry and Controlling Men*, Penguin, 2003.

In this volume, oriented toward women who are dealing with abusive relationships, Bancroft aims to first explain the roots of abusive behavior and then offer guidance with how to take steps toward ending the abuse or the relationship.

Chavkin, Allan, and Nancy Feyl Chavkin, eds., *Conversations with Louise Erdrich and Michael Dorris*, University Press of Mississippi, 1994.

In jointly treating both Erdrich and Dorris, who collaborated with or offered counsel to Erdrich in much of her early writing, this volume gives insight into the ways in which Erdrich's talents developed and her career flourished.

Hansen, Karen V., *Encounter on the Great Plains: Scandinavian Settlers and the Dispossession of Dakota Indians, 1890–1930*, Oxford University Press, 2013.

Hansen focuses on a period of particular relevance to the region of Erdrich's interest. In "The World's Greatest Fishermen," Lynette is of Norwegian heritage, which may play a part in the Indians', especially Delmar's, attitudes toward her.

Skinner, Alanson, *Political Organizations, Cults, and Ceremonies of the Plains-Ojibway and Plains-Cree Indians*, Trustees of the American Museum of Natural History, 1914.

This historical volume focuses on the two cultures most relevant to Erdrich's portrayal in "The World's Greatest Fishermen," in which the community is presumed to be a mix of Ojibway, as Erdrich's heritage would attest, and Cree, in that Uncle Eli identifies himself as "a real old Cree."

SUGGESTED SEARCH TERMS

Louise Erdrich AND The World's Greatest Fishermen

Louise Erdrich AND Love Medicine

Louise Erdrich AND Chippewa OR Ojibway OR Ojibwe

history AND Chippewa OR Ojibway

Turtle Mountain Band of Chippewa Indians

Native Americans AND alcohol OR abuse

Native American literature AND alcohol

Native Americans AND stereotypes

Native Americans AND genocide

Glossary of Literary Terms

A

Aestheticism: A literary and artistic movement of the nineteenth century. Followers of the movement believed that art should not be mixed with social, political, or moral teaching. The statement "art for art's sake" is a good summary of aestheticism. The movement had its roots in France, but it gained widespread importance in England in the last half of the nineteenth century, where it helped change the Victorian practice of including moral lessons in literature. Oscar Wilde and Edgar Allan Poe are two of the best-known "aesthetes" of the late nineteenth century.

Allegory: A narrative technique in which characters representing things or abstract ideas are used to convey a message or teach a lesson. Allegory is typically used to teach moral, ethical, or religious lessons but is sometimes used for satiric or political purposes. Many fairy tales are allegories.

Allusion: A reference to a familiar literary or historical person or event, used to make an idea more easily understood. Joyce Carol Oates's story "Where Are You Going, Where Have You Been?" exhibits several allusions to popular music.

Analogy: A comparison of two things made to explain something unfamiliar through its similarities to something familiar, or to prove one point based on the acceptance of another. Similes and metaphors are types of analogies.

Antagonist: The major character in a narrative or drama who works against the hero or protagonist. The Misfit in Flannery O'Connor's story "A Good Man Is Hard to Find" serves as the antagonist for the Grandmother.

Anthology: A collection of similar works of literature, art, or music. Zora Neale Hurston's "The Eatonville Anthology" is a collection of stories that take place in the same town.

Anthropomorphism: The presentation of animals or objects in human shape or with human characteristics. The term is derived from the Greek word for "human form." The fur necklet in Katherine Mansfield's story "Miss Brill" has anthropomorphic characteristics.

Anti-hero: A central character in a work of literature who lacks traditional heroic qualities such as courage, physical prowess, and fortitude. Anti-heroes typically distrust conventional values and are unable to commit themselves to any ideals. They generally feel helpless in a world over which they have no control. Anti-heroes usually accept, and often celebrate, their positions as social outcasts. A well-known anti-hero is Walter Mitty in James Thurber's story "The Secret Life of Walter Mitty."

Archetype: The word archetype is commonly used to describe an original pattern or model from which all other things of the same kind are made. Archetypes are the literary images that grow out of the "collective unconscious," a theory proposed by psychologist Carl Jung. They appear in literature as incidents and plots that repeat basic patterns of life. They may also appear as stereotyped characters. The "schlemiel" of Yiddish literature is an archetype.

Autobiography: A narrative in which an individual tells his or her life story. Examples include Benjamin Franklin's *Autobiography* and Amy Hempel's story "In the Cemetery Where Al Jolson Is Buried," which has autobiographical characteristics even though it is a work of fiction.

Avant-garde: A literary term that describes new writing that rejects traditional approaches to literature in favor of innovations in style or content. Twentieth-century examples of the literary avant-garde include the modernists and the minimalists.

B

Belles-lettres: A French term meaning "fine letters" or" beautiful writing." It is often used as a synonym for literature, typically referring to imaginative and artistic rather than scientific or expository writing. Current usage sometimes restricts the meaning to light or humorous writing and appreciative essays about literature. Lewis Carroll's *Alice in Wonderland* epitomizes the realm of belles-lettres.

Bildungsroman: A German word meaning "novel of development." The *bildungsroman* is a study of the maturation of a youthful character, typically brought about through a series of social or sexual encounters that lead to self-awareness. J. D. Salinger's *Catcher in the Rye* is a *bildungsroman*, and Doris Lessing's story "Through the Tunnel" exhibits characteristics of a *bildungsroman* as well.

Black Aesthetic Movement: A period of artistic and literary development among African Americans in the 1960s and early 1970s. This was the first major African-American artistic movement since the Harlem Renaissance and was closely paralleled by the civil rights and black power movements. The black aesthetic writers attempted to produce works of art that would be meaningful to the black masses. Key figures in black aesthetics included one of its founders, poet and playwright Amiri Baraka, formerly known as Le Roi Jones; poet and essayist Haki R. Madhubuti, formerly Don L. Lee; poet and playwright Sonia Sanchez; and dramatist Ed Bullins. Works representative of the Black Aesthetic Movement include Amiri Baraka's play *Dutchman,* a 1964 Obie award-winner.

Black Humor: Writing that places grotesque elements side by side with humorous ones in an attempt to shock the reader, forcing him or her to laugh at the horrifying reality of a disordered world. "Lamb to the Slaughter," by Roald Dahl, in which a placid housewife murders her husband and serves the murder weapon to the investigating policemen, is an example of black humor.

C

Catharsis: The release or purging of unwanted emotions—specifically fear and pity—brought about by exposure to art. The term was first used by the Greek philosopher Aristotle in his *Poetics* to refer to the desired effect of tragedy on spectators.

Character: Broadly speaking, a person in a literary work. The actions of characters are what constitute the plot of a story, novel, or poem. There are numerous types of characters, ranging from simple, stereotypical figures to intricate, multifaceted ones. "Characterization" is the process by which an author creates vivid, believable characters in a work of art. This may be done in a variety of ways, including (1) direct description of the character by the narrator; (2) the direct presentation of the speech, thoughts, or actions of the character; and (3) the responses of other characters to the character. The term "character" also refers to a form originated by the ancient Greek writer Theophrastus that later became popular in the seventeenth and eighteenth centuries. It is a short essay or sketch of a person who prominently displays a specific attribute or quality, such as miserliness or ambition. "Miss Brill," a story by Katherine Mansfield, is an example of a character sketch.

Classical: In its strictest definition in literary criticism, classicism refers to works of ancient Greek or Roman literature. The term may also be used to describe a literary work of recognized importance (a "classic") from any time period or literature that exhibits the traits of classicism. Examples of later works and authors now described as classical include French literature of the seventeenth century, Western novels of the nineteenth century, and American fiction of the mid-nineteenth century such as that written by James Fenimore Cooper and Mark Twain.

Climax: The turning point in a narrative, the moment when the conflict is at its most intense. Typically, the structure of stories, novels, and plays is one of rising action, in which tension builds to the climax, followed by falling action, in which tension lessens as the story moves to its conclusion.

Comedy: One of two major types of drama, the other being tragedy. Its aim is to amuse, and it typically ends happily. Comedy assumes many forms, such as farce and burlesque, and uses a variety of techniques, from parody to satire. In a restricted sense the term comedy refers only to dramatic presentations, but in general usage it is commonly applied to nondramatic works as well.

Comic Relief: The use of humor to lighten the mood of a serious or tragic story, especially in plays. The technique is very common in Elizabethan works, and can be an integral part of the plot or simply a brief event designed to break the tension of the scene.

Conflict: The conflict in a work of fiction is the issue to be resolved in the story. It usually occurs between two characters, the protagonist and the antagonist, or between the protagonist and society or the protagonist and himself or herself. The conflict in Washington Irving's story "The Devil and Tom Walker" is that the Devil wants Tom Walker's soul but Tom does not want to go to hell.

Criticism: The systematic study and evaluation of literary works, usually based on a specific method or set of principles. An important part of literary studies since ancient times, the practice of criticism has given rise to numerous theories, methods, and "schools," sometimes producing conflicting, even contradictory, interpretations of literature in general as well as of individual works. Even such basic issues as what constitutes a poem or a novel have been the subject of much criticism over the centuries. Seminal texts of literary criticism include Plato's *Republic,* Aristotle's *Poetics,* Sir Philip Sidney's *The Defence of Poesie,* and John Dryden's *Of Dramatic Poesie.* Contemporary schools of criticism include deconstruction, feminist, psychoanalytic, poststructuralist, new historicist, postcolonialist, and reader-response.

D

Deconstruction: A method of literary criticism characterized by multiple conflicting interpretations of a given work. Deconstructionists consider the impact of the language of a work and suggest that the true meaning of the work is not necessarily the meaning that the author intended.

Deduction: The process of reaching a conclusion through reasoning from general premises to a specific premise. Arthur Conan Doyle's character Sherlock Holmes often used deductive reasoning to solve mysteries.

Denotation: The definition of a word, apart from the impressions or feelings it creates in the reader. The word "apartheid" denotes a political and economic policy of segregation by race, but its connotations—oppression, slavery, inequality—are numerous.

Denouement: A French word meaning "the unknotting." In literature, it denotes the resolution of conflict in fiction or drama. The *denouement* follows the climax and provides an outcome to the primary plot situation as well as an explanation of secondary plot complications. A well-known example of *denouement* is the last scene of the play *As You Like It* by William Shakespeare, in which couples are married, an evildoer repents, the identities of two disguised characters are revealed, and a ruler is restored to power. Also known as "falling action."

Detective Story: A narrative about the solution of a mystery or the identification of a criminal. The conventions of the detective story include the detective's scrupulous use of logic in solving the mystery; incompetent or ineffectual police; a suspect who appears guilty at first but is later proved innocent; and the detective's friend or confidant—often the narrator—whose slowness in interpreting clues emphasizes by contrast the detective's brilliance. Edgar Allan Poe's "Murders in the Rue Morgue" is commonly regarded as the earliest example of this type of story. Other practitioners are Arthur Conan Doyle, Dashiell Hammett, and Agatha Christie.

Dialogue: Dialogue is conversation between people in a literary work. In its most restricted sense, it refers specifically to the speech of characters in a drama. As a specific literary genre, a "dialogue" is a composition in which characters debate an issue or idea.

Didactic: A term used to describe works of literature that aim to teach a moral, religious, political, or practical lesson. Although didactic elements are often found inartistically pleasing works, the term "didactic" usually refers to literature in which the message is more important than the form. The term may also be used to criticize a work that the critic finds "overly didactic," that is, heavy-handed in its delivery of a lesson. An example of didactic literature is John Bunyan's *Pilgrim's Progress.*

Dramatic Irony: Occurs when the reader of a work of literature knows something that a character in the work itself does not know. The irony is in the contrast between the intended meaning of the statements or actions of a character and the additional information understood by the audience.

Dystopia: An imaginary place in a work of fiction where the characters lead dehumanized, fearful lives. George Orwell's *Nineteen Eighty-four,* and Margaret Atwood's *Handmaid's Tale* portray versions of dystopia.

E

Edwardian: Describes cultural conventions identified with the period of the reign of Edward VII of England (1901–1910). Writers of the Edwardian Age typically displayed a strong reaction against the propriety and conservatism of the Victorian Age. Their work often exhibits distrust of authority in religion, politics, and art and expresses strong doubts about the soundness of conventional values. Writers of this era include E. M. Forster, H. G. Wells, and Joseph Conrad.

Empathy: A sense of shared experience, including emotional and physical feelings, with someone or something other than oneself. Empathy is often used to describe the response of a reader to a literary character.

Epilogue: A concluding statement or section of a literary work. In dramas, particularly those of the seventeenth and eighteenth centuries, the epilogue is a closing speech, often in verse, delivered by an actor at the end of a play and spoken directly to the audience.

Epiphany: A sudden revelation of truth inspired by a seemingly trivial incident. The term was widely used by James Joyce in his critical writings, and the stories in Joyce's *Dubliners* are commonly called "epiphanies."

Epistolary Novel: A novel in the form of letters. The form was particularly popular in the eighteenth century. The form can also be applied to short stories, as in Edwidge Danticat's "Children of the Sea."

Epithet: A word or phrase, often disparaging or abusive, that expresses a character trait of someone or something. "The Napoleon of crime" is an epithet applied to Professor Moriarty, arch-rival of Sherlock Holmes in Arthur Conan Doyle's series of detective stories.

Existentialism: A predominantly twentieth-century philosophy concerned with the nature and perception of human existence. There are two major strains of existentialist thought: atheistic and Christian. Followers of atheistic existentialism believe that the individual is alone in a godless universe and that the basic human condition is one of suffering and loneliness. Nevertheless, because there are no fixed values, individuals can create their own characters—indeed, they can shape themselves—through the exercise of free will. The atheistic strain culminates in and is popularly associated with the works of Jean-Paul Sartre. The Christian existentialists, on the other hand, believe that only in God may people find freedom from life's anguish. The two strains hold certain beliefs in common: that existence cannot be fully understood or described through empirical effort; that anguish is a universal element of life; that individuals must bear responsibility for their actions; and that there is no common standard of behavior or perception for religious and ethical matters. Existentialist thought figures prominently in the works of such authors as Franz Kafka, Fyodor Dostoyevsky, and Albert Camus.

Expatriatism: The practice of leaving one's country to live for an extended period in another country. Literary expatriates include Irish author James Joyce who moved to Italy and France, American writers James Baldwin, Ernest Hemingway, Gertrude Stein, and F. Scott Fitzgerald who lived and wrote in Paris, and Polish novelist Joseph Conrad in England.

Exposition: Writing intended to explain the nature of an idea, thing, or theme. Expository writing is often combined with description, narration, or argument.

Expressionism: An indistinct literary term, originally used to describe an early twentieth-century school of German painting. The term applies to almost any mode of unconventional, highly subjective writing that distorts reality in some way. Advocates of Expressionism include Federico Garcia Lorca, Eugene O'Neill, Franz Kafka, and James Joyce.

F

Fable: A prose or verse narrative intended to convey amoral. Animals or inanimate objects with human characteristics often serve as characters in fables. A famous fable is Aesop's "The Tortoise and the Hare."

Fantasy: A literary form related to mythology and folklore. Fantasy literature is typically set in non-existent realms and features supernatural beings. Notable examples of literature with elements of fantasy are Gabriel Gárcia Márquez's story "The Handsomest Drowned Man in the World" and Ursula K. Le Guin's "The Ones Who Walk Away from Omelas."

Farce: A type of comedy characterized by broad humor, outlandish incidents, and often vulgar subject matter. Much of the comedy in film and television could more accurately be described as farce.

Fiction: Any story that is the product of imagination rather than a documentation of fact. Characters and events in such narratives may be based in real life but their ultimate form and configuration is a creation of the author.

Figurative Language: A technique in which an author uses figures of speech such as hyperbole, irony, metaphor, or simile for a particular effect. Figurative language is the opposite of literal language, in which every word is truthful, accurate, and free of exaggeration or embellishment.

Flashback: A device used in literature to present action that occurred before the beginning of the story. Flashbacks are often introduced as the dreams or recollections of one or more characters.

Foil: A character in a work of literature whose physical or psychological qualities contrast strongly with, and therefore highlight, the corresponding qualities of another character. In his Sherlock Holmes stories, Arthur Conan Doyle portrayed Dr. Watson as a man of normal habits and intelligence, making him a foil for the eccentric and unusually perceptive Sherlock Holmes.

Folklore: Traditions and myths preserved in a culture or group of people. Typically, these are passed on by word of mouth in various forms—such as legends, songs, and proverbs—or preserved in customs and ceremonies. Washington Irving, in "The Devil and Tom Walker" and many of his other stories, incorporates many elements of the folklore of New England and Germany.

Folktale: A story originating in oral tradition. Folk tales fall into a variety of categories, including legends, ghost stories, fairy tales, fables, and anecdotes based on historical figures and events.

Foreshadowing: A device used in literature to create expectation or to set up an explanation of later developments. Edgar Allan Poe uses foreshadowing to create suspense in "The Fall of the House of Usher" when the narrator comments on the crumbling state of disrepair in which he finds the house.

G

Genre: A category of literary work. Genre may refer to both the content of a given work—tragedy, comedy, horror, science fiction—and to its form, such as poetry, novel, or drama.

Gilded Age: A period in American history during the 1870s and after characterized by political corruption and materialism. A number of important novels of social and political criticism were written during this time. Henry James and Kate Chopin are two writers who were prominent during the Gilded Age.

Gothicism: In literature, works characterized by a taste for medieval or morbid characters and situations. A gothic novel prominently features elements of horror, the supernatural, gloom, and violence: clanking chains, terror, ghosts, medieval castles, and unexplained phenomena. The term "gothic novel" is also applied to novels that lack elements of the traditional Gothic setting but that create a similar atmosphere of terror or dread. The term can also be applied to stories, plays, and poems. Mary Shelley's *Frankenstein* and Joyce Carol Oates's *Bellefleur* are both gothic novels.

Grotesque: In literature, a work that is characterized by exaggeration, deformity, freakishness, and disorder. The grotesque often includes an element of comic absurdity. Examples of the grotesque can be found in the works of Edgar Allan Poe, Flannery O'Connor, Joseph Heller, and Shirley Jackson.

H

Harlem Renaissance: The Harlem Renaissance of the 1920s is generally considered the first significant movement of black writers and artists in the United States. During this period, new and established black writers, many of whom lived in the region of New York City known as Harlem, published more fiction and poetry than ever before, the first influential black literary journals were established, and black authors and artists received their first widespread recognition and serious critical appraisal. Among the major writers associated with this period are Countee Cullen, Langston Hughes, Arna Bontemps, and Zora Neale Hurston.

Hero/Heroine: The principal sympathetic character in a literary work. Heroes and heroines typically exhibit admirable traits: idealism, courage, and integrity, for example. Famous heroes and heroines of literature include Charles Dickens's Oliver Twist, Margaret Mitchell's Scarlett O'Hara, and the anonymous narrator in Ralph Ellison's *Invisible Man*.

Hyperbole: Deliberate exaggeration used to achieve an effect. In William Shakespeare's *Macbeth,* Lady Macbeth hyperbolizes when she says, "All the perfumes of Arabia could not sweeten this little hand."

I

Image: A concrete representation of an object or sensory experience. Typically, such a representation helps evoke the feelings associated with the object or experience itself. Images are either "literal" or "figurative." Literal images are especially concrete and involve little or no extension of the obvious meaning of the words used to express them. Figurative images do not follow the literal meaning of the words exactly. Images in literature are usually visual, but the term "image" can also refer to the representation of any sensory experience.

Imagery: The array of images in a literary work. Also used to convey the author's overall use of figurative language in a work.

In medias res: A Latin term meaning "in the middle of things." It refers to the technique of beginning a story at its midpoint and then using various flashback devices to reveal previous action. This technique originated in such epics as Virgil's *Aeneid.*

Interior Monologue: A narrative technique in which characters' thoughts are revealed in a way that appears to be uncontrolled by the author. The interior monologue typically aims to reveal the inner self of a character. It portrays emotional experiences as they occur at both a conscious and unconscious level. One of the best-known interior monologues in English is the Molly Bloom section at the close of James Joyce's *Ulysses*. Katherine Anne Porter's "The Jilting of Granny Weatherall" is also told in the form of an interior monologue.

Irony: In literary criticism, the effect of language in which the intended meaning is the opposite of what is stated. The title of Jonathan Swift's "A Modest Proposal" is ironic because what Swift proposes in this essay is cannibalism—hardly "modest."

J

Jargon: Language that is used or understood only by a select group of people. Jargon may refer to terminology used in a certain profession, such as computer jargon, or it may refer to any nonsensical language that is not understood by most people. Anthony Burgess's *A Clockwork Orange* and James Thurber's "The Secret Life of Walter Mitty" both use jargon.

K

Knickerbocker Group: An indistinct group of New York writers of the first half of the nineteenth century. Members of the group were linked only by location and a common theme: New York life. Two famous members of the Knickerbocker Group were Washington Irving and William Cullen Bryant. The group's name derives from Irving's *Knickerbocker's History of New York.*

L

Literal Language: An author uses literal language when he or she writes without exaggerating or embellishing the subject matter and without any tools of figurative language. To say "He ran very quickly down the street" is to use literal language, whereas to say "He ran like a hare down the street" would be using figurative language.

Literature: Literature is broadly defined as any written or spoken material, but the term most often refers to creative works. Literature includes poetry, drama, fiction, and many kinds of nonfiction writing, as well as oral, dramatic, and broadcast compositions not necessarily preserved in a written format, such as films and television programs.

Lost Generation: A term first used by Gertrude Stein to describe the post-World War I generation of American writers: men and women haunted by a sense of betrayal and emptiness brought about by the destructiveness of the war. The term is commonly applied to Hart Crane, Ernest Hemingway, F. Scott Fitzgerald, and others.

M

Magic Realism: A form of literature that incorporates fantasy elements or supernatural occurrences into the narrative and accepts them as truth. Gabriel Gárcia Márquez and Laura Esquivel are two writers known for their works of magic realism.

Metaphor: A figure of speech that expresses an idea through the image of another object. Metaphors suggest the essence of the first object by identifying it with certain qualities of the second object. An example is "But soft, what light through yonder window breaks? / It is the east, and Juliet is the sun" in William Shakespeare's *Romeo and Juliet*. Here, Juliet, the first object, is identified with qualities of the second object, the sun.

Minimalism: A literary style characterized by spare, simple prose with few elaborations. In minimalism, the main theme of the work is often never discussed directly. Amy Hempel and Ernest Hemingway are two writers known for their works of minimalism.

Modernism: Modern literary practices. Also, the principles of a literary school that lasted from roughly the beginning of the twentieth century until the end of World War II. Modernism is defined by its rejection of the literary conventions of the nineteenth century and by its opposition to conventional morality, taste, traditions, and economic values. Many writers are associated with the concepts of modernism, including Albert Camus, D. H. Lawrence, Ernest Hemingway, William Faulkner, Eugene O'Neill, and James Joyce.

Monologue: A composition, written or oral, by a single individual. More specifically, a speech given by a single individual in a drama or other public entertainment. It has no set length, although it is usually several or more lines long. "I Stand Here Ironing" by Tillie Olsen is an example of a story written in the form of a monologue.

Mood: The prevailing emotions of a work or of the author in his or her creation of the work. The mood of a work is not always what might be expected based on its subject matter.

Motif: A theme, character type, image, metaphor, or other verbal element that recurs throughout a single work of literature or occurs in a number of different works over a period of time. For example, the color white in Herman Melville's *Moby Dick* is a "specific" motif, while the trials of star-crossed lovers is a "conventional" motif from the literature of all periods.

N

Narration: The telling of a series of events, real or invented. A narration may be either a simple narrative, in which the events are recounted chronologically, or a narrative with a plot, in which the account is given in a style reflecting the author's artistic concept of the story. Narration is sometimes used as a synonym for "storyline."

Narrative: A verse or prose accounting of an event or sequence of events, real or invented. The term is also used as an adjective in the sense "method of narration." For example, in literary criticism, the expression "narrative technique" usually refers to the way the author structures and presents his or her story. Different narrative forms include diaries, travelogues, novels, ballads, epics, short stories, and other fictional forms.

Narrator: The teller of a story. The narrator may be the author or a character in the story through whom the author speaks. Huckleberry Finn is the narrator of Mark Twain's *The Adventures of Huckleberry Finn.*

Novella: An Italian term meaning "story." This term has been especially used to describe fourteenth-century Italian tales, but it also refers to modern short novels. Modern novellas include Leo Tolstoy's *The Death of Ivan Ilich,* Fyodor Dostoyevsky's *Notes from the Underground,* and Joseph Conrad's *Heart of Darkness.*

O

Oedipus Complex: A son's romantic obsession with his mother. The phrase is derived from the story of the ancient Theban hero Oedipus, who unknowingly killed his father and married his mother, and was popularized by Sigmund Freud's theory of psychoanalysis. Literary occurrences of the Oedipus complex include Sophocles' *Oedipus Rex* and D. H. Lawrence's "The Rocking-Horse Winner."

Onomatopoeia: The use of words whose sounds express or suggest their meaning. In its simplest sense, onomatopoeia may be represented by words that mimic the sounds they denote such as "hiss" or "meow." At a more subtle level, the pattern and rhythm of sounds and rhymes of a line or poem may be onomatopoeic.

Oral Tradition: A process by which songs, ballads, folklore, and other material are transmitted by word of mouth. The tradition of oral transmission predates the written record systems of literate society. Oral transmission preserves material sometimes over generations, although often with variations. Memory plays a large part in the recitation and preservation of orally transmitted material. Native American myths and legends, and African folktales told by plantation slaves are examples of orally transmitted literature.

P

Parable: A story intended to teach a moral lesson or answer an ethical question. Examples of parables are the stories told by Jesus Christ in the New Testament, notably "The Prodigal Son," but parables also are used in Sufism, rabbinic literature, Hasidism, and Zen Buddhism. Isaac Bashevis Singer's story "Gimpel the Fool" exhibits characteristics of a parable.

Paradox: A statement that appears illogical or contradictory at first, but may actually point to an underlying truth. A literary example of a paradox is George Orwell's statement "All animals are equal, but some animals are more equal than others" in *Animal Farm.*

Parody: In literature, this term refers to an imitation of a serious literary work or the signature style of a particular author in a ridiculous manner. Atypical parody adopts the style of the original and applies it to an inappropriate subject for humorous effect. Parody is a form of satire and could be considered the literary equivalent of a caricature or cartoon. Henry Fielding's *Shamela* is a parody of Samuel Richardson's *Pamela.*

Persona: A Latin term meaning "mask." Personae are the characters in a fictional work of literature. The persona generally functions as a mask through which the author tells a story in a voice other than his or her own. A persona is usually either a character in a story who acts as a narrator or an "implied author," a voice created by the author to act as the narrator for himself or herself. The persona in Charlotte Perkins Gilman's story "The Yellow Wallpaper" is the unnamed young mother experiencing a mental breakdown.

Personification: A figure of speech that gives human qualities to abstract ideas, animals, and inanimate objects. To say that "the sun is smiling" is to personify the sun.

Plot: The pattern of events in a narrative or drama. In its simplest sense, the plot guides the author in composing the work and helps the reader follow the work. Typically, plots exhibit causality and unity and have a beginning, a middle, and an end. Sometimes, however, a plot may consist of a series of disconnected events, in which case it is known as an "episodic plot."

Poetic Justice: An outcome in a literary work, not necessarily a poem, in which the good are rewarded and the evil are punished, especially in ways that particularly fit their virtues or crimes. For example, a murderer may himself be murdered, or a thief will find himself penniless.

Poetic License: Distortions of fact and literary convention made by a writer—not always a poet—for the sake of the effect gained. Poetic license is closely related to the concept of "artistic freedom." An author exercises poetic license by saying that a pile of money "reaches as high as a mountain" when the pile is actually only a foot or two high.

Point of View: The narrative perspective from which a literary work is presented to the reader. There are four traditional points of view. The "third person omniscient" gives the reader a "godlike" perspective, unrestricted by time or place, from which to see actions and look into the minds of characters. This allows the author to comment openly on characters and events in the work. The "third person" point of view presents the events of the story from outside of any single character's perception, much like the omniscient point of view, but the reader must understand the action as it takes place and without any special insight into characters' minds or motivations. The "first person" or "personal" point of view relates events as they are perceived by a single character. The main character "tells" the story and may offer opinions about the action and characters which differ from those of the author. Much less common than omniscient, third person, and first person is the "second person" point of view, wherein the author tells the story as if it is happening to the reader. James Thurber employs the omniscient point of view in his short story "The Secret Life of Walter Mitty." Ernest Hemingway's "A Clean, Well-Lighted Place" is a short story told from the third person point of view. Mark Twain's novel *Huckleberry Finn* is presented from the first person viewpoint. Jay McInerney's *Bright Lights, Big City* is an example of a novel which uses the second person point of view.

Pornography: Writing intended to provoke feelings of lust in the reader. Such works are often condemned by critics and teachers, but those which can be shown to have literary value are viewed less harshly. Literary works that have been described as pornographic include D. H. Lawrence's *Lady Chatterley's Lover* and James Joyce's *Ulysses*.

Post-Aesthetic Movement: An artistic response made by African Americans to the black aesthetic movement of the 1960s and early 1970s. Writers since that time have adopted a somewhat different tone in their work, with less emphasis placed on the disparity between black and white in the United States. In the words of post-aesthetic authors such as Toni Morrison, John Edgar Wideman, and Kristin Hunter, African Americans are portrayed as looking inward for answers to their own questions, rather than always looking to the outside world. Two well-known examples of works produced as part of the post-aesthetic movement are the Pulitzer Prize–winning novels *The Color Purple* by Alice Walker and *Beloved* by Toni Morrison.

Postmodernism: Writing from the 1960s forward characterized by experimentation and application of modernist elements, which include existentialism and alienation. Postmodernists have gone a step further in the rejection of tradition begun with the modernists by also rejecting traditional forms, preferring the anti-novel over the novel and the anti-hero over the hero. Postmodern writers include Thomas Pynchon, Margaret Drabble, and Gabriel Gárcia Márquez.

Prologue: An introductory section of a literary work. It often contains information establishing the situation of the characters or presents information about the setting, time period, or action. In drama, the prologue is spoken by a chorus or by one of the principal characters.

Prose: A literary medium that attempts to mirror the language of everyday speech. It is distinguished from poetry by its use of unmetered, unrhymed language consisting of logically related sentences. Prose is usually grouped into paragraphs that form a cohesive whole such as an essay or a novel. The term is sometimes used to mean an author's general writing.

Protagonist: The central character of a story who serves as a focus for its themes and incidents and as the principal rationale for its development. The protagonist is sometimes referred to in discussions of modern literature as the hero or anti-hero. Well-known protagonists are Hamlet in William Shakespeare's *Hamlet* and Jay Gatsby in F. Scott Fitzgerald's *The Great Gatsby*.

R

Realism: A nineteenth-century European literary movement that sought to portray familiar characters, situations, and settings in a realistic manner. This was done primarily by using an objective narrative point of view and through the buildup of accurate detail. The standard for success of any realistic work depends on how faithfully it transfers common experience into fictional forms. The realistic method may be altered or extended, as in stream of consciousness writing, to record highly subjective experience. Contemporary authors who often write in a realistic way include Nadine Gordimer and Grace Paley.

Resolution: The portion of a story following the climax, in which the conflict is resolved. The resolution of Jane Austen's *Northanger Abbey* is neatly summed up in the following sentence: "Henry and Catherine were married, the bells rang and every body smiled."

Rising Action: The part of a drama where the plot becomes increasingly complicated. Rising action leads up to the climax, or turning point, of a drama. The final "chase scene" of an action film is generally the rising action which culminates in the film's climax.

Roman a clef: A French phrase meaning "novel with a key." It refers to a narrative in which real persons are portrayed under fictitious names. Jack Kerouac, for example, portrayed various friends under fictitious names in the novel *On the Road.* D. H. Lawrence based "The Rocking-Horse Winner" on a family he knew.

Romanticism: This term has two widely accepted meanings. In historical criticism, it refers to a European intellectual and artistic movement of the late eighteenth and early nineteenth centuries that sought greater freedom of personal expression than that allowed by the strict rules of literary form and logic of the eighteenth-century neoclassicists. The Romantics preferred emotional and imaginative expression to rational analysis. They considered the individual to be at the center of all experience and so placed him or her at the center of their art. The Romantics believed that the creative imagination reveals nobler truths—unique feelings and attitudes—than those that could be discovered by logic or by scientific examination. "Romanticism" is also used as a general term to refer to a type of sensibility found in all periods of literary history and usually considered to be in opposition to the principles of classicism. In this sense, Romanticism signifies any work or philosophy in which the exotic or dreamlike figure strongly, or that is devoted to individualistic expression, self-analysis, or a pursuit of a higher realm of knowledge than can be discovered by human reason. Prominent Romantics include Jean-Jacques Rousseau, William Wordsworth, John Keats, Lord Byron, and Johann Wolfgang von Goethe.

S

Satire: A work that uses ridicule, humor, and wit to criticize and provoke change in human nature and institutions. Voltaire's novella *Candide* and Jonathan Swift's essay "A Modest Proposal" are both satires. Flannery O'Connor's portrayal of the family in "A Good Man Is Hard to Find" is a satire of a modern, Southern, American family.

Science Fiction: A type of narrative based upon real or imagined scientific theories and technology. Science fiction is often peopled with alien creatures and set on other planets or in different dimensions. Popular writers of science fiction are Isaac Asimov, Karel Capek, Ray Bradbury, and Ursula K. Le Guin.

Setting: The time, place, and culture in which the action of a narrative takes place. The elements of setting may include geographic location, characters's physical and mental environments, prevailing cultural attitudes, or the historical time in which the action takes place.

Short Story: A fictional prose narrative shorter and more focused than a novella. The short story usually deals with a single episode and often a single character. The "tone," the author's attitude toward his or her subject and audience, is uniform throughout. The short story frequently also lacks *denouement*, ending instead at its climax.

Signifying Monkey: A popular trickster figure in black folklore, with hundreds of tales about this character documented since the 19th century. Henry Louis Gates Jr. examines the history of the signifying monkey in *The Signifying Monkey: Towards a Theory of Afro-American Literary Criticism,* published in 1988.

Simile: A comparison, usually using "like" or "as," of two essentially dissimilar things, as in "coffee as cold as ice" or "He sounded like a broken record." The title of Ernest Hemingway's "Hills Like White Elephants" contains a simile.

Socialist Realism: The Socialist Realism school of literary theory was proposed by Maxim Gorky and established as a dogma by the first Soviet Congress of Writers. It demanded adherence to a communist worldview in works of literature. Its doctrines required an objective viewpoint comprehensible to the working classes and themes of social struggle featuring strong proletarian heroes. Gabriel Gárcia Márquez's stories exhibit some characteristics of Socialist Realism.

Stereotype: A stereotype was originally the name for a duplication made during the printing process; this led to its modern definition as a person or thing that is (or is assumed to be) the same as all others of its type. Common stereotypical characters include the absent-minded professor, the nagging wife, the troublemaking teenager, and the kind-hearted grandmother.

Stream of Consciousness: A narrative technique for rendering the inward experience of a character. This technique is designed to give the impression of an ever-changing series of thoughts, emotions, images, and memories in the spontaneous and seemingly illogical order that they occur in life. The textbook example of stream of consciousness is the last section of James Joyce's *Ulysses.*

Structure: The form taken by a piece of literature. The structure may be made obvious for ease of understanding, as in nonfiction works, or may obscured for artistic purposes, as in some poetry or seemingly "unstructured" prose.

Style: A writer's distinctive manner of arranging words to suit his or her ideas and purpose in writing. The unique imprint of the author's personality upon his or her writing, style is the product of an author's way of arranging ideas and his or her use of diction, different sentence structures, rhythm, figures of speech, rhetorical principles, and other elements of composition.

Suspense: A literary device in which the author maintains the audience's attention through the buildup of events, the outcome of which will soon be revealed. Suspense in William Shakespeare's *Hamlet* is sustained throughout by the question of whether or not the Prince will achieve what he has been instructed to do and of what he intends to do.

Symbol: Something that suggests or stands for something else without losing its original identity. In literature, symbols combine their literal meaning with the suggestion of an abstract concept. Literary symbols are of two types: those that carry complex associations of meaning no matter what their contexts, and those that derive their suggestive meaning from their functions in specific literary works. Examples of symbols are sunshine suggesting happiness, rain suggesting sorrow, and storm clouds suggesting despair.

T

Tale: A story told by a narrator with a simple plot and little character development. Tales are usually relatively short and often carry a simple message. Examples of tales can be found in the works of Saki, Anton Chekhov, Guy de Maupassant, and O. Henry.

Tall Tale: A humorous tale told in a straightforward, credible tone but relating absolutely impossible events or feats of the characters. Such tales were commonly told of frontier adventures during the settlement of the west in the United States. Literary use of tall tales can be found in Washington Irving's *History of New York,* Mark Twain's *Life on the Mississippi,* and in the German R. F. Raspe's

Baron Munchausen's Narratives of His Marvellous Travels and Campaigns in Russia.

Theme: The main point of a work of literature. The term is used interchangeably with thesis. Many works have multiple themes. One of the themes of Nathaniel Hawthorne's "Young Goodman Brown" is loss of faith.

Tone: The author's attitude toward his or her audience maybe deduced from the tone of the work. A formal tone may create distance or convey politeness, while an informal tone may encourage a friendly, intimate, or intrusive feeling in the reader. The author's attitude toward his or her subject matter may also be deduced from the tone of the words he or she uses in discussing it. The tone of John F. Kennedy's speech which included the appeal to "ask not what your country can do for you" was intended to instill feelings of camaraderie and national pride in listeners.

Tragedy: A drama in prose or poetry about a noble, courageous hero of excellent character who, because of some tragic character flaw, brings ruin upon him- or herself. Tragedy treats its subjects in a dignified and serious manner, using poetic language to help evoke pity and fear and bring about catharsis, a purging of these emotions. The tragic form was practiced extensively by the ancient Greeks. The classical form of tragedy was revived in the sixteenth century; it flourished especially on the Elizabethan stage. In modern times, dramatists have attempted to adapt the form to the needs of modern society by drawing their heroes from the ranks of ordinary men and women and defining the nobility of these heroes in terms of spirit rather than exalted social standing. Some contemporary works that are thought of as tragedies include *The Great Gatsby* by F. Scott Fitzgerald, and *The Sound and the Fury* by William Faulkner.

Tragic Flaw: In a tragedy, the quality within the hero or heroine which leads to his or her downfall. Examples of the tragic flaw include Othello's jealousy and Hamlet's indecisiveness, although most great tragedies defy such simple interpretation.

U

Utopia: A fictional perfect place, such as "paradise" or "heaven." An early literary utopia was described in Plato's *Republic,* and in modern literature, Ursula K. Le Guin depicts a utopia in "The Ones Who Walk Away from Omelas."

V

Victorian: Refers broadly to the reign of Queen Victoria of England (1837-1901) and to anything with qualities typical of that era. For example, the qualities of smug narrow-mindedness, bourgeois materialism, faith in social progress, and priggish morality are often considered Victorian. In literature, the Victorian Period was the great age of the English novel, and the latter part of the era saw the rise of movements such as decadence and symbolism.

Cumulative Author/Title Index

C

D

E

F

I

J

K

N

O

P

Q

R

X

Y

Z

Cumulative Nationality/Ethnicity Index

Antiguan

Arab American

Argentinian

Asian American

Australian

Austrian

Bosnian

Brazilian

Canadian

Chilean

Chinese

Colombian

Cuban

Czech

Danish

Dominican

Egyptian

English

Eurasian

French

German

Greek

Haitian

Hispanic American

Indian

Indonesian

Irish

Israeli

Italian

Japanese

Jewish

Kenyan

Mexican

Native American

Nepalese

New Zealander

Nigerian

Peruvian

Philippine

Polish

Portuguese

Puerto Rican

Russian

Scottish

Sierra Leonean

South African

Spanish

Swedish

Trinidadan

Ugandan

Uruguayan

Vietnamese

Welsh

West Indian

Subject/Theme Index